AF352297

THE GERMAN NACHSPIEL

IN THE EIGHTEENTH CENTURY

The German Nachspiel in the Eighteenth Century

DAVID G. JOHN

UNIVERSITY OF TORONTO PRESS

Toronto Buffalo London

© University of Toronto Press 1991
Toronto Buffalo London
Printed in Canada

ISBN 0-8020-2771-7

Printed on acid-free paper

Canadian Cataloguing in Publication Data

John, David Gethin, 1947-
The German Nachspiel in the eighteenth century

Includes bibliographical references.
ISBN 0-8020-2771-7

1. Theater – Germany – History – 18th century.
2. Prologues and epilogues.   3. German drama – 18th century.
4. German drama (Comedy) – 18th century.
I. Title.

PN2652.J64 1991   792'.0943'09033   C90-095123-0

CATHARINAE

CONTENTS

ACKNOWLEDGMENTS

While many individuals and institutions deserve thanks for their part in the preparation of this book, my first expression of gratitude goes out to the unnamed, dedicated personnel of the libraries whose collections were indispensable for this research. In particular I wish to thank the staff of the Theatersammlung of the Austrian National Library, Director Oskar Pausch, his colleague Peter Nič, and Librarian Haris Baldič; of the theatre collection in the Städtisches Reiß-Museum, Mannheim, Director Liselotte Homering and Librarian Jürgen Hespe; and of the Theatermuseum, Schloß Wahn, Cologne, Director Roswitha Flatz. For full and generous access to their wonderful collections and for their expert advice I owe these people a considerable debt. Most of this book was written during a sabbatical year in Freiburg im Breisgau where much time was spent in the splendid University Library using its wide range of excellent facilities; the staff there, especially those in Reference and Inter-Library Loans, deserve special mention for their constant willingness to offer friendly professional advice and their obvious commitment to scholarly research. I wish to thank further the staff of the Zentralbibliothek der deutschen Klassik, Weimar, and the Wissenschaftliche Allgemeinbibliothek, Schwerin, for furnishing valuable copies and information. The librarians at the University of Waterloo have also contributed much to my research, notably the specialist in my discipline, Marsha Blok. This library, upon the sage advice of our beloved late colleague Igor Levitsky, had the foresight some years ago to purchase the entire eighteenth-century Austro-German theatre holdings of the Harvard Houghton Library on microfilm, a decision that has meant much for my work.

Several individuals deserve special mention and thanks: my dear Viennese friends Monika Bartl and Gertrude Lang, who helped me solve many an intricacy of local and dialect usage; Eckehard Catholy, who pointed me in the right direction when struggling with numerous interpretations; and Barbara Kaltz for rummaging on my behalf in the Bibliothèque Nationale. Reinhart Meyer must be singled out for his great generosity toward me in granting pre-publication access to a wealth of material he has collected on theatre in the eighteenth century; this, in addition to his publications, personal encouragement, and warm advice, leaves me much indebted. I thank the Director of the Handschriftenabteilung of the Austrian National Library, Vienna, for permission to publish the manuscripts found in Chapter 3. And I express great appreciation to Carl Hennig, Dagmar Jangl, and Cathy Claus for their considerable efforts and expertise in preparing the manuscript for publication. Camera-ready copy for the printing of this book was prepared by them in the Faculty of Arts at the University of Waterloo. Organization and layout of the material, aspects of style and linguistic felicity all came under the sharp eyes and conscientious scrutiny of Kathy Gaca and Lorraine Ourom of the University of Toronto Press, both of whom deserve much credit for polishing my work.

Finally, I acknowledge with sincere gratitude research funding from the Social Sciences and Humanities Research Council of Canada in support of my work. This book has been published with the help of a grant from the Canadian Federation for the Humanities, using funds provided by the Social Sciences and Humanities Research Council of Canada.

David G. John
University of Waterloo

THE GERMAN NACHSPIEL

IN THE EIGHTEENTH CENTURY

INTRODUCTION

Why a book on the Nachspiel? Anyone familiar with theatre activity in the German eighteenth century recognizes the term Nachspiel, but few understand fully what it means and the extent to which this form permeated the dramatic scene. The Nachspiel was one of the most frequent theatrical phenomena on German stages throughout the eighteenth century, yet it has never received a detailed study. To my knowledge there exists no scholarly article on the Nachspiel, no dissertation, no book, not even a chapter; information on it can be acquired only through brief accounts in literary lexica (at times mutually contradictory), through scattered references in most histories of German eighteenth-century theatre, or by reading the primary works themselves, if indeed you can find the texts. How many Germanists – even those occupied with the eighteenth century – can even name more than one or two Nachspiele; and seeking more information on Nachspiel texts, to which sources can they turn? There exists no bibliography of the Nachspiel, and even the lexical definitions combined cite only a handful of titles.

But is the Nachspiel a genre worthy of consideration on its own? There do exist after all some good studies of the German *Einakter* (Elise Meyer, 1920; Yüksel Pazarkaya, 1973) which make mention of the Nachspiel within the one-act tradition. Yet the word *Einakter* is not an eighteenth-century concept; it is a recent one used to describe a broad category of dramatic pieces by the rudimentary characteristics of structure and length. I contend that the Nachspiel deserves separate treatment, first because Nachspiel is a word used commonly in the eighteenth century to describe a type of dramatic work, carrying contemporary connotations which the modern word *Einakter* does not. I argue that the word 'Nachspiel' evoked in the eighteenth-century mind specific notions of what kind of work it was; indeed that the essential characteristics of the Nachspiel lay at the core of German-speaking theatre in its day. Further, I argue that the Nachspiel as genre changed during the century to carry at the end entirely different connotations, yet at the same time frequently retaining essential features and the spirit of the genre from earlier decades. While the Nachspiel is a genre, it is not a static concept to be easily defined; but neither is the tragedy, the novel, the lyric poem, or any dramatic or literary form.

As a dramatic work, the Nachspiel has two sides: text and performance; both must be considered to gain a clearer picture. In this case, however, the division between text and performance is particularly striking, for in the first half of the century, extant evidence of Nachspiel texts is scanty to say the least, while later on there is a wealth of material. This distribution of available evidence says more about the nature of the genre than about the thoroughness of library and archival collections, for indeed the early Nachspiel was foremost an improvised work with scanty text base or none at all; only later did it become what we might call a literary genre. This division necessitates a methodological approach that tries to come to grips with what the Nachspiel was like when performed, without the benefit of extant textual material. Further, when the text is available, it should not be given automatic priority for interpretation and understanding; rather, it serves as an aid, for what was written was not necessarily (or sometimes even similar to) what was performed in the eighteenth century.

In *Volk ohne Buch* (1970), Rudolf Schenda writes, 'Eine Sozialgeschichte der Lesestoffe sollte sich mit literarischen Fakten beschäftigen, die die verschiedensten Rückschlüsse auf möglichst viele, wenn nicht alle, sozialen Schichten der Gesellschaft erlauben' (32). His study is about works that deserve attention for their importance to readers of their age ('literarisch-gesellschaftlich'), not because they have become canonized by posterity for their timeless aesthetic merits ('literarisch-ästhetisch,' 34). While Schenda's primary focus is nineteenth-century prose, his approach is one with which I concur. The Nachspiel has been ignored by scholars because it cannot be argued to have those timeless literary merits so often touted, analysed, and praised. It deserves attention now, however, because it was enormously popular, indeed essential for the theatre scene of the age. Those who ignore the Nachspiel cannot possibly understand what theatre was like in the German eighteenth century.

The first chapter of the book, 'Towards a Definition of the Nachspiel,' surveys the genre designation first as it is described in modern literary lexica, turning then to eighteenth-century references which provide insight into contemporary undertanding of the word. From this base, Chapter 2, 'Repertoires and Performances of Itinerant Troupes and Standing Theatres,' looks at both the frequency and nature of Nachspiel performance first in eight major German-speaking centres throughout the century, then with a concentration on the activities of six major itinerant troupes whose travels covered virtually every nook and cranny of German-speaking Europe. This chapter establishes the popularity of the Nachspiel, changes in its fashion and function, and its essential traditional features, particularly the nature and function of the comic figure. Principal sources of information include contemporary accounts, histories of cities and companies, as well as repertoire and playbill collections.

Chapter 3, 'Three Unpublished Nachspiele,' makes an important bridge between the world of extemporized performance, i.e. without extensive or documentable text base, and the literary Nachspiel which dominated the latter part of the century. Here, three Nachspiele are published for the first time from extant manuscripts, the first of which is a mere scenario from which the Nachspiel was extemporized; the second a fully scripted work with dialogue, but containing as well clear indications of extemporized parts; the third also a full script. All three are analysed within the context of their performance at the time, including reference to contemporary actors, theatrical fashion, audience composition, and the physical properties of the stage. Chapter 4 begins the analysis of text-based Nachspiele. All examples discussed from this point are documented in published texts, which also constitute the 'Annotated Bibliography of the German Nachspiel' at the end of this volume. This chapter contains an overview of all Nachspiele in the Bibliography and leads to Chapters 5 and 6 which contain analyses of fifteen Nachspiele divided temporally into two groups, before and after 1770, the year (approximately) which marks a turning point in German-speaking Europe with the rapid rise of permanent theatres. Works selected for analysis cover the years 1722 to 1798 and each demonstrates in different ways key elements of the Nachspiel tradition.

Chapter 7 is devoted entirely to 'Acting: Talent and Rules,' for my previous analyses, as well as my investigation of the Nachspiel's function in the repertoires of itinerant troupes and on city stages, reveal that the genre played an important role in the development of acting technique. The emergence of standing theatres and permanent companies brought with it increased attention to the method of performance, much more formally than had been the case in earlier decades. From this study, Chapter 8 looks at a new type of Nachspiel as it emerged toward century's end, 'The Socio-Critical Nachspiel.' This chapter discusses many individual Nachspiele grouped thematically as they reflected current social conditions and issues, including further developments in acting and cultural debate.

The final analytical portion, Chapter 9, 'Between Text and Performance: Censorship,' concentrates first on developments in censorship which had such great impact on what was performed, where, and how; then a censored version of one Nachspiel, based on a censor's and prompter's copy, is edited and cited at length to demonstrate the concrete effects of contemporary legal censures on dramatic works.

Of the appended materials, the 'Annotated Bibliography of the German Nachspiel' is crucial, for it makes the primary works on which this study is based accessible to the reader. It contains all Nachspiele for which I have been able to find an extant text or reliable indication that one in fact exists. Entries carry full bibliographical documentation, including title-page information, internal divisions, prose or verse form, a list of personae and place(s) of action, a plot outline, the location of at least one extant copy, if known (with call number), brief comments on the work's significant features and history, and a reference to the pages of this study in which that particular entry is discussed at greater length. The Bibliography was compiled from many sources, chief among which are: Heinsius, *Allgemeines Bücherlexikon* (Appendix of *Schauspiele*); Kayser, *Vollständiges Bücher-Lexikon*; Goedeke, *Grundriß*; Binger, *Bibliography of German Plays on Microcards*; *German and Austrian Drama. Viennese Theatre 1740 to 1790* (Houghton Library, Harvard University); Asper, *Spieltexte der Wanderbühne*; Reinhart Meyer, *Bibliographia dramatica*; *Teatralia Zámecké Knihovny v Českém Krumlově*; *Teatralia Zámecké Knihovny z Křimic*; *Teatralia Zámecké Knihovny z Radenína*; and many historical studies. Consistent with my intention to investigate the Nachspiel as a genre in itself, the Bibliography contains only Nachspiele whose title-pages contain that explicit genre designation. Where it could be established that the entry was a German translation or adaptation of a work from another language (most often French), this information is included, as is information on anonymous authors and pseudonyms. Here I have relied largely on the title-pages themselves and Fromm's *Bibliographie deutscher Übersetzungen*, Holzmann/Bohatta's *Deutsches Anonymen-Lexikon* and *Pseudonymen-Lexikon,* and Schneider's *Deutsches Titelbuch.* While entries are not necessarily first editions, in each case I have used the earliest I could acquire, in most cases indeed the first printing, and in six instances I have also made use of manuscript versions (the three fully reproduced in Chapter 3 as well as *Blind und lahm, Der hinkende Bothe,* and *Der Magnetismus*).

Also included are two appendices. Appendix 1, 'Overview of Primary Works,' makes an analysis of structural and thematic characteristics of the Nachspiele considered in Chapters 3, 4, 5, 6, and 8. This analysis is a means to test the validity of those characteristics in quantifiable terms. Appendix 2 is a list of 'Documented Performances of Extant Nachspiele,' the sources for which are the many histories and repertoire lists cited in Chapter 2. Following the Bibliography are a bibliography of 'Secondary Works Cited,' an 'Index of Titles,' and finally an 'Index of Names' to which the study refers. Throughout my work, when citing primary sources, I have adopted the policy not to regularize spelling or punctuation according to modern conventions. Any exceptions to this policy are noted where relevant.

Many investigations of German theatre in the eighteenth century have served to broaden my understanding of the period. Among older works, Genée's *Lehr- und Wanderjahre des deutschen Schauspiels* (1882), Holl's *Geschichte des deutschen Lustspiels* (1923), and Rommel's introduction to *Die Maschinenkomödie* (1935) deserve mention as useful surveys, although Genée and Holl lack documentation and Rommel concentrates almost exclusively on Vienna. Aikin-Sneath's *Comedy in Germany in the First Half of the Eighteenth Century* (1936) is still an informative and entertaining little study of the early decades. Eduard Devrient's *Geschichte der deutschen Schauspielkunst* (1867) remains an indispensable classic, and despite its lack of documentation offers an invaluable fund of information from an author who brings his reader so close to the spirit of the contemporary scene. The only comparable modern study is Kindermann's *Theatergeschichte Europas* (1957-74) (Vols. IV, V), which offers similar depth and breadth.

The most enlightening broad treatments from more recent authors include Walter Hinck's *Das deutsche Lustspiel ...* (1965) with its detailed account of the intricate relationships between the *commedia dell'arte* and German theatre, Eckehard Catholy's two-volumed *Das deutsche Lustspiel* (1969, 1982), and two essays in Grimminger's *Deutsche Aufklärung*: Reinhart Meyer's 'Von der Wanderbühne zum Hof- und Nationaltheater' and Jochen Schulte-Sasse's 'Drama.' Together these essays provide an excellent concise survey with appropriate sensitivity not just to dramatic works but also to contemporary events that influenced them. Their treatment of dramatic literature against the backdrop of eighteenth-century society is much more helpful than the scanty essays on drama in Glaser's *Sozialgeschichte* (1980ff). Finally, Eike Pies's *Prinzipale* (1973) provides an indispensable guide to the documentation and activities of itinerant theatre companies in the century and Sybille Maurer-Schmoock's *Deutsches Theater im 18. Jahrhundert* (1982) gives a useful survey of staging, acting, and theatre life.

More sharply focused critical studies on which I have relied are cited at the appropriate place, but always economically in parentheses within the text itself instead of in notes. Except for one chapter in which editorial additions are used to clarify three reproduced manuscripts, this book contains no footnotes. To facilitate matters for the reader, all documentation is provided in brief parenthetical insertions which refer to the complete bibliographical information in the index of 'Secondary Works Cited.'

1

Towards a Definition of the Nachspiel

Modern Definitions

Most lexica of German literature and theatre provide definitions and descriptions of the Nachspiel. These are of unequal value, the chronological order in which they appeared revealing in most cases a sequence of heavy dependence on predecessors. Grimm's definition provides a starting point in a brief entry which separates the purely lexical meaning of 'nachspielen' (imitation) from the more formal and theatrically functional 'nachgespieltes stück, besonders ein dem hauptspiel folgendes spiel,' or the practice 'ein kleineres stück hinter dem hauptspiele folgen [zu] lassen oder dieses [zu] wiederholen' (*Deutsches Wörterbuch*, VII [1889], 130). Beyond this and some quotations from contemporary usage, Grimm directs us to several related words, of which 'exodium' is most fruitful. This Pauly-Wissowa defines at length, tracing its use as a comic, rhapsodic, or tragic theatrical form from classical Greek through Roman times (*Realenzyklopädie*, XII [1909], 1686-9). Using the word 'Nachspiel' as its German equivalent, Pauly-Wissowa draws attention to a variety of theatrical functions for the 'exodium,' including: parody of another work; an independent dramatic piece; a light work played after and in contrast to a previous tragedy (infrequent); or an improvised comedy played by amateurs after Atellan comedies or farces which in turn had been performed by experienced actors (most frequent). 'Exodia' were not always improvised, although the element of pantomime was usually prominent. A further definition from the nineteenth century is provided in Herloß-sohn/Marggraff's *Allgemeines Theaterlexikon*, which calls the Nachspiel 'ein 1-actiges Stückchen, welches zur Ausfüllung gegeben wird, wenn die Vorstellung zu kurz ist. Oft bringt auch der Dichter selbst ein N. an, wenn der Schluß seiner dram. Handlung in eine spätere Zeit fällt und als letzter Act daher nicht füglich gegeben werden kann' (V, 340). Two functions are named here, the Nachspiel simply as a filler for a short program and as an epilogue connected directly to the main work.

Edmund Stadler's description of the Nachspiel is still the most extensive we have to date (*Reallexikon* [2]1965, 'N,' 585-9). He begins with a brief definition: 'Meist kurzes heiteres Stück, das nach einem größeren gespielt wird, oft auch Nachkomödie genannt, selten Nach-stück.' He then moves to an extensive historical account of the genre from Roman *exodia* ('kurze improvisierte N.e, die aus dem Reiche des Niedrig-Komischen stammen und nach Tragödien und Komödien gespielt werden') to fifteenth- and sixteenth-century Netherlandic 'sotternien,' 'Possen,' 'Schwänke,' and 'kluchten,' played after longer works, and then to the sixteenth and seventeenth centuries, when the sung 'Jigs' of English wandering troupes penetrated German territory, sometimes in translation, with Pickelhäring often as the central comic character. Moving then to the German Nachspiel, Stadler begins with Jakob Ayrer's 'Singentspiele' of the seventeenth century, followed by 'Pickelhäring- und Possenspiele' popularized by Johann Velthen's troupe, and, at the turn of the century, by the replacement of Pickel-häring with Harlekin in short or longer comic works which included songs, several published by Christian Reuter from 1695. These pro-vided a prototype for the Harlekinaden as Nachspiele or Nach-Komö-dien played frequently by itinerant troupes in the eighteenth century. At the same time, German troupes such as those of Johann Velthen, Franz and Sophie Elensohn, Velthen's widow Katharina, Martin Müller, Johann Lorenz, Franz Wallerotty, Caroline Neuber, and past mid-century, Heinrich Koch, Franz Schuch, Joseph Memminger, Jo-hann Schönemann, and Konrad Ackermann commonly played Nach-spiele after longer works, often with Harlekin in the principal comic role, but increasingly with Hanswurst in the same function. In contrast to earlier musical models these troupes more frequently played purely spoken *Stegreifpossen* (i.e. improvised farces without songs, but some-times with dancing), designated as 'sehr lustige Nachspiele,' after longer works (the Hauptaktion), and decreasingly dependent on Dutch models. Now French, Italian, and to a lesser extent English predeces-sors became important (d'Allainval, Molière, Scarron, Kyd, de la Motte, Le Grand). Stadler cites numerous titles and refers to several reper-toires to justify his observations. As a result of Gottsched's influence on the theatre, writes Stadler, Nachspiele became less frequent after mid-century. Gottsched's celebrated *Deutsche Schaubühne*, which was to provide troupes with exemplary new material for their repertoires, contains only two Nachspiele (Quistorp's *Die Austern* and Luise Gottsched's *Der Witzling*). Repertoires of troupes such as Ackermann's increasingly played regular one-acters as Nachspiele, using Harlekin or Hanswurst less and less. 'Die Sitte, N.e zu veranstalten,' writes Stadler in reference to the final decade of the eighteenth century, 'wird endgültig aufgegeben.' Finally, he notes another Nachspiel tradition which he sees as an entirely different theatrical phenomenon: 'Neben diesen heitern N.en, die mit dem Hauptstück nichts zu tun haben, gibt es N.e, die mit ihm in Zusammenhang stehen.' He cites as examples Shakespeare's prelude and epilogue to *The Taming of the Shrew*, similar framing of Benedictine and Jesuit plays in the seventeenth and eighteenth centuries, and examples into the nineteenth century in which afterpieces had direct relation to the main action, like an epilogue. Some of this last group were even designated Nachspiele.

Since Stadler's account, little new has been added to our understanding of this genre. In his commentary to a reissue of Luise Gottsched's Nachspiel *Der Witzling* (1962), one of the few modern Nachspiel editions, Wolfgang Hecht describes the genre: '*Der Witzling* wird im Untertitel als *deutsches Nachspiel* bezeichnet, doch ist damit nicht der Gattungstyp, sondern allein die Aufführungsart gekennzeichnet: es sollte nach der Gewohnheit der damaligen Wandertruppen, als Aufheiterung nach einer Tragödie gespielt werden' (Gottsched, *Witzling*, 74). This suggests that the Nachspiel is not born of intrinsic structural characteristics, but rather of tonal and functional ones, a comic or light piece played as a contrast to a preceding tragedy. At the same time, Hecht claims: 'Eine literarische Wirkung des *Witzlings* ist nicht nachweisbar, und Aufführungen scheint das Nachspiel überhaupt nicht erlebt zu haben' (Gottsched, *Witzling*, 79). If this is indeed so, it must be difficult to conclude that this Nachspiel was played as a counterpoint to a preceding work, and even so it is only one example of hundreds.

Horst Steinmetz writes that the Nachspiel 'zwar gegenüber den komischen Teilen der Hauptaktion eine gewisse Selbständigkeit bewahrte, aber doch in der Art seiner Anlage und Durchführung große Ähnlichkeit mit ihnen hatte,' a claim that emphasizes tonal and thematic connections between the Nachspiel and previous work on the program, rather than the Nachspiel as light comic contrast (Steinmetz, [3]1978, 7). The definition in *Friedrichs Theaterlexikon* (1969) is a condensation of Stadler's, but stresses the Nachspiel's brevity and one-act structure, its placement after a longer piece but without thematic connection to it, and its usual comic content in contrast to the serious drama of the previous longer work ('komisches Gegenstück', p 300). Virtually the same as this are the accounts of Trilse (*Theaterlexikon*, 1977, 387), Wilpert (*Sachwörterbuch*, [6]1979, 535), Rischbieter (*Theater-Lexikon*, 1983, 939f), and *Metzlers Literatur Lexikon* (1984). Surprisingly, a number of modern lexica contain no entry on the Nachspiel at all, despite its prominence in the eighteenth century. These include Kosch's *Literatur-Lexikon* (1956) and *Theater-Lexikon* (1965), Kayser's *Kleines literarisches Lexikon* (1966), Krywalski's *Handlexikon* (1976), and Best's *Handbuch* (1982).

In her treatment of 'popular comedy,' Aikin-Sneath does devote some attention to the Nachspiel, but can list just two printed works of the genre (*Isaac und Rebecca; Harlequin, der ungedultig-hernach ...*), even maintaining that these are the only two 'that can be traced' (Aikin-Sneath, 55). Yüksel Pazarkaya's monograph on the German eighteenth-century one-act play (*Dramaturgie*, 1973) is based on a bibliography of some three hundred primary works, of which just fifteen are designated in their published or manuscript version as Nachspiele (the earliest 1743). Pazarkaya includes the Nachspiel among his general comments on the dramaturgy of the one-act play with the justification that many one-acters were played as Nachspiele (i.e. to close after a longer work) despite the absence of that designation on their title-pages. Yet early in the study he writes: 'Die Entwicklung des Nachspiels aus diesen Harlekinaden und Stegreifpossen zum schriftlich fixierten Einakter beweist sinnfällig die Unsinnigkeit der pauschalen Vermengung des Nachspiels mit dem Einakter' (Pazarkaya, 45). Nevertheless, once his emphasis is on text-based works, Pazarkaya abandons the distinction and consistently maintains the designation 'Einakter.' While his decision to do so is understandable considering the overall intention to examine the dramaturgy of the one-act play by means of 'eine dramatisch-poetologische Strukturanalyse' (25), my intention is to examine the Nachspiel as an autonomous genre and its contribution to the formation of another, much more general grouping, the *Einakter*. In doing so, not just text but also performance must play an important part. Mention must also be made of Elise Meyer's Leipzig dissertation of 1920 on the *Einakter* which does devote a chapter to the Nachspiel as autonomous work, but the slim study (66 typed pages) offers limited insight.

While some points of general agreement emerge from the above, there is also a good deal of contradiction. A major question must be raised about the basis from which all of the above works derive their definitions and understanding of the Nachspiel. While all cite secondary sources, particularly histories of literature and theatre, and some, especially Stadler and Pazarkaya, list titles on which they base their views, in no case could the primary text base from which these definitions derive be called extensive. Indeed, one must wonder in several cases if the writer had been exposed to any complete Nachspiel texts at all, or at least to more than a handful. Moreover, while Pazarkaya's study has a solid base in primary works, it is questionable whether the fifteen Nachspiel titles among his some three hundred justify the assumption that conclusions about the one-acter in general should also be applied to the Nachspiel in particular.

The Annotated Bibliography to the present volume includes 136 published Nachspiele or manuscripts ranging from 1702 to 1810. It provides a sufficiently broad primary text base against which to measure much of our understanding of the genre. The understanding can be divided into two parts, aspects relating to *structure* and *content*, and aspects relating to *function*. Within *structure* and *content* fall the questions of the Nachspiel's length, comic or tragic nature, the presence and role of a central comic character such as Harlekin or Hanswurst, and the presence of pantomime, music, songs, and dance. These questions can be answered with certainty when posed against the broad text base provided. But published texts or even manuscripts do not tell us enough about how a work was performed, to what extent the text or manuscript was honoured or altered in performance, and almost never give us information about other works performed beforehand or afterward on the same program. Beyond structure and content, dramatic *function* must be the second part of the Nachspiel definition. Under *function* fall questions of whether or not the Nachspiel was in fact always a theatrical afterpiece following a major one, as its lexical meaning would suggest; whether it was commonly related directly or indirectly to a preceding work, as comic counterpoint or otherwise; and finally, an aspect virtually ignored in the definitions above, how it related to audiences of the day. While the primary text base can help with these questions, more answers can be found by examining contemporary performance conditions, in other words the repertoires and production settings throughout the century.

In attempting a more comprehensive study of the Nachspiel, we must also be prepared to see it as a genre which possibly changed in structure, content, and function during these hundred years; or to con-clude that the term 'genre' is in fact a misnomer, or at least too vague to apply with accuracy to such a diverse group of dramatic pieces as the bibliographic and repertory bases represent.

Contemporary Understanding

Stadler's broad historical definition of the Nachspiel could be applied to any work occupying the final position in a multi-work program, not just those designated specifically 'Nachspiele.' So in the eighteenth century one could, for example, point to the many ecclesiastical and school dramas which commonly employed the structural division of prologue, drama text, and epilogue or operatic conclusion (*Nachmusik*). Such dramatic constructs abounded at least to the early 1760s – e.g. *Der gestraffte Ehr-Geitz in Ceadvalla Königen in Armuzia* (Auff der Schau-bühne vorgestellt von der studierenden Jugend deß Churfürstlichen Gymnasii Soc Jesu zu Landshuet, Golowitz, 1700); *Die Glückseligkeit eines fleißigen und gelehrten Studiosi* (Halle: Lehmann, [1727]); *Die IV. Betrachtung von Augustins Sieg über sich selbst* in Franz Neumayr, *Geistliche Schaubühne*, übersetzt von Johann Andree Schachtner (Augsburg & Innsbruck: Wolff, 1758). These works were often in two languages, the Latin original and German translation printed side by side, and the three structural parts closely related. But their epilogues are not comic and hence they do not belong within the same tradition as the focus of the present study.

Lessing actually fixes the first German use of 'Nachspiel' to refer to a comic afterpiece:

> Der Gebrauch, allezeit ein Nachspiel nach den neuen Stücken aufzuführen, ist erst 1722 aufgekommen. Man spielte vor dieser Zeit die neuen Komödien allein und begleitete sie erst, wenn sie acht- bis zehnmal waren vorgestellet worden, mit Nachspielen. Man glaubte alsdenn, daß das Stück anfinge, weniger zu gefallen. Diesen zuweilen ungegründeten Vorurteilen zu-vorzukommen, liess der Herr de la Motte gleich bei der ersten Vorstellung seines Trauerspiels 'Romulus', ein Nachspiel aufführen. Diesem Exempel haben hernach andere Komödienschreiber gefolgt ... (*Das Neueste aus dem Reiche des Witzes*, December 1751; *Werke*, vollständige Ausgabe, 8. Teil, 101)

Lessing is referring to a La Motte production on German soil in 1722, and although this must indeed have been an early use of the term 'Nachspiel,' Lessing's claim is not entirely accurate. That the term was used before 1722 is clear for example from *Die verachtete Eitelkeit der*

Welt, published in 1702, and designated specifically on the title-page as 'Nach-Spiel,' and from a 'lustiges Nachspiel' performed in 1710 in Frankfurt, as reported by Elisabeth Mentzel (Mentzel, 130). But Lessing's observation is concerned more with performance necessity and convention than semantics, and it is worth noting his belief that the Nachspiel was introduced to satisfy the audience as a welcome change from the ponderous tragedy preceding. Later on, Lessing wrote occasional further references to the Nachspiel, as in the *Hamburgische Dramaturgie*: 'Das Nachspiel kann handeln, wovon es will, und braucht mit dem Vorhergehenden nicht in der geringsten Verbindung zu stehen' (101-104. St., *Werke,* Hanser edition, IV, 693). This is a useful statement for our understanding, but stemming from the late sixties it should be seen as relevant mainly for the latter decades of the century; it may not be consistent with the nature and function of the Nachspiel in earlier years.

In the Preface to his own collected comedies in 1746/7, Adam Gottfried Uhlich noted the public demand for Nachspiele, similar to the way Lessing described the situation in 1722: 'Die Einrichtung von jedem Bande würde immer dergestalt beschaffen seyn, daß drey grosse und drey kleine Lustspiele darinnen wären. An den letztern haben wir bishero noch immer einen Mangel gehabt, und sie sind uns doch nöthig, da es einmal bey uns eingeführet ist, daß der Zuhörer für sein Geld eine Vor- und Nach-Comödie sehen muß' (*1. Sammlung,* v). When we compare this statement against performance evidence of the itinerant troupes in the coming chapter (Repertoires), it will be clear that Uhlich's statement tells only half the story. It was indeed so that the public demanded a Nachspiel, but it is not true that there was a dearth of them in the repertoires. What Uhlich means when he speaks of a 'Mangel' is the paucity of published, literary-based Nachspiele as opposed to the hundreds, if not thousands, of extemporized ones. His statement is supported by evidence of published Nachspiele in the Bibliography at the end of this study – it contains just twelve Nachspiele published in or before the year Uhlich wrote the above (one of which is his *Der faule Bauer,* itself not a particularly brilliant contribution to the genre). Uhlich's comment points to a necessary division in our examination of the Nachspiel: extemporized as opposed to text-based or literary works.

With the growing number of literary journals from mid-century, and a conscious cultivation of the theatre scene, more critics and theorists addressed themselves to the nature of the various genres. The extensive observations of one such critic, identified as 'J.F. He***rt,' show that the tension between extemporization and literary drama was central to the debate. He writes at length of Franz Schuch the Elder's highly successful Berlin engagement in 1754, performances characterized by their regular use of extemporization and the traditional comic figure in Nachspiele:

> Ich habe noch kein Wort von Komödien gesagt, in welchen Hanswurst erscheint, der Herr Schuch ist. Machte ich mich nicht einer lieblosen Gesinnung gegen mein Vaterland verdächtig, wenn ich einen Hanswurst rühmen wollte. Weg mit dem Schmuze vor gesitteten Leuten. Die Franzosen haben den feinen Arlequin von der Bühne verbannet, der doch das Theatre Italien mit sinnreichen Scherzen anfüllet, und wir erdulden den dummen groben H...W... Man sage nicht, das ist nun einmal der deutsche Geschmack, denn dieses heißt mit andern Worten, den Deutschen ergötzen grobe, niederträchtige Possen, und den Franzosen belustiget ein schöner, wohlanständiger Witz. Ich bin in diesen Gauckelspielen nicht gewesen aus Furcht ein jeder, der mich sähe heraus kommen, würde mit Fingern auf mich zeigen. Nur einmal führte mich, ich weiß nicht welcher Trieb in den Talismann, aber mir zum größesten Misvergnügen. Leider habe ich den H...W... in den Nachspielen oft genug angezeiget gesehen. Er macht allezeit den Beschluß. Ich werde der Nachspiele in dem Verzeichnisse nicht gedenken, denn sie haben wegen ihrer Ungereimtheit keinen Namen, und sie verdienen es auch nicht. (*Neue Erweiterungen*, IV, 221f)

This assessment makes it obvious first that crude Nachspiele were a constant theatrical presence in the fifties. The author's distaste for them seems to have two bases, one nationalistic pride, the other aesthetic. His preference for the French over his own countrymen is an unremitting tune of German theorists in the century, underscoring again and again a deep inferiority complex about their own stage when compared with that of their neighbours across the Rhine. This results here, as often in other documents, in an anxious disclaimer of the Nachspiel and what it represents. Heaven forbid that this be taken as the measure of 'der deutsche Geschmack'! The author takes pains to inform us that he himself has seen only one of these dreadful things – and is at a loss to guess 'welcher Trieb' drove him there – but insists that he avoids them in general 'aus Furcht ein jeder, der mich sähe heraus kommen, würde mit Fingern auf mich zeigen.' One suspects that had he given freer rein to his 'Trieb' and less to what others might think of him, he would have seen – even perhaps enjoyed – many more Nachspiele.

The author goes on to admit that when such classics as *Tartuffe*, *Canut*, *Zaire*, or *Iphigenia* are given, 'waren wieder leere Plätze,' whereas when they were not, 'Die Komödie war jedesmal gedrängt voll' (*Neue Erweiterungen*, IV, 223). The Nachspiel clearly had such a stranglehold on audiences that even this author, in private, would have to admit that it was indeed one undeniable indicator of German taste. He criticizes these audiences sharply for exercising in his view such crude preference:

> ... die wohlbestallten Herrn, werden ferner nach ausgeleerter Pfeife in der Komödie ihrem Bauche ungehindert eine Bewegung machen. Für ihr Geld müssen sie lachen, und zwar lachen, daß ihnen der Bauch schüttert. Die Tragödien besuchen sie nicht, dafür gehen sie lieber in die Kirche, da können sie umsonst weinen. In ihren Augen sind die Komödien bloße Gauckelspiele, und das lieben sie. Was sollen sie in den Trauerspielen machen, da man nur weinet und ermordet. Sind solche Menschen nicht hart gestraft, daß ihr Herz nicht die sanfte Empfindungen des Mitleidens, der Hoffnung, der Betrübnis, des Zorns in der Tragödie fühlet? Ja sie sind nur halbe Menschen, denn sie haben wenig Empfindungen der Menschlichkeit. Was soll man von dem Charakter solcher Leute denken, denen ein Gauckelspiel nur gefällt. (*Neue Erweiterungen*, IV, 223f)

Whatever one should think of these theatre-goers, they were more representative of German taste than the author. It is disturbing how he denigrates their character to the status of 'nur halbe Menschen' because they to him lack sufficient response to his grand list of human emotions. In fact this is never the fault of the audience. If anything it is the fault of the stage itself, the inability of dramatists and actors to present convincing works – that was the problem at the time. In accusing particularly 'die wohlbestallten Herrn,' the author tells much of the nature of those theatre-goers with such, for him, insufferable taste. They were the bourgeoisie with money, status, and influence, and if one class is to be taken as representative of the time, then surely this one must be a serious candidate. The author, as many others of his type, demonstrates blind intolerance and a pompous self-importance in refusing to accept popular entertainment as worthwhile despite its prevalence both in his time and indeed throughout cultural history.

In terms of aesthetics, the author complains bitterly about the Nachspiel's 'Ungereimtheiten' (*Neue Erweiterungen*, IV, 223), meaning its incongruities when compared with the author's sense of naturalness and verisimilitude. By contrast, he lauds the classical unities which to him represent the epitome of naturalness on stage. These unities of course were central to the standard aesthetic position of the time but soon after were recognized as the false construct that they are, albeit often necessary as rules of thumb for effective drama, yet in themselves an open admission of the fundamental unreality and unnaturalness of theatrical performance. By contrast, the Nachspiel was bounded by no rules at all. Later in our analyses of individual Nachspiele and comic figures the issue of naturalness will be important.

The author adds at the end of his treatise a bibliography of contemporary dramas, but as he said above, 'Ich werde der Nachspiele in dem Verzeichnisse nicht gedenken, denn sie haben wegen ihrer Ungereimtheit keinen Namen, und sie verdienen es auch nicht.' It is true that many extemporized Nachspiele were untitled, although many others were, and their documentation is a definite problem to be addressed.

We have Gottsched to thank for the first serious attempt to collect and publish a bibliography of German theatre in his *Nöthiger Vorrath* (1757-65). In the Foreword, he calls the work 'ein vollständiges Verzeichniß, wo nicht aller, doch der allermeisten dramatischen Stücke' (Gottsched, *NV*, I, [ix]). It is hence admittedly somewhat selective, but in it Gottsched is broad-minded enough to include works he himself considered bad (*NV*, I, [xvf]) and even offers the Nachspiel as an independent category (e.g. *NV*, II, 279, 281), thereby acknowledging it as a distinct genre. However, Gottsched's bibliography is entirely text-based, or literary; it takes no account of the extemporized Nachspiel. Further, under the subtitle Nachspiel he frequently lists works that were published as Lustspiele or Schäferspiele (e.g. *NV*, II, 284), all of which suggests that the Nachspiel for Gottsched was a concept that included several genres. He saw the Nachspiel as a functional entity, any short work that held final place on a program following a major one. This understanding must remain central to our consideration; it is an early sign that as the century progressed from extemporized to literary drama the notion of the Nachspiel became increasingly generalized to include a variety of sub-genres appearing in conjunction with longer works. Gottsched's publication of *Die Austern* and *Herr Witzling* in *Die deutsche Schaubühne*, a collection intended to represent all of the popular genres, illustrates again that he saw the Nachspiel as a genre in itself, however vaguely he defined it. There the two works carry the designation 'Nachspiel' on their title-pages, although Gottsched's introductory remark on *Die Austern*, that 'es nur ein Nachspiel ist' (Gottsched, *DS*, IV, [xxv]), suggests that he did not view the genre as very important.

Gottsched's inclusion of the Nachspiel as a genre in his *Deutsche Schaubühne* invites two questions: to what extent did further published

Nachspiele maintain the specific genre designation on their title-pages, and what did that indicate about the nature of those works? In 1770-1 Simon Nicolas Henri Linguet's *Beytrag zum spanischen Theater* (Hamburg u Riga: Hartknoch) appeared, containing German translations of his compilation of some Spanish plays. The originals carried the genre designation 'entremes,' in translation 'Lustspiel,' except for one, *Die Melonen*, which is designated in German as 'Nachspiel.' One can only speculate about why this was the case, the most obvious reason being that the translator saw in *Die Melonen* structural, thematic, tonal, or other characteristics which merited a different genre label. This speculation of course assumes that the translator had a prior conception of what a Nachspiel was, as opposed to the Lustspiel. But even if this was the case for him, there is a great deal of evidence to show that his contemporaries' understanding of the Nachspiel as genre was anything but clear. Increasingly from the sixties, plays designated as Nachspiele were published, but in many cases the same plays were republished with the genre designation 'Lustspiel' on their title-page. That can be said of many of the Nachspiele in the Bibliography at the end of this study. Clearly, in the later decades of the century, the designation Nachspiel was losing its meaning and becoming interchangeable with the more general designation 'Lustspiel.' Still, the fact that plays continued to be published specifically as 'Nachspiel' well past 1800 suggests that the term still held some meaning at the time, and it is one task of the following study to determine what this meaning was.

Critical discussion of the Nachspiel continued through the century's end. The Foreword to Heinrich Wilhelm Lawätz's *Die Diamanten* (1794) discusses the Nachspiel as genre and rejects it in favour of higher-quality pieces. Lawätz bases his opinions on the fact that such masters as Horace, Batteaux, and other French classicists made no place for short dramatic pieces (Lawätz, 7, 8, 11), which surely indicates their worthlessness. Molière, however, did write comedies in one act, but Lawätz condemns them as 'nicht anders, als Farcen – unbedeutende Possenspiele – Freudenfeste für den uncultivirtesten Theil der Gallerie' (12). He begins to remind us of the arrogance of J.F. H***rt above, continuing to echo that stance:

> Noch bis auf den Tag, – an dem ich dieses schreibe und der Leser das, was ich geschrieben habe, lesen wird – werden, selbst auf unseren regelmäßigsten und besten Bühnen, gleich nach den feinsten Produckten unserer besten dramatischen Dichter ... – Schnurren gegeben, die man Nachspiele nennt – ...

> Freylich, durch Nachspiele der gewöhnlichen Art werden die sanften,
> edlen und großen Gefühle, welche die Kunst mit der einen Hand in das
> Herz des Zuschauers gepflanzt hatte, mit der andern wieder ausgegätet –
> und die Thränen der Schwermuth oder Freude – diese schönen und ehren-
> vollen Thränen, die man seinen Augen entlockt hatte, auf eine unsanfte Art
> wiederum abgetrocknet, indem man ihn zum Lachen – und dadurch zu
> einer Thorheit verleitet, die er ungern begeht und gegen die sich seine
> bessere Empfindung mit starker Allgewalt sträubt. (13f)

Beneath Lawätz's complete disdain for the Nachspiel lies an aesthetic
bias which grants preference to melodramatic tragedy and sees comedy, particularly that of the Nachspiel type, as undermining that genre
in an almost immoral way. Yet Lawätz must admit in his foreword that
Nachspiele remained immensely popular, and he thus sees no way to
get rid of them for the moment. Still, he grasps eagerly at one solution
which he has observed in Hamburg: 'Auf einigen Bühnen, z.B. auf der
hamburgischen gehen mehrmalen diese sogenannten Nachspiele dem
Hauptstücke voraus, – und werden dadurch in Vorspiele umgewan-
delt' (14). The repertoires of standing theatres in Hamburg as well as
elsewhere will show that this was indeed sometimes the case, a fact
that makes the functional definition of the Nachspiel even more difficult. Just how important was its position in the program and its relationship to the preceding or following work? Lawätz approves of
playing the Nachspiel first because in order to maintain the primacy of
tragedy it is better to have the audience go home with this fresh in
mind, rather than

> mit dem lauten Gelächter [das Theater zu] verlassen, daß der gewöhnliche
> Zweck jener Nachspiele von der bisherigen Art ist, in welchen die einzelnen
> Scenen an einander genehet sind, wie die bunten Lappen des bekannten
> Lustigmachers, der in selbigen, nachdem er von den Bühnen verbannt wor-
> den ist, dennoch sein Wesen treibt, ohne daß derjenige ihn einmal bemerkt,
> der den Mann allein nach dem Kleide beurtheilt – und ihn folglich nun-
> mehro nicht kennt, weil er sein vielfarbiges Kleid mit einem einfarbigen ver-
> wechselt, und sich dadurch unkenntlich gemacht hat. (15)

Lawätz's diatribe is unintentionally valuable for what it tells us about
the Nachspiele he saw performed. They were clearly loosely structured
and dominated by a central comic figure, although without identifiable
garb. The role of the comic figure in the Nachspiel tradition needs to be
addressed at length.

A more positive position is presented by Franz von Bilderbeck in a Foreword to the two volumes of his own *Schauspiele* (1801) where he characterizes the Nachspiel as

> ... unter allen dramatischen Arbeiten ... die undankbarste ... Es ist Miniaturmalerei – weder an Entwickelung der Karaktere, noch an einer allmählich sich entfaltenden interessanten Intrigue ist dabei zu denken. Das Sujet zu einem Nachspiele kann und darf weiter nichts seyn, als entweder eine Karrikatur-Skizze, oder eine überraschende Anekdote, in einem gedrängten und raschen Dialog, launig oder beisend vorgetragen. Wir besitzen wenig gute Nachspiele, die Franzosen eine Menge – woher kommt das? Die Ursache davon wäre, sollt' ich glauben, selbst im Karakter beider Nationen leicht zu finden. (Bilderbeck, I, [xiif])

Bilderbeck's conception of the Nachspiel was obviously very different from that of Lawätz; indeed, they seem to be talking about two entirely different things. What he says here suggests that with 'Nachspiel' he simply means short comedy, especially since he praises the French for their Nachspiele, which were in fact as a rule designated as 'Comédie en un acte.' His characterization is based entirely on a literary form. However, Bilderbeck's genre designation of the plays in the two volumes following this introduction does not confirm his apparently clear grasp of what a Nachspiel was. *Erste Liebe* is designated there as a Nachspiel on its title-page, and also referred to as such in the Foreword. On the other hand, *Kleider machen Leute* is called both 'Nachspiel' and 'Posse' in the Foreword, but 'Lustspiel' on its title-page; similarly *Das Manuscript*. While the mixing of genre designations for the same work shows that Bilderbeck's understanding of 'Nachspiel' was anything but concrete, the fact remains that the term 'Nachspiel' must have had some significance, and some attraction for him, even if confused.

Bilderbeck was not alone in this confusion. At the end of the century and for the first decades of the next the following collections appeared (and there were others like them):

Nachspiele zum Behuf teutscher Theater. Hrsg v Georg Carl Claudius. Frankfurt u Leipzig: Brönner, 1783.

Nachspiele für Schauspielergesellschaften, die keine Operetten und Balletten aufführen können, oder wollen. Wesel u Leipzig: Röder u Heinsius, 1789.

Drei Nachspiele von Schletter. Brünn: Bauer, 1791.

Nachspiele für stehende Bühnen und Privattheater. Hrsg v W Vogel. 2 Bde, Frankfurt: Simon, 1809.

Jahrbuch deutscher Nachspiele. Hrsg v Carl v Holtei. 1. Jg.ff, 1822ff, Breslau: Graß, Barth u Co, Leipzig: Barth.

Despite what the reader might expect, all of these contain plays almost
exclusively designated as 'Lustspiele,' not 'Nachspiele,' on their title-
pages. Why then do they persistently and deliberately use the word
'Nachspiel' in their volume titles? The editors and publishers of these
volumes apparently saw the designation 'Nachspiel' as a point of
attraction for readers, hence buyers. It recalled a type of work with
high entertainment value, a throwback to the days when 'Nachspiel'
meant the comic climax of the performance, and while the works in
these volumes contain nothing of the outrageous bawdiness of that bygone era, it can certainly be said that their consistent intention is to appeal to popular taste. At the end of the eighteenth century and beyond,
the term 'Nachspiel' did not carry the same meaning as it did earlier,
but when used it did recall those early decades. Attempts to define it
through evidence from the century's end result only in vagueness and
confusion. Its pure form stems from the earlier great era of extemporized theatre and itinerant companies.

Finally, one notes with amusement that even the renowned literary
historian and bibliographer Karl Goedeke had difficulty with the genre
designation 'Nachspiel.' He erroneously lists the following as Nach-
spiele, when in fact their title-pages bear the genre designation
'Lustspiel': Löwen, *Die neue Agnese* (Goedeke, IV[1], 46); Bock, *Die Parodie*
(IV[1], 646); Schmid, *Die Parodie* (IV[1], 131); Weiße, *Walder* (IV[1], 131);
Schiebeler, *Schule der Jünglinge* (IV[1], 131); Kohusak, *Zeneide* (III, 369);
Die Gratien (III, 369); *Die Familie* (III, 370); Röpe, *Die ungewöhnliche
Liebeserklärung* (V, 252).

Clarification of the term 'Nachspiel' as it was used throughout the
century can result only from a re-examination of the two main sources
of information: performances of Nachspiele and written or published
evidence of the primary works. These, in turn, demand close inspection
of repertoires and theatre companies as well as analysis of texts. It is
hence along these lines of inquiry that the following study proceeds.

❧ 2 ❧

Repertoires and Performances
of Itinerant Troupes
and Standing Theatres
in the Eighteenth Century

The entries below comprise a broad and representative selection of German theatre repertoires (the stock of works) and performances (their actual occurrence on stage) in the eighteenth century. Readers should also consult the list of documented performances at the end of this volume. Of necessity the entries below cover much of the geographical extent of German-speaking territory, for what was typical in northern parts may have been quite different in other regions and so on. They take into account the entire century, for theatrical taste and convention certainly changed with time, even from decade to decade and year to year. Many highly reliable and virtually complete repertoire and performance lists, and many others which although fragmentary offer a variety of insights, provide the sources for this overview. Other names could be added to the cities and troupes selected below, but an attempt to present a complete picture would fill many volumes on its own.

The source material and subsequent repertoire and performance accounts have been divided into two groups: cities and itinerant troupes. By looking at activity in eight major centres and by six leading troupes, it is possible to assess changes in theatrical style and content over the century, most important the shift in focus from itinerant troupes to standing theatres. With the founding of standing theatres from about 1770 in virtually every major German city – Nationaltheater they were usually named, although there was no accompanying sense of nationhood – we witness a major change from the predominance of travelling actors to that of standing theatre conmpanies, and a complete reassessment of repertoires. The term 'Nationaltheater' is somewhat misleading as these theatres remained almost exclusively controlled by the court. State interest in them was largely based on the desire to encourage good social behaviour and morals, and to keep financial resources from flowing across political borders via itinerant companies from other lands (see Martens, 38, 48). These standing theatres increasingly had more or less permanent companies of actors instead of the constantly changing series of faces in the itinerant troupes. As regular employees under contract, they had less personal influence over what they performed and had to take heed constantly of the disposition and preference of their employers, which is not the same as tailoring one's efforts to the taste and demand of a paying general public. At the same time, Gottsched's theatre reforms were beginning to take root, and with them their originator's prejudices in favour of certain types and purposes of dramatic works and against others. Moreover, in major and minor centres alike, moral and political censorship of unacceptable theatrical thematics and expression was the norm in the last decades of the century.

The earlier repertoires and performances of itinerant troupes, however, offer a source of greater and freer theatrical energy from the beginning of the century until at least 1770. They also cover considerably greater geographic breadth than the analysis of eight cities can provide. The fate of such companies was to move constantly, among small centres and large, to find new sympathetic patrons and more responsive, financially generous audiences. They had to stay on the move either because their privilege to play had expired, or because their stock of plays had been exhausted, or simply because they could not pay their debts. Their repertoires and performances were geared much more to the taste of the common man than were those of the standing theatres later. Furthermore, lacking a single stage, good sets, costumes, and the like, their repertoires and especially the way they played them were naturally different from those of geographically fixed companies later on. This itinerant pattern creates extreme difficulties in identifying complete repertoires or performance schedules. In four cases of itinerant troupe principals, however, Franz Schuch, Heinrich Koch, Johann Schönemann, and Konrad Ackermann, we can rely on detailed historical studies. In two others, Caroline Neuber and Joseph von Kurz (Bernardon), we have extended examples of repertoires and performance programs sufficient to draw conclusions about their activities at least for certain periods. These six troupes were among the best known and most widely travelled during the eighteenth century. For many companies, however, especially before 1727, there exist no extensive accurate investigations of repertoires and performances, but a considerable amount of information on them will be presented during the discussion of the eight cities considered.

How reliable is the information provided by the reference works below? Their sources are primarily contemporary eighteenth-century theatre journals and diaries, of which there was a rapid increase after mid-century, contemporary theatre histories, and collections of *Theaterzettel* – playbills – on which actual programs were advertised. The journals, diaries, and histories, although providing a wealth of information, are far from complete, so too the collections of playbills known to the authors of these studies. But these playbills probably remain the most comprehensive primary documentation of eighteenth-century repertoires and performances. Many city and research libraries in German-speaking territory have collections of original playbills from their own immediate area, although naturally much more completely for more recent times than for the eighteenth-century, which is usually represented fragmentarily. But the original playbills of some major standing theatres remain available in complete form, as for example those of the Vienna Burgtheater in the Austrian National Library. Playbill collections of itinerant troupes are invariably fragmentary because of the very nature of their activity. The major collections of eighteenth-century German playbills available today are found in Berlin, Braunschweig, Budapest, Frankfurt (also on microfilm), Hamburg, Mannheim, and Vienna. More complete lists of playbill repositories and details of the holdings in these major centres can be found in Gebhardt (*Spezialbestände*, 1977) and Roob (*Sondersammlungen*, 1982). Yet even fine collections of playbills pose problems for the reconstruction of repertoires, for early playbills were often undated except for an indication of the weekday; and moreover, by comparing a specific playbill with a contemporary journal entry, it can sometimes be shown that what was actually played on a certain afternoon or evening was not exactly what had been previously advertised on the playbill – i.e. the program was changed at the last minute, perhaps, for example, because of sudden illness among the cast. Furthermore, when tracing performances of Nachspiele from playbills, there is the additional difficulty that the Nachspiel was often indicated without precise title. But it should be stressed that these problems are minor when set against the immense source of performance information that playbills provide.

Beyond those listed below, two further works should be mentioned as helpful for an overview of sources containing repertoires: Ralf Schuster's *Spielplanverzeichnisse* (1985) for standing theatres in the last decades of the century, and the unpublished collection of theatre materials by Oskar Fambach (Sammlung Oskar Fambach), now housed in an archive of the University German Department Seminar Library in Bonn, which concentrates on standing theatres toward and beyond 1800, with emphasis on Weimar, and holds a vast amount of unpublished reference material on individual performances, works, and personalities. One cannot fail to admire the enormous concentrated devotion of such scholars as Fambach, whose tens of thousands of precisely typed and handwritten slips of information based on many years of scrupulous sifting through sources form the essential Fambach archive; or, similarly, the eminent Franz Hadamowsky in Vienna, whose first major work appeared in 1934, with others steadily appearing until today and more to come.

Repertoires and performance data of specific cities follow alphabetically below. Itinerant troupes are then treated in chronological order, that is, with reference to their period of activity. Each section is preceded by a list of sources so that readers who wish to pursue individual topics further will have a concise bibliography at hand. The chapter ends with a summary of the nature and importance of the comic figure. In the course of analysing repertoires and performances, it will become obvious that his role was essential for the Nachspiel's success.

Clearly, choices have been made concerning which cities and which troupes are analysed in detail. The choices have been guided by the desire to be geographically and temporally comprehensive, by the availability of reliable source materials, and by the necessity to remain within reasonable constraints of length. While a reader may ask why such centres as Dresden, Leipzig, and Zürich are not analysed in detail, it should be remembered that coverage of itinerant troupes includes much more than the eight cities treated separately, for their travels were extensive. They played in Dresden, Leipzig, and many other German centres; and some in Switzerland, such as Ackermann who visited Basel, Bern, Lucerne, Solothurn, and Zürich repeatedly for dozens of performances. Thus the analysis of repertoires and performances in this chapter claims broad validity. Readers who wish further information on theatre activity in any German-speaking centre not treated in detail here should consult Franz Hadamowsky's most comprehensive list of historical sources (*Bücherkunde deutschsprachiger Theaterliteratur*, 1982) and Ralf Schuster's repertoire sources (*Spielplanverzeichnisse*, 1985).

CITIES

Berlin

SOURCES
Brachvogel, *Geschichte* (1877); Plümicke, *Entwurf* (1781); Schäffer/Hartmann, *Die königl. Theater* (1886)

COVERAGE
Samples from performances and repertoires from the beginning of the century to 1786 are considered, including complete performance lists of the Heinrich Koch and Carl Döbbelin companies 1771-81 and complete repertoires of seven theatres from 1786 beyond the end of the century (Potsdamer Stadttheater, Neues Palais in Potsdam, Prinzessinen-Palais in Berlin, Königliches Palais in Berlin, Charlottenburg Schloßtheater, Opernhaus, Schauspielhaus).

In the first half of the century the court theatre was the focus for theatrical activity, but there was also a regular series of appearances by itinerant troupes, seldom lasting as long as six months, on various stages, from palace and court theatres to temporary locations in public areas, such as those constructed on the Gendarmemarkt, before the city hall, and im Marstall, as well as standing structures such as the theatre on the Monbijou-Platz. A new Opernhaus was built in 1742, and Franz Schuch (the Younger), who took over his father's troupe after the latter's death in 1764, built his own theatre in 1771 on the Behrenstraße, in which Koch, then Döbbelin played. In 1775 the Königliches Komödienhaus, the first permanent theatre, was erected on the Gendarmeplatz, which became in 1786 the Königliches Nationaltheater (Schauspielhaus) under the direction of Johann Jakob Engel, then Karl Wilhelm Ramler and August Wilhelm Iffland.

Although Brachvogel includes no extended repertoires, he provides excerpts until 1786, those for the years before 1771 being particularly valuable. His account strikes the reader as reliable and well-informed, based on an exhaustive search of original source materials consulted (Brachvogel, *Vorrede*, VI-VII). Plümicke presents a complete record of performances by Koch's troupe from 1771 to 1775, the year of his death, and 1775 to 1781 by Döbbelin's, who succeeded Koch (Plümicke, 392-434). The information covers roughly four hundred performance dates and a thousand works. Brachvogel gives a representative picture of the Döbbelin repertoire 1781-6. Schäffer/Hartmann complement Plümicke and Brachvogel with alphabetical and chronological lists of works performed 1786-1885 in seven theatres with the total number of performances of each (Schäffer/Hartmann, 1-161). As these lists do not indicate the actual dates of each performance, combinations of works on a single program cannot be determined. The chronological list of works performed in what were essentially seven court theatres includes 493 titles.

ANALYSIS

From the beginning of the century, a passion for opera and various other forms of musical drama ruled Berlin alongside, and often intertwined with, the thriving theatre scene. Brachvogel's richly detailed account of the early decades, and the contemporary insights of Plümicke (an actor and playwright himself), show a regular series of German and foreign (especially French) itinerant companies vying for audiences. Common fare was the Hauptaktion with Harlekin or Hanswurst prominent, and Nach-Comödien in which the character seems to have enjoyed complete freedom to improvise. Plümicke summarizes the early years by means of what he claims to be the handwritten reflections of an early (unidentified) Hanswurst:

> Meistentheils musste die lustige Person zu Pferde, wo nicht in völliger Kleidung, doch unter einer Kappe mit Schellen, und während der Abkündigung, die nach dreimaligem Wirbel auf der Trommel erfolgte, mit einer Brille über die Nase erscheinen, statt des Zaums den Schweif seines Pferdes in die Hand nehmen, schnarren, lispeln oder durch die Nase reden, demnächst an öffentlichen Plätzen, oder den Hauptecken, ein gemahltes Bild aushängen, worauf alles das Wunderbare des zu gebenden Schauspiels mit lebhaften Farben aufgetragen war, vornehmlich aber auch die Ankündigungszettel über die Hälfte mit Unsinn und Rodomontaden anfüllen, weil sonst sogleich ein merklicher Schade bei der Einnahme verspürt wurde. (Plümicke, 174f)

With jester's cap and antics, holding his horse's tail, this theatrical envoy was in one sense a consummate fool, in another a veiled representative of social conscience. Amid much affected clamour he donned spectacles (a sign of learned authority), read a treatise (an act of governmental prescription), holding his horse by the tail, not the reins (allowing the beast, not the master, to lead, and at the same time risking faecal bombardment). The description shows that the comic antics were also pivotal for box office success, and despite some obvious reluctance, Plümicke acknowledges that such comic figures were essentially German and worthy of taking seriously as contributors to the development of a national theatre tradition as opposed to the foreign influence which dominated it for so long (Plümicke, 178f).

Brachvogel gives the most complete picture available of the first six
decades. Berlin's theatre history was intimately related to the tastes and
preferences of the Prussian king who held full authority over permission to perform, and who provided strong financial subsidies to
companies he wished to encourage, to the detriment of others. But the
theatrical dispositions of the three Prussian kings until 1786 differed,
which produced separate phases of theatrical development in these
years. Frederick I (died 1713) had no time for German troupes –
'deutsche Komödiantenbagage' (Brachvogel, 63) – generously supporting instead French and Italian companies at his court. Frederick
William I (1716-40) changed the climate abruptly with his support of
German troupes, particularly that of the renowned 'starken Mann' Johann von Eckenberg, whom he granted a privilege in 1717, named
'Hofcomödianten' in 1732, and assisted financially to the end of his
reign. Eckenberg played regularly at the court, but also enjoyed enormous popularity at other Berlin theatres with a wide range of citizens
in attendance. Famous initially for his acrobatics and carnival acts, he
developed to offer a wide repertoire including operettas, comedies,
and serious plays. A fascinating advertising sheet of 1725, complete
with fifteen dramatic pictures of Eckenberg's strongman antics, shows
what his public paid to see (reproduced in Hansen, Abb 59). It depicts,
among other settings, Eckenberg prostrate with enormous stones and
anvils on his body, Eckenberg lifting a horse, and bearing the weight of
five adults (including Hanswurst). Brachvogel shows that stock comic
characters such as Harlekin, Kolumbine, Pierrot, and Pantalon were an
integral part of his performances and recognizable immediately by
their traditional masks and costumes, but the central Harlekin was in
essence more a mixture of the German Hanswurst and his foreign
prototype than a continuation of the Italian tradition (Brachvogel, 70,
80). Frederick William ran a tight financial ship of state, which also applied to the theatre troupes he supported. Thus there were detailed
statements of his subventions, such as for the Eckenberg troupe's
monthly salaries in 1733. Here the money all goes to 'Bringhello und
Frau, Pantalon, Anselm, Zahnarzt und Frau, Pierrot, Theater Bediente
[a pittance], Arlequin und Frau' (Brachvogel, 78). It is easy to see where
the king's theatrical tastes and preferences lay at this point. A typical
playbill of the Eckenberg troupe from the thirties, which can be seen as
representative of performances at the time (Brachvogel, 82), announces
a 'lustige Haupt-Action,' *Der verliebte Frantzoss in Sachsen*, 'Mit Hanns

Wurst, einem abgedankten Soldaten, gekröhnten Poeten, curieusen Lufft-Fahrer auf den Blocksberg und endlich Bräutigam nach der alten Mode' (Brachvogel, 82). The title is followed by a detailed account of the many fantastical scene changes and adventures in which Hanswurst would be involved. He was clearly the centre of attraction in this main work, but also in the concluding piece: 'Den Schluß macht ein Tantz oder lustige Nach-Comoedie,' standard fare for the time in Berlin. Hanswurst's prevalence here is also an indication that Eckenberg made a regular practice of blending harlequin and traditional German comic types together, despite the official nomenclature of his comic figure in the king's monthly financial statements.

There is no doubt that the comic figure played extemporaneously in Eckenberg's troupe, or that his skill in doing so was his first claim to fame. But we see too that his role was also to provide social criticism. A manuscript from 1734 describing a work in which Hanswurst was central reflects a most daring example of this function:

> Den 8. Juni speisete S.K.M. [Seine Königliche Majestät] bey dem Grafen von Manteuffel in dem Ramin'schen Garten auf der Dorotheen-Stadt zu Mittag und Abend und wurde daselbst mit der bey sich habenden Suite auf das Magnifiqueste und Inventieuseste tracktiret, wie dann auch die hiesigen teutschen Hof-Komödianten auf dem theatro im Garten eine auf die Franzosen gemachte neue Pièce aufführen müssen, genannt, 'Den anfangs hitzigen und geistsprechenden, zuletzt aber mit Schlägen abgefertigten Frantzösischen Marquis!!'
>
> NB. Der zur selbigen Zeit allhier residirende Frantzösische Minister hieß Marquis de la Chétardie. (Brachvogel, 83)

Derision of the French could hardly be expressed in more powerful terms, a striking example of the comic stage being used as a tool for social and political satire with the obvious consent and collusion of a monarch who delighted in seeing the stage ridicule his Gallic neighbours. The Nachspiel *Harlequin, der ungedultig-hernach ...*, published after *Die Franzosen in Böhmen* in 1743, contains similar invective.

While Eckenberg enjoyed most of the king's favours before 1740, other troupes constantly tried to wedge their way into the theatrical scene, with limited success, which often led to bitter rivalries and confrontations with 'dem starken Mann' who used every trick to protect his turf. A court functionary wrote to the king on 16 May 1733 to report an incident in which the principal Franz Wallerotty had tried to enter Eckenberg's theatre, only to exit abruptly, beaten and bloody, the play interrupted, the public sent home, Eckenberg's inebriated wife jailed for the night (Brachvogel, 79). Still, Eckenberg managed to finesse for the king's continued support.

All changed abruptly in 1740 as Frederick II (the Great) ascended the throne. Frederick I's taste for foreign productions and troupes was suddenly rekindled and within two years Eckenberg was finished in Berlin. Subventions went now to visiting French and Italian troupes, and by the end of this reign in 1786 opera reached its zenith in the new opera house. Despite such heavy odds against them, a fresh series of German troupes with much greater ability and range than that of Eckenberg competed intensely for the Berlin theatrical market in the three decades after 1740. Johann Schönemann, Konrad Ackermann, Heinrich Koch, Franz Schuch, and Carl Döbbelin were the most prominent, each gaining footholds of varying security. Schönemann and Ackermann did not feature the traditional comic figure and were among the earliest principals to move toward regular theatre seriously, with the king's encouragement, so that the nature of theatrical productions in Berlin began to change. Schuch, however, stands out as a steady counterforce to this reform. While Schönemann and Ackermann maintained the Nachspiel as a distinct structural part of their programs without the *lustige Person*, Schuch represented the last bastion of this tradition, and with considerable success in Berlin from the forties until his death in 1764. Schuch himself played Hanswurst, and for him in Berlin, Hanswurst and extemporization always remained central, be it in longer works or in Nachspiele, which he played regularly. Before this famous Hanswurst's Berlin opening in 1754, city and church officials sought to blunt the barbs of his comic routines, 'ja den schändlichen Hanswurst mit seinen Zoten von der Bühne zu lassen,' to which the witty Schuch is said to have replied, 'Mein Herr Probst, wenn ich meinen Hanswurst weglasse, so ist es eben, als wenn Sie Ihren Teufel von der Kanzel lassen!!' (Brachvogel, 153). Hanswurst was obviously Schuch's tool for social criticism and commentary, something he knew that Berliners wanted. Of Schuch's repartee, Brachvogel writes,

Der Hieb saß, denn die damaligen Theologen konnten ihren Hanswurst, den Teufel, allerdings nicht entbehren!! – Schuch eröffnete seine Bude am 4. Mai [1754] und spielte bis 2. Juni Arlequinaden. Er war für die Berliner gerade jetzt der rechte Mann! – Die singende Römertugend im Opernhause hatte man satt! Sie war überlebt, bevor sie starb, die komische Oper aber, das Intermezzo, vermochte lange das herzliche Gelächter nicht zu erzielen, was Schuchs Harlequin, Mdme. Schuchs Kolumbine, Stänzels Anselmo wie Pantalon und Steins Crispin, Sganarell oder Tartaglia und Trufaldin erregten. Wie klug und vorsichtig dies Kleeblatt trotz tollster Ausgelassenheit

agirte, beweist, daß ihre Stegreifkomödie niemals gemein wurde, so daß
auch gebildete Leute an Schuchs Vorstellungen sich ergötzten! Bei Schuch
erholte sich eben Berlin von der Blasirtheit, zu welcher der Pomp der
Opern-Aera ihm verholfen hatte, von der Monotonie der antiquen Gattung!
(153f)

Comic extemporization in Schuch's troupe extended past his own depiction of Hanswurst to include other company members who shared
the freedom, utilizing masques which were the stock and trade of the
commedia dell'arte. Their success showed a bias in Berlin theatrical taste,
not just for artificial (and largely foreign) operatic pomp but for theatre
relevant to their own social circumstances. Their power extended over
not just the lowest class, but obviously the educated, and no doubt
wealthy bourgeoisie as well.

Schuch was not alone in his continuation of such comic types in
Berlin. Other troupes, most notably Andreas Bergé's, tried to capitalize
on public interest by offering the formidable presence of the *lustige Person* in Nachspiele until the seventies. Bergé was well-known for comic
pantomimes with dance which made use of *commedia dell'arte* characters. Their dancing was more a matter of athletic acrobatics and gymnastic fireworks than ballet, as this account shows:

Denke man sich z.B., daß derselbe [Harlekin], bei seinen losen Streichen er-
tappt, um seinen Verfolgern zu entgehen, an den Wänden der Decoration
emporlief und durch die Decke verschwand. Bald verdoppelte er sich, so
daß er aus der rechten Thür in dem Augenblicke trat, in welchem er durch
die linke schlüpfte, daß er wagerecht durch das Fenster oder den Spiegel
fuhr und verschwand … Einer Vorstellung entsinnen wir uns, in welcher
gar keine Rettungs-Auskunft dem Arlequin mehr blieb und er von den
übrigen Personen so bedrängt wurde, daß er voll komischer Verzweiflung
einen tüchtigen Ansatz nahm, um sich von der Bühne mitten in's Publikum
zu stürzen, was eine große Aufregung unter diesem hervorrief. Er verschwand wie der Blitz – im Soufleurkasten! (Brachvogel, 182)

Of particular interest in this description is Harlekin's unrestricted
movement both on and off stage. Indeed, he explodes the limitations of
the fictional dimension by breaking through scenery, changing appearance and character, and even projecting himself physically into the
audience. Such behaviour has important consequences for the notions
of theatrical illusion and communication between actor and public. In
this example, Harlekin is at the same time participant in the theatrical
illusion, destroyer of it, and even member of the audience watching.

This multi-dimensionality is a characteristic that will remain important for understanding the Nachspiel tradition.

From the seventies onward, central comic figures became rapidly extinct in Berlin as regular theatre dominated, particularly after construction of the Schauspielhaus and Döbbelin's emergence as the most influential principal (having received the king's privilege first in 1767) despite Lessing's view that 'Döbbelin ist ein Narr, das habe ich immer geglaubt. Wenn das deutsche Theater durch ihn hochkommen soll, so helfe ihm Gott' (Liss, 62).

According to Plümicke, the pattern for both Koch and Döbbelin in Berlin in the seventies was to perform a longer work, most frequently a comedy, followed often by a shorter one, again commonly a comedy, or a ballet; occasionally, short comedies were the only works on the program. In the latter part of the period examined the short ballet became increasingly prevalent and the short comedy less so. Also in the later years there was an increasing tendency to eliminate any kind of afterpiece at all. These short comic afterpieces exist in published versions, almost all as comedies in one act, and none show evidence of Harlekin or other traditional comic figures. The only sign of such a character is in three of Döbbelin's main titles. It is the short ballets that seem to have more connection to what can be documented as Nachspiel titles from earlier years. A number of these have titles identical to those of published Nachspiele, such as *Der bestrafte Hochmuth, Die betrogene Alte,* and *Die Maskerade.* This, along with the short ballet's increasing prominence, suggests that Koch and Döbbelin in Berlin transferred some of the function and content of the earlier Nachspiel to the ballet.

Among the works performed by the court theatres considered by Schäffer/Hartmann, there is a wide variety of spoken and musical drama as well as ballet. Included are a handful of one-act works they call Lustspiele but which were also published as Nachspiele: *Die beiden Billets, Der Instinkt, Der Magnetismus, Die Perücken, Der Scherenschleifer, Der sehende Blinde.* There is no sign of a central comic figure in any of the titles performed during this period, a clear indication that the move toward regular theatre begun in Frederick II's reign had gained firm footing.

Frankfurt am Main

SOURCES
Bing, *Rückblicke* (1892); Frankfurt, *Theaterzettelsammlung* (FZ); Mentzel, *Geschichte* (1882); Mohr, *Frankfurter* (1967)

COVERAGE
Before 1782 there was no permanent theatre in Frankfurt but rather a collection of temporary stages occupied by itinerant troupes for short periods, such as those of Caroline Neuber, Joseph von Kurz and Konrad Ackermann (Bockenheimergasse, Roßmarkt, Liebfrauenberg), and Theobald Marchand and Abel Seyler in the 'Comödien-Hauss' in Junghof (1774-7). Frankfurt's new permanent Komödienhaus was opened in 1782 (Mohr, 101), and in 1787 a 'Nationaltheater,' shared with Mainz, was inaugurated by the elector of Mainz, and housed a permanent company from 1792.

The sources above treat all activity throughout the century in excerpts and examples. In the form of 109 transcribed playbills advertising about two hundred works, Mentzel presents the complete performance records of the *französischen Komödianten* from 17 June 1741 to 25 May 1742 (429-39). As a contrast, she provides 180 transcribed playbills of German players, Franz Wallerotty's troupe, covering the period 30 August 1741 to 18 May 1742 (430-69). A detailed survey with samples of Nationaltheater performances from 1792 on is given by Bing, but in a form so densely packed with details of various aspects of the theatre's life that the complete repertoire is difficult to extract.

What gaps there are in the coverage by Bing and Mentzel are often filled by the extensive playbill collection of the Stadt- und Universitätsbibliothek Frankfurt am Main which begins with a sample from 1651 and runs through the end of the eighteenth century, virtually complete from 1782. The several thousand playbills are also available on microfilm for easy perusal.

ANALYSIS
The first three decades of the eighteenth century Mentzel characterizes as 'die Blüthezeit der tollen Haupt- und Staatsaktionen und des verwilderten Kunstvagabundenthums' (130). During this time there was constant competition among German and foreign troupes for the privilege to play in Frankfurt, and city officials proved a fickle group in their distribution of favours. Often their sense of public morality prevented them from according the right to play. A French company per-

formed opera and ballet before 1710 on a temporary stage, finishing their programs with a 'lustiges Nachspiel' played by Italian comedians (Mentzel, 130). In 1709 the troupe of Sophie Elensohn, widow of Franz Elensohn, occupied the Roßmarkt with programs filled with Haupt- und Staatsaktionen in which Harlekin starred in improvised sketches throughout. Her renowned attractiveness and clever manipulation of city officials ensured success for several years, unlike the experience of her rival Katharina Velthen, who played Frankfurt unsuccessfully in direct competition. Elensohn built a theatre in 1711 behind the Haupt- wache and for the next five years played during longer periods with considerable financial success. The nature of her performances can be understood from the following account of a contemporary viewer:

> Ausser 'den fürtrefflichen Schrullen und Schwänken des Harlekin' rühmt er besonders 'das abentheuerliche Geschrey,' welches schon vor dem Beginn der Aktion hinter dem Vorhang vernommen wurde, dann den Lärm der Trommeln und Heerpauken beim Aufziehen der Gardine und schliesslich den Prologanten, der mit fein gepuderter Perücke und glasirten Hand- schuhen hin und wieder auf der Bühne spazieren ging, das Publikum galant grüssen und den Inhalt des Stückes im Voraus berichten musste. (Mentzel, 144f)

Two elements stand out from this account, the overriding popularity of the comic figure Harlekin, and the fact that not the content of the work performed but rather the manner of performance was important. All possibility of dramatic tension or the like was destroyed by the 'Prologanten' who recounted dramatic events in advance. The audience knew the contents of these dramatic plots well – they did not come to see only them – rather, they came to see mainly the special effects and the improvisation of Harlekin.

The Stadt- und Universitätsbibliothek Frankfurt am Main contains a playbill of Elensohn's direct competitor Katharina Velthen from 28 October 1711. It advertises as 'Haupt-Action'

> Die Triumphirende Ehre Des höchstlöblichen Ertz-Hauses Oesterreichs In Der Glorieusen Erhaltung und Fortpflanzung Der Römischen MONAR- CHIE, Oder: Die durch die ohnlängst erhaltene grosse VICTORIE Derer Ho- hen Herren Alliirten in Flandern Vom Himmel selbst beglückte Wahl Eines Neuerwehlten Römischen Käysers ... Wenn solche Haupt-Action vorbey / so soll eine lustige / und allhier noch niemals gemachte Nach-Comödie den Beschluß machen / genannt: Arlequins singender Kind-Bett-Schmauß.

A printed 'Prologus' follows in its entirety (3pp), then a detailed plot summary of the five-act 'Haupt-Action' along with its epilogue. This summary makes it clear that 'Arlequin' is prevalent in that major piece as well as in the 'Nach-Comödie,' evidence that he and his comic antics provided a tonal link between the two. This and other playbills also show that 'Arlequin' typically played many roles during the course of the performance. Indeed as late as the 1740s there are many playbills with the note added after the main entry, 'Mit Arlequins Lustbarkeit durch und durch untermischt.'

A major fire interrupted theatrical activity in Frankfurt for several years after 1719, but in 1725 a troupe of German players from Prague under Albert de Fraine successfully offered German works with Harlekin once again. Despite his use of that name in advertisements, however, de Fraine himself actually played as Hanswurst. In the same year arrived the company of Johann Ferdinand Beck, known as Zahnbrecher and Hanswurst, for today's ears an incongruous combination of medicine and dramatic art, but not so strange in its own day – an indication of the carnival atmosphere in which he played his Haupt- und Staatsaktionen with Hanswurst to healthy audiences. Again from 1725 to 1730 there was a theatrical lull in Frankfurt, followed in the thirties by the successful engagements of Leonhard Denner (again with Haupt- und Staatsaktionen, but with a more refined 'Arlequin'), Anthonius Peruzzi with opera and Italian comedy, and Karl von Eckenberg, as in Berlin known widely as 'Der starke Mann,' purveyor of Haupt- und Staatsaktionen, Harlekinaden, puppet plays, and acrobatic spectacles. Again Mentzel quotes a contemporary who speaks of principals like Eckenberg and the great success which 'ein Gaukler ärndtete, der durch den Harlekin die grössten Unflätereien auf's Tapet brachte und Comödie spielen, Seiltanzen und Luftspringen in ein gezwungen widerliches Bündniss trieb' (Mentzel, 154). In 1736 Caroline Neuber came to Frankfurt with the avowed intention to play more respectable theatre – 'gereinigte Schaubühne' – and set up her stage on the Liebfrauenberg. One of her members, Heinrich Koch, would later form his own company and also be a member of Schönemann's. He was in charge of preparing and directing the Nachspiele. The Neuber's pattern in 1736-7 was to play major dramas of classical base or German imitations – not Haupt- und Staatsaktionen – followed by comic Nachspiele in which Harlekin was frequently the focus. Clearly a change in tone was beginning on the Frankfurt theatre scene which Mentzel reports:

'Was noch nie hierorts beschehen [sic],' schreibt eine der höheren
Gesellschaft angehörige Dame an ihren in Marburg studierenden Sohn

Ende October 1736 'Alles strömet in das Theater auf dem Liebfrauenberge.
Man erblicket nicht nur die fürnehmlichsten sondern auch Leuthe da, die
sonsten nur in der Kirchen sitzen und oft schon ein gar los Maul über der-
artige Kurzweil hatten ... die Comödianten ... führen allesambt einen stillen
ehrsamen Wandel und agiren gar ausnehmend schön und mit Respekt und
Sitte. – Vor zottigen Redensarten braucht man keine Angst mehr zu
empfinden, der Hans-Wurst kommt in der ernsthaften Action meist gar
nicht vor, erst zuletzt in dem Beschluss und dann ist er sehr manierlich und
ohne Unfläterey.' (169)

But it took much more than Neuber's resolve to change the taste and
demands of most audiences of the day. Still in the late thirties troupes
such as Eckenberg's continued to prosper, as did Wallerotty with many
Haupt- und Staatsaktionen and crude incorporations of Harlekin and
Kolumbine. But the tide was turning to a more refined comic figure,
one whose place became the Nachspiel rather than the main work.

In Mentzel's account of the French players (1741-2), it is evident that
the term 'Nachspiel' was used initially to designate a short work
following a longer comedy or tragedy, but this designation soon disappeared from the playbills and the short works were called 'Lust-
Spiele' instead, and sometimes indicated a musical supplement to the
action. Ballets or musical pieces were also used as independent units to
complete the program. The short 'Lust-Spiele' often indicate in their titles a central comic figure (*Arlequin ich weiss nicht was*, *Arlequin als Fürst
und Bauer*), while others were one-act comedies which can be documented in printed form. There is no apparent connection between main
and afterpiece, whatever form it took.

Mentzel traces the activities of numerous German troupes such as
those of Schuch, Ackermann, and Seyler, but her account of Wallerotty's troupe stands as the most instructive and detailed contrast
between German and French players. For Wallerotty the standard program consisted of a Hauptaktion followed by a Nach-Comödie, usually
untitled, or ballet. Hanswurst was frequently central to the Nach-
Comödie, and indeed often in the Hauptaktion as well. His presence
thus could have formed a thematic and/or tonal link between the two
parts of the performance. The fact that the Nachspiel was untitled indicates likely improvisation and perhaps such freedom was extended to
the ballets with which they shared the normal final position. Mentzel's
survey of Schuch's activities indicates a similar dependence on the
Nachspiel.

The central place of the comic figure in the Nachspiel for Wallerotty
as opposed to his sparse appearance in the French performances sug-

gests that such comic figures as Hanswurst, and even Harlekin, whose roots are French and Italian, are an essential distinguishing feature of the German stage at this time. Since this figure was most prevalent in the Nachspiel, it can be suggested further that this genre, as long as it contained the comic figure, was in itself most characteristic of the German tradition.

The rich Frankfurt playbill collection reflects these trends from a much broader perspective than Mentzel could provide. From the early forties the playbills show a gradual change in references to Harlekin and the Nachspiel. In one from 18 July 1741, the comedy *Der Reisende im Schlaff* is the main work, and we are told that 'in dieser Action wird sowohl mit angenehmen Arien als auch guter Lustbarkeit des Hanß-Wursts aufgewartet werden.' Then comes a description of three ballets to follow the main work, 'unter dem Titul: Der bezauberte Garten.' In these, 'Arlequin' is prominent. Finally, 'Den völligen Beschluß machet Arlequin mit einer lustigen Nach-Comödie.' Particularly interesting here is the use of both 'Hanß-Wurst' and 'Arlequin' to describe the comic figure on the program, the first in reference to the main work, the second to the ballet and Nachspiel. It is difficult to say today if in fact two different comic figures were involved here, or just one with two names. Whatever the case, this playbill is indicative of a trend to reduce mention of Hanswurst in favour of the name Arlequin or Harlekin. By the sixties, the name Hanswurst rarely appears, by 1780 not at all, although he could well have been hiding behind another nomenclature.

Two further playbills from 1742 (24 February and 17 March) provide evidence of another change occurring at the time. The first advertises that 'den Beschluß machet eine *modeste* Nach-Comödie,' the second that 'Die ganze serieuse Action spielet nicht länger als eine Stunde, deswegen sind unter der Action 5 *modeste* und lustige Intermedia' (emphasis mine). This is a shift from the stock adjective 'lustig' almost always attached to the advertising of Nachspiele until mid-century. It would seem that the reformatory spirit was having its influence in Frankfurt through a dampening of the excesses in the traditional comic genre.

Another trend evident from these playbills is the replacement of the *lustige Nach-Comödie* with a concluding ballet, often featuring Harlekin. These are prominent on many playbills from this time through the eighties, for example on Seyler's playbill of 22 April 1779 which has a main comedy by Regnard, and 'Hierauf folgt ein ganz neues, großes pantomimisches BALLET ... Betittelt: Das italiänische Theater.' Featured are numerous *commedia dell'arte* characters, including Harlekin.

The emergence of the concluding ballet in Berlin has already been noted, and the change in Frankfurt was concurrent with Ackermann's visit in 1755, a turning point for theatrical style in that city. Not only in the presence of a closing ballet, but also in the transformation of the 'lustige Nach-Comödie' to a regular one-act Nachspiel does this decade mark a change. In a representative playbill from 1755, Ackermann advertises, 'Den Beschluß macht ein gantz Neues Nachspiel in Prosa. Die beschwerte Mutter.' Neither Hanswurst nor Harlekin is mentioned. Mentzel's information on the sixties and seventies also shows that the Nachspiel by name, especially with the central comic figure, became less and less frequent as played by Marchand and Seyler.

Joseph von Kurz's visit to Frankfurt in 1768 is also well-documented in the playbill collection. Here, for the first time, the following note is appended to the advertised performance: 'NB Auf das Theater wird niemand, weder *bei der Probe*, noch währendem Schauspiele mit, oder ohne Geld, gelassen' (emphasis mine). This, along with many similar notations in the following years, indicates that the company did indeed have rehearsals for their performances, a fact important for our understanding of developments in acting and directing. In the analysis of individual Nachspiele later in this study, questions will arise about the nature of acting and the role of the director. The rehearsals at this early date would suggest that regulated acting and performance were becoming increasingly important as opposed to the purely improvised action of the early itinerant troupes.

Bing's account of the Nationaltheater repertoire (1792-1800), or 'Stadttheater' as it is called in his title, shows no evidence of Nachspiele with comic figures, only on occasion short comedies played to conclude the program. This is confirmed by the playbill collection which shows that short concluding comedies were performed only about once every eight performances in the nineties on the Nationaltheater stage. Remarkable among these, however, is the popularity of *Die beiden Billets* which was played repeatedly and published as a Nachspiel.

Gotha

SOURCES
Hodermann, *Geschichte* (1894); Schlösser, *Vom Hamburger* (1895)

COVERAGE
When the Weimar court theatre was destroyed by fire in 1774, the company took up residence in the Gotha Hoftheater, Schloß Friedenstein, a

standing theatre with contracted, salaried actors, pension scheme, and other institutional trappings. Hodermann presents a general history including the full repertoire and performance program from 1775 to 1779. It includes 176 works in 876 performances listed chronologically by première and subsequent performances (Hodermann, 141-71), followed by an alphabetical list by title (173-6). Schlösser duplicates this program with one minor correction and a slightly different organization of the material.

ANALYSIS

The normal pattern was to perform one longer work, usually a comedy but sometimes a tragedy or other serious work, followed by a shorter one, almost always a one-act comedy. As published, these comedies are categorized as Lustspiele; only two can be found published as Nachspiele (*Das Portrait, Der sehende Blinde*). In listing titles alphabetically, neither Hodermann nor Schlösser uses the category Nachspiel, and yet both use the word 'Nachspiel' throughout their texts to refer to the short works which customarily concluded the program; hence, purely as a functional term. None of these Nachspiele shows any evidence of a central comic character. Operettas were often played instead of these, but never ballets. Clearly the farcical Nachspiel-type and what may well have been for many companies the improvised short ballet were not to the refined taste of the court. Hodermann includes in his study long citations from the 'Theaterreglement' of 1775, including a section on 'Pflichten der Schauspieler' which among other restrictions prohibited extemporization absolutely: 'Alles extemporiren wird untersagt, und mit 4. bis 8 gr. bestraft' (Hodermann, 80) – quite a contrast to the custom earlier in the century in other places where freedom on stage was the essence of performance.

Hamburg

SOURCES
Lebrün, *Geschichte* (1841); Schlösser, *Vom Hamburger* (1895); Schütze, *Hamburgische* (1794); Wollrabe, *Chronologie* (1847)

COVERAGE
The famous Hamburg opera house built in 1678 was the centre of theatrical attention in that city until the 1730s when principal interest gradually shifted to theatre. Itinerant troupes performed on stages such as the Operntheater auf dem Gänsemarkt and the Komödienhaus am

Dragonerstall before Ackermann built a Schauspielhaus am Gänse-markt in 1764 where the Operntheater had previously stood. This be-came the site of the Nationaltheater from 1767 to 1769. Thereafter, nu-merous troupes played steadily in Hamburg on several stages, and for-eign troupes (French, Italian, English) also performed. (In the 1988 *Lessing Yearbook* Dieter Fratzke provides an excellent account of the physical structures in use during this period of Hamburg's theatrical development.)

While Lebrün, Schütze, and Wollrabe treat all theatrical activity in Hamburg from the beginnings through the eighteenth century, their works contain no complete repertoires or performance lists. Lebrün's and Schütze's anecdotal comtemporary overviews are large chron-ological accounts with samples from repertoires and performances. Wollrabe's chronology is similarly anecdotal with more attention to personnel than works and performances. Schlösser presents a complete repertoire and performance schedule of the Hamburg Nationaltheater from 1767 to 1769 (66-8) which includes 117 works in 507 perfor-mances, listed alphabetically by title with date of première, last perfor-mance, and number of performances overall.

ANALYSIS

The first decades of the century demonstrate a passion for opera in Hamburg, a love for musical drama which, while dampened toward mid-century, continued to 1800. At the same time the city was visited regularly by a steady stream of French, Italian, and also Dutch compa-nies, and a host of German itinerant troupes which dominated the the-atre scene until 1764. These include many of the major principals of the era (Johann Beck, Leonhard Denner, Carl von Eckenberg ['der starke Mann'], Johann Förster, Carl Hoffmann, Heinrich Koch, Johann Lein-haas, Ferdinand Müller, Caroline Neuber, Gottfried Prehauser, Johann Schönemann, Johann Spiegelberg), most of whom played the city on numerous occasions, for the theatre-hungry Hamburg citizens and the relative political liberalism of this free city made it a coveted location. Several of the names above are synonymous with central comic figures who specialized in extemporization (Beck/Hanswurst, Leinhaas/ Pantalone, Prehauser/Hanswurst), which tells much about the nature of performances on temporary stages in Hamburg at the time. Standard fare in the repertoires of most companies was the Hauptaktion containing a prominent role for Harlekin or Hanswurst and a *lustiges Nach-Spiel* or *Nach-Comödie*, often with songs and a ballet. As Schütze writes of Förster's performances in 1725, 'Je unnatürlicher, je widersinniger, je besser! war die Losung für das derzeitige Bedürfnis der Zuschauer wie der Schausteller' (Schütze, 55f). Lebrün, Schütze, and Wollrabe cite numerous representative playbills as evidence of the tenor of these productions from the beginning of the century right through to the sixties, Lebrün grouping them in an appendix amusingly entitled 'Kuriositäten' (363-92). A playbill from 14 November 1709 lists a performance by the 'Sächsisch-Hochteutschen Comoedianten' on the 'Neuer Markt' including 'eine gantz neue wohlsehenswürdige Haupt-Action, genannt Wett-Streit der Verliebten,' with a plot summary, then 'Nach Endigung der ersten Haupt-Action soll beschliessen eine lustige Nach-Comödie, genannt l'Esprit Francois oder der Frantzösische Geist' (Lebrün, 371f). Another from 1734 advertises a 'musicalischen Prologum, genannt Die danckbare Liebe ... Nebst einer Staats- und Haupt-Action ... betitult Der bis in den Tod getreue, beständige, und vor das Vaterland strebend- und sterbende CATO,' followed by a detailed description of the spectacular sets and arias of the Prologue, and finally 'Den Beschluß macht ein lustiges Nach-Spiel, genannt Die kostbare Lächerlichkeit' (Lebrün, 373-8). A third, also from 1734, promises the major piece 'Simson und Daelila, Mit Arlequin, einem lustigen Jäger, Hochzeit-Ritter, und interessirten Kuppler,' followed by 'eine extra lustige Nach-Comoedie' (Lebrün, 379f), which makes it clear that the comic figure was central to both the main work and Nachspiel. Similarly, a playbill of 1738 includes Arlequin in the main action and a Nachspiel to close (Lebrün, 381f). Of such a performance in the early fifties, Schütze writes: 'Die lustige Nach-Komödie enthält in leichten, wäßrichten, singbaren Reimversen eine Liebesavanturie der niedrigsten Gattung. Prügel und Zoten sind (mit Lessing zu reden) die witzigsten Einfälle derselben' (89). While there is little doubt that these works were coarse presentations, they were just as clearly the favourite of most of the paying public; many chroniclers such as Schütze seem unwilling to recognize their importance on this basis and investigate them further, preferring to adopt a cultivated tone of disdain, and saving most of their attention for so-called regular drama which was less interesting to the public at the time.

The year 1764 marked a turning point in the Hamburg theatre scene. Ackermann built his own permanent stage on the location of the old opera house after its demolition, a clear sign of the change in theatrical taste and at the same time an indicator that regular theatre, Ackermann's preference, was beginning to dominate. The age of the extemporized comic figure was at an end in Hamburg; the Nationaltheater with the Ackermann troupe as its core company was just three years from foundation, and most activity focused on this troupe and its fixed home.

From Schlösser's data and text we know that the normal procedure in the Hamburg Nationaltheater was to play a longer piece, usually a comedy but very often a tragedy, followed by a shorter one, usually a comedy in one act. None of these afterpieces had any apparent relation to the work preceding nor do they contain central comic characters or significant opportunities for extemporization. Most of them were published as short Lustspiele, three as Nachspiele (*Die dreifache Heirat/Die Maskerade, Die kranke Frau, Der sehende Blinde*). The Hamburg Nationaltheater under Lessing's influence maintained a structural pattern with the regular performance of Nachspiele to conclude the program, but without adherence to its earlier free-wheeling nature.

Although the enterprise of a Nationaltheater as such was unsuccessful in Hamburg, the physical structure remained, headed in turn by Friedrich Schröder after Ackermann's death in 1771 and by others thereafter. In 1786 Schröder founded an independent company which dominated the scene until 1796 before it dissolved amid a rash of artistic and contractual disputes. During these final decades foreign troupes, particularly French, remained prominent in Hamburg and provided ongoing competition for German companies, producing an unsettled atmosphere in the last decades of the century. This first attempt at a Nationaltheater was in the end the shortest-lived in any major centre, and in the long run the least successful. Nevertheless, Ackermann and the brief period of the Hamburg Nationaltheater incorporate a clear turning point in the nature and content of performance both there and soon similarly in many other centres, from the domination of extemporization and the heyday of the comic Nachspiel to an overriding emphasis on regular drama.

Mannheim

SOURCES
Martersteig, *Protokolle* (1890); Pichler, *Chronik* (1879); Sommerfeld, *Bühneneinrichtungen* (1921); Walter, *Archiv* (1899)

COVERAGE
Theatrical activity is covered from 1720 to the end of the century with particular focus on the celebrated Hof- und Nationaltheater under Dalberg's direction from its founding in 1779, with a complete repertoire and performance schedule from then through the end of the cen-

tury. Walter's work is the most important factual document, containing the full Nationaltheater repertoire (Walter, II, 249-377) and an alphabetical list by title of the 614 plays performed (II, 379-418). In addition, he provides a wealth of further material on playbills, scenarios, diaries, and theatre administration. Walter also includes the repertoires of the Theobald Marchand and Abel Seyler troupes in Mannheim for sixteen months of 1778/9. Pichler, Martersteig, and Sommerfeld supplement this basic tool with a wealth of information on production detail, personnel, and management.

ANALYSIS

Pichler's brief survey of the decades between 1742 and 1778 shows a strong foothold maintained by Italian opera with French drama and ballet at the court of Duke Karl Theodor. Meanwhile, itinerant German troupes, such as those of Johann Brunian, Arnold Porsch, Johann Tilly, and Joseph von Kurz, were actively supported by the general populace. Recorded details are sparse, but improvised Nachspiele with Bernardon or a central Hanswurst were clearly a staple of the repertoire.

Performance records of the Marchand and Seyler troupes show each program normally containing one or two works, often a longer followed by a shorter, with no apparent connection between the two. The short work, not designated Nachspiel, was most frequently a comedy or Singspiel. There is no evidence of a central comic character.

From 1779 it was normal to play either one long work per performance or a longer work (comedy or tragedy) followed by a shorter one (e.g. short comedy, Singspiel, opera or operetta). There is no evidence of a connection between main work and afterpiece, nor is a central comic figure evident, and towards 1800 there were even fewer of these shorter pieces to conclude. The term 'Nachspiel' is not used as a genre designation, but rather as a functional term and while most of the short comedies played as Nachspiele were published as Lustspiele, some were indeed published as Nachspiele (*Die arme Frau* [manuscript], *Die beiden Billets, Der Instinkt, Der Magnetismus, Die Martinsgänse, Der sehende Blinde*). Most of these saw frequent performance (*Billets* 32 times, *Magnetismus* 24 times) between 1779 and 1803. The Mannheim Nationaltheater thus maintained to a great extent the structural feature of the Nachspiel at the program's conclusion without using its genre designation or Nachspiele with a central comic figure and resulting improvisation.

Munich

SOURCES
Grandaur, *Chronik* (1878); Legband, *Münchener* (1901); Munich
Theaterzettelsammlung (MZ); Trautmann, 'Italienische/Französische/
Deutsche' (1887-9)

COVERAGE
Beyond activity in the court's Residenztheater, the main stage for
itinerant troupes in Munich was the Faberbräutheater. The Nationalschaubühne was founded in 1772, and by its official opening in 1778
had established a full company of performers and an extensive repertoire. In more modest terms, numerous Hüttentheater played a consistently important role in the theatre scene until they were banned in
1794. The Munich Theatermuseum has a modest collection of playbills
from the period.

Grandaur's chronicle, based, we are told in the Foreword, on archival material and many contemporary accounts, covers from 1765 to the
end of the century, but superficially in excerpts (Grandaur, 3-57). His
main focus is on the Nationalschaubühne during the years 1778-99, and
appendices include all titles performed, listed alphabetically (Grandaur, 213-38), though without performance dates or program combinations.

Trautmann's three lengthy (ponderous and often unfocused) articles
on German, French, and Italian troupes at the Bavarian court provide
many details of the competition for the privilege to perform and the
nature of works. For German players, the period 1671-1765 is covered
(French to 1745, Italian to 1765), with mention of many troupes and
some representative samples of their repertoires.

Legband's extensive study covers the entire century, although the
availability of documentation leaves treatment of the years before 1770
spotty. Franz Wallerotty's troupe was the most important itinerant
company in Munich from 1737 to 1762, but detailed documentation of
his repertoire and performances has not been preserved. Hence Legband tries to reconstruct the essence of these programs from their
performances in other centres such as Frankfurt, using historical studies as sources, especially Mentzel's. Legband presents a list of works
performed on the Faberbräu stage from 1782 to 1798 (488-98), albeit
with numerous gaps, and finally an extensive (though not complete)
repertoire of the Nationalschaubühne 1772-99 (421-87); the period 1772-
4 is documented sparsely, 1775-7 well, and 1778-99 extensively. In-

cluded is an alphabetical listing by title of the several thousand works performed on the Nationalschaubühne (501-25) and the Faberbräu stage (525-32) with information on dates of performance and program combinations.

ANALYSIS

The early decades of the century saw a series of French, Italian, and German itinerant troupes in constant competition for the privilege to play at the court theatre. This continued into mid-century until the Italian companies gave way, followed by the French as Munich became increasingly committed to the idea of a national German theatre. There was considerable influence on the Munich theatre scene from Vienna. Viennese troupes and comic stars (e.g. Brunian/Hanswurst) were frequent visitors at the court and temporary stages. Trautmann presents as representative for mid-century Bavarian centres a significant portion of the repertoire of Johann Schulz's troupe, including twenty-seven performances in 1748 and thirty-three in 1752 (Trautmann, 359-67). He describes the general tenor of their programs as 'ein ungeheuerliches Gemisch gespreizter Haupt- und Staatsaktionen und toller Hanswurstiaden' (Trautmann, 356), appending the transcribed playbills to prove his point. Hanswurst seemed ubiquitous, either in the Hauptaktion or in the *lustige Nach-Comödie* which frequently closed the program. One sample, similar to most of the other playbills from this time, will suffice:

> 6. August 1748: Demophoontes, König in Thracien / Oder: In einer Person Ein Bruder und Vatter / Bruder und Schwager / Bruder, und untadelhafter Bräutigam seiner Schwester. Mit Hans Wurst 1. Dem erfreuten Post-Träger. 2. Dem forchtsamen Secundanten. 3. Gefräßig verstellten Götzen-Pfaffen. 4. Dem verwirrten Hochzeiter. 5. Dem närrischen Ceremonien-Meister einer verwirrten Hochzeit. (Laut Vorbericht 'eine Uebersetzung aus dem berühmten Italiänischen Poeten Metasthasio, von Joh. Schultz'.) (359)

Wallerotty's performances were more rounded, but still presented ample opportunity for comic improvisation and crudity. Hanswurst was a frequent central figure in main works as well as in Nachspiele. In 1759 the Königliche Akademie der Wissenschaften (for the Kingdom of Bavaria) was founded, and in 1765 first moves were made to create a Nationalschaubühne. The venture had a patriotic flavour from the beginning in reaction to the heavy French influence, so German works and playwrights were encouraged, even to the extent of maintaining the credibility of the German troupes which performed improvised works with Hanswurst. In 1771 regularization of the theatre set in under the leadership of Johann Baptiste Niesser; thereafter, extemporization was discouraged on Munich stages. Yet it is clear by comparing the repertoire of the Faberbräu theatre with that of the Nationalschaubühne that the former represented one theatrical pole – traditional extemporization – and the latter regularized theatre. Indeed, they competed for audiences in Munich during the final decades of the century. In the early eighties, 42 per cent of works performed in the Faberbräu theatre featured Hanswurst or Bernardon (Legband, 195). Short comedies, also published as Nachspiele, were played there to the end of the century as well, and in addition often ballets instead of Nachspiele to close out the performances, as on a representative playbill of 2 March 1779 (MZ, *Theaterzettel*). Furthermore, until they were banned in 1794, the repertoires of the various Hüttentheater showed a wealth of extemporized works featuring Bernardon, Hanswurst, and the beloved Lipperl.

In contrast, the repertoire of the Nationalschaubühne from 1772 to 1799 shows only two works featuring Harlekin, four with Bernardon, two with Crispin, and two with Lipperl. The typical program consisted of one or two works, the second being one of a variety of short pieces from comedy to Singspiel to ballet, with no connection between the two evident, and frequently there were simply two shorter works together on the program. Legband uses the genre designation Nachspiel for works in his lists infrequently; Grandaur not at all. The short comedies exist in almost all cases in published form, some as Nachspiele (*Adel des Herzens, Die Aussteuer, Die beiden Billets, Die Bildsäule, Die Brandschatzung, Der fromme Betrug, Der Instinkt, Der Magnetismus, Die Maskerade, Das Rendezvous*). These works retained their popularity over time; for example, *Die beiden Billets* was performed eleven times between 1787 and 1798, *Der fromme Betrug* seven times from 1789 to 1796. The Munich performance of the *Bildsäule* stands as an interesting departure from performance of this popular work as documented in other theatres. In Munich it was performed as a ballet, a clear example of Nachspiel material making a transition to the ballet genre, reminiscent of the change in emphasis from Nachspiel to ballet in Berlin and Frankfurt. An interesting addition on some playbills after 1770, including one of the Kurz troupe, is the direction 'Auf das Theater wird Niemand, weder bey der Probe, noch unter wehrendem Schauspiel, weder mit, noch ohne Geld gelassen' (MZ, *Theaterzettel*). This phrasing recalls a similar note on a Kurz playbill in Frankfurt and likely indicates, as there, increased emphasis on rehearsal, acting, and directing.

A further anomaly offered by the performance records of the Munich Nationalschaubühne shows that the works called Nachspiele above were not played consistently at the end of the program. More often than not they were in fact played *before* other works (as in Hamburg, according to Heinrich Wilhelm Lawätz, cited earlier in Chapter one). Clearly the functional definition of the Nachspiel as a work to close the program does not apply to performances on the Munich Nationalschaubühne. However, the extemporized content of the traditional Nachspiel along with the central comic figure, especially Bernardon, remained strong in the competing Faberbräu theatre in the early eighties and the Hüttentheater until the end of the century.

Vienna

SOURCES
Alth/Obzyna, *Burgtheater* [1976]; Bauer, 'Catalogue' [1935], *Opern* (1955), *Josefstadt* (1957); Bergopzoom, *Theaterspiegel* (1788); Blümml/Gugitz, *Alt-Wiener* (1925); Hadamowsky, *Theater* (1934), *Wiener* (1966); Müller, *Genaue Nachrichten* (1772), *Geschichte* (1776); Rommel, *Alt-Wiener* (1952); Vienna *Theaterzettelsammlung* (VZ); Weilen, *Geschichte* (1899); Zechmeister, *Wiener* (1971)

COVERAGE
Historically and to this day Vienna has nurtured an extraordinary volume and range of theatrical activity. An overview of the extent of this activity can be gained from Anton Bauer's map of the 104 different Viennese theatres significant in the city's history, a huge list which does not include many temporary stages of the past (Bauer, *Opern*, XIf). Vienna is the only German-speaking urban centre where court and popular theatre existed symbiotically. As early as 1626 there was activity in the Hofburgtheater, and in 1709 an opera house, until 1846 the Kaiserlich-Königliches Hoftheater, opened. It is most commonly called the Theater nächst dem Kärntnertor or simply Kärntnertortheater (behind today's Staatsoper). It became the first German-speaking public standing theatre and from 1712 the home of Hanswurst and extemporized comedy. Renovated in 1748, it was destroyed by fire on 3 November 1761, rebuilt in 1763, and continued with extemporization only briefly until Joseph von Sonnenfels and others pressed for theatre reform in 1766. Thereafter the theatre was leased by the court from 1765 to 1785 to various entrepreneurs who complied with theatrical

reforms, and then was controlled solely by the court until century's end.

The Kärntnertortheater played a key role in Viennese theatre history throughout the century. Before 1770 this was the focal popular theatre, although there were many other temporary ones used by wandering troupes. The second court theatre was the Burgtheater, which with Empress Maria Theresia's permission was outfitted in 1741 from an unused Hofballhaus and by 1748 used as a proper theatre, to be renovated again in 1760. It was leased from 1752 to 1772 exclusively to French troupes, then to others as well until 1776. In 1776 Emperor Josef II founded the Teutsches Nationaltheater, which was housed in the Burgtheater and committed to the production of German *Sprechstücke*. It soon attracted large audiences, even to the detriment of its sister Kärntnertortheater, which suffered somewhat until 1785 when the court took it as well under its wing, thus maintaining two official and complementary organs for a wide range of theatrical activity. In the eighties, four major Volkstheater, public standing theatres, were founded, the Theater in der Leopoldstadt (1781), an der Wien (1787), in der Josefstadt (1788), and auf der Landstraße (1789). The Viennese theatre scene in the eighteenth century is without doubt the most extensively documented of any in German-speaking territory. In many ways its history can be seen as a special case, as Viennese of the time would have argued, for example, Johann Müller, who complained about a recent 'Chronology of German Theatre' (presumably Christian Heinrich Schmid's *Chronologie*) which, he pointed out, needed extensive corrections and additions because of its author's misunderstanding of the Vienna scene (Müller, *Geschichte*, 1-3).

In concentrating on the traditional *Volkskomödie*, Rommel presents a wealth of historical and anecdotal detail, particularly important for the years until 1770 for which complete documentation is unavailable. From 1781 documentation is virtually complete, and while Rommel does not present a full chronological repertoire of any particular theatre, to his extensive examples he adds a full title index, including thousands of works and performances.

Zechmeister's study is a necessary complement to others with its concentration on the Kärntnertortheater from 1747 to 1776. He provides a comprehensive chronological list of performances for the twenty-year period (Zechmeister, 399-562, 577f) as well as an alphabetical title register of works (582-612), information which includes hundreds of plays in their many performances. Hadamowsky (*Wiener Hoftheater*) completes the picture for the Kärntnertortheater to the end

of the century, including a complete chronology with dates of premières and repeat performances, information on set decorators, costume designers, other production miscellany, location of relevant texts
and playbills, and a complete register of works.

Coverage of the *Volkskomödie* continues from Rommel and Zechmeister to Hadamowsky (*Theater*) with his thorough treatment of the
Theater in der Leopoldstadt. Hadamowsky provides a daily account of
programs from 1781 through the end of the century along with an
alphabetical list of the many hundreds of works performed (Hadamowsky, *Theater*, 301-401). Blümml/Gugitz complete this part of the
picture with essays on the Theater auf der Landstraße, Theater an der
Wien, in der Josefstadt, zum Weißen Fasan, and miscellaneous temporary stages used by itinerant troupes, adding an alphabetical title index
of works performed (Blümml, 501-18).

In addition to these extensive modern studies of *Volkstheater* in Vienna, contemporary writers (and actors) supply additional information
on repertoires and performances, particularly Müller (*Genaue Nachrichten*) with information on the flood of *Marktspektakel*, marionette
theatres, and acrobat companies, and Bergopzoom on the broad theatre
scene in the late seventies. Even at the end of the century when numerous standing theatres were firmly established in Vienna and regular
theatre had gained sound footing, unconventional popular stages continued to emerge and flourish. An exemplary case in point is the
Wiedener Hetzamphitheater of the 1790s whose preserved playbills
testify to an almost unbelievable excess of showmanship and grandiose
spectacle in the form of *Tierkämpfe* – dogs and steers, bears and lions,
boars and oxen all performing on the same program (see playbills for
1789-92, 1794-1801 in Vienna Stadtbibliothek, Sig C77.250).

The history of the Burgtheater is covered from 1752 to 1776 by Zechmeister and from 1776 through century's end by Hadamowsky (*Wiener
Hoftheater*) and Alth/Obzyna. Zechmeister offers a chronological list of
works performed (399-562, 577f) and an alphabetical list of titles (582-
612); Hadamowsky a daily chronology of Burgtheater performances
(*Anlage*) and an alphabetical list of the 1,339 works performed 1776-
1810 (in both Burg- and Kärntnertor) with reference to location of texts,
playbills, designers, premières, and repeat performances (Hadamowsky, *Wiener*, 1-150). This list is clarified and enhanced by Alth/
Obzyna in their daily chronology of programs through the end of the
century, full title register of Burgtheater works, details of premières,
total number of performances, and often the cast list on a particular
day (gathered from handwritten notes on playbills, and diaries).

In addition there is Anton Bauer's extensive handwritten and unpublished card catalogue which stands virtually unused in the stacks of the theatre collection of the Austrian National Library. On thousands of cards Bauer traced performances of plays in all Viennese theatres, the results often overlapping with some of the studies above, but including further information on numerous other stages in Vienna and environs.

Finally, Viennese theatre history is extensively documented by large playbill collections in city archives and the National Library. The preservation of these playbills is one of the reasons scholars have been able to trace the theatre scene so thoroughly and, as was the case with Frankfurt am Main, they remain essential documents for an understanding of eighteenth-century Viennese theatre.

ANALYSIS

Documentation of the Viennese *Volkskomödie* reveals it as the vehicle which perpetuated the essence of the early Nachspiel, although not necessarily with the same formal structure as has largely been the case above. Rommel's title for his introduction captures the situation concisely: 'Literaturdrama und Spielstück.' From the beginning of the century, and even before, the Viennese tradition represents a coexistence between these two poles of stage performance, text-based theatre (regular theatre) and extemporization. The latter is at the heart of the Nachspiel, and its flourishing in Vienna shows this city as a continuing life force for the key elements of the genre. It is in Vienna that the central comic figure of Hanswurst was created by Josef Anton Stranitzky when he leased the Kärntnertortheater in 1712, beginning a grand tradition of Viennese Hanswurst figures from Gottfried Prehauser to Johann Eckenberg, Friedrich Weiskern, Franz Schuch the Elder, and Joseph von Kurz (Bernardon), each related to his predecessors, yet each at the same time individual and distinctive in costume and comportment. From this character stem a host of others in Vienna, particularly Kurz's famous Bernardon in mid-century, who enjoyed wide acclaim in other cities as well, and the many renditions of Kasperl. There is no doubt that such characters were the favourites of the Viennese populace throughout the century, nor that their popularity was anchored in an ability to entertain by comic improvisation. In the *Spielstück* it is only the performance that counts; in the *Literaturdrama* both text and performance, with the former sometimes gaining the upper hand. Audiences in the Kärntnertortheater before 1750 were usually treated to a double dose of their favourite comic figure, for he appeared both in longer works and in the Nachspiele which usually followed. The earliest extant playbills of the theatre from 1722 to 1728 give a good idea of the type of work performed and the principal focus of attention (*VZ*, *Stadtbibliothek*, Sig D5.996). They feature Hauptaktionen with prominent billing to Hanswurst, the promise that he will appear intermittently through the drama, and the further enticement of either a 'lustige Nach-Comödie' or 'Tanz' to conclude. The latter pair, apparently more or less interchangeable, is reminiscent of a trend to the alternation of ballets with Nachspiele to maintain audience interest in Berlin, Frankfurt, and Munich.

The tone and content of Kärntnertor productions began to change in the late forties. Zechmeister's chronology of the theatre from 1747 to 1763 shows a prevalence of Italian opera and pantomime, with many plays in French, a result of the repeated guest engagements by French and Italian companies, and also a testimony to the deep penetration of those two cultures into Viennese society, particularly into the upper classes. Yet the repertoire for the same years also shows German plays, including many Bernardoniaden and Hanswurstiaden. Despite the strong foreign influence catering to the upper classes, these elemental German comic forms were maintained. This period in the repertoire also reveals not many, but some, Nachspiel titles that can be traced to published texts (*Adel des Herzens, Der betrogene Betrüger, Fanny, Die Rekreation, Der Schatzgräber, Der sehende Blinde*), indicating some shift from pure *Spielstück* to *Literaturdrama*. Still, one cannot be sure just how closely the players did in fact honour the literary text. For instance, Gottfried Prehauser, famous as Hanswurst, also played roles in printed works such as *Der betrogene Betrüger*, and it is entirely likely that he treated the audience to some extemporized antics when the opportunity arose.

From mid-century to 1785, the Kärntertor- and Burgtheater played in direct competition. Until 1752 the Burgtheater played a regular fare of Italian opera, pantomime, French plays, and ballets, then adding more German comedies, while at the same time the Kärntnertortheater offered audiences many more German works and heavy doses of Bernardon, Hanswurst, and Harlekin as well as German ballet.

Zechmeister offers a fascinating account of the results of the direct competition between Kärntnertor- and Burgtheater in the fifties. The home of Hanswurst constantly outdid its highfalutin cousin in terms of attendance and profits, making the taste and loyalty of the Viennese public, including members of all classes, clear.

Fate and politics joined to change this pattern. To the fire which destroyed the Kärntnertortheater in 1761 was added during the sixties state pressure to discourage extemporization on the stage, with Joseph von Sonnenfels at the vanguard of reform. It reached its height when in 1769 extemporization was officially banned. The growing aesthetic and political movement to regularize theatre had reached Vienna and apparently taken it, at least temporarily. In the last decades of the century, the repertoire and performances of the Kärntnertortheater were markedly sobered and the official state support of the Burgtheater ensured its rise to prominence instead. From 1785 to the end of the century, when both Burg- and Kärntnertortheater were directly controlled by the court, the repertoires and even sets, costumes, and the like were often interchangeable. The Kärntnertor played German *Sprechstücke*, Singspiele, and ballet; the Burgtheater Italian Singspiele, also German *Sprechstücke*, as well as ballet.

The Burgtheater repertoire from 1776 shows no sign of the central comic figure or works in which he starred. As official home of the *Literaturdrama* and German *Sprechstück*, the plays were consistently German or translations into German, usually from the French. Most programs consisted of one long *Literaturdrama* or two shorter ones together, and among these there were many which can be documented as published Nachspiele (*Adel des Herzens, Die beiden Billets, Die beiden Portraits, Friederike von Rosenhayn, Der Instinkt, Der Magnetismus, Die Maskerade, Das Mündel, Nur ein Stündchen war er fort, Das Portrait, Der sehende Blinde, Was ist's?*). When played, these normally followed a longer work but without apparent connection to it. The Burgtheater became in this period a home for the Nachspiel as *Literaturdrama*.

Despite Sonnenfels and the censors, and despite all efforts to impose official aesthetic criteria on the stage, the *Spielstück* as staple of Viennese theatre was not so easily dismissed. From 1781 the Theater in der Leopoldstadt became its new home. Hadamowsky's record of the repertoire (*Theater*) shows forty-one separate plays in hundreds of performances with Kasper or Kasperle as their focus, the new king of extemporized comedy in Vienna in the last decades of the century. This character's habit of playing multiple roles in the same work, as Hanswurst was usually expected to do in the earlier Hauptaktionen, is evident from a representative playbill from 21 October 1781 when the main play was *Aller Anfang ist schwer*, in which Kasperle appeared 'als Friseur a la Mode, als Sesselträger, als Anstreicher, und als Stockmeister' (VZ, *Stadtbibliothek*, Sig C64525). There are also in Hadamowsky's record of the Theater in der Leopoldstadt thirty-six separate works starring Harlekin, in hundreds of performances stretching far into the next century. These characters clearly dominated that stage to 1800 and beyond. For the most part, they performed as central figures in longer works (Lustspiele in two, three, or four acts; farces in three acts; Singspiele; comic operas), but at times in one-act comedies as well. Often there were in fact two Hanswurst or Kasperl plays on the same program. This repertoire is reminiscent of that of the first decades of the Kärntnertortheater, and while once again the Nachspiel as designated genre does not play a prominent role, again it can be said that on the basis of activity in the Theater in der Leopoldstadt the key elements of the original Nachspiel permeated the primary works so that Nachspiele as additions were unnecessary.

In their analysis of the Vorstadttheater, Blümml/Gugitz devote close attention to the Theater auf der Landstraße for the brief portion of its history from 1789 until it closed four years later. In 1790 it played a great variety of musical and operatic works, ballet, and frequent Hauptaktionen with Harlekin and Kasperl. But when in 1791 the theatre came under the direction of Josef and Elise Kettner, to be succeeded by Christoph Seipp in 1793, the repertoire changed drastically, the short and lighter works disappearing almost entirely, the stage gradually dominated by lengthy dramas, tragedies, and opera. That proved to be the road to ruin for this theatrical enterprise – it closed, a failure, on 15 October 1793.

The Vienna scene demonstrates as no other both symbiosis and tension between state and popular theatre. Despite the censorship movement of the sixties, official discouragement, and then banning of extemporization, the tradition of *Spielstücke* remained vigorous and continued to enjoy support from all levels of society. In terms of the Nachspiel, Vienna is exemplary in cultivating what could be called both of its forms, *Spielstück* and *Literaturdrama*, but at the same time it is clear throughout the century that the *Spielstück* was the elemental form closest to the heart and theatrical taste of that society.

Weimar

SOURCES
Burkhardt, *Repertoire* (1891); Schrickel, *Geschichte* (1928); Sichardt, *Weimarer* (1957)

COVERAGE

The entire century is covered. In the early decades, Weimar was often visited by itinerant troupes and as early as 1733 a group of players was supported by the ducal court and outfitted with proper costumes. This tradition was continued until 1758 when the regent Duke Karl of Braunschweig dissolved the Hof-Comödianten in Weimar, beginning a period of relative quiet until 1768. But the interested involvement of Duchess Anna Amalia and the ascent of Duke Karl August brought long privileges to a number of established troupes into the seventies, including Heinrich Koch (1768-70) and Abel Seyler (1771).

After the ducal palace was destroyed by fire in 1774, Goethe's move to Weimar stimulated a particularly noteworthy Liebhabertheater which operated in a number of locations, from members' houses to temporary stages and from 1780 in the new Komödienhaus, built of wood in 1776 behind the ducal palace. Sichard provides a wealth of detail about technical features of the Liebhabertheater's stages, decorations, costumes, and a commentary on the repertoire and some one hundred performances (Sichardt, 130-72). In 1783 a court theatre was re-established by Duke Karl August with major influence from Goethe; professional actors were engaged, the Josef Bellomo troupe first from 1784 to 1791.

Burkhardt presents a detailed chronology of the 4,136 programs in this court theatre and its branches in Halle, Lauchstädt, Leipzig, Erfurt, Rudolstadt, and Naumburg (with slight omissions where sources were unavailable) from 1791 to 1817 (Burkhardt, 1-104). This is followed by an alphabetical list of the 648 works performed (including dramas, ballets, dances, and musical compositions).

ANALYSIS

Schrickel's survey of the early decades of the century shows that the itinerant troupes, even with court support, played a steady diet of harlequinades and farces, often called 'Nach-Spiele,' and often after a longer work, particularly comedies. Their repertoires also included a good deal of ballet. From Koch's arrival in 1768, repertoires became regularized and there are no more signs of the farcical Nachspiel, although ballets were maintained and by title indicate an affinity to the earthy subject-matter of many Nachspiele (e.g. *Die Bauernhochzeit, Hans und Grete, Der Kobold*, Schrickel, 55).

Sichard's overview of the Liebhabertheater shows that it was the norm to present one regular drama at each performance. Only one of those from her list is a published Nachspiel (*Der sehende Blinde*). On a number of occasions, however, the group played comedies whose titles are unrecorded, and also 'Extemporirte Comödie' (Sichardt, 146) which Goethe characterized in a diary entry of 1778 as 'Draussen allerley Tollheit, extemporirte Comödie' (*Tagebücher*, 59). Under his leadership, the group was keenly interested in the principles of acting, and this interest included the value of extemporization. Sichardt reminds us of Goethe's praise of extemporization through the *Prinzipalin* in the *Theatralische Sendung*:

> … man hätte mancherlei Nutzen herausziehen können, denn das Extemporiren war die Schule und der Probierstein des Acteurs … Es kam nicht darauf an, eine Rolle auswendig zu lernen und sich einzubilden, daß man sie spielen könne, sondern der Geist, die lebhafte Einbildung, die Gewandheit, die Kenntniß des Theaters, die Gegenwart des Geistes zeigte sich mit jedem Schritt auf das klärste; der Schauspieler war durch die Noth gezwungen, sich mit allen Ressourcen, die das Theater anbietet, bekannt zu machen …
> (*Werke* 231f)

Burkhardt's introduction gives an idea of the court theatre repertoire based initially on Bellomo's plays, about one-third comedies, one-third Singspiele and opera, one-third Schauspiel, Trauerspiel, or minor genre. Overall, for the period he examines, it was the pattern to perform one work only, less so two or three. When multiple short works were performed, they were frequently one-act comedies, with no apparent connection to each other. The term 'Nachspiel' is rarely used in the list. Once it is used to designate a second piece on the program: Lessing's *Der Schatz*, a comedy in three acts. Only two of the short comedies can be found as published Nachspiele: *Die beiden Billets*, which was taken over from Bellomo's repertoire and performed numerous times, often as the first work on the program, and *Die Martinsgänse*, which was performed once.

While it is evident that Goethe's direction of the court theatre in the 1790s left no distinctive place for the traditional Nachspiel, it had been very much alive in Weimar until the seventies. With the subsequent founding of the Liebhabertheater and then court theatre, evidence of the genre disappeared, but its essential element, extemporization, was obviously highly prized and even as Goethe and his colleagues moved to exclusively regular theatre, it played an indirect but important part in their productions.

ITINERANT TROUPES

Caroline Neuber

SOURCES
Reden-Esbeck, *Caroline Neuber* (1881); Sasse, *Friedericke* (1937)

COVERAGE
The life of the troupe from 1727 to 1755 is covered, during which time
Caroline Neuber is recorded to have played in nineteen towns and
cities as widely spread as Kiel, Straßburg, and Warsaw, but with concentration in Dresden, Hamburg, and Leipzig. While no complete
repertoire or list of performances is given, Reden-Esbeck provides a
detailed account of eight months in 1735, 8 April to 5 December (107-
10). The account includes seventy-five 'Schauspiele' (a mixture of
'Tragödien' and 'Comödien') in 203 performances. Separately, he lists
ninety-three 'Nachspiele' in 107 performances. Both Reden-Esbeck and
Sasse report further, but less completely, on other performance periods. The Neuber troupe was a training ground for later principals.
Among her company numbered at times both Heinrich Koch and
Friedrich Schönemann, each of whom founded his own troupe afterward and enjoyed far more success than his mentor.

ANALYSIS
While the Neuber troupe was founded officially by Johann Neuber, its
history shows that his wife Caroline was the driving force behind it.
From the period examined by Reden-Esbeck in detail, it is obvious that
Caroline Neuber played many more comedies than tragedies among
her major works. Further, when comparing the total number of Schauspiele and Nachspiele in the repertoire, seventy-five and ninety-three,
it is clear that Nachspiele represented the most prevalent genre by far.
In terms of performance, a comparison of 203 for Schauspiele with 107
for Nachspiele indicates that the troupe played a Nachspiel on more
than half of the programs; hence, these occupied a significant portion
of the performance activity.

Because the sources do not present the precise combination of works
on individual programs, it is impossible to say whether there was a direct relationship between the Nachspiel and its predecessor, but the
predominance of comedies in the repertoire indicates at least that a
tragicomic counterpoint between main work and Nachspiel was not
important. Whereas Reden-Esbeck is able to identify and list each

Schauspiel title, for the ninety-three Nachspiele only thirty-one specific titles are given, the other sixty-two simply being called 'Nachspiele ohne Namen.' These appeared on Neuber's playbills as 'Ein lustiges Nachspiel' or the like, and were improvised works which Reden-Esbeck discusses at some length. In general it can be said that they shared a common focus in a central comic figure such as Harlekin or Hanswurst and were crudely farcical. Among the thirty-one Nachspiel titles listed, five have specific reference to Harlekin, but this character likely played a major role in a number of the other improvised works as well.

Only a very few of the thirty-one Nachspiel titles listed in Neuber's repertoire can be traced to printed texts, and these were published largely as short Lustspiele, but one as a Nachspiel (*Der Dresdner Frauen Schlendrian*). However, many of the so-called Schauspiele listed appeared in published form, though two of them are designated in print as Nachspiele (*Der Klätscher, Die* [=*Das*] *Mündel*). The fact that Neuber played these two not as Nachspiele but rather as main works indicates that they did not fulfil the function of the Nachspiel for her troupe and its audience. Conversely, for the period under consideration, it is clear that the extemporized Nachspiel with central comic figure occupied a formidable position in the repertoire.

Although this is just one detailed segment of the troupe's history, it is possible to generalize about the entire scope of Neuber's activity with further information provided by Reden-Esbeck and Sasse. The essential features of her repertoire as examined for 1737 are valid for much of the first decade of the company's life. Beside a playbill of 1728 which features 'ein lustiges Nach-Spiel' Reden-Esbeck tells us that 'Die Stücke, welche die Neuber damals gab und gewöhnlich mit dem Lockworte "lustig" bezeichnete, waren elende extemporirte Burlesken …, waren aber von den gröbsten Späßen gereinigt, und [es] zeigte sich auch hierin das erste Bestreben die Schauspielkunst zu veredeln' (Reden-Esbeck, 66-8). Yet from the start this reforming spirit contradicted the wishes of audiences. Of the early thirties Reden-Esbeck reports, 'je länger die Neuber mit ihrer gereinigten Bühne sich in Hamburg aufhielt, desto mehr sehnte sich das dortige Publikum nach den unreinen Späßen des Hanswurstes' (Reden-Esbeck, 95). Eager to contribute to regularizing the German stage according to the standards of French classical, or literary, drama, and at the same time to find favour among those with artistic and political clout and gain the privilege to play, Neuber corresponded with Gottsched for years (1730-6), making known her intentions, dropping reference to Nachspiele on her playbills, and even banning Hanswurst ceremoniously in 1737. Thereafter,

Neuber continued to play extemporized works with central comic figures but they were given different names and played in a less offensive manner. Lessing tells us that Neuber advertised appearances of Harlekin but in fact had him play under the name Hänschen in an entirely white costume (*Werke*, Hanser edition, IV, 323). Significantly, the path of her troupe from then on was studded with impediments. Her relationship with Gottsched deteriorated into a feud by 1742 and thereafter the troupe had only occasional success and much hardship. Indeed, Neuber's reformatorial zeal, and particularly her emasculation of Hanswurst in the Nachspiel, can be seen as catalysts of her demise.

Joseph von Kurz (Bernardon)

SOURCES
Birbaumer, *Das Werk* (1971); Raab, *Johann Joseph Felix von Kurz* (1898)

COVERAGE
Both Birbaumer and Raab cover the years from Kurz's boyhood and first official stage appearance in Vienna's Kärntnertortheater (1737) to his death (1784). During this period Kurz played as comic Bernardon and in many other roles both as a member of other companies and as manager of his own, in Vienna (1737-40, 1744-60, 1769-71, 1781-3), Frankfurt/M, Mainz, and Cologne (1741-2, 1766-8), Prague (1753, 1760-4), Preßburg (1764), Munich (1765), Nürnberg (1766), and Warsaw (1771-81), where he was elevated to the nobility. Raab's study is chronological and anecdotal with examples of performances and texts, and one concentrated portion of Kurz's repertoire is presented. Birbaumer's study provides the most thorough analysis of Kurz's works available, but does not enlarge significantly upon Raab's account of the repertoire.

ANALYSIS
As Kurz was not primarily a troupe principal, it is inappropriate to speak of repertoire in the same sense as for unified itinerant companies. His repertoire was built around a performance style, extemporized comedy, and many titles he played can be found in the Viennese repertoires presented by Rommel, Blümml, and Zechmeister above. Kurz did play many works which by position and nature, and often by playbill advertisement, were Nachspiele, yet he is more appropriately understood as star performer in the *Hauptstück*. Throughout his career, he carried on the early tradition of the Hauptaktion with central comic

figure, steadily refusing to give in to regular theatre and maintaining the tradition of extemporization to the end. In doing so, he naturally ran afoul of theatre reformers such as Joseph von Sonnenfels, and such disagreements were at times the cause for his moving on.

Raab's longer excerpt from Kurz's repertoire is for the period 11 June to 2 October 1766 (Raab, 150-65). While some serious works were played, the main feature was clearly the comic work with Bernardon at the focus, either as 'Nach-Comödie,' 'Opéra comique,' 'Singspiel,' or other full-length work. Ballets and some musical pieces were also frequent, some of which carried titles otherwise known and played as spoken Nachspiele (*Der (hell)sehende Blinde, Der Scherenschleifer*), indicating a transference of Nachspiel material to other genres. The repertoire also includes the Nachspiel *Der falsche Verdacht, oder Bernardon der unschuldige Missethäter* (Raab, 158), which exists in manuscript form and is reproduced in full later in the present study (see p 80).

Kurz is one of the few of his age who epitomized the extemporized comic figure on stage. As Bernardon, his own creation and stage identity, he was a favourite in Vienna and other major, especially southern, centres for decades. Born into his father's itinerant troupe with the prototypical 'Wiener Hanswurst' Anton Stranitzky himself as godfather, Kurz played out Bernardon in extemporized scenarios beside Gottfried Prehauser, Stranitzky's successor as Hanswurst, Franz Nuth as Harlekin, and Johann Leinhaas as Pantalon, as potent a comic foursome as the eighteenth-century stage ever witnessed. The Bernardon character began as a young, ignorant, rude, and disrespectful type, initially one role in an extemporized play, but was soon so popular that it became Kurz's standard mask, as recognizable as Prehauser's Hanswurst, and after some time actually eclipsed Hanswurst in popularity. Raab offers this contemporary account of Bernardon's style and the audience's reaction to it around 1740: 'Nun stelle man sich ein hochansehnliches, hochgeneigtes Auditorium vor. Vierzig vollgepfrofte Logen, ein Parterre zum erdrücken und die Gallerien zum einbrechen. Die Gardinen aufgezogen,' and now the star appears: 'Bernardon kommt aus den Coulissen mit ein paar Seitensprüngen und einer lächerlichen Reverenz hervor.' He speaks:

Ich habe Appetit, denn der Tambour meines Magens schlägt schon Rebell und Vergatterung, aber meine Occasions-Laterne Colombine wird wohl wieder im Finstern auf der Treppe an einen Heyducken angestossen seyn, dass sie einen Geschwulst bekommt, der erst in dreyviertel Jahren aufgeht.

The audience reacts:

'Bravo, Bravo,' schreit das hochansehnliche, hochgeneigte Auditorium und klatscht 3 Minuten 45 Secunden, die Gallerie eine Minute weniger, ein paar Logen aber zwei Secunden länger. 'St. – St. – ' und eine allgemeine Stille zeigt die Begierde den Verfolg zu hören.

We witness a wildly enthusiastic audience, all applauding loud and long, the upper bourgeoisie and nobility in the loges the longest. The brief extended applause from these loges shows both the delight of the upper crust and their inhibition at expressing it too obviously. What makes this mixed audience so enthusiastic? Most of what Bernardon says is vulgar, revealing a primary motivation to satisfy his sexual and physical appetites. For the audience to approve so strongly is to indicate an identification with these acts – they share, vicariously, Bernardon's frustration and impending pleasure. That the comic personality and potential of Bernardon was undoubtedly known to them before he appeared ensured an identification between audience and fictional character even before his performance. And note that his appearance begins with 'ein paar Seitensprüngen und einer lächerlichen Reverenz' – obviously Bernardon's acrobatic, gesticular, and mimic abilities played a large part in his success. The 'lächerliche Reverenz' is a mimetic gesture, an imitation of aristocratic protocol through which Bernardon parodies with pointed economy the stuffy conventions of the pretentious bourgeoisie, the upper class, and the court.

Bernardon returns to the plot and, with the needs of his body foremost in mind, declares his love to Isabella:

'Was ist zu machen,' fährt Bernardon in seinem Monologe fort, 'ich werde zu Mamsel Isabellen gehen und sehen den Tambour meines Magens sowie meine äusserste Liebe zu befriedigen und zu krönen. Aber da kommt sie eben. Jetzt Bernardon nimm deine ganze Beredsamkeit zusammen, erwünschtere Gelegenheit einen Liebes-Antrag zu formiren, kann unmöglich erdacht werden. Wir sind hier überdies neben meinem Schlafzimmer und hier steht ein bequemer Sopha.

'Schönste Gebieterin! nachdem sintemalen, alldieweilen und demnach die Sterblichkeit aus dem Firmament der Sterne, gleichwie die hellglänzende Sonne in der Morgenröthe und Julius Caesar, der berühmte Philosoph, nicht minder der Alexander, der stoische Lehrer von der Liebe, also sag ich Ihnen, dass meine Gedanken durch die Wolken, wie die Sonnenstrahlen von der sterblichen Sterblichkeit, Glückseligkeit, Freude, Entzücken, Wollust und Vergnügen das Innerste meines verliebten Herzens durch die Liebe und Zärtlichkeit auf der Reitbahn des Cupido allezeit und jederzeit auf dem Mistbeete meines Herzens liebe und verehre, habe gesagt, sage und wollte sagen und verstummte und sprach.'

Again the audience reacts: '"Bravo, bravo," abermal ein Donner von 3 Minuten' (Raab, 13f).

The excerpt testifies to the enormous crowds Bernardon attracted to Vienna's Kärntnertortheater, and not just commoners but nobility as well, including the emperor and his family. His humour is a mixture of coarse sexuality and baroque bombast, often a parody of the classical imagery presented in the serious regular dramas of the day, and we can only imagine how much he added in gesture and mime. His language and movements suggest a freedom to mock even the manners of well-heeled patrons in the loges who, of course, enjoyed the show as much as any other group. (See further details of this theatre and discussion of an actual Kurz Nachspiel performance in the analysis of *Der falsche Verdacht*, p 88.)

Along with Franz Schuch, Kurz embodied the spirit of extemporization in the eighteenth century, and at the same time the essence of the early Nachspiel. His appeal to all classes, his reduction of thematics to an elemental level, and most of all the innate brilliance of his performance are features of his career that remain distinctive characteristics fundamental to the Nachspiel tradition.

Franz Schuch

SOURCE
Liss, 'Theater' (1925)

COVERAGE
Liss's Berlin dissertation, monstrously typed in single spacing with countless typographical errors and fuzzy text where his ribbon seemed to be failing, nevertheless stands as a gold-mine of well-documented and researched information on Schuch, the dean of mid-century comic figures. It is our loss that the dissertation has not been published, for it deserves equal prominence with the studies of Devrient on Schönemann and Eichhorn on Ackermann as essential documents for understanding the activities of leading itinerant troupes. The most valuable part of Liss's work remains his twenty pages of unpaginated appendices or 'Tabellen' in which he presents a thorough picture of the troupe under the subtitles 'Reisen der Truppe 1740-1770,' 'Bühnenverhältnisse,' 'Stammbaum der Schuchischen Truppe,' 'Rollenverzeichnis,' 'Repertoire,' and 'Bildliches Material.' In the troupe's thirty-one years of

activity from 1740 to 1771 (it was led by Schuch the Elder until his death in 1764, thereafter by his son), they performed in thirty-eight different towns and cities, repeating visits to most several times, on a total of forty-six different stages, from theatre buildings to improvised temporary locations with a broad concentration in the north (e.g. Berlin, Bremen, Danzig, Hamburg, Königsberg, Stettin), the most important centre of activity being Berlin. Often they played in one place only a few days, so the energy and dedication required by constant travel and reorientation to new surroundings and theatrical requirements was enormous. Over the years, the troupe had one hundred different members who joined and left from time to time as disposition and opportunity dictated, and Liss lists them all along with dates of activity, troupes from which they came and to which they went – a fascinating picture of the fluctuations in the itinerant theatre scene. The company included many who gained fame later with other troupes as well as in literary circles, for example Gottfried Uhlich (author and editor), Carl Döbbelin (later a leading principal in Berlin and Schuch's rival), Christian Stephanie (author), Sophie Hensel (to become one of the most renowned actresses of the age), Conrad Ekhof (later with Koch and Schönemann, an outstanding actor and one of the founders of the movement toward the improvement of acting), and Johann Brandes (author and chronicler). The stabilizing stalwarts, however, were Franz Schuch himself, troupe principal and celebrated Hanswurst, his wife Barbara (Kolumbine), and Johann Anton Stänzel (Anselmo), whose thirty-nine years with the troupe remain a record of loyalty on the eighteenth-century theatre scene.

In the section on repertoire, Liss provides as complete an account as possible of the some four hundred titles performed, along with more than a thousand performance dates.

ANALYSIS
While Schuch's Hanswurst is undoubtedly the key to his place in theatrical history, his repertoire shows great range and, in fact, a balance between traditional comedy, in which extemporization was frequent, and literary drama. As Liss puts it, '[Das Repertoire] trug einen Januskopf dessen eine Hälfte den Kenner im Parterre beobachtete, während die andere mit der Galerie liebäugelte: ein Stück Toga, ein Stück bürgerlichen Tuches, ein Stück Hanswurstjacke; das Ganze in Balletschuhen an ein Drahtseil gelehnt, ein Kind auf dem einen, die volle Theaterkasse unter dem andern Arm, das war das Wesen des Schuch-Theaters' (Liss, 2). Unlike the troupes who wished to be toadies

to theatrical reform, Schuch wanted foremost to play successful theatre, which meant pleasing audiences and selling tickets, and to do this he knew that extemporized comedy had to remain strong and literary drama its partner, not oppressor. With this duality in mind, Liss presents the repertoire in two halves, 'Das regelmäßige Theater' and 'Das extemporierte Schauspiel,' and within each there are several main groups.

'Das regelmäßige Theater' consists of 147 works divided as follows: Classical German and French *Tragödien*, twenty-four titles; *Bürgerliche Trauerspiele* by English and German authors, nine; Miscellaneous, eleven; Lustspiele by French authors, forty-one, many of which are noted as Nachspiele as well; Lustspiele by other foreign authors, seven; Schäferspiele by German authors, five; Lustspiele by German authors, thirty, many of which are noted as Nachspiele as well; Weiße's operettas, three; 'Neue Lustspiele,' a term from Schuch, most listed anonymously, several also as Nachspiele, seventeen. Within the considerable range of genres, we see that comic works outweigh tragic ones by just over two to one with a modest preponderance of French comedy over German (forty-one to thirty), both normal proportions for the age. About a fifth of the Lustspiele were in fact played as Nachspiele (twenty in all), but all but one (*Die Matrone von Ephesus*) were never published as such. Conversely, two Lustspiele in Schuch's repertoire not played as Nachspiele were nevertheless published with this genre subtitle (*Der Finanzpächter*, *Der sehende Blinde*).

An entirely different visage is presented by the other 'Januskopf.' 'Das extemporierte Schauspiel' is divided into: 'Haupt- und Staatsaktionen,' nineteen titles; 'Die Burleske,' forty-one; 'Gesungene Harlekinaden,' nineteen; 'Die Pantomime,' ten. Further, there is the 'Beiprogramm,' made up of: 'Das Festspiel,' twenty-five, short works written and performed for specific occasions in honour of dignitaries (discounted from the totals below), and 'Das extemporierte Nachspiel,' twenty; 'Gesungenes Nachspiel,' eight; 'Ballet,' eighty-nine, and 'Äquilibristik,' three. A final group is called 'Kindertheater,' which consisted of works drawn from across the repertoire, adapted and performed for and by children.

The material for Schuch's Haupt- und Staatsaktionen was drawn from Roman and Germanic sagas, historical events, and biblical stories, but any pretence of seriousness or tragedy was completely dispelled by the constant *Neben-Actionen* of Hanswurst. The 'Burlesken' were basically *Verwandlungsspiele* consisting of repeated comic metamorphoses of Hanswurst and Kolumbine (both prominently featured in many of the titles) which required them to change costumes and masks dozens of times. They often contained strong doses of satirical comment, and were in many cases adaptations of literary works listed among those in the 'regelmäßiges Theater' (Liss, 9, 94).

Liss warns us that the total of twenty-eight 'extemporierte Nachspiele' listed is misleading, for the repertoire presented here contains almost exclusively entitled works. Since such Nachspiele, in which Hanswurst was always central, were completely improvised, they were also often untitled, and there were many more of them than the number here indicates (Liss, 9), for we know that they were played at the end of most programs. In the case of Schuch's repertoire it is also difficult to separate the Nachspiel distinctly from other genres since Hanswurst was at the heart of the Haupt- und Staatsaktionen, 'Burlesken,' and 'Pantomimen' as well. Moreover, the extraordinary number of ballets cannot be discounted from the Nachspiel concept since they were also almost completely extemporized and functioned usually to close the program, either alone or alongside the comic work. Dancers and a choreographer were a regular part of Schuch's salaried personnel, but their performances were far from ballets in a classical sense, consisting more of gymnastic acrobatics and pantomime. Not far from these then were the 'Äquilibristik' performances (by gymnasts hired temporarily) which were circus-like acts on tightropes and such (Liss, 55). The ballet was for Schuch obviously both complement and alternative to the Nachspiel. Soon after him, other principals such as Schönemann and Ackermann used it as a replacement for the beloved Nachspiel in order to sanitize their repertoires of crude comic elements, but they learned from Schuch to draw the thematic content of their ballets from a world familiar and attractive to the common populace: the realms of the peasant, the shepherd, seasonal agrarian labours and pleasures, the handworker, the distant and exotic. Some of Schuch's ballet titles are: *Der lustige Bauer, Die böse Bäuerin, Die Hirten auf der Viehweide, Die Schäferflur, Der Frühling, Der Herbst, Die Heuernte, Die Weinlese, Die Nagelschmiede, Der Nachtwächter, Die Gartenlust des Chinesischen Kaisers,* and *Der Serail des Großsultans.*

One of Schuch's ballet titles, *Der falsche Verdacht,* is that of a work made famous by Kurz at the same time in Vienna (see later analysis, p 88), but it is impossible to tell if there is a closer connection. While the common title may well be merely a coincidence, the prominence of Hanswurst and extemporized comedy for Schuch is the same as that of the Viennese stage, the city where in fact he was born and lived long enough to absorb something of the legacy of Stranitzky. Then he became in a sense North Germany's counterpart to the Viennese Hanswurst, like Stranitzky and Prehauser immediately recognizable in the traditional comic costume of that character. While the name Harlekin is used in many titles of his extemporized repertoire, this should be understood to be in fact Schuch as Hanswurst until he retired from performing in the early sixties (Liss, 10). (Several portraits of Schuch exist – see later discussion, p 74.) In contrast to every other member of his company, Schuch played just one character almost exclusively (brief appearances in five other roles over twenty-three years), while others were assigned many. Even those few in the inner circle who were allowed to extemporize freely, Stänzel (Anselmo), Mme Schuch (Kolumbine), and one or two others, were required to fill many other roles (for example Stänzel had twenty-five). With Schuch's death in 1764, Northern Germany's greatest Hanswurst was gone and the Nachspiele which were his exclusive domain were soon transformed into much more tempered and restricted dramatic fare by his successors.

Heinrich Gottfried Koch

SOURCES
Prick, 'Heinrich Gottfried Koch' (1925); 'Verzeichnis der Tragödien und Komödien' [1750]

COVERAGE
Koch was an independent principal for twenty-five years from 1749 until 1775, during which time he made Leipzig his constant home base, performing at forty *Messen* there and remaining for longer periods during the years 1749-50 (Theater im Richtersgarten), 1750-1 (am Blumenberge), 1751-65 (im Quandtshof). The favour he enjoyed among audiences and city officials alike is shown by the fact that he built his own Komödienhaus on the Ranstädter Bastei in 1766, but in the early seventies he took up residence in Berlin. Prick's dissertation limits its focus to the years 1749-53 and includes numerous excerpts from the repertoire; more valuable for an overview, however, is the 'Verzeichnis' to which Prick refers (64). This is supposedly an appendix to her dissertation consisting of a transcript of a 'Verzeichnis' located in the Leipzig city library: 'Vgl. die genaue Abschrift dieses nur in einem Exemplar vorhandenen Buches in der Beilage zu vorliegender Arbeit' (65, note 1); and she reports that the copy transcribed contains not only a list of tragedies and comedies in Koch's repertoire before 1760, but handwritten on the facing pages a list of the Nachspiele performed as well,

which she has also transcribed. But there is no sign of such an appendix attached to her work. Curiously, a typescript of this 'Verzeichnis,' including the Nachspiele, is located without indication of author in the Austrian National Library (Sig 842773-CTh). It contains an alphabetical list of plays performed by Koch before 1760 with transcripts of playbills so that combinations of works are apparent. There is a separate extensive index of Nachspiele.

ANALYSIS

Prick's study of the years 1749-53 reveals Koch as a principal who like Neuber wished to move toward the regularization of German theatre but was unable to overcome the public's insistence on extemporization. Unlike his predecessor, he seems to have accepted this realistically, and while his repertoire contains a core of regular literary dramas, many translated from the French, the extemporized Nachspiel is constantly in evidence, often at the forefront. In the selection of works on his programs the clever Koch successfully walked a fine line between the taste of the public for extemporization and that of the cultivated and powerful, led by Gottsched. Koch's pragmatism and adroit theatre management are reflected by his hiring Johann Martin Lepper who previously had been a court jester and then principal of his own burlesque troupe. He was an odd fellow, exhibiting a passion for women's feet and footwear which he indulged by means of an extensive personal collection of women's shoes, stockings, and slippers with the names of the former owners attached (Prick, 67). Lepper was Koch's Harlekin, the central comic improviser in the Nachspiel as well as some other works, for the repertoire shows that frequently one work alone was performed, with Harlekin central. Singspiele, operettas, and light Intermezzi were also prevalent. Most of the Nachspiel titles contained in the 'Verzeichnis' were never published, which indicates their extemporized character, but many reveal through their titles the central presence of Harlekin. A few can be traced to published copies (*Die kranke Frau, Die Matrone von Ephesus, Die [=Das] Mündel, Das Portrait, Der sehende Blinde*). Koch evidently used the designation Nachspiel, which was bound to attract audiences, not just to give them the extemporization they wanted, but also to draw them gently into regular literary drama through comedies in one act. These became more prevalent in the late fifties and beyond, whereas the Harlekin-based Nachspiele were concentrated in the earlier years. It seems likely that external pressure to regularize the theatre toward literary drama, and Koch's own inclination to do so, gradually gained the upper hand after 1760.

Johann Friedrich Schönemann

SOURCE
Devrient, *Johann Friedrich Schönemann* (1895)

COVERAGE
The life of the troupe from 1740 to 1757 is considered, during which time they played in dozens of towns and cities concentrated in what was until 3 October 1990 East Germany, although the cities of Lüneburg, Braunschweig, Hannover, and especially Hamburg were also important locations. Devrient has recorded 319 different works played by the troupe in well over one thousand performances. Among the works in the repertoire, the most common were Lustspiele (149, almost half), followed by Nachspiele (62), with the Trauerspiel and Ballett a good distance behind, and thereafter several other genres. In actual performance, the frequency of both Lustspiel and Nachspiel must have been considerably higher than their proportions in the title register, as there was such a preponderance of them in the repertoire. Devrient divides his account of repertoire and performance into two parts: a chronological list of titles according to date of première, if known, along with the dates and places of subsequent performances, again if known; then the same list of titles arranged by author. In a third part Devrient lists chronologically the locations in which the troupe played, with specific dates of engagement.

ANALYSIS
Devrient's extensive information makes clear the importance of the Nachspiel in terms of sheer numbers of titles, although his account of performances is less complete. The chronological performance list shows an evolution over the seventeen years. For the first year of the troupe's life Schönemann played a number of tragedies, which attests to his intention to present regular theatre, as we learn from Devrient's historical account. But this intention was soon sacrificed (by 1741) to a preponderance of Lustspiele and Nachspiele which continued to the mid-50s. For the last three years of the troupe's life, however, there was a marked increase in performances of ballets at the end of the program and these appear to have replaced the Nachspiel to a considerable extent. While the overall frequency of ballets throughout the life of the troupe is well behind that of the Nachspiel, it indeed surpasses the Nachspiel's during these later years.

Schönemann's Nachspiele were performed at the end of the program after works of various genres, most frequently Lustspiele, with no obvious connection to them. Until 1747 some of their titles indicate the central presence of Harlekin, but Devrient lists no performance of a Nachspiel with Harlekin in its title later than that year. This absence makes clear Schönemann's avoidance of the central comic figure through most of the troupe's lifetime. The titles of most other Nachspiele listed indicate, however, that they were definitely comic works. Documentation of Nachspiel performance is a weakness in Devrient's statistics, for of the sixty-two titles listed he provides dates of premières and subsequent performances for only thirty-seven. Moreover, a full forty-nine are without author, a pattern of anonymity paralleled in the list only by the ballet, which suggests improvised performance in both cases. This supposition is reinforced by the fact that there are no extant texts for most of these Nachspiele and those for which authors and printings can be identified were published most frequently as short Lustspiele, less so with the subtitle Nachspiel (*Der bestrafte Hochmuth, Der betrogene Betrüger, Der faule Bauer, Das Portrait*).

Beyond this statistical evidence, Devrient provides us with glimpses into the nature of some of Schönemann's Nachspiele as well as some assessment of their importance:

> Die süße Zukost, mit der die schweren, oft wohl herben großen Stücke gereicht wurden, waren die Nachspiele und einzeln auch Vorspiele. Wenn wir sämtliche erhaltene Komödienzettel Schönemanns durchmustern, finden wir nur wenige Theaterabende der späteren Zeit, an denen man sich mit nur einem ernsten Stücke oder überhaupt nur einem einzigen Stücke begnügt hätte. Fast überall heißt es: 'den Beschluß macht ein lustiges' oder gar 'ein sehr lustiges Nachspiel', oder: Hierauf folget anstatt eines Nachspiels ein ... Schäferspiel. Und den völligen Beschluß wird ein sehenswürdiger Tanz machen.
>
> Diese Nachspiele sind das Gebiet, auf dem sich Harlekin ungehemmt noch tummeln durfte. Der lustige freche Vogel ist nie verschwunden. Er wurde aus den Hauptaktionen in die Nachspiele hinausgeschoben, um hier fortleben und zu warten, bis das ernste Drama auf eine höhere Stufe freierer Entfaltung gestiegen, um hier wieder emporzutauchen und, wie es Shakespeare ihn gelehrt, der tiefsten Tragik zu höchsten Wirkung zu verhelfen. (Devrient, 42f)

Devrient pays the Nachspiel a high compliment indeed in his depiction of it as a saviour for principal and public as they weathered the hard times of mediocre tragic works. Clearly the old comic figure of the

Haupt- und Staatsaktionen was very much at the focus of Schöne-mann's Nachspiele and the comedy he engineered was the main attraction for the audience. Devrient's final sentence elevates the Nach-spiel and comedy in general to a position of aesthetic importance in conjunction with its counterpoint in tragedy and points as well to our question of the relationship between the Nachspiel and preceding works. Repeatedly, evidence that Nachspiele were connected closely in content or tone to preceding works on the program is lacking, but if we are to argue as Devrient, the weak sister in the relationship was not the comic genre but rather its serious counterpart.

Konrad Ernst Ackermann

SOURCE
Eichhorn, *Konrad Ernst Ackermann* (1965)

COVERAGE
The life of the troupe in 1753-67 and 1769-71 is considered, including some three thousand performances in forty towns and cities from north (Hamburg, Königsberg, Danzig) to south (Basel, Bern, Zürich), east (Frankfurt/O, Breslau, Warsaw) to west (Straßburg, Colmar, Freiburg im Breisgau) with accurate information on 1,040 playing dates during which 1,357 performances of individual works took place. The reper-toire is listed two ways: chronologically according to performance date, so that it is evident which works were played in combination with oth-ers; and by author and title (with number of performances), which shows the popularity of individual playwrights and works. During this time, 332 different works were performed, for 298 of which Eichhorn has determined the author, hence for all but thirty-four. Ballets are ex-cluded from Eichhorn's title totals, but he does list ballets performed, these numbering some two hundred in six hundred performances, thus bringing the work total to over five hundred and performance total of individual works to almost two thousand.

ANALYSIS
Eichhorn divides the performed works by genre. From this division it is evident that Lustspiele were predominant (Eichhorn, 146). In a strong second place, however, were Nachspiele (93), with Trauerspiele (56) a distant third. If we consider the ballets here, however, with two hundred titles, they represent in fact the predominant genre for Ackermann. Of the thirty-four works performed whose author Eich-

horn could not identify, the majority are Nachspiele, and most of the ballets are listed anonymously as well. While many of these were not played from published or even handwritten texts, a few exist in print with the genre designation 'Lustspiel in einem Aufzug/Akt/einer Handlung' on the title-page, while eleven could be found with the title-page designation 'Nachspiel' (*Die ausgeschlagene Erbschaft* [*Adel des Herzens*], *Der bestrafte Hochmut* [*Johann Scherenschleifer*], *Der betrogene Kadi, Der faule Bauer, Der Finanzpächter* [*Finanzbediente*], *Die kranke Frau, Die Maskerade* [*Die dreifache Heirat*], *Das Mündel, Der Naturaliensammler, Das Portrait, Der sehende Blinde*).

Structurally, it is clear that Ackermann's Nachspiele occupied the final place in the program, after a longer work, or sometimes two shorter ones. The longer works were commonly Lustspiele, Trauerspiele, or Schauspiele, but most often by far they were Lustspiele, and there is almost no evidence to suggest that there was a connection between this longer piece and the following Nachspiel. The nature and frequency of Ackermann's Nachspiele also clearly changed over time in his repertoire. In the early years (1753-60) they were played frequently, later on less and less. In those early years the figure of Harlekin often appears in the Nachspiel titles, and this, combined with the fact that there is no documented evidence of a text, suggests strongly that these were largely improvised works with the comic figure as focal point. Later on, the Nachspiele were more frequently works which today can be documented as full texts, though more often than not as short Lustspiele. Finally, as the Nachspiel became less evident in the repertoire after 1760, there was a gradual surge of ballet performance, by the mid-60s played at the end of virtually every program. It would seem that the ballet, which shared with the Nachspiel anonymity of authorship and freedom to improvise, performed a similar function to the replaced Nachspiel in later years.

This transfer in function from Nachspiel to ballet is well demonstrated in the case of *Johann Scherenschleifer*, which Ackermann performed as a Nachspiel twenty-seven times between 1754 and 1770, but from September 1770 on only as a ballet. Similarly, *Die Maskerade, Die belebte Statue*, and *Die Weinlese* were ballets that were also well known as Nachspiele. Indeed, when surveying Ackermann's titled ballets, several prominent types or groups emerge which remind us of similar thematic focuses in Schuch's repertoire:

– ballets related to common trades or manual occupations (*Die verliebten Böttcher, Die Strohschneider, Die Nagelschmiede*);

- ballets related to social roles (*Der vom Müller betrogene Bauer, Der Bauernstreit, Der Bauernstreit über eingeschlagene Fenster*);

- ballets related to seasonal agrarian activities (*Die Lustbarkeit bei der Weinlese, Die Kornernte, Die Heuernte*);

- ballets related to traditional improvised comedy or comic figures (*Wettstreit zwischen Arlequin und Pierrot, Arlequin der verliebte Maler, Arlequin als Briefträger und Vorgeiger*);

- ballets related to exotica and fantasy (*Türkenballett, Das Serail des Großsultans, Chineserballett*).

We can see that Ackermann's ballets focused principally on themes and personalities in unquestionable rapport with the common man, a large component of his audience. They could identify with many of the characters, labourers and tradesmen like themselves, with their re-enacted social roles; and with seasonal tasks which were no doubt part of their daily lives. These ballets also maintained links with traditional comic favourites of the Nachspiel and extemporized theatre and in addition satisfied the audience's curiosity about the distant and exotic.

Ackermann employed *Tanzmeister* to direct this increasingly important portion of his repertoire. The second of these, Johann von Brunian, had careers as a puppeteer, tightrope-walker, actor, and acrobat before being charged with Ackermann's ballets, a background that indicates the principal's idea of appropriate professional qualifications. Obviously these ballets were more an extension of carnival acrobatics than refined dance, and indeed we should not forget that their performers were in fact often the same individuals who had become favourites in comic roles. An outstanding example lies in the person of Friedrich Schröder who had a wide reputation for his improvisational comic talent with Ackermann's troupe but who also performed regularly in ballets where he was 'mehr komischer Springer als ernsthafter Tänzer' (Eichhorn, 199). There are many anecdotes of Schröder's dancing, or more accurately comic acrobatics, in ballet. In a series of performances he is said to have outdone his rival Koch's feat of jumping to dislodge an object seven feet in the air by striking four tambourines nine feet above the ground with his foot, following this by springing aloft to pick an apple from a tree with his toes and delivering it to his mouth without use of the hands before landing (Eichhorn, 200)! While Schröder was doubtless a star, many members of Ackermann's company were required to do double duty as actor and dancer as well.

THE COMIC FIGURE

Throughout the repertoires of itinerant troupes it is evident that the comic figure played a central role, particularly in the Haupt- und Staatsaktionen and the Nachspiele of the early decades. Although this figure was present on the German stage in a bewildering array of variants developed by the individuals who played him, two stand out: Hanswurst and Harlekin (or Arlequin, Harlequin). As both recur in the analyses of individual Nachspiele following this chapter, a general definition of these two types now will later serve as a point of reference.

Hanswurst has been the subject of many studies, the definitive one, with copious documentation, by Helmut G. Asper (1980). Crucial to an understanding of Hanswurst, Asper rightly argues, is an awareness of his origin as 'der grobe Bauer' (129). He is not like Shakespeare's clever fool and not like Harlekin. This coarse earthy heritage results in the following characteristics: need for physical satisfaction (food, drink, sex); social clumsiness in contrast to the courtly manners of others with whom he interacts; impudence and blatant disrespect; materialism (constant plotting for financial reward); cowardice, yet boastfulness, particularly if he portrays a soldier; untruthfulness; scatological interest (often expressed in language); involvement with spirits and ghosts (Asper, 129-230). As far as the dramatic function is concerned, Asper stresses Hanswurst's 'Verwicklung in der Intrige' and improvised comic scenes ('lazzi'). He insists that, unlike Harlekin, Hanswurst through his actions gets drawn unwittingly into the intrigue; he does not construct, consciously manipulate, or direct it. Hanswurst is typically an accomplice to others who direct that intrigue, a letter carrier, a spy, a messenger, or the like (Asper, 210). In this subservient role he is subject to the authority of masters who do not hesitate to deliver the occasional blow to his back (*Buckel*) as a corrective or reprimand.

Other scholars have concentrated their analyses of Hanswurst within the broader context of the comic figure in general and his dramatic function. I see no contradiction between Asper's characterization of Hanswurst and that of Eckehard Catholy, who emphasizes his function outside the confines of the dramatic action, enjoying a special position between that realm and the audience, hence able to comment on events from a particular ironic perspective (Catholy, 1969, 124-5). The analysis of *Der falsche Verdacht* and *Das lustige Elendt* in the following chapter should be enough to demonstrate that this was indeed Hanswurst's function, at least in part.

Asper traces the name Hanswurst from the mid-sixteenth century and shows that common understanding of it changed. For theatre in the eighteenth century, however, his nature is firmly established. His most recognizable feature is undoubtedly his costume modelled on a Salzburg peasant which was established by Joseph Stranitzky in Vienna about 1712. This costume served many Hanswurst portrayers, with slight variation, throughout the century, all over German-speaking territory. Because of the wealth of pictorial representations of Hanswurst we can be quite sure of what he looked like on stage. (Many studies provide such evidence; again the best is Asper's which includes a host of plates.) Leading is the famous plate illustrating the old Vienna Kärntnertortheater with a jolly Hanswurst in front (Asper, Abb 150), reinforced by a separate copper etching of Stranitzky in the prototypical Hanswurst attire (Abb 37). Wearing a black beard, Stranitzky/Hanswurst sports a green pointed hat with a brim, a wide white neck ruffle, a long jacket with embroidered seams at the front, and baggy trousers, narrowing above the ankles, embroidered at the sides and on the cuffs. These are complemented by a black belt, into which is stuck a blunt wooden sword, and black shoes. Embroidered on his chest are the initials 'HW.' Other pictures of later Hanswurst portrayers show only slight variation from this prototype. Franz Schuch's depiction omits the embroidery, sharpens the sword, and adds a top-knot made of gathered hair; it carries the motto 'Castigo ridendo mores' (Asper, Abb 52), which adds credence to Catholy's interpretation of his function. Gottfried Prehauser, Stranitzky's direct successor as Hanswurst in the Kärntnertortheater, appears virtually identical to the Schuch depiction, as do Johann Reck, Johann Zelius, and Johann Brunian (Asper, Abb 64, 54, 71, 72), except that the initials 'HW' embroidered on the chest have been replaced by a red heart. There is no doubt that contemporary audiences would have recognized instantly any of these or their generic cousins throughout German-speaking territory and immediately expected some of the stock character traits to reveal themselves.

Three further visual representations raise an important question. A porcelain depiction of Hanswurst from about 1770 shows him with customary pointed hat, ruffle, beard, belt, and sword, but in a chequered costume like the one we will see to be typical for Harlekin (Asper, Abb 152). A second porcelain depiction also shows him with a chequered jacket (Asper, Abb 154). A third, a pictorial board game from the nineteenth century entitled 'Der deutsche Hanswurst und seine auswärtigen Vettern,' shows the so-called 'deutscher Hanswurst' in a chequered costume as well, surrounded by six other famous comic figures (Pickelhering, Jean Potage, Pierrot, Pulcinella, Jack Pudding,

Bajazzo; Asper, Abb 161). These three depictions of Hanswurst show that some people had a different idea of what Hanswurst looked like than what the prototype above provides. It seems reasonable to assume that the outward features of Hanswurst in time experienced some variance. The striking difference between the Hanswurst of these three examples and Stranitzky's model is their chequered attire, typical for Harlekin, as we will see, which suggests that the two comic figures were blended in the minds of some despite all one may argue to the effect that Hanswurst was distinctive. Later analyses will strengthen this assumption by discussing comic characters in some Nachspiele who appear to have attributes of both Hanswurst and Harlekin.

There is also a host of studies on Harlekin of course, particularly because, unlike Hanswurst, he has an international heritage and reputation in Italy, France, Austria, and Germany, to name only the main countries. From the German-speaking perspective, Otto Driesen (1904) and Hermann Flasdieck (1937) have written thorough accounts of his heritage, and more recently Walter Hinck (1965) and Günter Hansen (1984) have explored Harlekin and his *commedia dell'arte* cohorts extensively with respect to the German stage in the eighteenth century. Our concern now is not with his heritage or appearance in other countries, but rather with Harlekin on the German stage.

Harlekin is typically a clever comic figure with wit and spirit – 'esprit.' He is a thorough fun-maker and often, accompanied by the like-minded Brighella, highly active in the intrigue, even to the extent of directing and manipulating it. Often he exhibits a comic childish helplessness and enters complications with misguided and naive incomprehension, as a result suffering frequent punishments, often in the form of beatings. He acts impulsively, without reflection, according to his nature and innate *joie de vivre*. Nevertheless, he demonstrates repeated cleverness at extricating himself from difficulty. He is vulnerable to love, direct and passionate in romantic expression, and in this respect is usually paired with a servant girl, frequently Kolumbina (or Kolombine, Colombina), who in turn has her own distinct characteristics. Harlekin characteristically enjoys a special position in terms of the dramatic action, both involved in its fiction but also slipping out to play the role of ironic commentator, and in doing so establishing a direct bridge to the audience. He traditionally takes great licence in extemporized comic routines and the role always requires an actor with considerable acrobatic, gestural, and mimic ability.

Like Hanswurst, the Harlekin role underwent much interpretation and variation depending on period, location, and portrayer. But he too was immediately recognizable by a distinctive costume which remained more or less the same. Even today there is a common public conception of Harlekin's appearance all over the world. Günther Hansen provides a wealth of pictorial evidence supporting our understanding of this costume in the eighteenth century (see his Abb 85, 116, 152, 198, 199 covering the years 1720 to 1758). Harlekin wears a suit consisting of a coat to mid-thigh, fastened at the front with buttons, and trousers beneath narrowing to cuffs just above the ankles, with coat and trousers both made of multicoloured rhomboid-shaped (sometimes triangular) patches sewn together. These reflect his humble social origin and vagabond nature. Harlekin wears a belt outside his coat into which a blunt wooden sword is stuck and wears on his head a brimmed hat with a feather rising from the front. His face is darkened, usually by a beard, but also on the upper part by makeup or a half mask; on his forehead are the nubby traces of horns, these and the darkened face the vestiges of devilish origins.

In Italy and France, and in visiting companies from those countries in Germany, Harlekin was just one of a troupe of well-known comic figures. The analyses of individual Nachspiele ahead discuss some examples in which Harlekin appears alongside one or more of these (Pantalon, Colombina, Brighella, Scapin, Trivelin). Their respective identities within the comic tradition will be outlined there as necessary.

Although highly popular in the repertoires of itinerant companies in the early decades, and the bastion of Vienna's Kärntnertortheater until mid-century, the figure of Hanswurst by name appears to my knowledge in only two extant Nachspiele of the eighteenth century, *Der falsche Verdacht* and *Das lustige Elendt*, both manuscripts, both of which follow in their entirety in the next chapter. I have found no published Nachspiel with the character Hanswurst. From mid-century, with the theorists' rejection of Hanswurst carrying sway, with the text-based drama gaining firm footing, and the standing theatres quickly dominating, Hanswurst seemed to have no place. Harlekin is, however, very much present in published Nachspiele until the end of the century, and it is natural to wonder just how much of the German Hanswurst was assimilated into these representations. Among other things, the analysis will attempt to show the true face of this comic figure on the German-speaking eighteenth-century stage.

❧ *3* ❧

Three Unpublished Nachspiele

The three Nachspiele following appear here for the first time in published form. Although the Bibliography at the end of this volume includes eight Nachspiele published before 1746, none of those reflects the wealth of comic elements revealed by these manuscripts. The fact that they were not published in their day testifies to the primacy of performance over text before 1750. The first, *Der falsche Verdacht*, is unique since it is not a document with specific written dialogue but rather a scenario of the action, and hence in performance was necessarily completely improvised. *Das lustige Elend* consists of a partially scripted dialogue; numerous scenes are only sketched and thus had to be improvised by the cast as well. These Nachspiele provide valuable links between performances of itinerant troupes and the text-based Nachspiele of later decades.

Analysis of the Bibliography will show that some 65 per cent of all extant Nachspiele until 1810 were published during or after 1770 (see p 140) and were usually the work of identifiable authors. This proportion is evidence of the primacy of the literary work, or of text over performance. Their authors were interested in the theatre, of course, and were also in many cases actors at one time or another, but it is unlikely that they were as intricately involved, or knew the performance conditions, stage, and public for which their works were written, as were the authors of these manuscripts. This applies especially to *Der falsche Verdacht* and *Das lustige Elendt* which are unmistakeable products of the mid-eighteenth-century theatre scene in Vienna, more specifically that of the Kärntnerthortheater. They were written for that stage, the actors who performed there, for a loyal public, and foremost with an eye to effectiveness on stage – *Bühnenwirksamkeit*.

Because of their obscurity, these Nachspiele have largely escaped critical attention. The two Viennese manuscripts have been dealt with to some extent within Walter Lehr's dissertation 'Die szenischen Bemerkungen in den Dramen des Altwiener Volkstheaters bis 1752' (1965) to which I owe many insights. Ulf Birbaumer gives only passing attention to *Der falsche Verdacht* in his study on Kurz (1971). Helmut Asper lists all three manuscripts in *Spieltexte der Wanderbühne* (1975, pp 111, 115), which provided my initial means of access to them.

Der falsche verdacht
ein nachspill.

Personen

Odoardo, gnrhab dnr Colombina
Celio dns odoardo dihrnnhtnr bohn, nin aúsgnloßanenns mnnsch
Bernardon dns edof brnidnrs bohn, nin arenns ninfältignr tropff
Colombina, nin iúngnforstann pupillin dns odoardo.
Haußwúrst, dns odoardo gneurnhtnune dinune amant dnr colombina

Scena 1.ma
Bernardon allni

so ist ganz znorichbnu nit ninnue manhtnl brhlagt sich dnr hi arm, d ihm
Srin vathr gnstorbnu, d ist d gröstn conih d ihm srin vathr nicht
so vill hintnrlasn, als nin bohn ime stand ist zú anbring, nr sich von hanr
fortgnronchnt in neillnne srin stúhel brod nonitnr zú súch, allnin nr
habn nin hrimlich Grannhhrit, din sich d nr in nin jnhr nonn sphonn
falln, gnst habn nr hnin gnld mnhr, hnin credit aúch nicht, drúme mueßn
nr bntnlnn gnhnn. d nniß srni abnr so ineheßhlich, d hin ihm glaúh neny
gntehnn, nr neill am nächstnn bnhtnn haúß anstogghenu, d nr srin
heúngnr stilln honnn: hrrit miseremini mei. fangt an zú singnn.
Scena 2.da
Bernardon. Odoardo.

dnr Odoardo gnhel vor ihm vorbny, bernardon last sich abnr nicht stör
nnhlich fragl ihn dns odoardo neas dihn rnhalu music brdnúhe, nr sagl nr
sich nin pauper studiosus, odoardo fragl cujus classis, dnr bernador sagl
spittelbenjium, odoardo neundnol sich d nr so gúl redn fragl ihm, neni rahnel

{138ʳ}   *Der falsche verdacht*

ein nachspill.[1]

Personen

Odoardo, gerhab[2] der colombina.
Celio, des odoardo Schwester-Sohn, ein ausgelaßener mensch.
Bernardon, des odo{ardo} bruders Sohn, ein armer einfältiger tropff.
Colombina, ein ungehorsame pupillin[3] des odoardo.
Hanswurst, des odoardo gewesener diener, amant der colombina.

*Scena 1.*ᵐᵃ

Bernardon allein.

Er ist ganz zerrißen mit einem mantel: beklagt sich daß er so arm, daß
ihm sein vatter gestorben, daß sey daß gröste creütz, daß ihm sein vatter nicht so vill hinterlaßn, als ein sohn im stand ist zum anbringn: er
sey von Linz fortgereiset in willens sein stückl brod weiter zu suchn,
allein er habe ein heimliche krankheit, die sey daß er in ein jedes
wirthshaus falle, jetzt habe er kein geld mehr, kein credit auch nicht,
drum müße er bettlen gehen, d'leüth[4] seind aber so unhöfflich, daß sie

---

1 Manuscript in the österreichische Nationalbibliothek, Wien, Handschriftensammlung, Cod. 13.193 fol. Bleistift-Paginierung 138ʳ-141ʳ. The following text is an exact
   rendition of the original with the following exceptions:
   {…} = editorial addition to text;
   […] = letters/words partially illegible;
   [– -] = illegible letters;
   the characters ÿ and m̄ in the ms are rendered as y and mm respectively;
   minor alterations in punctuation, capitalization, and completion of abbreviations in
   text for consistency;
   footnotes to clarify obscure vocabulary (references: Grimm, *Deutsches Wörterbuch*;
   Schmeller, *Bayerisches Wörterbuch*; Macchi, *Wörterbuch der Italienischen und Deutschen
   Sprache*; Küpper, *Wörterbuch der deutschen Umgangssprache*).
2 Gehrhab, Vormund
3 die Pupille, das Mündel, die Minderjährige
4 Leute

ihn gleich wegpeitschen, er will am nächsten besten Hauß anklopffen,
daß er sein Hunger stilln könne: schreit miseremini mei: fangt an zu
singen.

Scena 2.da

Bernardon. Odoardo.

Der Odoardo gehet vor ihm vorbey, bernardon last sich aber nicht
störn. endtlich fragt ihn der Odoardo was dise esels music bedeüte, er
sagt er sey ein pauper studiosus, odoardo fragt cujus clahsis,[5] der
bernardon sagt Spittelbergium,[6] odoardo wundert sich daß er so gut
rede, fragt um sein vatherstadt, {138ᵛ} Bern sagt er sey ein Linzer.
odoardo fragt wie lang er schon von Linz verreiset seye. Bern sagt [vor]
8 wochen, der odoardo wundert sich daß er so lang auf der reis
geblieben, Bern sagt es gebe alles zu vill wirthshäuser und bierhäusel in
diser reis. Odoardo ermahnt ihn, er soll lieber einn Herren suchn, in
dienst gehen, alß disem luderleben nachziehn. Bern ist willens, dises
zuthun, er wiße wohl, daß er wohlgewachßn, allein bis dato habe er
keinn findn könen: er sey noch im stand etwas rechts zuwerdn, seine
lehrbrieff und attestata, daß er fleißig g'studirt habe, habe er bey sich:
odoardo list solche; fragt ihn abermahl um alles, bernardon voller
forcht[7] vermeinend es seye ein bettelrichter:[8] odoardo sagt er sey sein
vetter. (der hanswurst hört zu) er wolle ihn ins Hauß nemmn, weiln er
den hanswurst aus dem haus gestoßn, so solle er auf dn Celio obacht
haben, wie auch auf die colombina, weiln sie ein liederliches leben
führen, wan er was siht, sonderbahr wan der hanswurst sich ins hauß
schleichet, solle er ihms glei sagn, er soll mit ihm gehen, er werd ihm
unterdeßn ein anders kleid gebn, bis der schneider fertig seyn wird,
mit einm neüen.

---

5   classis (Lat); Klasse, Abteilung; cuius classis = aus welcher Klasse/Abteilung?

6   Spittelberg, since 1850 part of the 6th (changed in 1861 to 7th) District of Vienna
    (Neubau). Before that, an area in Vienna first recorded in 1525 (*Brockhaus*, 13, 320).
    Bernardon's claim here likely means that he was really educated on the streets of the
    Spittelberg District, and along with Odoardo's subsequent observations comprises a
    local joke on the education and language of the people of that area. The Spittelberg
    District in the eighteenth century was renowned for its bright mixture of ethnic in-
    habitants and tangle of streets containing a high density of 'Beisel' (pubs) where not
    just beer and entertainment but also lady friends were plentiful. Wolfgang Mayer
    catches the flavour in his 'Historisches Leben und Treiben am Wiener Spittelberg'
    (1985).

7   Furcht

8   Bettelvogt; Richter, der über Bettler verfügt

Scena 3.^{tia}

Hanswurst. Celio, hernach **Colombina.**

der hanswurst verwundert sich, daß ein solcher Herr, einn solchn
lumpen für einn vetter erkennn möge, wan ers auch wäre, so solte ers
verläugnn: erzehlts dem dazu kommendn Celio, was er gesehen hat,
daß den bernardon d'läuß schier ins hauß oder zimmer getragen
haben; celio beklagt sein unglück, sonderbahr weiln er kein geld habe,
gibt sein silberne uhr, alß daß leste was er hat, dem hanswurst zu ver-
setzn, hansw. versprichts sobald er sich aus dem hauß wird schleichn
könn, gibt ihm unterdeßn 6.fl., der Celio ist voller freüd, die Colombina
erzehlt, was sie vom bernardon gesehn hat, daß er ins haus alß
vet{139ʳ}ter, und auch alß hoffmeister aufgenommn wordn auf ihre
thatn obachtzugebn. sie versprechen einander hilff, ihn wan er das
mindeste schwätzn wurde so zu mortificirn,⁹ daß er g'wis gern wider
aus dem hauß gehen wurde. sie fangen an zu spiln,¹⁰ sagen sie fragen
um den altn nichts, der alte soll crepieren,¹¹ soll sich lieber aufhenck-
hen, und dergleichn: hanswurst g{e}ht ab.

Scena 4.ta

Bernardon, dazu **Odoardo.**

Bern: gehts so zu, warts nur, ich wils schon meinm vetter sagn, die
colombina lauffet wechk: der bernardon setzet sich nider, repetirt was
er gehört, der alte soll crepieren. der celio gehet auch, weiln er den
odoardo siht kommn, odoardo trifft den bernardon spilend an, hört
was er sagt, ermahnt ihn, er soll nicht mehr spiln, soll gedenkhn daß er
den andern mit einm gutn exempl vorgehen müße, dismahl verzeihe er
es ihm noch: der bernardon will sich excuhieren¹² hochgeehrtester
Herr Vetter, wird nicht angehört, gehen ab.

---

9 totprügeln
10 spielen (Glücksspiele, Karten oder dgl)
11 krepieren, verenden, sterben
12 excusieren, entschuldigen

Scena 5.ta

Colombina. Celio. Hanswurst.

Erzehlen einander was ihnen pahsirt, lachen darüber, fangen
widerumb an zu spilen, der hanswurst sagt ihnen, der bernardon habe
ihm zugesehen, er habe g'sagt, er [w]erds seinm vettern sagen, celio
geht gleich wech, der hanswurst voller sorgen, will sich versteckhn, die
colombina sagt, er soll sich niderlegen, sie wolle eine canapé[13] aus ihm
machen, sie deckht ihn zu, gleich darauff kombt

Scena 6.ta

Colomb. Odoardo. Hansw, hernach **Bernardon.**

Od. voller Zorn, fragt wo die compagni[14] seye, die spiln und sauffn
könn, Colombina excuhirt sich, sie wiße von nichts, sie sey allein hier
gewesn, {139[v]} der odoardo wills nicht glaubn: colombina sagt es sey
einn solchn nicht zu glaubn, der selber nicht vill werth ist; odoardo siht
den tepich, fragt was dise canapé hier thu: sie sagt sie habe ihn wolln
ausklopffn, damit er doch sihe daß sie fleißig gearbeitet habe: der
odoardo wils nicht recht glaubn, befihlt ihr niderzusetzn, er setzt sich
auf den Hanswurst, sie will lang nicht, weiln sie den altn lieber fort
hätt, sie habe gar vill zu thun, es schickhe sich nicht, der odoardo befihlt ihrs, er fangt an ihr ein lehrpredig zumachn, sie soll sich beßern,
sie soll an seine gnadn gedenkhen und der hanswurst rührt sich: das
canapé ist schon alt, drum trags gleich morgen zum sattler, daß ers fest
macht; fangt wider an zu redn, endtlich hebt sich der Hanswurst, und
laufft davon, der odoardo falt auf d'nasen, der bernardon, ders gesehn
hat, schliefft[15] auch hinein, der odoardo hebt die deckhn auf, siht den
Bernardon, voller verwunderung und zorn, will sich excuhiern, wird
weggepeitscht.

Scena 7.ma

Colomb. Odoardo. Hansw, dazu **Bernardon.**

die Colombina sucht dem bernardon ein übles spill zu machen. der
odoardo erkent zwar seine kindereyn, doch er verhofft wan er wird

---

13 Canapée, Lectulus, Sofa
14 Compagnie, Consortium, Gesellschaft
15 schlieffen, schlüpfen, gleiten

bekant werden, er werde es laßen, fangt wider sein alte lehrpredig an,
der hanswurst kombt, die colombina siht ihn, [mac]ht complimenten,
der odoardo sagt, er brauche ihre buckerl nicht, und dises öffters, so
bald er anfangen will zu redn. endtlich nimbt der hanswurst den
odoardo, treht[16] ihn, sagt der colombina sie soll bald gehen, der alte
wurd nicht so bald sein leichpredig endn: der odoardo zürnt sich, daß
sie solche g'späsl[17] macht, sie will nichts drum wißn: der hanswurst
verbirgt sich hinter der colombina, sagt sie soll lieber fortlauffn:
odoardo erzürnt sich, schaut um und um, fragt sie was hintn g'murt
hat, sie will nichtß davon wißn vom murren: der Hanswurst küzlt[18]
ihn mit seinm steckhen {140r} zwischen d'füß, zweymahl, der bernardon sihts, geht ab ein steckhn zuhohln: der odoardo zürnt sich, der
hansw. schlagt ihn auf den buckel; der bernardon sagt, wart du schelm
ich will dir lehrnen, der hanswurst laufft ab, der odoar siht den berna,
macht ihn aus,[19] und geht fort: der bernardon schreit, hochgeehrtester
Herr Vetter. die colombina lacht ihn aus, der bernardon zürnt sich über
sie, sie sagt, daß wan er mit ihr halten will, er gute täg[20] soll haben, soll
er aber fort fahrn mit seinm zuschwäzen, soll er gnug verdruß haben.
der bernardon: nent sie einn teüffel, sie soll ihn in kein versuchung
bringen, sie sey ärger alß ein alraunel,[21] geht ab.

*Scena 8.*va

Colombina. Hanswurst.

Der hanswurst beklagt sich daß er nirgends aus dem hauß wischen
kan, daß der alte alle thüren verschloßn hat, die colomb sagt er soll sich
nur nicht förchtn, sie werde schon ein mittel finden, sie sey willens mit
ihm und dem celio durchzugehen, sobald sie werde die schlüßel dem
odoardo stehln könn damit sie daß kostbahrste, was er besitzt mit-
nehmn könne: der hanswurst will gehen und dem Celio davon
nachricht zugeben, weiln er aber den bernardon und hernach den
odoardo siht kommn, so versteckht er sich untern tisch.

---

16 While ms is clear here, this word does not fit the sense; possibly a copy error, the
scribe intending 'dreht'.

17 Spaß

18 kitzelt

19 schimpft ihn aus

20 Tage

21 Alraun, Wurzel der *Atropa mandragora*; Alraundelberin: kluge Frau oder Hexe, die
nach Alraunen gräbt

*Scena 9.*na

Odoardo. Bernardon dazu.

Bern soll aufdeckhen, tragt holzerne teller, der odoardo greinet[22] mit
der colombina, daß sie ihn last hölzern teller aufdeckhn, sagt dem
bernardon er soll nur g'schwind aufdeckhn, vorheüt seits schon gut,
der odoardo fangt an zu eßn, der hanswurst nimbt auch vom tisch, ist
mit, gibt die beinl aufs teller des bernardons, er wundert sich, der
odoardo auch, siht endlich die hand des hanswursts auf dem tisch,
steht auf, nimbt ein licht, und hohlt ein steckhn. {140ᵛ} der Hanswurst
laufft fort, der bernardon schliefft unter den tisch, der odoardo trifft
ihn wider an, schlagt ihn, hochgeehrtester Herr vetter, schreit er. die
colombina wird vom odoardo in ihr zimmer g'schafft, sie will nicht
unter villn vorwand, gehet ganz stat,[23] hanswurst siht daß sie fort-
gangn ist, folgt ihr nach, schliefft dem odoardo zwischen d'füß, der
bernardon lacht, will auch durchschlieffn; der odoardo siht ihn aber.
der bern will sich aber ausden,[24] der odoardo peitscht ihn fort:
odoardo ist müd von allen disn sachen, sizt sich nider, er erkent, daß so
lang der bernardon im hauß, er ville ve[r]drüslichkeiten gehabt, er sey
zu gut, daß er sich um frembde leüth und freund so vill plagen mag, er
wolle sein reichtum in friden vertzehrn und schlafft ein: die colombina
sihet daß er schlafft, freüt sich über dise gute gelegenheit, sie stilt ihm
die schlüßel. der bernardon, der darzu kombt, reist ihr die schlüßel
wech, sagt, warts ihs verfluchtn leüth, is[25] gehts so mit meinm herren
um, colombina laufft davon, der bernardon will zeigen daß er ein ge-
treüwer diener von seinm Herren ist, er w[ill][26] hingehen, die schlüßel
wider hineinsteckhen, hernach wan er munter wird, wird er ihms
sagen, will sie hineinlegen, der odoardo wi[rd][26] munter, ergreifft ihn
bey der hand, wischt sich d'augn aus, erkennt ihn, trohet ihn nebst anderen auch mit dem zuchthauß. der bernardon hochgeehrtester Herr
Vetter, ich bin unschuldig, erzehlt wie es zugegangen ist. der odoardo
fangt an zu zweiffln, weilen er so einfältig, so wurde er auch aufrichtig
seyn: er sagt er soll sich mit ihm versteckhen, er werde villeicht etwas
erfahren können.

---

22 greinen; murren, zanken
23 ruhig
24 ausdehnen
25 ihr
26 Ms binding obstructs text at this point.

Scena ultima

Alle.

der hanswurst klagt über den alten, daß der alte stock alle seine thürn
{141ʳ} verspehrt,[27] daß nicht einmahl ein mauß hinaußschlieffen kan;
die colombina klagt auch daß der alte kein schlüßel steckhen last, daß
man ihm et[was] aus seinm kasten nehmen kunt, wan man in der noth
ist, oder braucht, der hw. fragt ob sie die schlüßln erwischt; sie erzehlts
und daß der esel der dumme bernardonische teüffel dieselben ihr
abgejagt habe: der celio sagt, sie brauchen keine schlüßel; er habe ohne
disem instrument dem alten geizhals sein schaz trüherl gefundn, es
gehe zu ihrer flucht [nichts] mehr ab, sie sollen kein zeit verliehren; der
hansw. aber ist in sorgen wie sie bey der hausthür hinaus gehen
wurdn: die colombina sagt sie müßen dieselbe aufsprengen, der
odoardo kombt hervor mit dem bernardon, sagt er kumme[28] ihnen die
mühe zu erspahren, und daß trüherl wurde auch zu schwer zutragen
seyn, sie stehen alle erstaunt. der bernardon lacht sie alle aus, is[29]
hien[z]en,[30] habs mi gnug g'fopt,[31] jetzt wollen wir sehen: odoardo
sagt, er erkenne nun, daß der bernardon bey seiner einfältigen
ehrlichkeit daßjenige allzeit entgelten habe müßn was die anderen bey
ihrer falschen weisheit verschuldet haben: er seye diser sachn müd,
den bernardon will ich mit einem stückel geld nach haus schickhen,
dem H. celio will ich obwohlen nichts schuldig bin, auch ein
wegzehrung mitheilen, bey der colombina hört ohne dem mein
gerhabschafft auf, du kanst dir also einn mann aufsuchn: aus disem
siht man, daß die aufrichtigkeit nicht gnug ist, sein glück zumachn,
wan mann nicht auch vernunfft darneben besitzet.

Dating, Authorship, Performances, Adaptations

Because Bernardon is the central character and appears as an itinerant
student, Lehr dates the manuscript 'um etwa 1745,' and definitely

---

27 versperrt
28 komme
29 ihr
30 In the ms this word appears to be 'hienxen' which makes no sense. The 'z' suggested
   here creates 'hienzen' = 'dummen,' which maintains the sense of the text; Hienz =
   dumme Person. This may be a case of scribal error.
31 zum Narren gehalten

before 1752 when Maria Theresia's censorship laws prohibiting extemporization came into effect (Lehr, 414; a full discussion of the question of censorship has been reserved for a later chapter; see p 269). This is consistent with our knowledge of the activities and whereabouts of Joseph von Kurz, the creator and portrayer of this comic figure. Lehr directs us also to Alexander von Weilen's discussion of the play in *Euphorion* (VI, 1899), in which the author notes a performance by Johann [=Joseph] Memminger's troupe on 4 January 1767, under the title *Der falsche und ungegründete Verdacht: oder Bernardon der unschuldige Missethäter mit Hanns-Wurst dem geschickten Narrenfopper und groben Possenträger nebst Colombine und Lisette den ungleichen Freundinnen der Mannspersonen* (Weilen, 1899, 358f; see also Blümml, 16). Weilen quotes the 'Vorbericht' on the playbill: 'Bernardon spielt heute die Haupt-Rolle. Sein Character ist ein dummer, unschuldiger Student, welcher durch die Bosheit falscher Leuthe in alle gestellte Netze fällt und sich nicht verantworten kan. Alle fremde Verbrechen werden ihme aufgebürdet, er hat keine Schuld. Wie beklagenswerth ist sein Schicksal! Aber wie lustig und lächerlich seine Einwürfe' (359). 'Einwürfe' point directly to Bernardon's extemporized actions which permeate the play. Weilen notes further a performance of the same work on 25 October 1769 in the Theater in der Leopoldstadt, except that Bernardon is replaced by 'Casperle' (359; see also Blümml, 17). As Lehr points out, these performances were versions of a comedy 'die auf unser Stück zurückgeht' (Lehr, 414), but since the original is purely a scenario requiring improvised enactment, it is difficult to determine the extent to which these later versions differed. Moreover, the 'Vorbericht' cited above mentions Lisette as one of the characters and she is absent from the manuscript version before us.

Weilen's account is supplemented by Otto Schindler ('Theatergeschichte von Baden bei Wien,' 1971, I, 177f) who fixes the playbill cited above in Brünn, adding documented performances in 1753/4 in Vienna and in 1766 by Kurz in Nürnberg (the latter also in Raab, 158). Of the 1769 performance with Casperl (or Casperle) replacing Bernardon, he notes that Casperl was played by Johann Laroche who was famous in the role. From the eighties the play continued to be popular until 1813 as a vehicle for Casperl, with the modified title *Der guthherzige Vetter oder Casperle, der unschuldige Mißetäter*. Schindler refers to the Nachspiel as 'die vielgespielte Weiskern-Burleske' and also cites the *Répertoire des Théâtres de la ville de Vienne* (1757) as listing *Le faux Soupçon, farce allemande, de Weiskern*. Whether the well-known Viennese actor and playwright Friedrich Weiskern was the author of the manuscript before us, or merely adaptations of it, is uncertain. Schindler does insist, however, that it is not by Kurz himself, although I can see no reason for such a statement.

To Schindler's supplements we can add information from Anton Bauer's handwritten file cards in the Vienna National Library, which list the author as Kurz and a performance in the Kärntnerthortheater 'um 1765' with Casperle instead of Bernardon, and also one in the Theater in der Leopoldstadt, 25 October 1769. The card carries a description of the central characters, including several 'nebst Colombina und Isabella, den ungleichen Freundinnen der Mannspersonen.' Isabella is present in neither the manuscript before us nor the 1767 version described by Weilen.

Of particular significance among the adaptations is the change from Bernardon to Casperle, a response to the theatrical taste and fashion of the day, and one which supports the suspicion voiced earlier with regard to Hanswurst and Harlekin that central comic figures were often replaceable, or were impure mixtures and blendings. We know in fact that the famous Casperle (Kasperl) of the Viennese Leopoldstadttheater Johann Laroche retained many of Hanswurst's characteristics, including use of local dialect, peasant manners, beard, jacket and trousers, a red heart stitched on his chest with 'Kasperl' embroidered onto it, a wide-ranging freedom to extemporize, and direct contact with the audience (see Devrient, *Geschichte*, II, 17).

The titles *Der falsche Verdacht* and *Der ungegründete Verdacht* were also used by Friedrich Ludwig Schröder and P. Moriz von Brahm respectively for their three-act and one-act comedies played in the last decades of the century, but these works bear no other relation to the Nachspiel under consideration now.

Analysis

The personae are, as Lehr puts it, 'die Hauptvertreter des Wiener Stegreifspiels um 1750' (416). Odoardo is the grumpy old gentleman, likely played by Weiskern who established himself in father roles with a particular brand of Odoardo; Celio, a throw-back from the *commedia dell'arte*, is a peripheral character without definite comic attributes; Bernardon is Joseph von Kurz's famous comic creation, a dim-witted bumbler, and almost certainly played by Kurz himself. Twice in the play the author emphasizes the fact that Bernardon is from the city of Linz, which was Kurz's birthplace (Scenes 1, 2). Colombina and Hanswurst together form a common variation on the classic pairing also from the *commedia dell'arte* of Colombina and Harlekin. In that tradition, Colombina was originally a person of peasant heritage, but alert and self-confident, though sometimes naive. She developed into a clever servant with an active role in the intrigue, usually protecting and furthering her mistress's romantic interests. Colombina's predominant characteristic is the inability to hold her tongue, especially in matters of secrecy, which leads her often to speak the truth with refreshing bluntness. She is usually in love with her counterpart Harlekin, but does not make it easy for him and is often fickle or unfaithful, often conspiring against him or bringing him under control with physical threats. There are many visual depictions of Colombina, and she often took on disguises, but normally she wore a low-cut dress (suggesting voluptuousness), in a style appropriate for a servant of the upper class (see Hansen, Abb 84, 148; Karl Riha's *Commedia dell'arte* provides an excellent concise summary of the chief *commedia dell'arte* characters, complete with colour pictures). However, it is likely that in the work at hand, when matched with Hanswurst, she wore a costume more suited to a lower servant or peasant type. We can expect that Hanswurst, in turn, appeared much as we have described him earlier. When the play was performed about 1750, this role was likely filled by Gottfried Prehauser, Colombina by Maria Nuth or Christine Lorenz, called by her adoring public 'die schöne Lorenzin.'

As the play opens we are told that Bernardon appears 'ganz zerrißen mit einem mantel' (Scene 1). When taken under Odoardo's wing, he receives 'ein anders kleid ... bis der schneider fertig seyn wird, mit einm neüen' (Scene 2), and we can assume that this new attire was familiar to the audience from past performances. Bernardon had a number of standard costumes in various roles, for example his famous 'Kölner Soldat' (see Raab, 14), but was best known for a black Spanish costume reminiscent of a 'Scaramouche,' the first role in which he had appeared as Bernardon by name (see Rommel, 365).

While Lehr does not present a detailed analysis of the extemporization in the work, his insightful summary of what must have occurred is worth quoting at length:

> Die Vertreter jeder einzelnen Charaktertype waren so 'aufeinander eingespielt', daß genaue Angaben über die Inszenierung einer solchen Posse, die ja erst im Augenblick ihrer Aufführung Leben gewann, völlig überflüssig waren. Gerade bei diesem Genre von Komödien konnte sich die ganze vis comica der Darsteller unbehindert entfalten. Die Wirkung wurde nicht erzielt durch genaue Einübung, sondern durch die Spontaneität, durch die momentanen Einfälle der Schauspieler. Der Text, den wir vor uns haben,

bildete nur das Gerüst, eine Art 'Gedächtnisstütze', die in groben Umrissen die markantesten Situationen festhält, während die Durchführung, die Nuancen, sämtliche Details buchstäblich erst während der Aufführung neu geboren wurden ... Der Canevas besteht im Grunde nur aus einer Kette von aneinandergereihten Schelmenstreichen. Aktion und Reaktion der einzelnen Figuren ist prinzipiell immer gleich, nur die Individuallösung stets eine andere. (419)

It is impossible to reconstruct completely the comic nuances of language and gesture employed by these practised performers as they brought the scenario to life. However, the manuscript provides many indications of the directions that improvisation took.

A clear line of distinction must be drawn between Bernardon and Hanswurst. Bernardon is spontaneous, naive, even childishly comical, thus easy prey for his oppressors, qualities that ensure the audience's sympathy. With his frequent laments and cries to his master for understanding and justice, he tugs at the sentiments of his doting supporters in word, gesture, and every suffering expression. Obviously the star, he carries the first scene alone, and we should not underestimate the immediate reaction of welcoming glee as the beloved Bernardon first stepped out onto the stage before his loyal audience, a scene similar to that cited earlier (p 60). Bernardon sets the tone, beginning by informing his listeners of the background action, creating a bond of knowledge and understanding shared by none of the other characters. His story is melodramatic – poverty, rags, a deceased father, hunger, mistreatment – an exaggeration of sentiment designed to draw the audience into its fabricated spell. Bernardon's penchant for the tavern, which is likely the real cause of his destitute state, links him with many comic figures, and he also ends his solo appearance here in keeping with this tradition – in song, providing a link to the following scene as Odoardo reacts to 'diese esels music' (Scene 2). Bernardon's song was likely familiar to the audience and may have varied according to time and place. We know from Raab and many extant examples that Kurz was a prolific writer of both songs and Singspiele, most of which he played in himself (Raab, 12).

Bernardon's simplicity and honesty remain as recurring motifs throughout the play, so we could expect the linguistic and gestural means he used to express them in Scene 1 to be repeated often, as in Scene 2, which he also dominates, this time repeating the details of his plight to Odoardo, and upon each contact with the other characters in later scenes. When tricked and compromised before his master, he is beaten, 'wird weggepeitscht' (Scene 6); Hanswurst 'schlagt ihn auf den buckel' (Scene 7); Odoardo 'peitscht ihn fort' (Scene 9), traditionally the common reward of Hanswurst and Harlekin, but here arousing sympathy for Bernardon. On such occasions his only defence is to plead innocence to his master with a lament that is a variant on that begun in the first scene: 'hochgeehrtester Herr Vetter, ich bin unschuldig, erzehlt wie es zugegangen ist ... ' (Scenes 7, 9).

Under Odoardo's guidance, the simple Bernardon undergoes a certain degree of moral development. First of all there is no more sign of his drinking. Then his master 'trifft den bernardon spilend an, hört was er sagt, ermahnt ihn, er soll nicht mehr spiln, soll gedenkhn daß er den andern mit einm gutn exempl vorgehen müße, dismahl verzeihe er es ihm noch' (Scene 4). It is not clear exactly what the nature of this gaming is, or with whom Bernardon is playing (no other characters are listed as present), but it is obviously a practice to be frowned upon, and presumably some sort of gambling activity. Admonished by his master, Bernardon avoids gaming for the rest of the play, while other characters continue to do it. Gambling and drinking become signs of their corruption as opposed to Bernardon's moral superiority. In contrast to Bernardon, when Odoardo preaches a moral lesson to Colombina – 'er fangt ihr ein lehrpredig zumachn, sie soll sich beßern' – it has no effect (Scene 6).

Bernardon's fundamental honesty and loyalty to Odoardo are what ensure justice and reward in the end, for it is only his power to convince through complete absence of deception that convinces his master of his innocence: 'der odoardo fangt an zu zweiffln, weilen er so einfältig, so wurde er auch aufrichtig seyn ...' (Scene 9), and 'odoardo sagt, er erkenne nun, daß der bernardon bey seiner einfältigen ehrlichkeit daßjenige allzeit entgelten habe müßn was die anderen bey ihrer falschen weisheit verschuldet haben' (Scena ultima). The character of Bernardon and its consequences in the play together amount to an endorsement of the attributes of simplicity and honesty in human beings. Added to this is an indirect praise of Odoardo as a representative of the monied class for his ability to recognize these qualities and his fairness and good judgment in the end.

Hanswurst and Colombina stand in strong moral contrast. Hanswurst is first designated in the personae as 'des odoardo gewesener diener,' and we know that in fact he had been thrown out by the master, 'aus dem haus gestoßn' (Scene 2). The role of servant is common to Hanswurst, but the blackness of his character here is worthy of note, as well as the fact that along with Colombina he is a thorough manipulator of the intrigue. Whereas Hanswurst traditionally was drawn unwittingly into a supporting role for such complications, that function is taken over here by Bernardon. Our first encounter with Hanswurst in the play underscores his duplicity. Odoardo instructs Bernardon '(der Hanswurst hört zu)' (Scene 2), surreptitiously learning of Bernardon's task to watch his own activities and neutralize his presence: 'wan der hanswurst sich ins hauß schleichet, solle er ihms [Odoardo] glei sagn.' Seeing all, the audience is thrust into a position as buffer between the good Bernardon and the outcast Hanswurst; the latter represents a constant threat to the well-being of the household should he succeed in infiltrating it once again. Hanswurst's first words are to denounce the good Bernardon, vow his ruin, as well as that of his master. Evidently this was to be expressed in crude and cruel terms – 'mortificirn ... der alte soll crepieren, soll sich lieber aufhencken, und dergleichn' (Scene 3). The nature of his character is underscored by the activity presented in immediate conjunction, gambling: 'sie fangen an zu spiln,' which occurs just moments before Bernardon is caught doing the same and reprimanded. While not evident from the scenario, a connection may have been made to show that Bernardon's gambling activities are a result of his new contact with these corruptive elements in the household, for the motif of gambling is continued in relation to both Hanswurst and Colombina soon after as they 'fangen widerumb an zu spilen' (Scene 5) and then, even worse, as Odoardo complains of 'die compagni ... die spiln und sauffn' (Scene 6). In addition to having these vices, Colombina and Hanswurst are thieves, their plot to steal the master's money forming the core of the intrigue.

Despite the blackness of his character, Hanswurst is nevertheless the leader of the three central comic gags (*Streiche*) in the play, hiding under a canopy to imitate a sofa (Scene 6), hiding behind Colombina and tormenting Odoardo (Scene 7), and hiding under the table with similar results (Scene 9). All three involve deception, and all three unfairly trap Bernardon into a situation of apparent guilt with resulting unjust punishment. While these central incidents all contribute to the underlying moral differentiation between the two characters, they were also likely the comic high points in the play, so even in this nasty incarnation, Hanswurst performs his traditional role as instigator and leader of extemporized action. In the first, hiding under the canopy to simulate a sofa on which Odoardo sits, he rises suddenly so that 'der odoardo falt auf d'nasen' (Scene 6). Although Odoardo in general represents a steady, respectable, positive moral force, he is also a somewhat stuffy representative of the monied class, and the vision of him sprawled in humiliation no doubt caused much mirth among the audience.

In the second incident Hanswurst 'verbirgt sich hinter Colombina' (Scene 7), how or where exactly is difficult to say, although likely in one of the stage wings. From this position he whispers to her in the presence of Odoardo who hears and becomes annoyed. Hanswurst tickles and teases him with a stick, remaining undetected and leaving Bernardon to take the blame. Again Odoardo is made to look foolish, presumably to the audience's delight.

In the third, Hanswurst hides beneath the table while Odoardo attempts to dine. From that position he adroitly helps himself to part of the meal, no doubt a master play of timing and sleight-of-hand, concluding in discovery, escape, and blame once more for Bernardon. The object of the humour again is Odoardo, consistently the serious foil for the joker Hanswurst. Satirical disrespect for self-righteousness was obviously part of the licence granted to Kärntnerthortheater comics.

Much of what has been said of Hanswurst's character can be applied to Colombina as well. We learn from Odoardo early that she leads 'ein liederliches leben' (Scene 2). As Hanswurst's ally she is also a gambler and a drinker, and she repeatedly shows herself to be a cool, bare-faced liar with the standard line 'sie wiße von nichts' (Scene 6). She is also a thief, finally stealing the master's keys while he is asleep (Scene 9). Although Columbina is traditionally a clever manipulator and cohort of Hanswurst, like him in this work, the blackness of her character is unusually extreme. Thus when Odoardo throws her too out of his household and withdraws his support from her permanently (Scena ultima), the audience is given a moral message to take home. Not only will wickedness and duplicity receive their just rewards, but as Odoardo puts it, 'aus disem siht man, daß die aufrichtigkeit nicht genug ist, sein glück zumachn, wan mann nicht auch vernunfft darneben besitzet' (Scena ultima). In other words, honesty (like Bernardon's) is praiseworthy, but not enough to ensure happiness. One must also be aware of the tricks and treachery that the world brings to one's doorstep. It is neither Bernardon nor Hanswurst who is given this final word, but Odoardo, a serious character not a comic one. The moral message of 'aufrichtigkeit,' as well as the practical one of 'vernunfft,' was evidently meant for the audience to take seriously.

Two further important factors in the performance of the work should be taken into account: the language and the stage. With only a scenario to work from, we cannot reconstruct the innumerable wordplays and local references that surely accompanied the action, providing a source of constant laughter. We do know, however, that the language was the warm, rich, colourful, and wonderfully expressive Viennese dialect that still today is a most fertile linguistic ground for subtle nuance and local wit. Usually Hanswurst spoke dialect, the others a higher form, Odoardo likely High German. Yet despite such differences, the language of all characters bore some degree of local colour. There may be no dialect in the German language more suitable for comedy of this type, with its prevalent diminutives, the familiar '-erl' ending on substantives, which softens every such word to an expression of familiarity and identification. Viennese of the time was also rife with adapted foreign words, hence offering enormous opportunity for misunderstandings, comic mispronunciations and misuse, and characterization through the use and abuse of terms. It was also abundant in formal expressions of address, respect, title, and honour, a practice still prevalent in Austrian German today. Exaggerated respect for rank and position can be exploited magnificently as an ironic device when applied to individuals whose actions really call for descriptions of a very different nature, but of course Viennese is also so rich in *Schimpfwörter* that it would hardly come up short on that count.

It is almost certain that the play was performed on the Kärntnertor stage. This theatre was renovated in 1748 and the plan is still accessible today (see copy in Lehr, 486; Birbaumer also compares it with other stages Kurz used, 395-405). The stage was relatively small, comprising an area with the dimensions 7.87 metres at the front, 5.33 metres at the back, with a depth of 8.49 metres from backdrop to the front. This playing area had two parts, divided by the curtain line which (Lehr assumes, 487) divided the stage into front and rear, the rear some 7 metres deep, the front the remaining approximately 1.49 metres. Loges extended over this front stage area on one side, as did the emperor's box on the other. The rear part of the stage was outfitted with six sets of movable, sliding wings, spaced 1.25 metres apart, which could be drawn together toward the middle in pairs to create a shallow or deep playing area or to change backdrops, and which also provided many alternatives for characters to enter and exit. Beyond the front stage was an orchestra pit, then a horseshoe-shaped auditorium with parterre measuring 13.13 by 8.10 metres, around which were twenty-three narrow loges (for the nobility, Lehr, 487).

This plan gives some clues about the performance of *Der falsche Verdacht*. The Nachspiel clearly requires at least two different scenic sets: the street in front of Odoardo's house and probably its façade as the play begins; and inside his house, where the remaining scenes play, possibly in more than one room. These changes could be easily arranged by manipulating the sliding wings. In Scenes 2 and 7 respectively, when Hanswurst listens to the conversation of Bernardon with Odoardo and then hides behind Colombina, we can assume that he employed one of the nearby wings. With emperor and nobility in the loges (the emperor very close to the action!), other citizens in the parterre, we can assume a broadly mixed audience with representatives from all classes but the lowest. Thus the moral lessons of the play and the fun poked at the serious-minded Odoardo may well have engendered varied responses. Yet all would likely have joined uniformly in the pure fun created by Bernardon and by Hanswurst's antics. The most striking detail of the theatre plan for understanding the play is the overall size of the stage and theatre. The stage was clearly small and shallow, even shallower if the wings were drawn for some scenes, and most important, the front stage which extended right under the emperor's nose into the parterre opened the way for the characters to get right out among their listeners and fans. In fact, no one in the theatre sat more than 17 metres from the front of the stage! The overall effect of the small stage and its thrust into the parterre created an atmosphere of proximity and intimacy in which virtually every nuance of gesture and expression could be seen by all, every aside heard, every grunt and sigh captured. It was a perfect setting for the power of extemporized theatre to weave its theatrical magic.

Das Lustige Elende.

ein Nachspiel.

Personen

H: Hr: von Habenichts.
Frau v: Habenichts.
Leander, ein Burgros Sohn.
Anselmo, ein Lanzheuaua.
HW: diener des Leanders.
Colombina, Mädl der Fr: v: Habenichts.
Corporal und Wacht.

Isabella H: v: Habenichts Tochter

Requisita

Eine Boutelie wein.
Ein glaß.

Zimmer mit Tisch und Sessel.

St: H: frau v: Habenichts am Tisch.
hat ein Boutelie mit wein. und ein glaß.

Arie: 1. darunter zählt sie geld. und trinckt. nach aria wird
geklopft.
H: v: und Herein, dazu St: zu Leander.
Leander unterthänigster diener frau v: Habenichts, wie befinden
sie sich?

{22ʳ}

Das lustige Elendt

ein Nachspiel.[1]

Personen

{22ᵛ}

H. von Habenichts.
Frau v Habenichts.
Leander, ein Burgers Sohn.
Anselmo, ein Kaufmann.
HW, diener des Leanders.
Colombina, Mädl der Fr. v. Habenichts.[2]
Corporal und Wache
Isabella, H. v. Habenichts Tochter.

Requisita

Zwey Putelie[3] wein.
Ein glaß.

{23ʳ}

Zimmer mit Tisch und Sessel.

Scena 1

Frau v. Habenichts am Tisch,
hat ein Putelie mit wein, und ein glaß.

Arie 1: darunter zählt sie geld, und drinckt. *nach arie wird geklopft.*

Fr.v.H.: nur herein, *dazu*

---

1 Manuscript in the österreichische Nationalbibliothek, Wien, Handschriftensammlung, Cod. 13.160, fol. Bleistift-Paginierung 22ʳ-28ᵛ; auf dem Einbandrücken
   eingepreßt: CJ Nʳᵒ·12. Castelli Nʳ·46 u. 47. The following text is an exact rendition of
   the original with the same exceptions as those discussed at p 80 n. 1 above.
2 Colombina is called Lisette throughout the text, however, except twice in Scene 12.
3 Flasche, 0,7 l.

Scena 2

Leander

Leander: unterthäniger diener frau v. Habenichts, wie befinden sie sich?

Leander: Man siehet ihnen doch nichts an, sie sehen Ja recht gut aus.

Fr.v.H.: Sie Flatiren[4] H. Leander, dan ich sehe mir schier gar nicht mehr gleich, also zwar, das ich mich Recht schämen muß wann mich jemandt besuchet.

Leander: und ich sage, das sie noch so artig sindt, das sie ein jeder vor ein frauenzimmer von 18 Jahren ansehen muß.

Fr.v.H.: Ja, vor zeiten wohl, dan man nannte mich nur die schöne frau v. Habenichts, aber jetzo …

Leander: auch jetzo noch wären sie im standt ein jedes Herz in Contribution zu setzen.

Fr.v.H.: dieses haben mir schon viele brave Junge Herrn versichern wollen, und weilen es H. Leander bekräftiget, so därft ich es bald glauben, dan die Leuthe wollen mich {23ᵛ} be[i]schwadieren,[5] ich habe eine gewisse Scharme im gesicht, welche dennen H. Mannsbildern, oder vilmehr ihrer freyheit sehr gefährlich sein solte.

Leander: ich hätte nur die Ehre haben mögen, sie in ihren jungen Jahren zu kennen.[6]

Fr.v.H.: Ja, das glaub ich: fragen sie nur meinen Mann. dieser ist seiner Lebtag weit und breith, 7. 8. meillen in der weld herum gereiset, und hat mir doch oftmahls zu geschwohren, das er keine schönheit, die der meinigen nur von weiten gleichete, gefunden.

Leander: so werden sie in ihrer Jugend sehr viele anbetter gehabt haben?

Fr.v.H.: ach! freylich; einer wolte mir eins mahls einen Diamantring von 8000 fn.[7] schäncken, ich solte ihm nur einen eintzigen kuß geben, aber weit gefehlt, davor beware mich der güttige himmel, alles in der weld, nur dieses nicht.

Leander: so kan sich dero H. Liebster glückseelig schätzen.

Fr.v.H.: O, der liederliche halunck weis nicht was er an mir hat, ich spare alle Xrº.[8] zusammen, ich getraue mich nicht einmahl ein

---

4   schmeicheln

5   Perhaps from 'schwadern,' verbal form of 'Schwaderei, Geschwätz'

6   in ms: können

7   unit of currency, likely 'florin' ('Florin, Gulden')

8   abbreviation for 'Kreuzer,' a small unit of currency; the coin itself was marked on one side with an 'X.'

saitl[9] wein zu trincken, und er schlampt Tag und Nacht in denen wirths-häusern herum, das ich ihn offt in einer wochen nicht einmahl nüchtern sehe. {24ʳ}

Leander: (das glaub ich, weil du selbst alle Tag besoffen bist.)

Fr.v.H.: ich habe mich eine Zeit her recht übel befunden, deswegen ich den H. Doctor Clistirium um Rath gefragt.

Leander: hat er ihnen nichts verschrieben?

Fr.v.H.: Ja, einen holtz-tranck,[10] welchen ich in dieser flaschen verwahre. *zeigt die flaschen und trünckt.*

Leander: der holtz tranck siehet aus, wie der schönste wein.

Fr.v.H.: er hat aber einen infamen geruch, pfuj. *beidelt sich.*[11] wan ich nur etwas hätte, das ich den abscheulichen geruch könte aus den hals bringen.

Leander: nur ein glaß wein darauf gedruncken Madame.

Fr.v.H.: Vermeinen sie es solte gut sein, H. Leander? holla Lisette.

Scena 3

Lisette.

Lisette: was schaffen[12] sie?

Fr.v.H.: geschwind, drag mir eine Putelie wein herauf.

Lisette: ist dan diese schon leer?

Fr.v.H.: in dieser ist ja nur mein ordinari[13] holtz-tranck, meine Medicin.

Lisette: Ey ja wohl holtztranck, es ist wein, ich hab ihn ja gekostet wie ich ihn herauf getragen.

Fr.v.H.: halte dein maul, oder ich schmeiß dir die Putelie {24ᵛ} ins gesicht, du Rabenfüeh.[14]

Leander: ärgern sie sich nicht Madame, es möchte ihnen schaden.

Fr.v.H.: gleich schier dich fort, und trage mir eine Putelie wein herauf.

Lisette: ich kann nicht in den keller.

F.v.H.: und warum?

Lisette: der Herr hat den schlissel mit genohmen.

---

9 Seidel, Flüßigkeitsmaß, 0,3 bis 0,5 l.

10 Holztrank: Trank aus arzneilichen Holzarten bereitet, Holzkur

11 beutelt sich, a gesture of distaste

12 verlangen

13 gewöhnlicher

14 Rabenvieh

Fr.v.H.: solte man sich nicht gleich zu todt ärgern, der Liederliche Lumpenhund weiß, das mir alle augenblick etwas zustöst, da ich dan statt einer Labung einen Löffel voll wein nehme.

Lisette: (ja, es muß aber ein löffel seyn, der wönigstens ein paar Maß haldt.)

Fr.v.H.: jetzo nimt er gar den keller schlißel mit.

Leander: hierzu ist noch Rath zu schaffen, (zu Lisette) da habt ihr einen Thaler, bringet eine gute Putelie wein.

Lisette: gleich soll er hier sein, *und ab*

Fr.v.H.: (lächelt) daß ist halt wahr, der Herr Leander ist ein Herr, der wenig seines gleichen hat, ich glaube, das ihn alle frauenzimmer lieben müssen.

Leander: ich verlange nicht von allen, sondern nur von einer geliebet zu werden, und sie könten mir am besten verhilflüh[15] sein. {25[r]}

Fr.v.H.: ich? (was gilts, er ist gar in mich verliebt) ich könte ihnen behilflich seyn? belieben sie nur zu befehlen.

Leander: wan ich nicht beförchten darf, etwan mit einer langen Naze abgewissen zu werden.

Fr.v.H.: sein sie doch nicht so wunderlich, ich bin auch nicht von stein, ich weis wohl, wo einen jungen Menschen die schuch trücken.[16]

Leander: so darf ich nun mein anliegen frey bekännen?

Fr.v.H.: frisch gewagt ist halb gewonnen, bey der liebe muß Curage sein.

Leander: so bitte ich dann meine liebe zu der freylein Isabella zu billigen, und mich mit dero ja-word zu beglückseeligen.

Fr.v.H.: so ist dan der Herr in meine Tochter verliebt? (ich habe geglaubt in[17] mich)

Leander: also ist es, es stehet demnach bey ihnen Madame, mich glücklich zu machen.

Fr.v.H.: ich habe nichts darwieder, allein mein Mann will ein wenig Hoch mit ihr hinaus, jedoch, lassen sie mich nur sorgen, ich werde das beste dabey thun.

dazu

---

15 verhilflich, behilflich
16 Schuhe drucken
17 in ms: 'ich'

{25ᵛ}   *Scena 4*

Lisette mit wein.

Lisette: hier ist der wein.
Fr.v.H.: ich mus ihn geschwind kosten, ob er besser ist, als der meinige,
schenck ein.
Lisette: (sie wird wohl so lange kosten, biß nichts mehr darinen ist)
Fr.v.H.: der künftige Herr schwiegersohn soll leben.
Leander: ich bedancke mich Madame.
Fr.v.H.: gehe Lisette, führe den H. Leander zu meiner Tochter, ich
werde gleich nach kommen.
Lisette: Soll ich die Putelie mit nehmen?
Fr.v.H.: die werde ich schon nach bringen.
Lisette: H. Leander, sie belieben mir nach zu folgen. *ab*
Leander: mit dero Erlaubnuß Madame.
Fr.v.H.: ich werde gleich nach kommen. (trinckt) es lebe der H. Lean-
der. (lobet Leander) *gehet mit der Putelie solche gut auf zu heben.*
Aria 2: *Jung gewohnet*
            Alt gethan und ab.

Mitel zu. Strada.[18]

                                 Scena 5

Habenichts begegnet den **Anselmo**.

ihre Complimenten. **Anselmo:** verlangdt sein geld, haben ihre Sc:
Concertata,[19] hernach beklagendt **Anselmo** *ab.*
Aria 3: Habenichts seine Aria *tanzen springen caresiren* und auch *ab:* ins
haus.

---

18 Strada (Ital.): street. After Scene 4 presumably a change in set from 'Zimmer' indi-
     cated before Scene 1 and carrying through Scenes 2-4 to 'Strada' here, where Scenes 5
     and 6 take place before the set reverts to 'Zimmer,' as indicated just before Scene 7.
     'Mitel zu.' may thus mean 'Mittelvorhang zu,' an instruction to draw or drop the cen-
     tre curtain, or movable wings, thus dividing the stage into two sets.
19 haben ihre Sc: Concertata: either from Latin 'concertare,' to have a verbal dispute,
     which suits the context of the present scene in which von Habenichts and Anselmo
     argue about money; or from the Italian 'concertare,' to concert, plan, arrange, re-
     hearse, which could refer to their combined extemporization here. See further discus-
     sion of this term in the analysis which follows.

{26^r}   *Scena 6*

HW begegnet der **Lisette.**

Lisette: gehorsamer dienerin Herr **HW.**
HW: unvergleichlicher diener Jungfer Lisette.
Lisette: wie leben wir?
HW: wie befinden wir uns?
Lisette: so, so, la, la.
HW: wo ist deine frau?
Lisette: bey deinen herrn.
HW: was macht sie?
Lisette: ist das fragens werth? sauffen thut sie.
HW: warum bleibst du nicht bey ihr?
Lisette: weil ich dabey nicht vonöthen bin.
HW: nicht vonöthen sagst du? bey deiner frau ist der Major daß Sauf-
fen, der Minor das speyen,[20] und die Conhequenz[21] köhret[22] man mit
den besen aus, und also haben bey dergleichen Disputationes die
stuben menscher[23] am meisten zu thun.
Lisette: das erfahre ich armes Mädl am besten.
Nb[24] **HW:** offenbahret ihr seine Liebe, lazirt sich.[25]
Lisette: jezo habe sie nicht zeit davon zu r{e}den, er soll sie auf den
Abend besuchen. *ab.* **HW:** lobet sie und auch *ab.* {26^v}
Zimmer

Scena 7

Leander und **Isabella.**

Versbrechen einander Ewige Treu,

Isabella ab. zu **Leander.**

---

20 speien, erbrechen
21 Consequenz
22 kehret
23 Stuben-Mädchen
24 The 'Nb,' presumably 'nota bene!' appears slightly to the left in the margin and likely
    alerts the players to the upcoming improvised scene.
25 Verb from the noun 'lazzo' (Ital.), 'drollige Gebärde, wunderlicher Einfall, Schwank,
    Posse,' used in *commedia dell'arte* to indicate a comic improvised action or scene.

Scena 8

Frau v. Habenichts besoffen.

Frau v.H.: fraget ob der handel richtig. **Leander:** ja, bittet, sie wolle ihm behilflig sein das er Isabella bekomme, etc. *Lazo,*[26] wegen brautkleid, und wovon haben wir geredet etc. er soll sie hierin in ihr zimmer be-kleiten. **Sie** falet, **er** hebet sie auf, **sie** verspricht ihn ihre Tochter. **er** küsset ihr die Hand. *Sie ab. dazu*

Scena 9

H. v. Habenichts hat das lezte gesehen.

H.v.H.: (Ey du alte verliebte Runckunckel[27])
Leander: gehorsammer diener H. v. Habenichts!
H.v.H.: ich brauche keinen solchen diener, der zu meiner schande meine frau bedienen will.
Leander: Holla nur nicht so hitzig.
H.v.H.: seid nur ihr nicht so hitzig, oder wan ihr ja überflissige Hitze habt, so gehet in die apotecken, dan in meinem Hause werdet ihr schwehrlich ein Recept vor eure hitze finden, hab{t} ihr mich ver-standten? {27ʳ}
Leander:[28] freulich habe ich eure grobheit verstandten, und Rathe euch, unterlasset eure unhöflichkeit, oder ich will euch etwas andres weißen.
H.v.H.: und ich Rathe euch, brauchet Respect vor einen Edelmann oder …
Leander: wer weiß in was vor einen wirths hauß ihr euren adels brief versetzet habt?
H.v.H.: das sagt mir ein schelm nach.
Leander: das ware zu viel (*gibt ihm eine ohrfeige. od. z[i]eht von, leder*)[29]
H.v.H.: Ihr seyd kein Edelmann.

---

26 See n. 25 above.
27 Runckunckel, Rungunckel, Runkunkel, Spott- u. Scherzname für alte Weiber; proba-bly from 'Runkel, Runkelrübe'
28 Preceded by a deleted line, still legible as 'H.v.H.: und ich Rathe euch, brauchet Reßpeckt vor.' The line appears in full in the ms. after Leander's present speech.
29 Presumably the players are given the option here of having Leander deliver a blow by hand or actually make a challenge with his sword drawn from a leather sheath. See Küpper, *Wörterbuch der deutschen Umgangssprache* (490): 'vom Leder ziehen = energisch einschreiten; streng, unnachsichtig vorgehen. Gemeint ist ursprünglich, "das Schwert aus der Lederscheide ziehen" 1700 ff.'

Leander: du bist ein verzagter bernhäuter.[30]
Aria 4: *du bist ein solcher Mann etc. und ab.*
H.v.H.: O du Ehrlicher backen etc. *ruft* holla. *dazu*

Scena 10

Frau v. Habenichts

Fr.v.H.: ich habe mirs wohl eingebildet, der volle zapf wird da sein.
H.v.H.: ich habe nicht gezweifelt, das die verliebte Maderazen wird
heraus kommen.
Fr.v.H.: in was von einen bierhauß hast du wieder gesoffen? {27ᵛ}
H.v.H.: mit was vor einen Kerl hast du Carehsirt?[31]
Fr.v.H.: was? ich Carehsirt?
H.v.H.: was? ich gesoffen?
Fr.v.H.: freylich gesoffen, du bist ja stern voll.
H.v.H.: freylich Carehsirt, ich hab es Ja selbst gesehen.
Fr.v.H.: Bachus brueder.
H.v.H.: Venus schwyster.
Fr.v.H.: wein zapfer.
H.v.H.: alte Rungunckel[27]
Fr.v.H.: Lumpenhundt.
H.v.H.: Carfunckel im offenloch.
Fr.v.H. / H.v.H.: hald das Maul, oder ich {zerbreche} dir halß und bein.

Duetto

Aria 5: *[N]as[s]er bruder altes Lueder etc.*

Scena 11

Lisette. unter der arie bringet Lisette wein und glaß.

Entlich **H. v.** und **Fr. v. H.** ab.

Lisette: Ey, so wolte ich nicht länger hier in diensten bleiben, und solte
ich heute noch einen Man nemmen.

---

30 Bärenhäuter, Faulenzer
31 caressiert, liebkost

Scena 12

HW hat opserviert.

HW.: da steh ich schon zu diensten, wan du mich heurathen wilst.
Lisette: es wäre alles recht, Mein Lieber HW, wie werden wir uns aber mit ehren ernähren können? {28ʳ}
HW: warum dan nicht, ich kuple, und du machst gelegenheit, so werden wir uns wohl mit ehren durchbringen.
Lisette: diese profeshion ist gar gefährlich, dan ville sindt schon deßwegen auf den branger[32] gestelt worden.
HW: O! das versteht sich.
Lisette: wie mancher ist schon wegen der kuplerey außgebäutscht[33] worden?
HW: das tragt sich auf den buckel auß.
Lisette: Ja, viele sindt schon auß den Land verwisen worden.
HW: daß hat seine geweisten weege.
Lisette: freylich hat es seine gewisene weege.[34]
HW: Er habe vor zwey Jahr besoldung bey seinen herrn stehen,
Colom:[35] sie habe auch noch 50 fn.[36] erspartes geld, wollen zusammen heurathen etc:
Aria 6: *M{ein} Hanserl M{ein} schatz*[37]
HW: *singt seine Arie.*
Aria 7:[38] *ein schönes weib ein sack voll geld etc.*

---

32 Pranger, Pfahl, an dem ein Missetäter zur Schau gestellt wird
33 ausgepeitscht
34 There is a word-play here between the two on 'verwisen,' 'geweisten,' and 'gewisene,' and the clever Lisette appears to have the better of it; 'geweisen' = verstärktes 'weisen'; basic meanings are 'sich umsehen,' 'weis machen' (jn aufklären, jm zeigen), 'etwas erweisen' (nachweisen, beweisen); past participle 'geweist' or 'gewiesen,' 'gewisen'; in common combination with 'Weg,' as in 'lieben hat seinen geweiseten wege,' 'es hat alles seinen gewiesenen weg' (Grimm, 4/1,3,5460). To Lisette's observation that procurers have been known to be banished, Hans Wurst replies with the equivalent of 'There is a way to get around everything.' She answers with a pun carrying the possible multiple meanings 'Of course there is a way / Of course you had better keep an eye out (sich umsehen) / Of course that remains to be seen.'
35 To this point, Colombina has been referred to as Lisette.
36 Unit of currency, likely 'florin' ('Florin, Gulden')
37 This opening of the aria stands in the left margin beside the text describing Colombina's savings and aspirations. There is no precise indication of when or by whom it is sung, but the context suggests that it is her aria.
38 This aria is not numbered in the ms. Consequently, the final aria in Scene 15 is numbered incorrectly as 'Aria 7.'

und hernach **Colomb.** *ab.* zu **HW** welcher sich Reterirt,[39] wan er dan Anselmo sihet.

Scena 13

Anselmo mit **wache.**

will den H. v. Habenichts Arediren[40] lassen, gehet ins hauß. *ab mit wache.* Nb. *Sc.14 stehet hinten.*[41] *Zimmer*

Scena 14

H. v. Habenichts. Fr. v. Habenichts. Isabella. hernach **Anselmo** mit **wache.**

Anselmo: will sein geld, oder den H. v. [Habenichts] in Areht[42] führen. {28ᵛ}
Isabella: bittet bey Anselmo vor ihren vatter, es ist aber alles umsonst. **Anselmo** schafet der wache den H. v. Habenichts mit sich zu führen. **wache** wollen ihm anbacken,[43]
a tempo dazu

Scena 15

Leander. HW und **Lisette.**

Leander: spricht gut[44] vor den H.v. Habenichts. **Anselmo** ist damit zu frieden. **H.v.H.** gibt ihm zur danckbarkeit seine Tochter. **Anselmo:** muß gleich alß beystandt[45] da bleiben. **HW** haltet bey Leander an, um heurathen zu dörfen, Erkenet die Lisette, und mit den Chorus, folget das
Aria 8:[46] *Corus.*

Ende

---

39 zurückzieht
40 arretieren, festnehmen, verhaften
41 presumably an instruction to Anselmo re his positioning in preparation for the following scene.
42 Arrest
43 anpacken
44 verspricht zu bezahlen
45 Trauzeuge
46 In ms incorrectly as 'Aria 7'; see n. 38 above.

Dating, Authorship, Performances, Adaptations

Lehr dates the manuscript in or before 1741 and assumes its author to be Franz Nuth (359). He bases this assumption on the fact that a work was published entitled *Das lustige Elend zwischen zwey betrunkenen Eheleuten*, ein neues Lust-Spiel, in Versen von drey Aufzügen (Verfertiget von Franz Anton Nuth. Linz: Pramsteidel, [1760]). Lehr was aware that this published version is in verse and in three acts, the manuscript prose and in one act, and goes on to call the published version 'Das Original,' the manuscript the 'sicher später entstandene Handschrift,' but does not explain how he draws this conclusion. He was also unable to examine the copy of the published version which he traced to the collection of the Schloßbibliothek Radenin in Czechoslovakia. This rare copy is listed in the *Theatralia zámecké Knihovny z Radenina* (1962; p 13, No. 72 [Lehr gives 62]), the collection now under the jurisdiction of the Czechoslovakian National Library. This copy is in fact incomplete, missing pp [24-5] and [55-7]. A complete copy is available in the Harvard University Library (Sig *GC7 A100 B750 v.126, on the catalogue card listed erroneously as 59 pp instead of 63). The three acts have eleven, ten, and eight scenes respectively.

The published text is in alexandrines, the persona list largely the same as in the Ms except as follows:

Manuscript	*Publication*
Leander, Burgers Sohn	Leander
Anselmo, Kaufmann	Geronte, Kaufmann
Hans Wurst	Crispin
Colombina	Lisette
Corporal und Wache	Wache appears in III,3 but is absent from the list of personae
Absent	Lelio, Leanders Freund
Absent	Furbon, ein Bandit

These changes in personae result in significant differences for the published version. It would not be especially productive for the present study to do a detailed comparison of the manuscript (Ms) and publication (P) now, but a few points of difference resulting from these personae changes will serve to illustrate. The change from 'Leander, Burgers Sohn' (Ms) to simply 'Leander' (P) is insignificant, as Leander's bourgeois status is repeatedly emphasized in the text of P; nor is the change from Anselmo (Ms) to Geronte (P) of great importance. The change from Hans Wurst (Ms) to Crispin (P) reflects a development similar to what we saw in adaptations of *Der falsche Verdacht*, the interchangeability of comic figures. In P, Crispin has a much different and greater role than Hans Wurst in the Ms; he is more intricately involved in the intrigue and essential for its resolution. Lelio and Furbon are new characters in P and provide an entirely different twist to the plot. Lelio tries to steal Isabella from Leander, which results in some exciting skulduggery including a murder off-stage. Crispin is instrumental in outwitting Lelio and ensuring Isabella for Leander in the end. Further, unlike in the Ms, in P there are very few stage directions suggesting extemporized action, no signs of 'Lazzi,' and the full dialogue for all scenes is given. P is a play whose interest derives primarily from the excitement of the intrigue, while the Ms relies little on intrigue and puts most emphasis on the comic potential of the cast. The theme of class conflict between nobility and bourgoisie, present in both versions, is much more pronounced in P. *All* of the arias in P are different from those in the Ms (judging from the first lines given in the Ms). Many phrases and almost entire sentences are identical in both versions, but P has more scenes and often its scenes follow a different order than comparable scenes in the Ms.

If anything, P's attributes suggest that it is a later version than our Ms. The change from Hans Wurst to Crispin, from Colombina to Lisette, from extemporaneous action to fully scripted dialogue, from a scanty intrigue to a much more complicated one, and the fact that a published version is much more likely to follow a manuscript than the reverse, all indicate that it is more reasonable to consider the Ms to be the original in this case, and the publication an adaptation. This, however, does not clear up the questions of authorship and dating.

There are recorded performances of *Das lustige Elendt* on 7 April and 25 May 1741, 10 January 1742, and 8 September 1755 in Frankurt am Main (Mentzel, 444, 448, 463, 485), as well as in Brünn (bei Wien) 1767 and Vienna 1769 (Blümml, 22). It was advertised on the playbills as an 'Operette-Comique' instead of a 'Nach-Comödie,' and performed after a longer work (see Mentzel, 444 and Frankfurt playbill collection). In each case arias are advertised, but they range in number from seven to ten, with one even promised in Italian. Obviously the play was popular, but it is difficult to say whether these performances were closer to the Ms or to P. It is most likely that the play was given at the Kärntnertortheater, although this is not documented. Lehr also points to the emendations within the manuscript (e.g. the addition in the margin of Scene 12 – see note 37 above) as evidence of the play's popularity; because of repeated performance, alterations were necessary from time to time to provide variety (Lehr, 364). The documented performances do indicate that the work was written in or before 1741, when Nuth was active, as Lehr had surmised, although Nuth's authorship must still remain in doubt.

Emmanuel Schickaneder's comic opera in three acts, *Die Lyranten oder Das lustige Elend* (1776), has nothing in common with the work under discussion.

Analysis

The personae of the work can be divided into three constellations: the representatives of the nobility, Herr and Frau von Habenichts and their daughter Isabella; representatives of the rising wealthy bourgeoisie, Leander and Anselmo; and the servant class, Hans Wurst and Colombina.

The aristocratic couple is indeed a sorry pair, drowning their troubles in drink, and the name they share – 'Habenichts' – tells us at once of their dispossessed state. Frau von Habenichts is a pitiful yet sympathetic character who assumes Leander in fact to be courting *her* (Scene 2), and is a woman left with only memories of a brighter past when she was young, beautiful, and admired by abundant suitors, even her husband. Little of the refinement of a lady is left as she clings desperately to her wine bottle and resorts to rough language in altercations with Colombina or her husband. Still astute, she recognizes from the start the financial advantage of accepting Leander's offer to marry Isabella, and this for her obviously supersedes considerations of social rank. In comic terms, Frau von Habenichts is the image of the aging, fading female desperately hoping for one last romantic fling, and thereby cheapening herself to the point of ridicule. The actress portraying the role has outstanding comic opportunities in depicting her increasingly intoxicated state as the play progresses.

Herr von Habenichts desperately asserts the superiority of his class without any of the noble bearing that should accompany it. Painfully aware that financial difficulties have nullified the social advantages of his rank, humiliated by the preying creditor Anselmo, threatened with imprisonment, powerless against the impudent taunts of Leander, he resorts to aggressive behaviour as his only defence. This is directed frequently at his wife who must bear the burden of most of his frustration. Scene 10 is the highlight as a full-fledged battle of insults rages, the rapid-fire dialogue and colourful vocabulary providing a comic highlight, but the whole underpinned by the misery of their circum-stances.

In strong contrast stand Anselmo and Leander who clearly hold power because of their wealth. From the perspective of the aristocracy, they represent a new, unpleasant, and aggressive force, a threat to the established social structure and social code. We learn little of Anselmo's character – it seems enough to know that he is a merchant – but witness in him dogged persistence and hard-heartedness as he uses the force of the state to press his claim to the point of having his debtor incarcerated if payment does not follow. This is how a member of the bourgeoisie achieves satisfaction. By contrast, Herr von Habenichts is helpless to achieve satisfaction in aristocratic terms by fighting a duel with Leander, for as a member of the bourgeoisie Leander cannot serve as a suitable opponent (which is altogether fortunate for the cowardly Habenichts in this case).

Leander himself is a well-defined character with more than one face. Confident and charming, he shows a certain sensitivity to the pitiful Frau von Habenichts in Scene 2, but much would depend on how the actor played his role. Through asides, expressions, and gestures, Lean-der could ridicule Frau von Habenichts at will if he wished, particu-larly when she assumes his overture is meant for her. He wants some-thing that only she and her husband can give – Isabella – so his polite-ness is to some extent self-serving, but the text as it stands suggests that he does not exploit her vulnerability as he could. Later, however, he is impudent and cruel to Herr von Habenichts (Scene 9), showing absolutely no respect for his status or age. He insults him, strikes him, and possibly even challenges him to a duel. To some extent his be-haviour here can be explained by the fact that Herr von Habenichts be-gins the meeting so aggressively, believing incorrectly that Leander has made a pass at his wife. Yet in the final scene of the play we learn that Leander has satisfied Herr von Habenichts's creditor (the bourgeois way to honour), although again his own interests are very much fur-thered by doing so. Leander is a fairly complicated character who, de-pending on how he was played, could be depicted as an obnoxious representative of the *nouveau riche* or a man with new-found social clout who retains some regard for the fading nobility.

This character grouping makes the underlying theme of the comedy clear from the outset. It is a comic statement on social change, the grad-ual impoverishment of the aristocracy in favour of the rising wealth and power of the bourgeoisie. We will see many Nachspiele with a similar theme later in the century, but it is surprising to find it so strongly here in a document from about 1741. Herr and Frau von Habenichts are truly in desperate straits, their predicament particularly evident when they come face-to-face with either Anselmo or Leander. In Scene 5, which is only sketched, we are told that Habenichts and Anselmo meet and 'haben ihre Sc: Concertata.' They likely have an argument about money, the severity of which cannot be determined. Lehr provides a useful explanation of the term *Concertata*, fixing it as an indication of free dispute which could carry on for an undetermined length of time. Sometimes it could only end when actors off-stage had changed costumes and were ready for the next scene, though this is not the case here (Lehr, 258). Clear stage directions in Scenes 13 and 14 indicate the ominous presence of the 'Wache,' and even an attempted arrest, which further cloud the predicament of the Habenichts couple.

Also central for this theme is the altercation between Habenichts and Leander in Scene 9. Normal addresses of politeness and respect are turned by Leander into 'eure grobheit,' a verbal slap in the face, and then the impudent question, 'wer weiß in was vor einen wirths hauß ihr euren adels brief versetzt habt?' This really cuts to the bone, for it is as true as it is cruel. Habenichts has in effect been stripped of his rank, and is indeed squandering his last assets on drink. Then comes the last straw: Leander 'gibt ihm eine ohrfeige. od. z[i]eht von, leder,' absolutely outrageous, almost unthinkable behaviour towards an aristocrat, and the strongest sign in the play that the poles of power have been reversed. It is Habenichts who should be doing the slapping here, not Leander. Then there is the apparent option for Leander to either deal a blow or draw his sword. Either way, Habenichts is powerless since the code of his class requires him to fight a member of equal status to achieve satisfaction.

The themes of class conflict and social change assume earnest dimensions. But how seriously should we take them in a work that also includes Colombina and Hans Wurst, and was to a great extent extemporized comedy with constant interruptions by arias which destroy any illusion of dramatic realism? Right after his confrontation with Anselmo, for example, Habenichts breaks into song; similarly Leander at the end of his altercation with Habenichts. These elements tell us not to overestimate the heavy-handedness of the class theme, although it is strongly present and of great interest for our understanding of important social changes obviously occurring at the time.

As representatives of the servant class, Hanswurst and Colombina are at home in customary roles. But while they are traditionally drawn into the intrigue, sometimes even playing a major role in it, here they have little involvement in the central action and in effect form a comic counterpoint to the other set of lovers, Isabella and Leander. Their relationships run parallel to the same conclusion of marriage, so that the classic comic union with general harmony is achieved at the end. This is another reason for de-emphasizing the serious thematics. The presence of this comic pair, the constant irreal dimension underscored by the arias, the comic aspects of the Habenichts themselves, and the harmonious assembly of all characters together for the final chorus all tell us to understand the work in expanded terms, as a representation of rejuvenation and hope, the essential underlying message of the comic mode.

There is obviously a great difference between the Colombina and Hans Wurst of this work and those in *Der falsche Verdacht*, more evidence that narrow definitions of such comic figures are dangerous. In costume, however, they were likely in their customary recognizable garb, Hans Wurst likely played by Gottfried Prehauser in performances of the forties in Vienna, Colombina by Maria Nuth. The interchange of the names Colombina and Lisette in the play shows further that she is a diluted original, taking on broader qualities of the soubrette or clever female servant. (See Scott-Prelorentzos for detailed analysis of this comic type; the change from the name Colombina to Lisette also occurs in the *Nachspiel zur berühmten Komödie List gegen List*, discussed later; see p 203.) But the soubrette Lisette is very often an active intriguer, while Colombina/Lisette here is peripheral, contributing in conjunction with Hans Wurst as a simple, playful, and charming couterpoint to the portentous love intrigue of Leander and Isabella.

Hans Wurst too plays a complementary role to the central action, appearing in just four of the fifteen scenes, and first appearing only in Scene 6. Nevertheless, he does show some of the characteristics we have come to expect. Scene 6 with Colombina is a delightful little gem of playful affection, ending with this stage direction for him: 'Nb HW: offenbahret ihr seine Liebe, lazirt sich.' Hans Wurst is to extemporize this scene completely, but in a way certainly familiar to the audience. He is to act out the essence of his character – 'offenbahret sich' – to expose to the audience his inner feelings. He is the only character to do this in the play, an indication that he represents something special in the work for those watching it.

At the beginning of Scene 12 we are told that he 'hat opserviert' the previous acrimonious exchange between the Habenichts, presumably half-tucked away behind one of the stage wings. This is consistent with his frequent role as an outsider with full knowledge of the central events, but belonging himself to a different realm and able to comment from that perspective. His later meeting with Colombina, a repetition of the tenderness in Scene 6, is a culmination of his naive confession of love and a stark contrast to the unpleasant conflict between the Habenichts. Scene 12 ends with two arias (one added in the margin), one his solo, the other a duet, a musical union of Hans Wurst and Colombina, a wonderfully fanciful escape from the misery of the central characters. It is meaningful too that just at this point Colombina is again referred to by that name instead of Lisette, an indication that in the musical exchange her true character comes to the fore.

In the Ms only first lines of arias are given, in some cases not even that, so we can assume that they were popular and well known to audiences. Lehr has done great service in discovering the text of two of them in Max Pirker's collection (Lehr, 371-3), indeed the two that close Scene 12. First is Hans Wurst's 'ein schönes weib ein sack voll geld':

1.

Ein schönes Weib, ein Sack voll Geld,
Seynd zwey sehr gute Sachen,
Mit welchen man kan in der Welt,
Sein Glück am besten machen.
Wen dieser sich nicht trösten kann,
Der bleibet ein geschlagner Mann.

2.

Wie mancher Bauer ist schon offt,
Durchs Geld zum Herren worden,
Wie mancher Mann kommt unverhofft,
Durchs Weib in Ritter-Orden,
Je mancher kriegt gar eine Cron,
Und weiß offt selbsten nichts davon.

3.

Und also hoff ich mit der Zeit,
Auch noch zu avanciren,
Dieweil mein Weib mit Höflichkeit,
Weiß jeden zu charmiren,
Zuckt mich die Stirn, so heists: Gedult!
Wer weiß, wie ich es hab verschuld.

(Pirker, II, 171f; Lehr, 372)

Then comes the duet 'Mein Hanserl Mein schatz':

1.

Col. Mei Hannserl, mei Wursterl, mei Schatz,
      Ich schenck dir den vorigen Platz.
HW. Ich schwör dir die vorige Treu
      Mei Weiberl mit Freuden aufs neu.

2.

Col. Das Zancken bey Mann und bey Weib,
      Schadt beyden, dann sie seynd ein Leib;
HW. Mei Hertzerl drum brume ja nicht,
      Weil dir selbst am härtesten gschicht.

3.

à 2 Was du wilst, das will ich halt a
Col. Arbeitst du? Arbeit ich halt a;
HW. Faulentzt du? Faulentz ich halt a,
à 2 Wie dirs geht, so geht mirs halt a.

(Lehr, 372f; he refers to the aria's source in the work *Bernardon der acht-mal verwandelte, und Hanns Wurst der gezwungene Holz-Hacker*; see Asper, *Spieltexte*, 102.) Actually in the Ms the second of these songs appears first, but it is a marginal addition, and the sense would indicate that it was sung second, which I assume.

Hans Wurst's aria reveals a little more of his customary character, particularly his constant drive for money. His approach shows that he is not quite as innocent as we have assumed so far, for the song and previous dialogue both show his willingness to engage in somewhat sleazy, if not illegal, and certainly socially unacceptable activities to line his purse. But that is secondary to the charming flood of warmth, affection, and loyalty conveyed by the subsequent duet.

Let us turn now to some specifics of how the play was performed. I assume that it was seen repeatedly on the Kärntnertor stage, which means that all of the physical facts discussed in relation to *Der falsche Verdacht* again come into play. *Das lustige Elendt* probably had two or three different scene settings. Scene 1, the text tells us, plays in a 'Zimmer,' the Habenichts home. This continues to the end of Scene 4. Here there is a direction 'Mitel zu. Strada.' Thus the scene changes to the street, perhaps showing the façade of the house, perhaps not. 'Mitel zu' indicates that an intermediate curtain or pair of wings was drawn, likely the latter, as the plan of the Kärntnertor theatre shows no evidence of a mid-stage curtain. One might expect the street/façade set to be depicted on the backdrop, the wings drawn to produce the room, but this does not seem to have been the case. The set seems to be further forward on the stage, perhaps so that the action occurs closer to the audience and its immediacy and effect are heightened. At the end of Scene 5 Herr von Habenichts goes 'ab: ins Haus,' suggesting that he went through a door, which would mean that the street scene included a depiction of the house's façade with a functioning entrance. Upon his exit, Scene 6 continues on the street. Scenes 7-12 revert to the 'Zimmer,' so a change must have been made in between, likely by pushing the wings of the street scene aside. Scenes 12 and 13 return to the street, again requiring movement of the wings, although the precise point of the change is not noted. We recall that Hans Wurst 'hat opserviert' Scenes 10 and 11 (as indicated at the outset of Scene 12), but it is unclear where he stood to do this. It seems likely, however, that Scene 12, between Columbina and him, occurred on the street as did their first meeting in Scene 6. It is also unclear where the guard and Anselmo are standing in Scene 14, for Scenes 14 and 15 again play in the 'Zimmer,' but he and the guard are clearly to be seen. Thus it is likely that by manipulating the wings both street and room sets could be viewed at the same time. In addition to this use of stage mechanics, the arias suggest that beyond the proscenium and stage extension the orchestra pit was filled and alive.

We recall that the Kärntertor was not large, with no member of the audience more than seventeen metres from the stage and loges overhanging the front extension beyond the proscenium. In concert with the orchestra, it is likely that performers moved to front stage to sing, bringing the action out into the audience. That the arias were almost certainly well known increased this feeling of intimacy. These were also surely accompanied by extended gestural communication, even extemporized routines, as we might surmise for example from the title of Herr von Habenichts's aria in Scene 5, 'tanzen springen caresiren.' But beyond the arias themselves, the proximity of actors to audience for all parts of the performance afforded outstanding opportunities to elicit reaction through expression, gesture, and extemporized play. The text contains many specific notations showing that this aspect was foremost in the writer's mind.

Some of the stage directions in the text are the usual prosaic necessities, 'ab,' 'dazu,' or the like, but even these are at times extended to indicate the pace required, as 'a tempo dazu' (Scene 14). Indeed, the entire work was likely played at rapid-fire speed. Other directions require facial expressiveness, as Frau von Habenichts 'lächelt' (Scene 3), or extended gestural actions, as 'darunter zählt sie geld, und drinckt'

(Scene 1), 'zeigt die flaschen und trünckt' or 'beidelt sich' (Scene 2). Frau von Habenichts's gestures and movements must have been particularly challenging to perform as she must move from these early scenes to Scene 4 where she again 'trinckt,' but this time 'gehet mit der Putelie,' stopping to deliver an aria on the way. Imagine her standing there at centre stage swaying to the music, slurring out the song, tottering over the orchestra pit, and all right under the emperor's nose! Then in Scene 8 she is truly 'besoffen,' and now required to deliver a 'Lazo,' a completely extemporized comic routine, probably the familiar one of the staggering drunkard, here doubly funny as it is a woman. This scene ends with a fall to the ground, Leander's assistance and courtly kiss, and immediately the surprise entry of Habenichts. Split-second timing was essential.

While Frau von Habenichts builds her routine from scene to scene, Lisette and Leander assist, and their asides in the text (indicated there by parentheses) suggest that they too were communicating directly to the audience in word and gesture. On her lady's spoonful of 'medicine' Lisette comments wryly, 'es muß aber ein löffel seyn, der wönigstens ein paar Maß haldt' (Scene 3); and as Frau von Habenichts nips to sample the wine, Leander remarks to the audience, 'sie wird wohl so lange kosten biß nichts mehr darinen ist' (Scene 4). Each such aside required the speaker to turn to the audience and communicate directly, often with suitable gestures to accompany the comment. An intoxicated woman with senses dulled could pretend to let even the loudest asides pass by unnoticed.

One could well make the claim that the work in fact dissolves from its text base into almost complete extemporization. In the Ms the dialogue for the early scenes is extensive, even complete, while more and more as the play moves along, fully scripted scenes give way increasingly to mere notes and scenarios. Already the dialogue action of Scene 5 is indicated only in this way. Scene 6 (Hans Wurst and Colombina) begins with scripted dialogue but ends with his *Lazo*, a mere outline of what is to follow. Scenes 7 and 8 had to be completely extemporized; Scene 12 dissolves into extemporization; and the remainder of the work, Scenes 13 to 15, is extemporized completely. In total, including the interspersed arias, one can fairly say that the entire work is more an exercise in extemporaneous comedy than anything else.

A final comment on the language. Observations similar to those made about *Der falsche Verdacht* are in order here, but with the advantage that the text of some of the actual dialogue can help us be more specific. Lehr assumes that Hans Wurst spoke Viennese dialect as usual, the others High German, with Colombina somewhere in between (Lehr, 373). Even if he is right in claiming that most spoke High German, then it was of a type heavily coloured with Viennese accent, vocabulary, and local reference (as it is today). We cannot be sure how much of what we read in the Ms is a reflection of the author/scribe's linguistic state or how much shows exactly what the actors said. We can also only guess at their pronunciation. I cannot see from the text, for instance, that Hans Wurst's language is markedly different from that of the other characters. Certain patterns are, however, unmistakeably present in the text:

- the wealth of humorous *Schimpfwörter* (e.g. Rabenvüeh/Rabenvieh, Lumpenhund, Sc 3; wein zapfer, alte Rungunckel, Carfunckel im offenloch, Sc 10);
- colloquial or dialect sound shifts, including d>t (trücken, Sc 3); t>d (drag, Sc 3; hald, Sc 9); b>p (Putelie, passim; opserviert, Sc 12); p>b (Versbrechen, Sc 7; außgebäutscht (Sc 12); anbacken (Sc 14); ü>i (schlissel, Sc 3); ie>üe (Rabenfüeh, Sc 3); and ei>eu (freulich, Sc 9);
- local or regional references, such as the currencies 'florin' and 'Xr⁰·' = 'Kreuzer' (Sc 2), the liquid measure 'saitl' = 'Seidel' (Sc 2).

All of these indicate a strongly flavoured Viennese accent, dialect, and linguistic usage. Language is of course, besides gesture, the chief medium of the stage, so its importance is paramount. As we said of *Der falsche Verdacht*, the language of *Das lustige Elendt* was a major contributor to its overall comic effect.

Personen

Jörgel   liebhaber der urschel
Bartel   vetter des jörgel
Jockerl   vetter der urschel
Kiesel   liebhaber der urschel
Urschel   tochter der jockerl
Ascheuttl ein alte kugglerin
Wilhelm   gefangner
Lorenz   sein trabant
Cunz   sein trabant

{105ʳ}

Die Bauren

Ein Nachspill.[1]

Personen

Görgel, liebhaber der urschel.
Bartel, Vetter des görgel.
Jockerl, Vatter der urschel.
Hiesel, liebhaber der urschel.
Urschel, tochter des[2] jockerls.
Aschewettl, ein alte kuplerin.
Wilhelm, pfleger.
Lorenz, sein trabant.
Cunz, sein trabant

{105ᵛ}

Erster Auftrit.

Iörgel.

G. Es ist wohl ä harte sach um lieb, und wan man sich in was vernart
hat: sonderbar wan einem der geyer einn vetter darzwischen macht,
der nichts alß brumt: ich bin so vertiefft in unsers nachbahrn tochter
die urschl, daß ich gar dulle[3] werdn möchte, ich möcht gern, wan sie
nur wolt, aber wan d'braut nicht lust hat, wird selten hochzeit: doch
wir wurden uns noch vertragen: daß ist aber gar der teüffel, mein vetter und mein nachbahr oder der vatter von meinem mensch[4] schlagen
und rauffen sich alle tag mit einander, alß wan sie doll[3] wärn: ich soll
von meinem Vetter erben, drum darff ich nit zürnen, und nichts thun,
was er nit gern sihet, aber secht, wer kämbt doher gestulpert.

---

1 Manuscript in the österreichische Nationalbibliothek, Wien, Handschriftensammlung, Cod. 13.193 fol. Bleistift-Paginierung 105ʳ-113ʳ. The following is an exact rendition of the original with the same exceptions as those discussed at p 80 n. 1 above.
2 In ms 'der,' likely a scribal error
3 toll
4 (das) Mensch = Mädchen

Anderter Auftrit.

Görgel.[5] Bartel. Iockerl.

B. Es glaubts kein mensch aufm lichten breiten gotsboden, was daß für ä kreutz ist, wan me nu sulchen leühtfertigen ehrvergeßenen nachber hat.

G. (daß ist der bärtel, mein zukunfftiger schwigervatter wans grath![6] ich will ä wengerl[7] auf d'seythen tretten, und hürn was drauß werden wird) O[8]

B. o mei hahn! o du armer hahn! o du krumper[9] hahn, s'is kein hahn in dem gantzen viertl der meinem hahn gleich gewesen wäre. {106ʳ}

I. (hols der hencker: i kans nimmä leyden, niä macht mir der poßn[10] in d'läng zu vill: ich stech dem bärtl noch ä mahl ä meßer in baug[11] daß iem der pfifferling zur wunde rausfährt. o mein armer budel,[12] wie haben dich d'schelmen verbrennt.)

B. o mein armer hahn!

I. (warum haben dich heilose leüth so getribilirt.[13] nu ich schwere, sie habens nit dir, aber wohl mir gethan.)

B. wer raset dan dorth?

I. wer macht sich dorten so breit?

B. hoho! es ist der jockl selber.

I. Gott grüße euch nachbahr Bärtl, und geb eüch so vill glück, alß ihr werth seyt.

B. und eüch Jockel so vill ihr verdienet.

I. ich denk allzeit, ich verdien beßer glück alß du.

B. was hat dir mein hahn gethan, daß ihms beyn entzwey geschmißn?

I. da soll mein budel antworten: ich wird dir d'goschen[14] so verbrennn, daß der bart aussehnen[15] soll, wie meinem budl d'haar.

B. du darffest mihr nit vill wesens machen, so will ich dir alle beydn hie[x]en[16] in kleine trümmer zerschlagen, daß du auf denn finger heim

---

5   In ms here: Iorgel; similarly in character lists of Scenes 2, 3, 4, 6
6   wenn es glückt
7   wenig
8   exit; hereafter in text as {geht ab}
9   krummer
10 Possen, Streiche, Späße
11 Bauch
12 Pudel
13 geneckt, zum besten gehabt
14 Mund (abwertend)
15 aussehen
16 Haxen, Hachsen, Beine

kriechen solst: wan mei hahn so schlecht wech daß ben[17] zerbrochen,
so wolte ich nicht ä solches leben machen.
I. ich schmis[18] dir uf dei hahn, was is um ä hahn, mein budel ach! mein
budel, der hat sich allzeit wacker mit den andern hundn im dorff
herumbißn: er hat bey der nacht beßer g'wacht alß zehen
muschketierer: nur schad is, daß er nit teüsch reden könn: o du armer
budel. {106ᵛ}
B. mei hahn hat mer verstand im hirn g'habt, alß mancher kalender
macher: ich schmiße dir auf deinen schäbigen hund.
I. du hast vill zu schmeißen? wirds ämahl heraus käme, daß du meine
zäun zerbrochen, und niderg'rißen hast: du wirst wohl sehen wies dir
gehen wird.
B. wie wirds dir aber gehen, der mir d'junge bäumer unten
abgeschelt,[19] daß sie haben ausdörren müßen? wars nicht du? he!
I. wer war der, der der herrschafft d'forelln ausm bach g'stohln, und
hernach dieselbe in der stadt verkaufft, wars nicht du? he!
B. wer war der, der mir alle bougerdin piren[20] g'stohlen, und hernach
in der stadt verkaufft. wars nicht du? he!
I. hat nit dein bui[21] meinen pferden die schweiff[22] ausgeraufft und
hutschnür daraus gemacht? he!
B. hat nit dein weib kalck in teich g'worffen, daß der große hecht hat
müßen abstehen?[23] he!
I. hast mir vill vorzusteßen.[24]
B. halts maul, sonst nieth[25] ich dich.

Dritter Auftrit.

Görgel dazu.

G. (des dings wird kein end. sie krigen schier einander beym kopff:)
frid! frid! gott grüs eüch alle beede.
B. nu schau, was hast do zuschaffen?
I. wo führt dich der henckher hieher?

---

17 Bein
18 schmeiße or scheiße
19 abgeschält, die Rinde abgenommen
20 Art von Birne?
21 Bube
22 Schweif, Schwanz
23 sterben
24 vorzuwerfen
25 niete, prügle, schlage

G. ich kumm[26] in frid und frindschafft. s'is schad, daß is[27] eüch so mit
einander kifelt,[28] einer ist mein vetter, der andere kunt noch woll mein
Vatter werden, wan es wohl glückhet, und ihr {107ʳ} hollundert einander,[29] wie die kleine beschmißene kinder.

I. i solt dein vatter werdn? i wolt lieber mei tochter lebendig schinden,[30] unds leder im schinder verkauffen, alß in eine solche freind-
schafft kämen.

G. is doch der schad nit ä so erschrecklich. Vetter i will ein andren
hahn geben, und ihr nachbehr wan der hund stirbt, so will ich einn
beßern verschaffen, von eüwres hunds vatter muttern, bruders sohn
schwester kind, oder zucht, wie mes heist, und solte ich meinen neün
hut und grünen hosentrager darauff setzen.

B. du hast vill zu verschenckhen, du bettelhund du, gehe mir auß den
augen, so weith dich deine beyde beyn tragen. {geht ab}

I. gehe, sonst will ich dich so zurichten, daß dich der bader[31] schmiren
soll.

G. mei einfältiger rath wäre, mer[32] machten fride, und ...

I. was? und ...

G. und ... ich kans nit sagen. ihr möcht büß[33] werdn.

I. nu ney, so red ...

G. wan ir mer wolt?

I. was.

G. wan ir mer wolt!

I. was soll i dan wolln? nu hurtig! herauß.

G. wan ir mirs eheder zuisagt.

I. nu ja! wan sichs offte thun läst.

G. nu d'hand drauff.

I. da hast d'hand, was wilst dann nu?

G. wan ihr mer wolt ... wan ihr mer wolt ... eüwre ... i weis nit wie
mer ist ... eüwre ... eüwre tochter geben. {107ᵛ}

I. ho ho! daß is ä andres werck ... daß ding hab i dir nit zuigsagt ... nei
... daß nit ...

G. ir habt mer ja d'hand darauf geben.

I. nä ... nä ... auf daß ding nicht. {geht ab}

---

26 komme
27 ihr
28 keifen, zanken
29 heult einander an, schimpft einander aus
30 die Haut abziehen
31 Wundarzt
32 wir
33 böse

Vierter Auftrit.

Görgel. Bartel.

G. daß heißen d'stadtleüth ä kurb:[34] jetzt weis i bey meiner treü nit was
i anfangen soll: i hab kein zeügen, i hab kein gutn freund … er hat mirs
zuig'sagt.

B. hörst dus junger rotzleffel,[35] warum must du dein nasn in unseren
pfifferling[36] steckhä: s'is ä schand und sünd vor den irrlichen[37]
leüthen, daß solche junge schlenckln[38] denen alten alle augenblick
übers maul scheren.

G. ich habs im besten willen gethan.

B. s'is dir in halß geschmißen, s'is dir um d'urschel zuthun nit um unsern frindschafft.

G. ja nu vetter! wers dann so böse gemeinet. ich meyn, wir kuntn mit
gott und ehren wohl ä paar werdn.

B. ä paar werden: daß mus und wird nit geschehen: i will mein alten
hals daran setzen, du solst nichts von mir erben: ich will lieber mei
haab und guth ins hundsloch werffen, alß daß mei geld do hin g'rathen
solt.

G. Vetter macht mit mir was ir wollet, s'ist mir unmüglich, i kans nit
laßen, ir könt nit glauben, wie mer ist: denckht offten wie eüch war, da
ir bey der nacht zu meiner mamm[39] g'fensterlt habts. {108ʳ}

B. sich der leichtfertige vogel, solst du mir mit solchen poßen aufge-
zogn kommen? raum mer s'hauß, komme mir dein lebtag nimmer, geh
mer auß den augen, sonst wird ich an dir zum armen sünder. {geht ab}

G. wie mus mer jetzt seyn, soll ich mi allzeit so zerhudln[40] laßen: s'is ja
zu allen dingen rath, alß wider den todt nit, es wird ja auch do ä mittel
seyn. {geht ab}

---

34 Korb

35 Rotzlöffel, Schimpfwort für jungen unerfahrenen Menschen

36 Angelegenheit

37 ehrlichen

38 Schlingel, frecher Kerl

39 weibliche Verwandte

40 plagen, quälen, schlecht behandeln

Fünfter Auftrit.

Hiesel. Urschel.

H. s'ist schon zwey jahre, daß i um d'urschl gebuhlet ha, sie hat mer
aber nichtß alß ä korb über den anderen gemacht: unser alte aschevettl
hat mer den rath geben, ich solt hier ä wengerl auflauren, und solte
sehen, daß ich sie mit g'walt krieg, sie wurd schon dem himmel
danckhn daß ich sie behielte: o säht, da kombt sie schon.
U. ach ich unglückseelige, wie foltert eft[41] die liebe mein gemüth?
H. (wan i di ä mohl[42] krieg, so will i di schon lehrnen herrisch[43] reden)
U. o Görgl, warum ist der streitt zwischen meinem vatter, und deinm
vetter so grimmig, warumb wird er nicht hingelegt durch unser
vereinigung.
H. (hörcht, was der toifel kan.)
U. der hiesl der limmel[44] marteret mich ohne end, er ist nur gebohren
um zu sehen, wie vill untugend, grobheit, laster, und schelmerey in
seinem hertzen steckhe.
H. (solte sich wohl ä mensch einbilden, daß ein solches undanckbahres
mensch aufm gottsboden leben solte: ich mus raus, und sehen, wie
meinen sachen zurathen.)
U. ach himmel, da kumbt mein feind daher! {108ᵛ}
H. glück zu mein schatz, wie stehts?
U. es gehet mir ärger, alß zu erdenckhen.
H. au wehe wie traurig, weil ihr den görgel nicht kriegn kunt. i bin so
gut alß er, und wohl no anderthalb centner beßer.
U. daß kan seyn: gott behüt mich. *will gehen.*
H. nei, wir, wir müßen mit einander was reden, ihr habt mi lang gnui[45]
bey der nasen herumg'führt, nu g'schwind d'bratzn[46] her! auf d'zusag.
U. ich bin nicht vor eüch, und ihr nicht vor mich gebohrn, drum suchet
eine andere aus, die eüwer beßer würdig.
H. ihr bildet eüch groili[47] vill ein: ich geh nit vom fleck, bis ir mi nit
nembt, i weis daß mein zaplndes hertz aussiht, wie ä welcker rättig:[48] i
kan mi nimmer zum narrn halten müßn:

---

41 oft; or aft = hernach, dann
42 ä mohl, einmal
43 wie die Herren, vornehm (Hochdeutsch)
44 Lümmel, flegelhafter ungezogener Mensch
45 genug
46 Bratze, Tatze, Hand
47 greulich
48 Rettich

U. geht von hier, wohin ir gehört.

H. gib d'bratzen her, sonst …

U. was? mit mir, he! nachbahrn, freünd, vatter, helffts, rettets.

H. halt d'goschen, sunst wirds nit gut werdn mit uns zwey. du stelst di nur so büs,[49] du wirst wol wider gut werden.

Sechster Auftrit.

Iörgel. Urschel. Hiesel.

G. du leichtfertiger, redlichkeit vergeßener, treüloser landlaufferischer schelm und dieb.

U. nur zu, errettet mich von disem galgenvogel. {geht ab}

H. du lugner, du kirchdieb, wart nur, ich will di schon no niätn.[50] {geht ab}

G. gehe nur, i will di schon verklagen, du schelm, du hießlischer[51] hiesel. {109ʳ} daß ist mein glück, daß i der urschl z'hilff kommn bin, wan is nit gethan hätt, so wärs wohl g'sungen g'wesen. jetzt will i vor d'lange weil du[52] der frau aschevettl gehen, und … just kumbts raus.

Siebender Auftrit.

Aschevettel. Iörgel.

A. wär sich nit ä wencherl[53] in d'welt schickhen kan, der stirbt, und verdirbt, s'ist alles blut theür. die contribulation[54] mus fallen, me hats, oder me hats nicht. drum kan me mir nichts nachsagn, wan i ä bißl auf mein s[äc]hl[55] schau: i bin in großer grusachtbahrkeit[56] in unserem dorff, sie meinen, i kan ä bißl hexen; nei i thu nichts übels, i hilff allen leüthen, i hab ein mitleidliches herz, und i brauch zu allem schöne ge-bettl:[57] i mus schauen, ob i was heüt erwischn kan. gott grüs dich du schöne liebe sonne: beschere uns ä guts vetter, so freüwn sich die Städter.

---

49 böse

50 nieten, prügeln, schlagen

51 likely a play on words between 'Hies' = 'Dummkopf,' the proper name 'Hiesel,' and the adjective 'häßlich'

52 zu

53 wenig

54 Distortion of 'Contribution' = a type of tax

55 Säckel

56 Grusel, Schauder der Angst, Furcht + Achtbarkeit = Befürchtung

57 Gebetlein

G. gott geb eüch glück frau aschevettl!

A. hax, fax, max, stracks, und backs, der engel uriel bliß in sein horn.

G. gott geb eüch glück frau aschevttl, hört ir nit wohl?

A. es zanten[58] die tannn, es zanten die eichen, s waßer hat mögen einm die keye[59] erreichen.

G. gott geb eüch glück zum drittenmahl.

A. gott danck eüch mein liebes kind, gott verzeichs, ir störet mich in meinem gebett.

G. is habts eüwre gebettlein alle an einer schnur.

A. was, ir nent mi ein alte hur, ach lieber gott was erlebt me nit auf seinen alten tägen.

G. ey ney, ich hab g'sagt, ir bettet fleißig an der schnur. {109ᵛ}

A. daß ist was anders, liebes kind, halts mir nicht vor übl, alte leüth hören und sehen nit recht: wo gehet der weg hin?

G. zu eüch: i hab halt ä schwäres anligen, d'urschl meines nachbahrn tochter, acht meiner nit vill, i aber hab sie gar lieb: was soll i jetzt anfangen: was rathet ihr mir?

A. ho! mein lieber görgl, ich hör und sih nit wohl, s'ist halt ä elendes ding um ein alts weib.

G. so will ich laut reden, was rathet ir mir?

A. s'ist mir ein flus fürs ohr g'falln: d'alte weiber sind alzeit flüßig.

G. so will i schreyen, was rathet ir mir?

W. heüt ist ä unglückseeliger tag, heüt verstehe ich nichtß.

G. i verstehe dich schon, du altes rabenfell; da habt ir ein hartn guldn.

A. ja! ja: s'ist war, wan mä ä silber auf d'pulsader legt, so ist gut vors verlohren g'hör: ir habt von der urschl g'redet: nit war.

G. daß rindvieh hats doch g'hört! ja, von der urschl.

A. o mein liebes kind, i meins troili[60] mit dir, i ha gestern in mond g'schaut, d'urschl halt di auch vor einn narren.

G. daß ist nit möglich.

A. i wils glei in der hand sehen: wan bist auf d'welt kämä, beym tag?

G. i woäs nit: mei muetä hat g'sagt, es sey an walburgi abend geschehä, grad wie der hahn gekrät, d'sonn hat aber no g'schlaffen.

A. so ists in der nacht geschehä.

G. hürt doch, wie sie gut rathä kan.

A. i mus dirs doch sagen. du beckombst d'urschl nit.

G. sie hats mir offt zuig'sagt.

---

58 zanteln, zanzen, oft und stark zanken; or zänken, hin- und herziehen; or gaffen,
     hohnlachen, grinsen, weinen; or klaffen, schallen, tönen, klappern
59 Kaie; Kai = Weg am Wasser, Damm
60 treulich

A. sie halt dich vor ein narrn. {110[r]}

G. daß ist unmenschlich, und unmögli.

A. i glaub wohl, i mus es beßer wißen alß du, du wirst ein hüpsch alts weib, wie i bin heürathen: folge nur gutn rath, weils no zeit ist.

G. was glaubt dan die alte hex?

A. i hab 4 misthauffen im hoff, also sicht wie vill ochzen i hab, der kleinste davon, ist größer alß du: i ha ä bißl geld au no: gc! sag! wan dich d'urschel nit mag, wilst mi dan nehmen?

G. etliche jahr mus i mi drüber bedenckhen.

A. nu b'sin[61] di nit lang, i bin wohlg'wachßen au, nur zuig'sagt.

G. i mus mi bedenckhen: aber da kumbt der pfleger, gehn mer auf d seithn. {gehen ab}

Achter Auftrit.

Wilhelm. Lorenz. Cuntz.

W. immer schade ist, daß mich die leüth nicht kennen. ich bin ein hoffmann, ich bin ein politicum. der tausende verstehet nicht, was in disem kopff steckhet: aber wo kein ansehen, daß ist kein forcht, und wo kein forcht, da pravieren[62] die bauren nicht: ich hab eüch beyde zu mein[er] leibguardi aufgenommn, nicht anderst, alß ein kleiner fürst, deme stäts ein paar hexscharen[63] aufwarten, und ob ihr zwar noch heu und mistgabel statt der courtisanen[64] traget, wirds sich mit der zeit schon geben. versprecht ihr mir getreüv zu seyn.

C. ja herr!

W. esel sag! g'streng'herr!

C. esel, g'strenger Herr!

W. kanst nit ein knicker[65] mit einem krumpen Lorenz[66] dazu machen, meinst du hast mit einem hundsbubn, oder deines gleichn zuthun, villeicht wird man mi no gar eüwr gnadn, oder eüwr Lenz[67] geben {110[v]} noch einmahl versprecht ihr mir getreüv zu seyn?

C.L. ja g'strenger Herr!

W. und zu thun und zu laßen, was ich gebiete und verbiete?

C.L. ja g'strenger Herr!

---

61 besinn'

62 'parieren' = 'gehorchen'; also possibly a word play with 'bravieren' = 'einherstolzieren'

63 Hartschiere, Trabanten

64 Partisanen

65 Knick, Knicks

66 krummer Lorenz, Bezeichnung einer Verbeugung, Reverenz

67 Abbreviation for 'Exzellenz'

W. daß war recht! nun werde ich verhör geben. sihe ob wer vor der thür, und sag ihnen daß sie bescheidn, und mit repete[n]z[68] herein trettn, und mir den gebührendn ehren titl geben: heüt gib ich audienz zwar, doch sie kosten mich vill arbeit, ich schwitze schon im voraus.

Neunter Auftrit.

Alle.

Alle. g'strenger herr!
W. he! holla!
Alle. g'strenger Herr!
W. so schreyt nicht alle, wie d'besoffene baurn, red einer nach dem andern.
B. g'strenger Herr!
I. halts maul du, i mus z'erst reden.
B. s'ist erstunckhn und erlogen, s'ist an mir.
I. du kanst vill redn, du kanst nit lesen, nit schreibn wie i.
B. du tag dieb, du …
W. he! respect, sonst musts alle in kotter.[69]
G. geltn ihr g'streng, ich bin der erste.
A. nei s'ist an mir, s'trifft mein redlichkeit. d'weiber habn dn vorzug.
W. was sagt d'urschel dazu.
U. ich will den anderen zeit laßen, hernach kan villeicht mein sach g'sprochen werden. {111ʳ}
W. wohl! also bärtel was hast vor ein klag!
B. i hab g'wüst, daß i der erste bin: herr pfleger s'ist gar ä große sach. i hab so ä schelmischen nachbarn am Jockel, daß ichs unmenschlich sagn kan; er hat ohn schuld meinem hahn, der der beste hahn, der schönste hahn, der gröste hahn, der g'scheidste hahn im dorff ware, ein beyn entzwey geschmißen. wan er im an kopff getroffen hätt, so hät er ihm d' hirnschaaln zertrümmert: drum bitt i den H. pfleger gar schön, daß mein nachbahr so g'strafft werde, daß im d'rippen knachen.
W. hast ausg'redt?
B. nei, i ha no vill wider den hiesel.
W. was sagt Jockel zu dem hahn?

---

68 Reverenz
69 Gefängnis

I. was hahn! die bestien salva veni g'strenger herr[70], haben mir mey
budel so zugricht, als wan er 4 jahr in der märing[71] gelegn wäre.
W. was sagst zu dem hahn, sag ich?
I. zum hahn hab i nichts g'sagt,[72] wie i ihn d'beyn abg'worffen hab, hab
i ihn lauffä laßn: s'ist nit so vill an einn hahn geleg als an einn hund: er
hat mir hernach solche schandfleck angehenckht, alß wan ich sein beü-
telschneider, oder schupuzer wär.
W. ir seit böse bubn allzwey: is[73] zanckht eüch für und für: ich wird
eüch so abstraffn, daß sich andere daran bespeculiern[74] solln: wie
stehts um die[75] hiesl?
H. wie sols stehen, schlecht. der görgl hat mir ä halb schock[76] blaue
fleck geschlagen, drum sagen ihm ihr gestreng, daß er den bader zahle,
oder daß i ihm au so vill schlagen darff.
W. görgl, ich hab di ein von frömbsten gehalten.
G. wie mes macht, so gehets. der dieb, oder wie mä häist der {111ᵛ}
hiesl mit züchten zu reden, hat die hand von der urschl abzwingn
wollen, i bin just dazu kommn, und
W. wie ists urschel?
U. es ist nicht anderst.
I. ja daß ist die gründliche wahrheit: wan der H. pfleger kein einstehn[77]
nicht macht, werden unsern menscher nitmehr sicher seyn.
W. genug geplaudert. wir werdn schon wißn, was wir zuthun habn.
H. i kan nicht davor, d'aschevettl hats mir g'rathen.
A. was? hiesel schambst dich nit so z'liegen; je ney ihr g'streng glaubt
solche kindische sachen von mir nit, i hab den lugner über 3 jahr nit
gesehen.
H. was? nit gesehen! hab i dir heüt no aufm freythoff[78] 2 groschn
gegebn, um den rath, den du mir gegeben.
A. so lieg schelm, bin i nit schon über 6 jahr in kein kirchn gekommn
aufm kirchhoff noch weniger.
H. hast nit ein groschen lang g'sucht, der dir ins beyn haus[79] gefalln.

---

70 *salva venia,* mit Verlaub (zu sagen), gestrenger Herr
71 die Merung (Mering), Ablauf des Klos; Jauche
72 a word-play on Wilhelm's question
73 ihr
74 denken, lernen
75 dich
76 Anzahl von 60 Stück, in allgemeiner Verwendung ein unbestimmter Mengebegriff
77 Einverständnis, Eintracht
78 Friedhof
79 Beinhaus, Ossarium, Karner

A. ist erstunckn und erlogn, ä todtenkopff hab i g'sucht, der zu villn
sachn gut ist.
W. ich vermeinte du wärest in 6 jahrn in keinn kirchn gekommn, ich
will dich schon finden.
A. mir g'schicht vor dem himmel, und der welt unrecht.
W. schweig, dich wird ich schon caranzen.[80] hät der jörgl noch was?
G. i mein ihr g'streng, wan mä einem ein sach zu sagt, so sollt man es
halten, der Jockl hat mir auf d'urschl Hand zugegebn.
I. i hab im wohl was zuig'sagt, doch nicht daß ding, was er meint.
G. es wär ja kein üble sach, wan ihr d'urschl und mich mit recht wolt
{112ʳ} zusamen helffen.
A. das wär mir ä fräßn:[81] hast du mirs nit versprochn, daß ist wohl un-
freündlich, daß einer zwey weiber auf einmahl nemn will.
G. i hab dir den teüffel, und sein mutter zuig'sagt.
A. nit? hast mir doch einn thaler drauff gegeben.
G. lieg teüffel lieg.
W. ich mus mich bedenckhen!
A. du must mi hahn, du solst mi hahn; und i will di habn.
G. ein teüffel solst habn, du altes rabenfell, du bockreiterische hex!
A. was? du greiffest mich noch an meinn erlichen namen an? daß soll
dir schwer ausbrechen.[82]
W. ich mus mir schon ein ansehen machen: her du Bartl, und Jockl; is[83]
zwey alte lumpen, is haderkatzen, die kein bedenckhen traget, wegen
einn einaugigen hund …
B. er hat zwey augen.
W. und schäbigen hunds willn, alle nachbahrn in rumonbus[84]
zubringn, und mein richterliches ambt so liederlich, und umsonst zu
beschwern, du Bartl solst heüt 3 dutznt alte harte reichsthaler straff erlegen, den hund 3 mahl des tags auff deinn schultern, daß ganze jahr
auf und abtragen, darauf ein viertljahr in kotter.
B. daß ist ämahl zu tirannisch.
W. du Jockerl, weiln du die händel angefangen, solst 24 guldn in gold
baar noch vor abends dem gericht erlegen: hernach ein halb jahr, alle
tag 25 prügel im kotter empfangen: darauf des lands verwisen, solte
man dich im dorff antreffn: so solst du dein straff nicht mißen.[85] {112ᵛ}

---

80 karunzen, kuranzen, prügeln
81 das wäre eine (schöne) Sache
82 schwere Folgen haben
83 ihr
84 Perhaps scribal error for 'in rumoribus' = 'ins Gerede (bringen)'
85 In ms: wißen

I. ey ey daß ist ä theürer hahn; schonet doch meiner graun haar! es ist
ja auf mein eichel[86] unbillich.

W. schweige man mus exempln statirn:[87] die urschl soll dafern sie ihrn
willen drein gibt dem görgl verheürathet werdn.

G. o! wo ist ä seeligerer mensch auf der ganzen welt, alß ich, ich be-
danckhe mich zu tausendmahlen.

U. weils es mir daß recht zuerkenet, so mus ich mirs schon gefalln
laßen ihn zu nemmn.

A. hat mä sein lebetag, solche ungerichtigkeit gesehen, dis fischperl
kriegt ein mann, und i nit; d'jungn fischen denn alten weibern alles vor
der nasen wech.

W. halt dein maul du plaudergoschen, du wirst dein theil schon
bekommen; du hast wegen deinen hexereyen, kuplereyn, und anderen
händln zwar schon lang den holtzstos verdienet. ich will doch noch
gnädig mit dir handlen, und die gnad vor recht gehen laßen: du solst
zuschaun wie der galgenmäßige strick der hiesel auffgeknüpfft wird
werdn. hernach sollen dir d'ohren abgeschnittn, die stirn mit einn
glüendn eisen getzwickht werden, zuvor aber wird ich dir die flöhn
von deinem kuplerischen buckel mit hundert und fünffzig streich ab-
jagen laßen.

A. sey der richter kein narr!

W. ich will dir schon lehrnen! kein gnad ist zu hoffn.

A. was? ich habs ja nit so übel gemeint.

W. und ich meins nicht übel.

H. und i soll henckhn, i bin noch z'jung dazu, i habs ja nit verstandn.
{113ʳ}

W. nichts da, du verstehest es jezt.

I. i bin nitmehr so böse, thut eine vorbitte.

W. die zwey sind keiner vorbitt würdig.

B. daß erbarme, dens erbarmn kan, und dens angehet.

G.U. wir bitten beyde g'strenger Herr!

W. ja es soll eüch gnad widerfahren, doch bey geringster klag, wird ich
eüch schon zu verexequiren[88] wißen.

B. wir bedanckhen uns gar schön, wir wollens uns eine witzigung[89]
seyn laßen.

---

86 Beteuerungsausdruck = 'Eid'
87 statuieren, festsetzen
88 exekutieren, vollziehen, ausführen
89 Lehre

W. gebt einander d'händ, lebt hinführo schwägerlich: is zwey solts
zwar auch gnad findn, doch auf künfftige beßerung, und daß ir eüch
morgen zusamen geben läst.
G. du i wolt lieber 4 wochn henckhn, alß disen bären heürathen.
H. hast gut z'reden, i leb au gern.
I. o wie war mir so bang.
B. o wie eng war mir der pelz.
A. o wie hat mi der buckel g'jucht.
H. o wie eng war mir der halß.
G. o wie froh bin i, daß i di hab.
W. also mus man denen baurn mores lehrnen.
A. also wird mein alte tugend, und treüwe auführung belohnt: ich lad
alle zusamen auf mein morgige hochzeit, und hiemit gute nacht.

Authorship, Dating, Performances, Source

Although this manuscript is found in the same volume as *Der falsche
Verdacht* in the Austrian National Library, it cannot be assumed to derive from the same year [1745] or even decade. Nevertheless, its place
in this collection suggests that it too stems roughly from the mid-eigh-
teenth century. The only comment on *Die Bauren* that I have discovered
in the critical literature comes from Alexander von Weilen in a brief
note (*Euphorion*, 2, 1895, 632). Following Goedeke's lead (V, 304),
Weilen assumes Joseph von Kurz to be the author, a supposition very
difficult to accept considering the language (not Viennese dialect) and
content of this Nachspiel. It has almost nothing in common with Kurz's
other works. The author of *Die Bauren* remains unknown and I have
found no documented performances. This frustrating void has its
compensation however in the Nachspiel's source (and I am grateful to
Eckehard Catholy for pointing me in this direction). *Die Bauren* is an
unknown version of one of the classics of seventeenth-century German
comedy, Gryphius's *Die gelibte Dornrose*, the 'Schertz-Spill,' intertwined
with his 'Gesang-Spil' *Verlibtes Gespenst* (1661), which, one suspects,
was performed and adapted many times, although to my knowledge
there exists no scholarly study of such adaptations. None of the basic
critical works – Powell's *Gryphius. Gesamtausgabe* (1972), Mannack's
edition (1962), article (1964), and book ([2]1986), Catholy's *Lustspiel I*
(1969), and Wentzlaff-Eggebert's book (1983) – explores this aspect. *Die*

Bauren contains nothing of Gryphius's 'Gesang-Spil,' but a comparison with *Die gelibte Dornrose* yields worthwhile results.

Analysis

With the exception of two characters (Lise Dornrose and Wilhelm von hohen Sinnen) who speak High German, *Die gelibte Dornrose* is written in the Lower Silesian dialect (Catholy, *Lustspiel*, 1969, 150: 'niederschlesisch'; Powell, however, refers to it as 'niederländisch' in Gryphius, *Gesamtausgabe*, VIII, 251). Two comparable characters (Urschel and Wilhelm) speak High German in *Die Bauren*, the rest a dialect that suggests Bavarian: e.g. the words 'wengerl' for 'wenig,' 'goschen' for 'Gosche,' 'haxen' for 'Haxe,' 'kunt' for 'konnt,' 'bratzen' for 'Bratze,' and the expression 'g'fensterlt' to describe the amorous practice of climbing a ladder to visit one's lady-love. But other elements contradict a Bavarian heritage. There is a clear tendency in the dialect of the manuscript towards lightening the typically Bavarian dark vowels 'a,' 'o,' 'u' to 'i' and 'ü.' Also, there are none of the typically Bavarian diphthongs 'ua,' 'ia,' 'ea'; the indefinite article 'ä,' frequent in the manuscript, is not Bavarian; the manuscript contains the word 'ämal' for 'einmal' and 'nit' for 'nicht,' instead of the Bavarian forms 'amuol' and 'ned.' The sound change in the manuscript from 'g' to 'ch,' as in 'weg>wech,' is also not Bavarian. In general terms, the manuscript does not show signs of some typical Bavarian grammatical patterns that we might expect, such as the use of double negatives. Several words suggest that other dialects are mixed in: the ending on 'mueti' and 'groili' looks Alemannic; the tendency to 'i' and 'iu' sounds and the use of 'nu' for 'nun' and 'nit' for 'nicht' suggest Franconian; and the word 'beede' is Saxon.

This curious mixture composes a linguistic puzzle to which I cannot supply a satisfactory solution. Nevertheless, the text of the play is entirely understandable and hence open to full analysis. As a basis from which to compare *Die Bauren* with its source, I shall use Eberhard Mannack's 1961 edition of Gryphius's two plays and refer as well to Eckehard Catholy's analysis of them in *Das deutsche Lustspiel* (1969). Because *Die Bauren* is an adaptation of only *Die gelibte Dornrose* and not *Verlibtes Gespenst*, the significance of the thematic interplay between Gryphius's 'Gesang-Spil' and 'Schertz-Spil' need not be a point of comparison here.

The personae compare thus:

Die gelibte Dornrose	**Die Bauren**
Greger Kornblume	Görgel
verlibt in Dornrosen	liebhaber der urschel
Bartel Klotzmann	Bartel
Kornbl. Vetter	Vetter des Görgel
Jockel Dreyeck	Jockerl
Dornrosen Vater	Vatter der Urschel
Lise Dornrose	Urschel
Matz Aschewedell	Hiesel
verlibt auff Dornrosen	liebhaber der urschel
Frau Salome	Aschewettl
eine alte Kuplerin	eine alte kuplerin
Wilhelm von hohen Sinnen	Wilhelm
Arendator des Dorffs	pfleger
Villdünckall	
Cuntz und Lorentz	Cunz, Lorenz
zwey junge Bauren	trabanten

The parallels are obvious, the only changes being the shift of the name Aschewettl from rejected lover to procurer, and consequently the addition of the name Hiesel and deletion of Salome. The meaning and humour underlying the names Kornblume, Dornrose, Klotzmann, and Dreyeck are lost in their more prosaic renditions in *Die Bauren*, as is the ironic village name 'Villdünckall,' yet both works play in a similarly anonymous village setting so that their action achieves a certain universality within that sphere.

Here is a structural comparison:

Die gelibte Dornrose	**Die Bauren**
Erster Aufzug	*Auftritte 1-4*
Starts with Greger's mono-logue	Starts with Görgel's mono-logue
Greger, Bartel, Jockel: dispute, ending with Greger's monologue	Görgel, Bartel, Iockerl: dispute, ending with Görgel's monologue
Zweiter Aufzug	*Auftritte 5-6*
Matz's overture to Lise, her refusal, Greger's intervention	Hiesel's overture to Urschel, her refusal, Görgel's intervention

Dritter Aufzug
Greger seeks Salome's help

Vierter Aufzug
Wilhelm enters with his entourage, briefs them; joined by others, Wilhelm intervenes to restore justice and order

Auftritt 7
Görgel and Aschewettl the same

Auftritt 8-9
The same

It is fair to say that virtually the same events happen in the same order in both works with comparable characters. Within parallel scenes, many details are also the same, for example the dispute over the cockerel (Scene 2); Hiesel's admonition to Urschel not to speak such highfalutin German (Scene 5); Aschewettl's metaphors, ailments, and financial conniving (Scene 7); and Wilhelm's braggadocio with his men (Scene 8). Yet while the two works contain many virtually identical sentences and turns of phrase, *Die Bauren* is definitely not just a translation of Gryphius's original. There are too many differences of detail. A complete summary of these now would not contribute to an understanding of the Nachspiel at hand, and hence the discussion below will concentrate on the relevant aspects of thematics and dramatic presentation.

Like its source, *Die Bauren* plays in a realistic milieu, as Catholy has pointed out (*Lustspiel*, 1969, 152f). The general theme is a classic one for comedy, love and marriage, the central action emanating from a love triangle made up of the natural pairing of Görgel and Urschel with Hiesel as rude pretender. This is complicated by the family feud fuelled by Urschel's father Jockerl and Görgel's cousin Bartel, which endangers the marriage and undermines Görgel's legacy. As both Mannack and Catholy have pointed out, the situation is the same as in Shakespeare's *Romeo and Juliet*, and shares with it the possibility of a tragic outcome were it not for external intervention, a device common to ensure the happy end comedy requires.

Like Gryphius, the author of *Die Bauren* depicts some of the farmers as a crude lot. The early altercation between Bartel and Jockerl (Scene 2) is rife with rough language, crude allusion, and frightening viciousness. Their pattern of life is depicted for us by images of maimed animals, destroyed property, and stolen produce, and when Jockerl promises his enemy 'ä meßer in baug' we are inclined to believe him.

Hiesel is of the same ilk. His approach to Urschel is characterized by aggression, crudity, and finally a physical attack (Scene 5).

The viciousness of these men hardly seems appropriate for a comic work and stands in stark contrast to Görgel and Urschel. After the initial monologue of Scene 1, Görgel's first words to the warring relatives are 'frid! frid! gott grüs eüch alle beede' (Scene 3), a friendly and civilized expression which becomes a *leitmotiv* when paraphrased three times later to Aschewettl: 'got geb eüch glück frau aschevettl!' (Scene 7). Urschel too is presented as a person of finer stuff than those around her, which is underscored, as in the source, by her use of High German. As in Gryphius, Hiesel admonishes her for it here, suggesting by 'so will i di schon lehrnen herrisch reden' that she as a peasant has no business aspiring to realms beyond her status. But she does nevertheless, and with Görgel represents a refinement of character that in thematic terms suggests nobility despite her lowly social rank (Catholy, *Lustspiel*, 1969, 150).

As in the source, Wilhelm makes it possible for this nobility to triumph over the underside of humanity in the world from which Görgel and Urschel stem. Wilhelm has two entirely different faces, the first shown in the introductory entrance with Lorenz and Cunz (Scene 8). Here he begins with what is essentially a monologue, strutting and boasting, asserting his authority and importance over his witless underlings. His self-classification as 'hoffmann' and 'politicum' and his lament about the lack of respect he receives only serve to make him look ridiculous when held against his ignorant misuse of language and absurd entourage of dim-wits with pitchforks. But what Wilhelm lacks in humility and education is compensated for in the final scene by his self-assertion and obvious sense of justice, a courtroom scene in a barnyard with all evidence of past conflicts recounted once again in painstaking detail. Wilhelm shows himself to be placid, instinctively clever and just, making sure each has his full turn to speak ('hast ausg'redt?'), threatening the full force of the law if he does not receive respect ('he! respect, sonst musts alle in kotter'), describing the harshest of punishments for all guilty parties, followed by munificent clemency when he hears them repent. Wilhelm's clear judgment satisfies all and gives him the aura of a superior being from another realm who creates harmony from a situation of chaos. And while harmony in this case can be realized only through an external force, still, the final message of the play is not merely a defeatist Baroque abandonment to higher powers. Wilhelm's actions serve as a 'witzigung' recognized and understood by all who are reconciled to his judgment, and Wilhelm has indeed accomplished his goal 'denen baurn mores [zu] lehrnen.'

Die Bauren contains no stage directions to indicate how the actors should play their parts. However, the text itself forces us to infer considerable action, both individual and ensemble. First on the stage is Görgel, and as Catholy has emphasized with respect to Greger's initial monologue (*Lustspiel*, 1969, 152f), Görgel here has a primary opportunity to distance himself from the fiction of the stage and establish intimate personal contact with the audience. We have seen this as a device of comic improvisation in the previous two manuscripts, but here Görgel uses the opportunity to describe the background events of the action and the predicament in which he finds himself. It is an exercise in aesthetic alienation from the fiction of the stage. With Görgel clearly at his wit's end and needing help, who should provide it but the audience, at least through their moral support? So the bond and the spectators' role are established, even though the tone is not that of extemporized comedy. We must not forget as well that at the core of this play there is a bitterness with the potential for tragedy. Görgel's appearance before the audience is an encouragement for them to think about the play as a moral piece by lifting it as a deliberate fictional example before their eyes. Görgel continues this special relationship between dramatic fiction and the audience at the beginning of Scene 2 as he overhears the start of the dispute before commenting – presumably to the spectators – and exiting; and further, at the end of Scene 4 he again uses a monologue to express his frustration, much as he did at the beginning of the play.

Unlike its source, however, direct contact with the audience is employed by more than one character in *Die Bauren*. Görgel's rival Hiesel begins Scene 5 alone on stage and explains the background of his desire for Urschel. We can almost sympathize with his frustration as well until he betrays himself with the vow 'daß ich sie mit g'walt krieg' which alienates any spectator who might be on his side. This monologue is a direct parallel to Görgel's and in effect sets up the audience as an informed, if biased, arbitrator of the developments to come.

Beyond these two examples, we can turn to the end of the play when Aschewettl surely turns directly to the public with her final words: 'ich lad alle zusamen auf mein morgige hochzeit, und hiemit gute nacht.' This is a classic comic convention to signal the conclusion of the dramatic fiction and distance the speaker from it. Not only does Görgel stand outside that realm, and even Hiesel at one point, but also Aschewettl, the only truly funny character in the play. Such a farewell to the audience as this is frequently the pleasant task of the central comic figure, and Aschewettl assumes that role here. This is appropriate, for it is she who provides much of the humour of the play. Her curious character, her charms, mysterious verbal allusions, deafness with resulting misunderstandings, her misplaced lust for a young man, and no doubt her appearance too were all a rich mine for laughter.

It could well be argued that Wilhelm is a fourth character who breaks through the play's fictional dimension. His first appearance on stage with Cunz and Lorenz begins with a long speech about himself. Cunz and Lorenz are such dimwitted puppets that he could scarcely be thought to be addressing them, and even if he did they would not likely understand. Wilhelm philosophizes on life and his lot, the kind of thing most of us do from time to time, and all with the bias that our efforts are not recognized sufficiently by the great wide world. I would argue that Wilhelm here is holding what amounts to a monologue before the audience, with the dual purpose of amusing them in the stock role of transparent braggart as well as forming a bridge to his function in the final scene. There he is essentially aloof as judge and absolute authority, completing the judgment in which the audience has been involved since Görgel and Hiesel addressed them. Wilhelm's direct relationship to the audience is, like Görgel's and Hiesel's, not comical; rather it serves to underscore the fictional dimension of the work and the lesson to be distilled from it.

Wilhelm's comic contribution is also strong, first in Scene 8 when he puts Cunz and Lorenz through their paces. His cry of 'esel sag! g'streng' herr' virtually demands a farce of gesture and mimicry in response, and that is what occurs. With their exaggerated bows and mispronounced salutations, the antics of Cunz and Lorenz contribute a double source of humour, laughter at their stupidity and satire on the pretensions of the upper class. Wilhelm makes possible the injection of this parodistic element.

Numerous other scenes likely required adroit movement. The second, in which Bartel and Jockerl have their vicious dispute, must have included a good deal of pushing and shoving to match the verbal abuse. The end of Scene 5 must have shown Hiesel in chase after Urschel, Scene 6 beginning with Görgel's saving entry and certain tussle with his rival – Hiesel complains to Wilhelm in the final scene that 'der görgl hat mir ä halb schock blaue fleck geschlagen.' While the content of these scenes is potentially brutal, they may well have been comical as well. Beatings of a sort are after all a stock-in-trade for comedy. Despite the coarseness of the characters involved here, we must not rule out the possibility that contemporary audiences saw them foremost as objects of ridicule and mirth, an assumption strengthened by the final scene. Here the pace becomes frantic, the full cast involved, emotions high, no doubt at times all shouting and contradicting at once (or Wilhelm would not need to threaten the lot with jail). There is still plenty of brutality and aggression in this scene, and the pacing must have been furious, but the fact that in the end (as in *Das lustige Elendt*) all join in harmonious agreement, and resolve to live the lives Wilhelm has wisely arranged, shows that the comic elements, in execution and theme, should be seen to have primacy.

Finally, although we are dealing here with a different dialect than in the previous two manuscripts, the comedy of *Die Bauren* rests just as much on language as did those. Indeed, one can hardly read a line of this play without finding some word-play, insult, metaphor, or linguistic distortion to smile or laugh about. Language that is funny in text can be hilarious in performance. From harsh verbal attacks such as 'rotzleffel,' 'd'goschen verbrenn,' 'rabenfell,' or 'erstunckhn und erlogen' to crude metaphors of a poodle who looks 'als wan er 4 jahr in der märing gelegn wäre' or a knife wound so deep 'daß iem der pfifferling zur wunde rausfährt' (Scene 2), to Wilhelm's distortions with his lackeys ('pravieren,' 'courtisanen,' 'eüwr Lenz,' 'repetenz,' Scene 8) or Aschewettl's 'hax, fax, max, stracks, und backs, der engel uriel bliß in sein horn' (Scene 7), or a host of others, *Die Bauren* is a constant barrage of spirited, entertaining, at times uproarious, language.

Die Bauren is unique among the Nachspiele considered in this study. No other is set in such a seemingly realistic peasant milieu or presents characters with the raw edge of these. It has in common with the previous manuscripts, however, an obvious attention to effective performance, elements of traditional comedy, and serious thematics beneath the surface. As we move to analyse published Nachspiele now, these points of focus will remain central.

4

The Extant Nachspiel:
Text and Performance

The Bibliography at the end of this volume contains 136 titles, a large proportion of the extant eighteenth-century Nachspiele (manuscripts and published texts), yet a fraction of the Nachspiele actually performed in these years. Of all titles listed, 114 have been located and analysed for this study. This primary corpus stands as the literary residue of an extemporized genre which was one of the most popular in the first seven decades of the century and held considerable interest thereafter. By date of their appearance as texts, the located titles fall into these groups:

Year span	Number of titles
1702-19	1
1720-29	1
1730-39	1
1740-49	16
1750-59	14
1760-69	8
1770-79	22
1780-89	25
1790-99	12
1800-10	12
Undated	2
Total	114

The slim representation for the first three decades shows the Nachspiel's then-undocumented character, but also the reluctance of authors and companies to publish their most popular plays at the risk of literary piracy. It is, moreover, in keeping with the general state of dramatic publication at the time. Before 1750 the list of plays published in German, especially works which were not just translations, was small, whatever the genre. This is the reason for the customary lament at the time of company directors, theatre critics, and historians that there was simply a shortage of German works to perform. However, there was a shift in this pattern between 1740 and 1759 when published Nachspiel production increased significantly, as did production in all genres, for by then Gottsched and other reformers had identified the stage as a vehicle for social comment, education, and change. The drop in production during the sixties stands out as an anomaly, perhaps explicable in socio-historical terms such as the major interference of the Seven Years' War. In conjunction with the foundation of standing theatres throughout German-speaking territory (theatres whose burgeoning audiences had a voracious appetite for new plays) and also as a consequence of the general encouragement of German playwrights, there was a productive surge in all dramatic genres in the seventies and eighties, including the Nachspiel. D.C. Seybold's Foreword to his *Hirten der Alpen* demonstrates that authors such as he were writing specifically in response to contemporary theatrical needs: 'weil ich etwa kurz zuvor in einem Journale oder in einer Zeitung Klagen über Mangel an Nachspielen gelesen hatte' (7). The increased productivity began to wane for the Nachspiel by the nineties, and by the first decade of the next century it was on its way out as a published genre. As a clear temporal dividing point in the Nachspiel's publication history, the year 1770 is a useful pivot for analysing the genre as a literary phenomenon. This date also coincides with the beginning of the widespread movement to found standing theatres.

The analyses in this chapter and in Chapters 5, 6, and 8 refer to the 136 works in the Annotated Bibliography. Readers will need to consult the bibliographical descriptions, plot summaries, and comments there from time to time. Of this number, I have located and studied 112 Nachspiele which could also be dated, and grouped them according to categories summarized below.

– Nachspiele translated or adapted from French and other languages (FR): 26

– Nachspiele in 2-3 acts (2-3): 10

– Nachspiele published after and bound to a previous work (CP): 13

– Nachspiele with music, songs, dance (MSD): 24

– Nachspiele with traditional comic figure or devices (TC): 32

– Nachspiele with serious thematics/social criticism (SC): 69

To see these categories tabulated by title, please refer to Appendix 1 beginning on p 293. The abbreviations FR, 2-3, CP, MSD, TC, and SC are used there in the same way as above.

Nachspiele Based on French or Other Foreign Models

	Total	FR
1702-1769	41	11 (27%)
1770-1816	71	15 (21%)

Before 1770 there was much dependence on French (and other foreign) models, which lessened somewhat in the later decades of the century. This was perhaps one sign that the general encouragement of German writers to create original dramatic works for their own new theatres was contributing toward the nationalization of German drama. And this was true for virtually all genres. There is of course no doubt that both French and Italian theatre had an enormous influence on many aspects of the German stage in the eighteenth century. Heinz Kindermann describes 'Das Paradigma der Comédie française' (*Theatergeschichte der Goethezeit*, 37-43) and Walter Hinck provides a solid assessment of the importance of both *commedia dell'arte* and *Théâtre italien* to begin his important study (*Das deutsche Lustspiel*). My investigation of the Nachspiel also provides repeated evidence of such influence. The repertoires considered earlier showed constant infiltration of French and Italian troupes and their plays into German court, itinerant, and standing theatres. The later chapter on Acting will pay due notice to the French classical models used by German actors for decades. Gottsched's French-based reforms gain repeated mention. The chart above, Appendix 1, and the Annotated Bibliography show many Nachspiele translated or adapted from the French, and in others French names and allusions are not infrequent. As far as Italian influence is concerned, the two Viennese manuscripts discussed earlier, *Der falsche Verdacht* and *Das lustige Elendt*, show through their personae, character constellations, and intrigues the direct influence of the *commedia dell'arte*, and other published Nachspiele such as *Harlequin, der ungedultig-hernach* and *Das Nachspiel zur berühmten Komödie, Erklärte Fehde oder List gegen List* do the same. And virtually every time the German name Harlekin is mentioned in this book, his French and

Italian relatives Arlequin and Arlecchino inevitably come to mind and contribute to the image.

Nachspiele in 2-3 Acts

Ten of the Nachspiele in the Bibliography have a multi-act structure. In several cases (*Der betrogene Alte*, 1747, 21 pp; *Die Chymici*, 1771, 54 pp; *Die Gespenster*, 1757, 46 pp; *Wildheit und Großmuth*, 1784, 27 pp) their dramatic action is simply not complicated enough to justify such major internal divisions, nor is their length. While in each of these early works the internal division seems arbitrary and not born of dramatic necessity, the structure of some later multi-act Nachspiele makes more sense. *Heyrath aus Liebe* (1781, 80 pp) and *Die jungen Rekruten* (1781, 35 pp) are musical works with numerous arias and songs which would extend them to full-length performance. The latter was also written for school performance, which may have caused the author to insert needed pauses. *Hochzeittag* (1789, 52 pp) and *Kaiser Joseph auf der Reise im Amthause* (1799, 80 pp) both have a large cast and relatively complicated dramatic intrigue, as do *Die kleinste Lüge* (1800, 51 pp) and *Der Weihnachtabend* (1803, 40 pp) which also call for more than one place of action and for set changes. While in some cases the internal division into more than one act can be readily explained by dramatic necessity, changes of set, length, or complicated intrigues, it is significant that all but two of these Nachspiele appeared after 1769 when the rush was on to stock the repertoires of standing theatres. Moreover, these eight are all German plays (as opposed to translations or adaptations), meeting the growing demand for works by native authors. Such realities of the theatre scene at the end of the century probably had as much to do with writers' efforts to produce longer works as did the intrinsic necessities of the dramas themselves. There are also enough examples of Nachspiele in more than one act to call into question the statement in many current definitions of the genre that the Nachspiel is exclusively a one-act work.

Nachspiele Connected to a Previous Work (CP)

	Total	CP
1702-1769	41	10 (24%)
1770-1810	71	3 (4%)

The repertoires analysed in Chapter 2 revealed little connection between the Nachspiel and other works on a specific theatrical program. This is largely substantiated by the publication history. Surprisingly, however, ten of the thirteen published Nachspiele with such a connection appeared before 1770, suggesting that in the earlier part of the century the relationship between Nachspiel and previous work was much more significant than later on. Of these thirteen works in the Bibliography, only one, *Die Klatschen* (1757), was published with a longer preceding work (*Die Menechmes*), without apparent thematic or structural connection to it except for a shared title-page. The others certainly do have a connection to a previous work. In the case of *Isaac und Rebecca* (1722) and its subsequent Nachspiel, the relation between the two works is both thematic and theoretical. First, both deal with the theme of marriage, one seriously, one comically, providing a light-hearted counterpoint. But the more important connection between the two lies in Jodocus's foreword to the reader where he discusses the works on aesthetic grounds, justifying their stylistic attributes within the context of his age (see p 155).

Der betrogene Alte (1747, published after *Der verlohrne Cranz*), *Der hinkende Bothe* (1758, after *Die Rechnung ohne Wirth*), and *Comödie ohne Tittel* (1750, after *Der Krieg der Götter*) all focus on the theme of war and reject the social upheaval brought on by military campaigns in Germany and Europe. The Nachspiel is a vehicle to extend the thematics of the longer preceding work and casts it in new light with the aid of comic – in two cases extemporized comic – characters and devices. In the case of *Harlequin, der ungedultig gemachte Hahnrey* (1743, after *Franzosen in Böhmen*), parody of French manners and affectation is the shared thematic focus, as is the method of using characters from traditional comedy to communicate social criticism and satire with considerable freedom for comic improvisation. *Die Franzosen*'s focal character is Hansspringinsfeld who appears alone on stage in the first scene and carries out a mimed routine (17). Such extemporization is continued throughout, as can be seen in explicit stage directions to that effect: 'ad Spect[atores]' (24f); 'NB Diese Scene wird wieder extemporiert' (30f); 'H[ansspringinsfeld] als Harlequin gekleidet' (Scene vii); 'Nun wird extemporiert' (44f). Hansspringinsfeld plays on several levels, assuming new points of view, postures, and appearances throughout the work. His primary function, beyond pure entertainment through extemporized comedy, is to stand apart from and comment on the themes of French affectation in manners and dress, separating himself from the dramatic action not only by means of soliloquies, but even physically during communal scenes, as when we are told that he withdraws to the farthest 'Prospect-Fliegel, und siehet zu' (26). His behaviour is at times reminiscent of the coarsest of comics in the early decades of the century, including swine-grunting noises (47f), reference to poking one's nose into another's anus (74), parading in drag as a French Madame (II, ii) and participating in physical beatings (61). With the thematic point of it all to ridicule French affectation, his role is meaningful in terms of the emergence of German consciousness and self-pride.

The Nachspiel to *Die Franzosen* then picks up and continues both thematics and method of presentation. Again the personae include a mixture of French, German, and traditional comic characters, in this case Harlequin and Columbina. But here Harlequin is not the omniscient commentator as was the case before. Instead, he is the butt of the joke, manipulated, deceived, and humiliated by his wife with assistance from the other characters. It is also the others who comment on him, not the reverse. Considering the anti-French tone of *Die Franzosen*, it is difficult to know how a contemporary reader or audience would react to its Nachspiel. Here, Harlequin is not a positive figure, and in a sense deserves to be deceived. Yet Columbina and the French are not positive models either, depending on deception and infidelity to gain advantage. Although the Nachspiel does not continue the direct satire on the French which occupies central position in *Die Franzosen*, it is likely that German audiences would lend their sympathies to Harlequin, their traditional favourite, and turn against Columbina and her lovers. Thus, the Nachspiel, using different means, accomplishes an end similar to that of the full-length work. While today we can only speculate on whether or not Nachspiele in the first decades of the century were connected closely to previous works on the progam, the author of *Die Franzosen* and its Nachspiel seemed to be conscious of locating these works in the literary tradition of the time, and thus, it would seem, optimistic that theatre could have impact not only on the stage but also through a reading public (see further analysis, p 162).

Also from mid-century, *Die neueste Verheyrathung* (1759) has strong thematic and structural similarities to the work after which it was published. *Bauer-Arzt* presents a traditional comic love triangle in which the marriage of two young persons (Selinde and Listig) is blocked by a powerful father who has promised his daughter to another, largely to solidify his own financial position. Nevertheless, the young lovers prevail over the father's authority in the end, a reversal which forecasts many later dramatic treatments of the same theme, and one which indirectly criticizes contemporary paternalistic authority and lays a foundation for some shift in social power. The play also contains many elements of traditional comedy. Munter is like a *lustige Person* in his freedom to extemporize, as in the stage direction 'Hier macht Munter allerhand närrische Fragen ...' (11). Ließchen is his female counterpart with similar freedom; so too Listig, as seen in this stage direction applying to him: 'hier können allerhand lustige Fragen an den Doctor gethan werden, endlich spricht er ferner' (23). Pinsel, the main character, exhibits characteristics of coarse comic figures earlier in the century with his penchant for gluttony, licentiousness, and his apparent stupidity. The Nachspiel following continues the theme of marriage with further connections to traditional comedy, from the father's name, Pantalon, to beatings, coarse language, gluttony, cuckoldry, and extemporization. The entire fifth scene 'Stellt erstlich den Schulmeister mit seiner Schule vor, welche nach Belieben *extemp.* können' (51); similarly, the entire Scene 11: 'Arlequin (mit den Schuljungen treibt allerhand Possen)' (56). Beneath this bawdy surface, however, lies a theme as socially relevant as that of the preceding work. Arlequin's self-auctioning to the highest female bidder whom he then marries comments ironically on accepted methods of matchmaking in contemporary society in which monetary advantage prevailed over human inclination or compatibility, as it still does in many cases today. (See further analysis p 174.)

The theme of marriage also connects *Isaac und Rebecca* (1722) to its Nachspiel, and in similar fashion the Nachspiele *Die Heyrath der Thorheit* (1757) and *Eurydice* (1759) are joined to the plays that precede them (*Die verliebten Thorheiten, Der Hochzeitstag*), but these links are less intricate than in the works discussed above. Finally, the *Verbesserungen und Zusätze* (1744) have direct and explicit relation to the previously published *Geistlichen auf dem Lande* (1743). They contain an attack upon all that their predecessor represents, but the dramatic potential of this Nachspiel is minimal, the primary intention clearly being literary persiflage (see details in John, *Krüger. Werke* and Van Cleve, *Harlequin besieged*).

Three Nachspiele published after 1770 in connection with preceding works are *Die frohe Frau* (1775), written in response to Klinger's *Die leidende Frau* (or *Das leidende Weib*), Lederer's *Die jungen Rekruten*, connected with *Der Chargenverkauf* (1781), and Ayrenhoff's *Nachspiel zur berühmten Komödie Erklärte Fehde oder List gegen List* (1789). *Erklärte Fehde* is a translation of Dumaniant's *Guerre ouverte*, and Ayrenhoff's *Nachspiel* is essentially a satirical continuation. The personae reveal a conscious affiliation with the *commedia dell'arte* tradition in names such as Pantalon, Brigella, and Columbina, and the action makes generous use of such devices as disguise, sexual innuendo, exaggeration, beatings, traditional costumes, and the play within a play (see detailed discussion p 203). Thematically, the Nachspiel completes an unresolved sub-plot of the work it follows, but by shifting the venue to the world of traditional comedy, it debases and trivializes its predecessor and at the same time ridicules the manner of its French characters and the tone of Dumaniant's work itself. A Venetian gondolier is substituted for the ship's captain of the original, and a hectic whirlwind of disguise, beatings, sexual innuendo, and deliberate confusion replaces the pretentiously refined comedy. The Nachspiel becomes a humorous statement on both French manners and literary style.

Die frohe Frau also makes a literary statement, but with much more serious intention. It provides insight into the intense feuding surrounding Storm and Stress authors such as Klinger and reflects the heightened critical involvement of German readers and theatre-goers toward the end of the century. In this case an enormous conservative resistance to the emotion, libertinism, and social criticism of the new writers is reflected. In effect this is a piece of literary criticism in dramatic form, with no relationship whatever to the traditional attributes of the Nachspiel, which indicates a new and separate function for the genre. It is one of the many Nachspiele that tackle serious themes, including the state of theatre and literature, in the last three decades of the century (see detailed analysis p 264).

Lederer's *Die jungen Rekruten* shares thematics with the previous military drama *Der Chargenverkauf* and their dual title-page makes it clear that they were to be played in conjunction. This Nachspiel was constructed especially for school performance and delivered a light-hearted lesson on the seriousness of the military draft. Despite its playful tone, when set against the preceding drama this Nachspiel must have carried a stern message to the young men who played and watched it – further evidence of the Nachspiel's later function as a conveyor of serious thematics.

Nachspiele with Music, Songs, Dance (MSD)

	Total	MSD
1702-1769	41	10 (24%)
1770-1810	71	14 (20%)

Regardless of time frame, it is evident that the Nachspiel is a genre which frequently makes use of music, song, and dance as part of its theatrical composition. This characteristic was evident from the earliest decades of the century even among works without written documentation. The activities of itinerant troupes made it clear that they used drums and other instruments to announce and advertise their programs when arriving at a new venue, and the 'divertissements' which composed an integral part of the Haupt- und Staatsaktion and *lustiges* Nachspiel commonly continued the entertainment in musical form. We know too that for Schuch, Schönemann, Ackermann, and other troupe principals, the Nachspiel often became interchangeable with operettas or ballets to complete an evening's program, some titles even identical with spoken Nachspiele. From the percentages given above, it is clear that the published Nachspiel shows a close alliance with musical performance throughout the century, not just before the establishment of standing theatres. This mixture of drama and orchestral accompaniment, song, and dance indicates that the Nachspiel is a theatrical form which cuts across several genres and reflects diverse trends of its age. Another strong indication of this will be seen in the many Nachspiele after 1769 which centre upon socio-critical themes more commonly associated with the serious Lustspiel, with sentimental comedy, and even with tragedy. When it comes specifically to musical drama in the century, one thinks naturally of opera, then in a lighter vein of the operetta and the Singspiel, each of which formed a significant part of the repertoires of both itinerant troupes and standing theatres. In fact, musical accompaniment in some form was so much a part of German theatre in the century that specific reference to it in texts probably illustrates only a small portion of the musically enhanced theatre that actually took place. The Singspiel as independent genre was especially popular from 1760 to the end of the century, consisting of a primary dramatic action, with interspersed songs as a complement (as opposed to opera in which the musical parts dominate). The genre's popularity on German stages can be traced back to the popular Jiggs played by itinerant English troupes in German territory in the sixteenth and seventeenth centuries, works consisting of dialogues interspersed with popular melodies, songs, and dances. The single striking catalyst was, however, Coffey's *Devil to Pay* in its several German translations and adaptations, most important being those of Christian Felix Weiße (text) and J.C. Standfuß (music) in 1752, then Johann Adam Hiller who wrote new music for it in 1766. Elements of the French *opéra comique* as well as the *opera buffa*, both popular in German areas, also had their effect on the new genre. In the sixties and seventies, Singspiele began to appear at a rapid rate and were important not just for their place in the repertoire, but perhaps even more so for the aesthetic debate on the relationship between dramatic and musical performance they triggered, a debate conducted actively by Weiße, Hiller, and other prominent contemporaries such as Goethe and Wieland to the end of the century.

The Nachspiel titles in the Bibliography containing elements of music, song, and dance fall naturally into two subcategories, those with musical features as tangential additions to the dramatic action, and others that use music and dance as essential structural and thematic elements. Of the twenty-four Nachspiele under consideration now, fourteen include musical features only to a minor extent, ten in a major way.

Minor use of musical features may be represented in a closing song, usually by the full cast, in which the action is summarized and a resulting light-hearted word of advice passed on to the audience (*Die Melonen*, 1771; *Christen in Abyssinien*, [1780]; *Der Perücken zweyter Theil*, 1791; *Die Heirathslustigen*, 1801); or a combined closing song with ballet (*Die Rekreation*, 1766; *Die Bildsäule*, 1782); or a concluding ballet or musical piece alone (Nachspiel to *Isaac und Rebecca*, 1722; *Der bezauberte Gürtel*, 1748; *Eurydice*, 1759). But a minor use of music is not limited to closings. It is also represented by an orchestral introduction (*Minna*, 1799); a single aria (*Matrone von Ephesus*, 1764; *Fanny*, 1772; *Juliane Dürrbach*, 1783); or interspersed songs (*Er ist es selbst*, 1808).

More significant are the ten Nachspiele in which music and dance are essential features. Two of these in fact bear a dual genre designation on their title-pages: *Harlequin, der ungedultig hernach* ... (1743) is called a 'Sing-Spiel als eine lustige Nach-Comödie' (contrary to the entry in the *Reallexikon*, [2]1977, III, 832, which states that with *Mit Lottchen am Hofe*, 1767 'erschien zum ersten Mal ein Original-Singspiel'); and *Die jungen Rekruten* (1781) is called 'Eine komische Operette ... als ein Nachspiel.' *Die verachtete Eitelkeit der Welt* (1702) is subtitled 'Musikalisches Nachspiel' and indeed appears to be an entirely musical piece including arias and operatic dialogue. Other works in the Bibliography could also be easily designated Singspiele (*Das lustige Elendt*, [1741]; *Der Prahler*, 1761; *Heyrath aus Liebe*, 1781; *Die Wolken*, 1782). All of these contain a variety of songs, arias, duets, and choral pieces which either complement the dramatic action at every turn or even constitute a much greater part of the work than the spoken word. *Die Wolken* is especially instructive because of the preliminary notes to the reader in which both its theatrical success in Frankfurt and the critical backlash are outlined. (The playbill of its performance is also preserved in the Frankfurt Stadt- und Universitätsbibliothek collection.) It cuts even further across genre designations than the other examples, being not just Nachspiel and in effect Singspiel, but showing strong features of the bucolic Schäferspiel and including ballet as an important element as well. (Other titles in the Bibliography also show strong characteristics of the Schäferspiel; see, for example, *Hirten der Alpen, Rosalia*.)

Three further examples are of particular interest in their use of musical motifs. In *Heyrath der Thorheit* (1757), the dramatic action is suddenly and permanently disrupted by a jolly carnival group from outside the action which takes over the play with a flourish of ebullient song, dance, and merrymaking. The dramatic action of the socio-critical Nachspiel *Das Liebhabertheater vor dem Parlament* (1790), which in itself results in a complete failure to come to grips with the problem at hand, is literally annulled by the sudden magical entrance of an allegorical entourage, led by Thalia, which lifts the problem to a higher dimension of reality and provides an elevated dénouement. The magical tender lyrics of Rosalia in the Nachspiel of the same title (1777) are the key to reversing the action and assuring a conclusion of unproblematic bliss. In each of these works, music and song represent a dimension of reality above the mundane world of the dramatic action; in each, the spirit of the audience is released by music to enjoy a few brief moments of magical harmony in another realm. With this strong representation of musical Nachspiele, it is evident that throughout the century the mixture of dialogue and musical accompaniment was an ongoing characteristic.

Nachspiele with Traditional Comic Elements (TC)

The works in the Bibliography show an enormous wealth, variety, and prevalence of comic themes, characters, structures, and devices, as can be seen from their plot summaries and the subsequent comments. These for the most part represent a continuation of comic elements present for centuries in many cultural traditions, stretching back to classical times at least. However, this is not what makes them a distinctive part of the German Nachspiel tradition. My analysis in Chapter 2 of the repertoires and performances of itinerant troupes, the carriers of the Nachspiel from the beginning of the century, showed certain comic elements that were central to the Nachspiel's continuing popularity.

These include primarily: the presence of a familiar central comic figure; the freedom to improvise or extemporize; pantomimic elements; the freedom to stand outside the dramatic action and address the audience directly; internal commentary on the dramatic action; coarseness in language and gestures; physical and verbal abuse; general confusion and raucous behaviour; and indirect social criticism. Early Nachspiele also made frequent use of such traditional comic structural devices as the love triangle, mistaken identity through disguise, impersonation or concealed heritage, and eavesdropping to create separate levels of understanding. Most important among all of these, however, was the freedom to – indeed the necessity to – extemporize. Here, mime (the silent playing out of a part with expressions and actions) and gesture (motion of the body to convey or emphasize emotions, ideas, and opinions, etc.) were most important. It is with reference to these elements that the term 'traditional comedy' is used in the following analysis. The central question now is: to what extent were they maintained in published Nachspiele? On the basis of these prevalent elements the works listed in the Bibliography have been considered in relation to their traditionally comic (TC) nature, giving the following results:

	Total	TC
1702-69	41	17 (41%)
1770-10	71	15 (21%)

The decrease in the use of traditional comic elements in published Nachspiele from 41 per cent before 1770 to 21 per cent thereafter indicates a general change in the nature and tone of the genre. Still, their prevalence in more than a fifth of the Nachspiele published after 1769 is surprisingly high considering the fact that the German theatre scene had by then undergone a stringent phase of moralistic and theatrical regularization; extemporization in particular had been officially banned in many places. It is also difficult to say entirely on the basis of what we can now read in texts just how much improvisation and pantomime went on during the performance on stage of any of the Nachspiele in the Bibliography. In all likelihood there was much more than the texts alone indicate; hence, the figure of 21 per cent represents an absolute minimum. The table in Appendix 1 also shows that a change occurred in the appearance of traditional central comic figures such as Hanswurst and Harlekin. Before 1770, such a character is present in nine of the published Nachspiele, thereafter only three; and no published Nachspiel contains the figure of Hanswurst. In most examples the central comic figure is Harlekin. The drive to cleanse the theatre of coarse traditional extemporized comedy, as exemplified in Hanswurst, had clearly been successful in terms of the published Nachspiel, but this should by no means be understood to mean that what that figure stood for and how he went about his craft had disappeared completely with the name, as the analysis of individual works below will show. His disappearance should also come as no surprise considering the fact that he was foremost a non-literary figure. We must also be cautious in assuming that the Harlekin named among the personae of published texts was in fact attired and played according to the tradition associated with that name. Schuch, we saw, commonly used the name Harlekin in titles although it was in fact himself as Hanswurst who played that role. No doubt the Harlekin of published texts was at times played as a mixture of Italian, French, and German comic types.

One could approach this group of Nachspiele by tracing individual comic elements through a number of works; however, such an approach would divert attention from the overall impact of many elements working simultaneously, for it is their cumulative effect that made individual works successful. Accordingly, the following discussion treats each work as a dramatic whole. As the size of the Bibliography does not permit intensive analysis of every work, fifteen Nachspiele have been selected which cover the range in time from six published before 1770 (discussed in Chapter 5) to nine thereafter (discussed in Chapter 6). In the latter group, the works selected cover the last three decades of the century, including three from the 1770s, five from the 1780s, and one from the 1790s. What is said about these works could be broadened to include many other titles in the Bibliography, as the plot summaries of works not discussed here and the information in Appendix 1 demonstrate. The three Nachspiele published from manuscripts in Chapter 3 are also omitted from the discussion here.

There are two central questions now: what traditional Nachspiel elements are evident in each of the works? and to what extent are these elements as strongly represented in the later group as in the earlier one? The works below are treated in chronological order so that the temporal division between them is clear. Plot summaries for all are available in the Bibliography.

As texts tell us only part of the story about stage productions, the following discussions attempt to keep in mind how the actors interpreted these texts and what effect their interpretations had on the audience. Indications of performances carried on the title-page of many of the Nachspiele in the Bibliography tell us when and where they were produced – e.g. *Adel des Herzens, Die alte Bekanntschaft, Der betrogene Kadi, Die beyden Portraits, Der Blinde aus Leichtgläubigkeit, Eurydice, Der Instinkt, Die jungen Rekruten, Liebe und Vaterland, Das Liebhabertheater vor dem Parlament, Die Rekreation, Die verachtete Eitelkeit der Welt, Was ist's?*, and *Die Wolken*. Otherwise, this information can only be gained by searching repertoire lists, playbill collections, and other historical sources. This has been fruitful in the case of many of the Nachspiele discussed below, but did not lead to success in every instance (see Documented Performances, p 299).

5

The Nachspiel as Text
before 1770

Isaac und Rebecca (1722)

This play and its Nachspiel by the mysterious Jodocus of Thüringen (whose name does not appear in Jöcher, Jördens, Meusel, the *ADB*, or the *Deutscher Biographischer Index*) is among the rarest in the Bibliography with only the single extant copy in Weimar known. But it is not simply this quality that calls for attention, it is the publication's importance as a theoretical tract and a singular example of contemporary theatre as well. On the surface, the theme of marriage connects the two works beneath the title *Isaac* and its *Nach-spiel*, but the comic Nachspiel is more of a tonal contrast than a serious extension of the theme. In the pairing – a serious work based on biblical history followed by a comic one featuring the central figure of Harlequin – we see a variation on the typical dramatic combination of the Haupt- und Staatsaktion with 'lustiger Nach-Comödie,' the bread and butter of itinerant troupes. Here, however, the comic figure is excluded from the main work.

The title-page provides a number of clues about how the works should be understood. The Nachspiel is untitled, but characterized by the action 'Worinn der Harlequin fünff, in einer Person sich nicht wohl zusammen schickende Bedienungen / Nehmlich Eines Herren-Dieners, Nacht-Wächters, Bier-Rüffers, Thor-Hüters, und Kuh-Hirtens zusammen verwaltet.' This listing of Harlequin's multiple identities reminds us of early playbills for Haupt- und Staatsaktionen in which Hanswurst was the star in many roles. It also shows that his execution of these roles is of central interest and suggests that the character is multi-dimensional in function and meaning. Within the play Harlequin in fact plays six roles, the five above as well as his own character. Ordinarily, the Nachspiel was a shorter supplement to the main work, but in this published version it is virtually the same length, indicating the importance the author attached to the comic element, which he also addressed seriously in the foreword. On the title-page we are told further that the works to follow, that is, not just the serious one but also the Nachspiel, are intended 'Zur nützlichen Ergötzung.' Jodocus's dramatic purpose is the classic Horatian combination of instruction and entertainment, much discussed as the century progressed, rather abused by Gottsched with his unbalanced pedagogical emphasis, but championed by Johann Elias Schlegel in the 1740s and others thereafter.

Jodocus's serious approach to the nature and function of his work is spelled out in some detail in his foreword to the reader. The rambling argument of the first two pages in favour of open rational discussion suggests that he had been involved for some time in a debate, without much clarity emerging from it, and that he expected criticism about these works. Indeed the sense of frustration that resulted from that discussion seems to have caused him directly to write them:

> Kan man aber seinen Zweck dadurch nicht völlig erreichen / so muß man schon darmit zufrieden seyn / wenn daher auch nur bey etlichen die Mühe gespahret wird / daß sie sich mit unnützen Raisonniren nicht lange aufhalten. Und eben dieses hat mich bewogen / diesem kleinen Werkchen / welches ich schon vor einiger Zeit in denen Recreations-Stunden aufgesetzet / eine Praefation vorzusetzen / und in derselben unterschiedenen zu vermuthenden Judiciis entgegen zu gehen. Denn man findet erstlich Leuthe in der Welt / welche bloß nach ihrem Goût die Sachen zu beurtheilen pflegen / und davor halten / es sey schon genug / ohne gegebene Raison zu statuiren / daß etwas nicht tauge / wenn es ihnen nur nich gefället. Diesen nun mag ich ihre Empfindung / so sie haben / nicht disputiren / so wenig als ich Lust habe / jemanden seinen Geschmack abzustreiten / wenn derselbe saget / daß ihm eine gewisse Speise oder Tranck nicht schmecke; Allein sie werden mirs nicht verdencken / daß ich sie eines Fehlers beschuldige / wenn sie nach ihrem Geschmacke anderer Leuthe ihren urtheilen / und dasjenige / was ihnen nicht schmecket / durchgehends vor abgeschmackt halten. Sonderlich aber sollen dieselbe wohl erwegen / daß in Sachen / welche den Verstand angehen / es niemahl auff ihr Gefallen / sondern auff den Beweiß ankomme. Ich werde also nichts darnach fragen / wenn jemanden / ohne Anführung gnugsamer Ursachen / diese meine wenige Arbeit nicht gefallen sollte. (ivf)

This author was obviously convinced about his own skills of rational argumentation, but just as clearly realistic about the lack of them in his opponents with their penchant for praising or condemning without objective basis. Through underlying personal disdain for their type, he asks only that they keep their opinions responsibly to themselves. His own approach to theatre is clearly more liberal, as witnessed by the works at hand which in many ways offend the aesthetic taste of those he addresses here. His explicit assuredness about the instructive nature of these works is really quite remarkable:

> Allein / ich zweiffle sehr / daß man in diesen wenigen Bogen gar keinen Nutzen antreffen werde. Denn zugeschweigen / daß man fast durchgehends die Comoedien / welche nicht mit schändlichen Sau-Possen / und ärgerlichen Vorstellungen angefüllet sind / alß eine nicht unnütze Sache passiren läßet / so findet man insonderheit in nachfolgenden Theatralischen Aufführungen solchen moralische Reflexiones, welche allerdings auf die Berförderung so wohl der zeitlichen / als ewigen Wohlfarth abzielen. (v)

It is most important to notice that Jodocus is talking here of both the serious *Isaac und Rebecca* and the comic Nachspiel – 'nachfolgenden theatralischen Aufführungen' – so that his ambitious and confident claim to present material of moral value should be understood to apply to both. In this first published Nachspiel to be considered in detail here we see that the intention goes far beyond superficial comic amusement to include serious comment on the values of the day. Such serious intentions established themselves as a pattern to the end of the century. Jodocus's concept of the comic Nachspiel, however, does not include outlandish crudity and tasteless demonstration – 'schändliche Saupossen und ärgerliche Vorstellungen' – trademarks of the Haupt- und Staatsaktion and the early German comic figure, and characteristics that stirred the moral indignation of theatre reformers for decades to come. Jodocus shows himself here as a a liberal reformer in his own right, a pioneer of the modified comic figure, cleansed of unnecessary crudity. What he saw as important to maintain, however, the more sophisticated and multi-faceted comic person and the underlying social and moral commentary, was also what enabled the Nachspiel tradition to continue thriving.

Jodocus proceeds in the foreword to address his Nachspiel more specifically:

> Weiter stelle ich mir auch vor / daß vielleicht denen allzuernsthafften Gemüthern die Beyfügung eines lustigen Nach-Spiels zu der vorhergehenden Biblischen Historie nicht anständig und geschickt genug vorkommen werde. Gegen diese nun wolte ich mich wohl mit der Gewonheit / da man nicht nur schertzhaffte Nach-Spiele zu serieusen Vorspielen zu setzen /

sondern auch gar in Tragoedien kurtzweilige Zwischen-Scenen einzumi-
schen pfleget / zu defendiren suchen / wenn ich nicht besorgete / daß man
in Theologicis und Moralibus die Gewonheit nicht so / wie in der Jurispru-
dentz, möchte passiren lassen: Dannenhero muß ich solchen auff eine andere
Arth begegnen / und ihnen zu bedencken geben / ob sie es wohl vor
sündlich / oder ungereimt halten können / wenn in einer Schrifft so wohl
Tugend- als Lasterhaffte / oder auch solche Personen / welche in ihrem
Verstande merckliche Fehler spühren lassen / vorgestellet werden. Wolten
sie dieses bejahen / so würden sie selbst wieder die Heilige Schrifft reden /
und die Moralen, wie auch Historische Bücher verwerffen müssen / solcher
Gestalt aber ihren Mangel des Verstandes gar sehr verrathen. (vi)

The passage again reflects something of contemporary theatrical fashion, this time the *Zwischenspiele* usually starring the comic figure, frequently interspersed within the Hauptaktion, even if this was tragic.
Jodocus mentions the practice as one way of justifying his own mixing
of biblical and comic motifs, but in the end does not rely on that defence alone. Rather, he cites biblical and historical tradition as carriers
of both positive and negative characters which serve as instructive
moral examples to readers. The Nachspiel builds on this tradition, he
argues, at the same time sounding very much like a forerunner of
Gottsched with his juxtaposition of characterized virtue and vice.

In the remainder of the foreword the author raises six criticisms of
his two plays in anticipation of his opponents' reaction, answering each
in turn. They focus on aesthetic considerations, verisimilitude in language, the division of acts and scenes, the verse form (of *Isaac und Rebecca*), word order in verses, elisions, and other metrical details. Some
of these are relevant for his Nachspiel. Of its language, which contains
many examples of comic linguistic misuse, he writes: 'Was im übrigen
die in dem Nach-Spiele enthaltene und unrichtig formirte Lateinische
Terminos anlanget / so ist gewiß / daß es Leuthe genug giebt / welche
dergleichen Fehler vielfältig begehen / und sich nicht wenig dabey einbilden / wenn sie solche in grosser Menge vorbringen können: Weswe-
gen denn auch in dieser Vorstellung nichts wider die Probabilität be-
gangen worden' (ix). The misuse of foreign terms, especially Latin and
French, was of course nothing new for Jodocus. There are many examples in theatre for at least a century before. The speakers themselves
customarily bear the brunt of the ridicule because of their modish pretension to learning which cannot mask their own true ignorance. Such
is also the case in Jodocus's Nachspiel, but the grounding of his defence
here is in the dramatic requirement of verisimilitude ('Probabilität'),
which points directly to Christlob Mylius's and Johann Elias Schlegel's

insistence on *Wahrscheinlichkeit* as a necessity in drama that should override even the mimetic precision of *Wirklichkeit* (see Mylius, 'Abhandlung'; Schlegel, 'Abhandlung'). The argument that drama should be grounded in probability rather than reality was one of the major aesthetic breakthroughs of the age in German theatre, but rarely, if ever, attributed to one as early as Jodocus. Still, that is clearly what he is thinking of here. This aspect of his progressiveness is noteworthy for the development of the aesthetics of theatre in Germany and also a signal that he understood the essential strength of the Nachspiel genre. Linguistic misuse here is a reflection of society and certain social types; hence by ridiculing them in his Nachspiel he is providing models for behavioural correction. Beyond this, the crux of his argument that such types are legitimate in comedy because they are probable in reality has greater significance when applied to the entire Nachspiel genre. Contemporary critics of the Nachspiel and its central comic figure customarily focused on his 'unnaturalness,' arguing that he had no place in a genre which should depict the reality of life. Here is Gottsched's famous statement on comic figures from the *Critische Dichtkunst*: 'Eben die Gründe, die wider jene [Hans Wurst, Pickelhering] streiten, sind auch allen diesen Geschöpfen [Peter, Crispin] einer unordentlichen Einbildungskraft zuwider, die kein Muster in der Natur haben' (654). What Gottsched failed to understand, as Lessing and Möser pointed out, was that the comic figure, in his apparent unnaturalness, reflected fundamental truths about human nature in society – that is in fact what always guaranteed in the end such a high level of public interest in him. Thus his 'unnaturalness' was but a superficial screen for the core of natural truth beneath. Many examples in the following analyses illustrate how essential this type of naturalness was to the comic figure.

The Nachspiel to *Isaac und Rebecca* relies on numerous traditional comic devices including caricature and satire, verbal misunderstandings and linguistic misuse, physical pratfalls, beatings, gestures, and mime play. The comic names of the personae and their town already provide a basis for understanding them and indicate as well the two social strata involved – civic officialdom, the judge and his assistant Leberwurst and Rundhut, and the simpler folk, the rest. With this division, a potential for social comment is immediately present. Of particular interest is the presence of Harlequin, many of whose actions are typical of what the audience could expect from this name, and indeed his costume in the play might also have been in keeping with their expectations.

The action begins with the judge and his assistant, whose language from the start begins the satire of their type:

Leberwurst. Bons Dies [guten Tag], Herr Culege, Bons Dies.
Rundhut. Cramerschies [Krämerscheiß?], Herr Culege, Cramerschies.
Leberwurst. Es ist eben gut / daß wir einander antreffen; ich muß was wichtiges mit euch reden / das unsere Pulcey-Sachen [Polizei-Sachen] consternirt [konzerniert, betrifft]. (44)

Thus they ramble on throughout, building an image of ridiculous pompous ignorance. The matter they must discuss is the appointment of a successor to Matzpump in the five jobs on the title-page, and of course they choose Harlequin. Thus the action becomes focused on what they want as authoritative figures as opposed to what Harlequin understands and delivers. By the end, he has thoroughly botched all five jobs and prepares to sneak away, which suggests his defeat, but in fact the reverse is true. In the course of his negotiations with his superiors he manages to escape the beatings usually reserved for him, adroitly causing his superiors to tumble over each other to the ground and even doling out a flogging to the judge himself (64). This physical retribution exerted over the higher powers is supplemented by constant verbal and gestural ridicule, as in Scenes 8 and 9 when Harlequin plays the fool in his role as 'Herrendiener,' relying on a verbal misunderstanding to achieve his ends:

Harlequin. (Er tritt vor ein ander Hauß.)
Halt / ich will hier einmahl anklopffen.
Hullerdiepuller / Hullerdiepuller!
   (Er klopfft dabey starck an, es komt aber Niemand drum rufft er weiter.)
Hoya / Hoya! Herauß / herauß!
   (Stephen Rundhuth komt herauß.)
Rundhut. Wer ist hier? Du pochst ja trefflich an. Was wilst du?
   (Harlequin macht viel Reverentze vor ihm.)
Harlequin. Mein Herr Culege Rundhuth soll einmahl hieher kommen.
Rundhut. Was? heißt du mich Culege? Kerl / bist du in dem Rumpelsdorffischen Machstratum?
Harlequin. Ja / Herr Culege, ihr wißt ja wohl / daß ich Herrendiener bin / und der Herr Richter Carsten Leberwurst hat mir befohlen: sage / mein Herr Culege Rundhuth soll einmahl hieher kommen? und eben so habe ichs bey euch ausgerichtet.
Rundhut. Wo soll ich hinkommen?
Harlequin. Gleich da gegenüber / folgt mir nur nach, und geht fort.
   (Harlequin stellt sich vor Ihn.)
Rundhut. Du grober Klotz / du mußt als Herren-Diener nicht vorher gehen.
   (Harlequin tritt ihm zur rechten Seite.)

Harlequin. Nun ist es recht.

Rundhut. Noch nicht. Du mußt hinter mir hergehen.

   (Harlequin geht hinter ihm her mit Spanischen Schritten biß auff den be-
stimmten Platz. Von da laufft er vor des Richters Hauß, und pocht starck.)

Harlequin. Holla / Holla! Heraus / heraus! Herr Richter.

   (Er kommt heraus.) (62f)

Harlequin continues in similar fashion with Leberwurst.

The scene is really about power in society, the 'Rumpelsdorffischen Machstratum,' as Rundhut calls it indignantly, serving as a fictitious comic model for what the play's audience may well have experienced in their daily lives. What counts for Rundhut, Leberwurst, and their type is a guaranteed position near the top of the hierarchy, but Harlequin's mixture of doltish buffoonery and clever manipulation enables him to penetrate the structure and gain influence at the expense of those who hold power but lack his innate cleverness. With the address 'Herr Culege' he utilizes a verbal misunderstanding to accord himself the same rank as his superiors. This is the essence of the traditional comic figure: blundering incompetence on the surface; clever resourcefulness beneath.

Rundhut calls Harlequin 'grober Klotz' because he bungles the social protocol, and the apparent coarseness of his character is frequently brought out elsewhere in the text as well. For example, at his first meeting with Ursel he immediately lunges for physical favours (56), eliciting this response: 'Seht doch / Alber Hanß / Hanß Wurst / latt mech unge-heyet / oder ech wells miner Motter säge' (56). With this Harlequin's real heritage is revealed. He is in fact the traditional German Hanswurst thinly disguised, but when he lapses into his old ways, his roots become unmistakeably unearthed again. We recall Jodocus's comments on crudity in his foreword, and in later Nachspiele will see other examples of comic figures bearing the name Harlequin who nevertheless carry strong characteristics of the German Hanswurst. Harlequin is in effect Hanswurst's literary incarnation. His costume on stage would be one of the keys to his identity, and while there are no costume indicators in Jodocus's text, some later works do provide such clues.

It is Harlequin's apparent ignorance in this Nachspiel that gives him such licence, a freedom exploited to its fullest in gesture and mime. His exaggerated 'Reverentze' and exit behind Rundhut 'mit Spanischen Schritten' are mimed parodies of social pomposity. As 'Herrendiener' his social status is low, but when he makes use of such opportunities for mime play he is the 'Herrendiener' no more, but rather a character outside the structures of social reality and hence immune from classification according to its strata. This extraordinary status is also suggested in the text by the fact that his name alone is always typeset in Roman characters, while all others are consistently in *Fraktur*.

In the forty pages of text there are roughly two hundred stage directions, some brief, many lengthy and requiring extended improvised action. This wealth of extra-textual activity indicates the premium the author put on movement, gesture, and mime. It also suggests a play with great potential for interplay between actors and audience, for gesture and mime are vehicles usually directed more to the public than to others on stage. They establish private interpretive links outside the action between the actor and his public.

The bulk of the stage directions in this Nachspiel relate to Harlequin, many offering opportunities for minute extemporized scenes similar to the marching exit above. His initial entry on stage illustrates their importance. The first scene ends with Rundhut and Leberwurst deciding to sit and think together about the problem at hand, and so they strike this pose: '(Sie stellen sich beyde in positur, und dencken, ohne die geringste Bewegung zu machen, der Sache starck nach)' (46). At this point Scene 2 begins with Harlequin's entrance thus:

> (Der Harlequin, welcher mit einen grossen Räntzel von der Reise kommt, tantzt lustig herum / und wie er die beyde Rumpelsdorffischen Männer stehen siehet, setzt er seinen Stock wieder den einen, sagend.)
> *Harlequin*. Hier muß gewiß eines vornehmen Herrn sein Garten seyn; Denn da stehen ein paar recht künstliche Statuen.
> (Er will seinen Räntzel an den andern anhencken; Sie regen sich aber alle beyde, und Harlequin schreyt darauff gantz erschrocken.) (47)

Harlequin's first action in the work is an extemporized dance, quite possibly one familiar to the audience. It is impossible to say from the text alone what freedom he took here, how the dance was structured, or how long it lasted, but it is certain that he could improvise the little scene as he wished. Such an entrance was characteristic for the comic figure in unpublished Nachspiele, and this Nachspiel shows a literary continuation of that tradition, as will other examples later on. The extemporization here is doubly effective because it has been prepared unwittingly by the silent pose of the two officials. In Harlequin's initial comment – 'ein paar recht künstliche Statuen' – and treatment of them as inanimate objects, he already begins to satirize their self-importance. From the start, then, the playwright removes these objects of satire from the world of dialogue and places them at the mercy of Harlequin in his realm – pantomime. It is significant too that Harlequin enters their world as an outsider, his knapsack symbolizing a nomadic quality; as an outsider he is not part of the social structure that prevails in Rumpelsdorff, and hence he stands free to treat it with caustic objectivity.

Many of the stage directions offer potential for mimic improvisation similar to that above, and each, when exploited, must have created a bond of extra-textual understanding between Harlequin and the audience. So by the end, as he decides to make an escape from the turmoil he has created, he takes his leave directly from the audience by stepping out of the action to perform a final piece just for them:

> (Er spielt ein Stückgen auff der Maul Trumpe [Mundharmonika], nachher sagend:)
> Nun so geht es denn fort / und ich sage noch zu letzt grossen Danck / und eine gute Nacht.
> (Er spatziret tantzend mit seinem Räntzel zum Thore hinaus, und ist also hiermit das
>
> ENDE.

In leaving, Harlequin picks up once again the extemporized dance with which he began, taking his pack to move on, and seems to end the action by walking right out of a stage direction through the door. Harlequin in effect escapes the dramatic fiction we have just seen when it ends on stage and lives on separately, to return again, as we shall indeed witness.

Harlequin, der ungedultig-hernach aber mit Gewalt gedultig gemachte Hahnrey (1743)

This work's simultaneous publication with *Die Franzosen in Böhmen* and their shared depiction of French characters and morals makes its socio-critical dimension clear from the start, and the theme of cuckoldry highlighted in its subtitle places the comedy in an ancient thematic tradition. As central figures, however, Harlequin and Columbina represent in name the more recent comic types of the *commedia dell'arte*, whereas in character and function they represent much of what we would expect in the central comic figures of the German Nachspiel. There can be little doubt about what Harlequin in this play was intended to look like. The title-page of one edition of *Die Franzosen in Böhmen* (Pilsen, 1743) includes a copper engraving depicting the affected French characters in the play in all their splendour, and behind them, a distant observer in the background, is the figure of Harlequin in typical chequered attire (engraving reproduced in Hansen, Abb 252, 253). In the brief Foreword, the anonymous author claims that the work presents 'eine artige und wahrhaffte geschehene Liebes-Begebenheit' with place of action 'in dem Dorff Quirlequitsch bey Pirlepump nicht weit von Rumpelshausen' (102). This simultaneous claim of plot authenticity alongside the fanciful location sets up a deliberate ironic interplay between the worlds of reality and fiction. Such too is the composition of the personae, on the one hand the French characters who could be found in any comedy of French manners, or even in contemporary society, on the other Harlequin and Columbina who only come alive on the stage. The Foreword further contains a curious encouragement to the reader as he 'durchlaufft die paar Blätter zu einem kurzen Zeit-Vertreib,' suggesting that the author had in mind a new reading public which did not exist for the Nachspiel when it was solely extant in performance. This signals an awareness in this early work of the trend toward the 'textualization' of drama which was to predominate after 1770.

The first action of the play is indicated in the stage direction 'Harlequin. Stoßt die Columbina zu dem Hause hinaus' (104). Obviously we are dealing here with a coarse comic type, not a refined Harlequin figure. The action would be just as appropriate to begin a Nachspiel much earlier in the century with Hanswurst at the focus. Such underlying physical brutality is a motif throughout the work, either in concrete actions or in linguistic expression. Soon after, Harlequin's crudity is underscored in this address to his wife:

> Du Ehr-vergeßnes Raben-Aas!
> Wilst du mir nicht pariren [gehorchen]?
> So werd ich dich mit diesem Maaß
> Auf deinen Buckel schmieren;
> Du sollst mein Weib für mich allein,
> Und nicht für die Franzosen sein. (zornig),

which is followed at once by the stage direction: 'Schlägt sie mit seiner Pritsche etlichmal herum, sie fängt an so starck und laut zu schreyen, daß es in den Ohren ergellt, wie der bösen Weiber Brauch ist, die ihren Männern untreu sind' (105f). The rough language, the beating, the vocabulary of 'Pritsche' and 'Buckel' are characteristic of coarse Nachspiele and comic figures, the 'Pritsche' according with our knowledge of this Harlequin's costume. But it is the comic figure who traditionally receives the beating instead of doling it out. Contemporary audiences would notice this reversal and begin to suspect a change in perspective. This, along with the content of the above speech and its subsequent stage direction, leaves us wondering where our sympathies are meant to lie, with the husband who is being blatantly deceived by a conniving wife and her modish lover, or with the wife who is subjected to such abuse. The author's editorial comment in the stage direction on the nature of Columbina's screams seems to indicate his loyalties with the husband at this point, but later scenes and speeches, as well as the end of the play, leave us with a different impression of where he stood. We sense an underlying mixture of themes that is disturbing and complex. In addition, this internal editorial comment could have effect only on a reader of the work, not an audience, for whom it would pass unknown – but the comment might indicate the author's assumption of contemporary audience reaction to the beating. Like the curious remark in the Foreword, the comment suggests that this author had a reading public very much in mind.

Whatever thematic information is to be drawn from this early scene, one thing is clear: extemporized action is very much part of this play. The beating incident is undetermined in length or detail, so that it was a matter of the theatrical sense of the actors and their judgment of what would entertain the audience. With such initial freedom, the characters Harlequin and Columbina could turn audience sympathies one way or another; in other words, the nature of the extemporization could have a significant effect on the thematic message of the play.

Stage directions and the often resulting freedom to – even necessity to – extemporize continue to play a major role in further scenes, and often much more subtly than cursory reading of the text would suggest. When, to start the action, Harlequin pushes Columbina out of the house in the first scene, we are told in the stage direction simply 'Columbina weint' (104). Then in the beating scene cited above, 'sie fängt an so starck und laut zu schreyen ...' (105), and soon after before the judge Partout, 'Hier fängt sie wieder an aus allen Kräfften zu schreyen und zu weinen ...' (106). Conversely, in answer to her tears, 'Harlequin lacht höhnisch' (105). But then a dramatic reversal begins. The judge Partout pronounces his sentence, incriminating not Columbine but Harlequin, and concludes his judgment with an echo of Harlequin's own cruelty to his wife: 'Partout ... (Lacht etlichemal recht sehr höhnisch durch die Nase)' (107). From this point the roles are reversed as Columbina quickly gains the upper hand in her deceit, until at the end of the play Harlequin is made the complete fool and penitently submits to his punishment:

Harl. (Kniet vor ihr nieder, und küßt ihre Hand weinend.)

...

(Küßt den Pantoffel an ihrem Fuß, und weint.)

Similar stage directions continue to the end, requiring him to adopt the teary pose which earlier was characteristic of his wife (118f). In accepting defeat, Harlequin must also accept his subservient role and the humiliation along with it. The mimic reversal is an outward sign of his inner change.

Beyond these actions which convey in essence the course of the play, there are many other uses of stage directions which further indicate improvisational freedom. For a brief time after Partout's judgment, which concludes with his kissing Columbina before the very eyes of her husband, Harlequin and Columbina make amends, but by now clearly with the accepted understanding that she has a lover. He has lost all power and authority, even dignity, within the context of the play, so precisely at this point he escapes that sphere and turns to a new ally – his oldest and most loyal – the audience:

> *Harl.* (Küßt sie auch,) singt aber auf der Seite ad Spectatores.
> Von Herzen kan der Kuß fürwar nicht seyn. (108)

The line given here is surely only the first of a longer song, and presumably one well known to the reader and audience (a similar feature was present in the manuscript of *Das lustige Elendt*). Harlequin thus steps out of the play and meets the audience on different but mutual ground, a neutral zone familiar to and pleasurable for both.

Columbina has two arias soon afterward, but, in contrast, there is no indication that either is specifically sung to the audience. The first was likely intended to be parallel to Harlequin's above, following it almost immediately:

> Dem Himmel sey geklagt!
> Wie bin ich doch geplagt!
> Weil ich bey diesem Mann
> Nicht courtesiren kan.
> Er geht zum Bier und Wein,
> Ich soll alleine seyn.
> Nein, das geschiehet nicht,
> Weil es mein Herz nicht spricht. (weint.) (109)

The texts of this and a subsequent aria by Columbina are given in full, suggesting that they were either new to readers and audiences or at least not as well known as that of Harlequin. All of these arias were interruptions of the action and, as all song, required accompanying gestures. They are also all in effect commentaries on the action from without. The text of Columbina's song above helps to prepare us for the logic of the play's conclusion when we witness Harlequin's humiliation.

The image given of him in Columbina's aria here is one of a drunken lout who neglects his wife and thus, not surprisingly, does not enjoy her love. It is a reinforcement of Partout's judgment of Harlequin just before:

> Du hast das Weib nicht lieb,
> Die gleichwohl niemal nicht,
> Lebt wider Ehr und Pflicht;
> Drum schlage sie nicht ferner so
> Du grober Ochs in Folio! (Bedroht ihm.)
> Sonst kriegt sie gar den Zieb. (107)

This too could well have been sung, although there is no clear indication to that effect in the text. Despite the judge's own questionable character and compromised position, Partout's words contain a truth which Harlequin must acknowledge and which the audience or reader, based on the opening scene of the play, understands as well. We begin to sink into a rather murky and unpleasant thematic complex in which the traditional favourite is justifiably condemned for his cruelty and neglect – but neglect of a wife who is herself ready to deceive him, and with the very judge who pronounces sentence: a black picture of both marriage and justice. When Harlequin objects, questioning Partout's integrity, the judge just brushes him aside with the remark that the French are not so meticulous when it comes to such matters – a condemnation of his countrymen to be sure, but perhaps a wider group in the minds of the author, audience and reader; after all, the name of the judge is 'Partout'!

The judge's words here also contain an odd reference to Harlequin as 'Du grober Ochs in Folio,' meaning either 'Ochs in größtem Maße,' or perhaps again a veiled indication of the author's thoughts of this play as a published text, for the word 'Folio' is now and was then most commonly associated with a large page format. Published dramas in the eighteenth century very rarely appeared in folio (2°). They were most likely to appear in octavo (8°) or, infrequently, in quarto (4°). Conversely, manuscripts were frequently written on large sheets, which when folded over once created the folio format. This 'grober Ochs in Folio' may well be one of the many comic figures who normally never found his way past the manuscript folio sheet into publication, remaining forever undocumented, or at most sketched in a manuscript plot; in other words, the Hanswurst of the earlier decades.

The final scene of the play fixes this subtle literary undertone in an almost emblematic fashion:

(Hinten wird aufgezogen, da stellet das Theatrum ein Zimmer vor.
Harlequin sitzt in der Mitte, hat eine Crone von Hirsch-Geweyh auf dem
Kopfe. Auf jeder Seite stehet eine Wiege, von jedweder Wiege gehet ein
Band, so Harlequin auch in jeder Hand hältet, und die Kinder sachte wieget,
unter dem Wiegen singt er:)
Erschröckliche Marter! und grausame Pein!
Indem ich dem Weibe nun dienstbar muß seyn,
Ich kehre die Stube, ich wasche das Zinn,
Weil ich bey dem wiegen gedultig auch bin
    Ein Hahnrey! ein Hahnrey!
Der Rübezahl hat die Franzosen gebracht,
Die mich so tyrannisch zum Hahnrey gemacht.
Mein Weib, der Karnickel, bringt mich in das Grab,
Weil ich auf dem Haupte die Crone jetzt hab
    Als Hahnrey! als Hahnrey! (119f)

For this single concluding scene a new theatrical set is required and a
different dimension of the stage is used to present Harlequin as a living
image of the classic cuckold's appearance and pose, without dramatic
action, just his song directly to the audience. The detail with which the
author sets this conclusion through the lengthy stage direction is evidence of the importance he attached to it. Cuckold themes are a com-
monplace in comedy, as is the image of the deceived husband in cuckold's horns. The stag horns specified here draw particular attention to
the motif of sexuality, an attribute traditionally associated with the central comic figure, but here reversed to represent him as a victim of the
licentiousness of others. It is difficult to think of another work in which
this conclusion is stamped into the audience's mind with such visual
impact. Why is Harlequin reduced to such humiliation at the end? True
enough, he has been a negligent husband and a coarse partner, but that
alone would scarcely justify such a definitive image of the arch-cuckold
in the final scene. The author's awareness of readers in the Foreword,
Partout's categorization of Harlequin as a Folio fool, the powerful emblematic quality of this final scene – these elements may suggest an underlying dialectic between the non-literary and literary worlds. Based
on his character and actions, Harlequin/Hanswurst in this play represents the comic figure in decline, and with him the decline of the non-
literary work. In the final scene, the change is documented in literary
terms by means of an emblematic topos brought to life on stage; in en-
tering the new age, Harlequin/Hanswurst moves from his position of
independent sovereignty on the unpublished folio sheet and the non-
literary stage to become cuckolded by social and literary convention, a

loss of freedom which inevitably means his demise. The play carries an underlying comment on theatrical and literary evolution in the eighteenth century.

The text also has curiously insistent lighting directions throughout. After Scene I, in which Harlequin and Columbina are introduced and their relationship set, Scene II begins with the direction 'Es wird Nacht gemacht' (106), Scene IV with 'Es bleibt beständig Nacht und finster' (110), and Scene IX '... es bleibet beständig Nacht bis zum Ende des Spiels' (118). Only the first scene seems to be bright. Ostensibly the playwright wanted to project a growing atmosphere of gloom in contrast to the brightness at the play's outset. Thus the feeling of malaise begins before we sense the disturbing thematic undertones suggested by Partout's duplicity and witness Harlequin's humiliation in the final scene. With no edifying characters, an all-pervading gloom, and the fall of a theatrical favourite, we are left with a feeling of loss and unease, perhaps precisely the comment the playwright wishes to make on theatre and society in his day.

Der betrogene Alte (1747)

Despite its setting and publication (possibly fictitious) in the Netherlands, this work shows a wealth of characteristics that place it firmly within the tradition of the German Nachspiel. Harlequin is central to the action and key to the comic resolution. As in *Harlequin, der ungedultig-hernach*, he is immediately distingished from the other characters by the fact that from the outset his name is printed in Roman type, the others and the rest of the text in *Fraktur*. It is he who suggests the possibility of a play-within-a-play which provides both a contemporary commentary on the siege of Bergen op Zoom and a theatrical vehicle to separate the stodgy Truglieb from Charlotte. It is he, too, who is the focus of the internal play. In effect, then, Harlequin plays two roles, within the outer framework, already a theatrical fiction, and within it in the artificial world of the play-within-a-play, so that a constant ironical interplay between the two levels of reality exists. This is deepened by the active involvement of the audience who were likely aware of the historical facts on which the action is based, a third level, onto which the other two are projected. Historically, blame for the fall of the Dutch town Bergen op Zoom after the siege of 1747 was laid at the feet of eighty-six-year-old General Isaac Kock Baron Cronström, and his parallel in this Nachspiel is the 'Alte' of its title, old Saur-Aug.

Early in the work Harlequin establishes his first direct contact with the audience through the remark '*ad spect.* Wenn nichts dazwischen kommt' (83), an ironic comment on Charlotte's and her father's claims of honour. The stage direction '*ad spect.*' makes clear from the start what licence the author intended his comic figure to enjoy and sets up a direct avenue of communication between Harlequin and the audience beyond that understood by the other characters in the play, and one which makes the audience omnipotent viewing partners. Socially and politically, the audience was likely aware of the military siege on which the play is based, so all references to that event were understood in one sense as direct contemporary comment. But we can judge something of the personal character of this audience by the way in which most of the comment is communicated, for the overriding parallel between the military siege and the winning of Charlotte lays every allusion open to sexual double entendre. Just after Harlequin has made his initial comment '*ad spect.,*' Charlotte draws this parallel between the allegorized city under siege and herself: 'Wie muß denn die Vestung by Dero Jungfer Tochter aussehen, Denn ich glaube, daß sie nicht anders, als die Meinige gebauet ist' (84). What would the men in the audience be thinking of at this point? No doubt their fantasy would be further titillated by Harlequin's retort: 'Mademoiselle. Sie werden doch kein so starckes Kyck in de Pott haben, als Berg op Zoom,' to which this time Charlotte responds '*ad spect.*' 'Es liegt so hoch, und so tief, wie das Meinige' (85). This is a wonderfully clever little word-play involving the phrase 'Kyck in de Pott,' and the reality of the Bergen op Zoom siege and Charlotte herself. With it, the intimacy between audience and Harlequin has now been extended to include Charlotte. We must wonder at this point whether this is really Harlequin's traditional partner Columbina renamed, and further, how she appeared on stage. It is likely that Harlequin was wearing his traditional bright chequered costume and possible from Charlotte's role that she could be readily identified through a Columbina costume (as in *Der falsche Verdacht*, p 80). Charlotte's reference to Kyck in de Pott recalls the title-page of the 1747 edition which records this town as its place of publication. But there is no such place – it is a deliberate fiction. 'Kyck in de Pott' (or 'Kijk-in-de-pot') is Dutch for 'Look in the pot!' or 'See for yourself!' so the title-page begins a deliberate deceit of unobservant readers while alerting others to the play's double entendres. Its admonition 'Look for yourself!' tells us to be on guard for double meanings, and these apply not only to the social and political events surrounding the siege of Bergen op Zoom. When Harlequin uses the Dutch words in direct conjunction with the banter about Charlotte's body parts ('sie werden doch kein so starckes Kyck in de Pott haben, als Berg op Zoom'), her rejoinder, 'Es liegt so hoch, und so tief, wie das Meinige,' adds a distinctly sexual dimension to the ambivalent Dutch place-name. It must have elicited a howl of delight from the men in the audience.

With the tone of sexual innuendo set, one must suspect that statements such as the following were also loaded with double meaning: *'Harl.*[to Charl.]: O Schatz! ich mach dich sodann zum Marschall bey meiner ganzen Armee, und will dir die schönste Canone zum Präsent geben' (87). As husband and wife with their little clan of children in tow, Harlequin and Charlotte become General and Field Marshall leading their troops into battle. Surely the potency of the 'Canone' on the battlefield has something to do with Harlequin's own reproductive weapon – after all, Charlotte's 'Vestung' had been quite specifically located just moments earlier. Lines like this simply beg us to imagine the speaker's concurrent gestures on stage.

The siege is re-enacted in the play-within-a-play; Truglieb moves to defend Jungfer Wahr-Ehr, taking up a protective position in front; Harlequin uses the crucial moment again to turn *'ad spect.'* with 'Dieser machts recht, jetzt hat er sie hinten, was wirds geben, wenn er sie erst vornher bekommt' (89). The answer no doubt flew through the active imagination of every licentious audience member (and reader).

The entire siege scene requires broad use of improvised gesture and mime play. We are told in a general stage direction, set off by indentation from the rest of the text, that 'Der Streit währet annoch, biß *Harlequin* und Spitz-Sinn den verstellten Ausreiß nehmen [die Flucht ergreifen]. Charlotte laufft mit Ihnen' (89). We cannot know exactly how this scene was played or for how long, but the stage direction tells us that it was certainly extemporized. This leads us to suspect that much more improvised play took place in other parts of the work. Through this major extemporized scene, the comedy dissolves into its conclusion; the play-within-a-play is ended, the fiction on stage reverts to the first level with old Saur-Aug realizing suddenly that he has been duped, with the lovers Truglieb and Wahr-Ehr fittingly united, and with Harlequin and Charlotte escaping both realms. To summarize the action's meaning:

Harl. guckt hinter den Tapeten hervor, und sticht mit dem Finger auf Sauer-Aug den Gecken. Wie steht's nun, ist die Jungfer nun doch so rein und unüberwindlich?

...

*Charl.*So wird man von der Knechtschafft frey,
Harl. und bleibt dem Rechten aufgehoben.
Der wenn das *Fas* nicht helffen kan,
durchs *Nefas* alles wohlgethan. (90)

Once they have escaped the action on stage, Harlequin, and presumably Charlotte beside him, confirm their position as outsiders by speaking from the other side of a curtain ('hinter den Tapeten'), from there combining ironic word and rude gesture to make final pronouncement on old Saur-Aug and his pretence of morality. His daughter, the test of his principles, has fallen in the siege. Saur-Aug is an archetypical representative of false morality, of the old and rigid, of conservative convention and the status quo. The final rhymed couplets lift the comment about him to the level of a general social statement. Liberation from 'Knechtschafft' means not just the freeing of citizens in the military siege of Bergen op Zoom, but also the release of a young woman from her domineering parent, and a victory over his false morality and social conservatism. The final juxtaposition of 'Fas' and 'Nefas,' or 'what is permitted' and 'what is not,' tells us that it is not through legitimate means that the victory is won, but through illegitimacy, which is an affront to the rules of society. As final commentator on the action, Harlequin here performs a function that had been Hanswurst's in the Nachspiel since the beginning of the century.

Der bestrafte Hochmuth oder Johann Scherenschleifer (1751)

While the text of this work does not readily reveal the wealth of traditional Nachspiel elements evident in the previous three, the character of Johann, the play's continuing popularity for several decades, and its numerous printings make it worthy of attention. Something in it obviously caught the lasting fancy of theatre-goers at the time, which is evidenced by the play's repeated regeneration through revision and adaption, under either of its two titles, even becoming a ballet, as for example in Ackermann's repertoire. The latter alone suggests its inherent mimic qualities and a central theme and plot development that could be comprehended and enjoyed even without dialogue.

The play's lasting popularity is the result of this mimic potential as well as of an undercurrent of contemporary satire. The plot is simple: a young woman from the wealthy bourgeois class is redressed for her vanity and pretentious aspirations to join the nobility – a moral lesson in modesty on the one hand, a social one on the other. Such thematics can be found in dozens of works from the period and could not in themselves have given this one its continuing attraction. While Lotte is put in her place, that place is beside Leander, a wealthy young businessman, who is portrayed entirely in a positive light. Lotte's folly is an indication of social aberration, but when she gratefully accepts Leander in the end, there is no sense of having lost something valuable in failing to marry into nobility – rather, her recognition of the advantage of identifying with the wealthy bourgeoisie is a confirmation of the growing superiority of this class. The work thus stands as an early illustration of the transfer of power from upper to middle class which characterized social developments in the latter decades of the century.

Johann is identified simply as 'ein loser Vogel,' hence belonging to no identifiable social group and standing outside the bounds of class identification. This is important, for in a play whose essence denies the worth of the noble class in favour of the wealthy bourgeoisie, use of Johann as the engineer of the action avoids direct class conflict while the bourgeoisie reaps the benefits of Johann's role. His position as a social non-entity who satirizes character types and conventions is common to the function of the traditional comic figure, as is his principal means to fulfil this function. In the pivotal sixth and seventh scenes of the play he appears 'in gräflicher Kleidung, nebst einem Laufer' and plays the role so convincingly that both Anselmo and Lotte are fooled into accepting a marriage contract. These scenes contain a noticeable wealth of stage directions which enhance the basic comic devices of disguise and mistaken identity. Johann uses frequent asides, speaking 'heimlich,' which can only mean that he shares his observations on the action with the audience. He is playing a three-dimensional role now, the count, Scherenschleifer, and commentator on the other characters in covert coalition with the audience, as here:

> (heimlich) Entsetzlich frecher Stolz! Ja, Schöne, es ist wahr,
> Sie sind das Meisterstück, das die Natur gebahr. (13)

Although there is insufficient indication in the text to say exactly how Johann played the role as count, the impersonation obviously called for extensive improvised mime play, and one suspects from the work's popularity that a good deal of parody on affected courtly manners was included. In sum, despite his name, Johann plays in effect the same role as a Hanswurst or Harlequin comic figure. We are witnessing an absorption of those characters into persons bearing different names.

Die Bauern vom Stande (1756)

Like the former, this work contains a steady undertone of social commentary, beginning with the title which expresses a contradiction in social terms and draws attention to class divisions. The unreal world of comedy can sometimes accomplish what is impossible in contemporary society: the gentleman Erast remains faithful to Lucinde even after she loses social status; both they and Maturin/Collette are then moved to marry for love, without consideration for social position. A liberal attitude prevails, and in the course of the work frequent aim is taken at the insincerity and pretension of the Parisian upper crust. But the work is by no means revolutionary in spirit, for only through the discovery that Maturin is a man of means is his marriage with Collette sanctioned, a reinforcement of the class-conscious conservatism represented by her father Orontes.

The work was published in German almost thirty years after its original, which invites the assumption that such thematics were of interest in Germany about one generation later than in France. Its subtitle informs us that it is 'Aus dem Französischen,' which suggests translation rather than adaptation of Romagnesi/Biancolelli's *Les paysans de qualité*. This suggestion of direct translation raises a general question with regard to all Nachspiele based on, translated, or adapted from French models. Even in a straight translation, differences always emerge, and in cases of adaptation there can be enormous adjustments made to the original. Only by comparing translation or adaptation with its source can we fully see what elements were particularly important for the German adapter of the work.

The main link in this play with the Nachspiel tradition is through the figure of Trivelin. He is throughout an entertaining and impudent comic servant who reminds us often of the *lustige Person*. In fact, in the French original this character is named 'Arlequin.' The change of name to Trivelin is the only significant variation among the personae and a reflection of the German adapter's awareness of the sensitivity toward comic prototypes such as Hanswurst and Harlekin by mid-century. Otherwise Trivelin and Arlequin are very much alike. The German work reduces the original's nineteen scenes to sixteen, omitting the Prologue and closing 'Divertissement' in which dancers and musicians perform, as well as the accompanying 'Vaudeville' which in the original consisted of several characters, including Arlequin, singing verses which summarize and expound upon the action. Arlequin's verses there read

> Nous ne manquons point d'Auteurs
> Leur veine est fertile,
> Mais il est des connoisseurs
> Qui frondent leur style;
> Aux écrits qu' Apollon dément
> Où livre-t-on la guerre,
> Où décide-t'on sainement?
> C'est dans le parterre.
> (Romagnesi/Biancolleli, *Les paysans* ...
> [Paris: Briasson, 1729], p 57)

Here, ultimate authority for the judgment of theatrical works is placed in the hands of the audience as opposed to the literary critics – an affirmation of the primacy of performance over text.

Both versions are rich in stage directions requiring gestures and mimed actions from several characters, but most extensively in a single scene involving Arlequin/Trivelin in which the comic character has the farmer remove his boots:

> (Trivelin treibt allerhand Possen mit dem Bauer, um sich die Stiefeln ausziehen zu lassen, der endlich nach einem großen Theaterspiele zu Ende kommt …)
>
> …
>
> (Er springt und hüpfet, hebt dem Bauer Stöße mit dem Fuße, der endlich nach den Possen des Trivelins abgeht.) (29)

The same scene in the original is as follows:

> Arlequin fait des lazis avec le Paysan pour faire tirer les bottes, qui en vient à bout après un grand jeu de Théatre; quand Arlequin est débotté il saute de joie, embrasse le Paysan et son Maître.
>
> …
>
> Il saute, donne des coups de pié au Paysan, qui s'en va après les lazis d'Arlequin. (*Les paysans*, 40)

The passages are very close, both suggesting a lively scene which demands considerable extemporized pantomime by Arlequin/Trivelin and includes the familiar motif of physical beating so common in the traditional Nachspiel. This freedom to improvise, along with his generally impertinent behaviour, makes Trivelin a character akin to German comic figures in the early century, but without the same degree of crudity or nominal identification with a comic type, no doubt more of a tactical decision on the part of the author than anything else. Instead, Trivelin appears simply in the servant role, a type that became increasingly important toward the end of the century as Hanswurst and Harlekin were gradually forced out of the limelight, if only in name.

Die neueste Verheyrathung (1759)

The list of personae in this work sets up an immediate connection to the comic tradition. Pantalon and Arlequin are central, all others of secondary importance. Pantalon (Pantalone) was a core character in the *commedia dell'arte* ensemble. He was a Venetian merchant, respectable, and dignified, and characteristically interested in money and financial advantage. Sometimes portrayed as sickly, with a penchant for complaining of his ills, he is recognizable in pictures from his pose, bent forward, hand resting on his hip, an attempt at elegance. Despite his years, Pantalone is quick to snatch at romance, and is then carefree, even careless in conduct, which results in his being vulnerable to the deceit of younger women and their lovers. He is sometimes portrayed as a father who carefully and suspiciously guards his nubile daughter, or who tries to exert authority over his son, only to be outwitted by both (see Riha, 28f). It is this last characteristic that is evident in the Nachspiel at hand.

The play begins, as did *Harlequin, der ungedultig-hernach*, with Arlequin at the focus:

> Pantalon (schläget den Arlequin hinter der Scene und unter währenden
> Schlagen kommen sie heraus ... und Pantalon sagt:)
> He du Hauß-Zucht-und Ehebestia! du ungerathener Sohn ... (42)

Immediately a coarse tone prevails and our sympathies are drawn to the object of the abuse, Arlequin. This tumultuous start sets the mood of a work rooted in the physical as opposed to the intellectual sphere. Soon after, in conversation with his father, Arlequin describes his lot in these terms: 'Hört nur, wenn ich nun so am Feuerheerd stunde, und über mein schlecht Abendbrodt seufzte (denn ihr wißt wohl, daß ich ein großer Liebhaber von Fressen bin) so sahe ich von ohngefehr in die Höhe, und da wurde ich gewahr, daß in der Feuermauer viele Degenscheiden hingen, aus Hunger langte ich eine herunter, und fraß solche mit dem größten Appetit auf' (43). His foremost concern is his belly and how to fill it, just like his cousin Hanswurst, whose name itself is half sausage. But to whom is the text in parenthesis directed? The party to whom Arlequin's gluttonous tendencies are familiar indeed – the audience. This first aside in the play rekindles Arlequin's intimacy with them and sets up his dual role as player and commentator on the work. Further culinary humour follows soon after, reinforcing his intense physicality once again. He describes his meals with his past master as

> Eine Wassersuppe und Sallat um 10 Uhr,
> Eine Wassersuppe und Sallat um 12 Uhr,
> Eine Wassersuppe und Sallat um 2 Uhr,
> Eine Wassersuppe und Sallat um 4 Uhr,
> Eine Wassersuppe und Sallat um 6 Uhr,
> Eine Wassersuppe und Sallat und so
> währet es bis in die Nacht hinein, daß ich endlich bald selbst zu einen Sallat
> geworden wäre. (45)

The passage is both a call for sympathy for this poor creature who we all know must have his belly filled and an exaggerated repetition which by its very monotony on the printed page suggests that it was intended to be accompanied by a generous portion of gesture and mimicry for full effect. This grounding of Arlequin's character in the physical world is both traditional and important for the work at hand.

The crux of the plot is Pantalon's attempt to get his son a job, the first attempt a physical occupation with the shoemaker, the second an intellectual one with the schoolmaster. In each Arlequin shows himself as absolutely incapable or doltish, but each time we are left with the impression that his failure is elected rather than inevitable. His attraction to the physical world extends only as far as what is necessary to satisfy his own bodily needs for the moment; he is aware of the advantage of a position that would ensure comfort in the long term – this is why he eventually seeks a wife to support him – but not at the cost of actual labour. A position in the intellectual sphere is absolutely out of the question for it has nothing whatever to do with his natural inclinations.

The second scene depicts Arlequin's trial with the shoemaker Peter as he drinks and sings 'valalteria' at his tasks, the topos of the simple-minded, happy, and devoted craftsman. Arlequin's actions throughout the scene consist of mimicking the master, but in doing so he carries out a selective process, imitating precisely and with delight the actions that appeal to him (the song 'valalteria' which he repeats throughout the scene, his nips at the bottle), but failing miserably to emulate the master in anything to do with the actual trade of shoemaking. The first stage of the lesson ends abruptly with '(er schmeist den Vater und Petern zugleich übern Haufen und wie sie liegen spricht er: hast du nicht gesehen?)' (47). 'Hast du nicht gesehen' is a precise parroting of what Peter has been saying all along during the instruction period. The second try starts off better: 'Arlequin (arbeitet ordentlich, trinkt aber sehr fleißig dazu und singt *valalteralt)*' (48). Briefly, Arlequin seems to be an acceptable apprentice, but soon makes it quite clear that he has no intention of harnessing himself to something so practical and to so much work.

At this point he decides to auction himself off as a husband (Scene 4), standing centre stage and calling for bids. Liesgen, we are told, '(steht auf dem Parterre und ruft) Schuster-Liesgen will dich haben' (50). Her location while making this bid is significant. She clearly takes up a position off-stage on the parterre of the theatre, among the audience; in other words, she becomes one of them. As in *Harlequin der ungedultig-hernach*, Arlequin's escape from the unpleasantness of the fictionalized action in which he finds himself trapped on stage is made possible once again by his oldest and most sympathetic ally, the audience itself, and at the same time the play gains a dimension that it did not have before. From the fairly meagre textual account of this scene, it is difficult to say just how it was played, but one would suspect that the auction took some time, during which Arlequin must have tried his best to cajole the audience into supporting him and bidding for his services. How successful he was would depend on his talent for extemporized communication with the bidders, but at best he would have evoked from them some verbal response to his offer before the bidding finally closed with Liesgen's cry.

Pantalon's final attempt to engage his son in a productive occupation follows and takes up the remainder of the play. Scene 5: '(Stellt erstlich den Schulmeister mit seiner Schule vor, welche nach Belieben *extemp.* können.)' (51). The extemporization only hinted at in earlier scenes now takes over the play with more characters enjoying absolute freedom on stage in a scene that requires them to take matters completely into their own hands. Only when they are thoroughly spent does the dialogue begin with Arlequin assuming a role as pompous superior. This character change requires its own new set of physical and linguistic mannerisms, in other words, a harlequin metamorphosis. With such remarks as 'Point de tout, mein hochgeehrtester Herr Schulmajor' (52), Arlequin uses a combination of linguistic inaccuracy (correctly 'Pas du tout ... Schulmeister') and probably physical gestures to satirize the affected gentleman scholar. He is then put to a test of knowledge in which he reveals profound ignorance while employing such comic devices as parrot-like repetition of questions, verbal misunderstandings, and hidden prompting from Liesgen, all of which are accompanied by stage directions requiring movement and gesture. Yet despite his obvious incompetence the candidate gets the job when the licentious schoolmaster discovers that Liesgen, one of his favourite pupils in more senses than one, is Arlequin's partner: 'Da hat er meine Hand, er soll den Dienst haben, gehe er nur geschwind in die Schule, ich will unterdessen die Frau Liebste ein wenig spazieren führen. (gehn ab.)' (56). In the end it is not knowledge or ability that wins Arlequin the position, it is the sexual attraction of the schoolmaster to Liesgen, a physical primacy which offsets all thoughts of higher matters.

From this point on the work dissolves rapidly into completely extemporized mayhem. The entire following scene (11) appears in the text thus: 'Arlequin (mit den Schuljungen treibt allerhand Possen),' followed by Scene 12, the last, again quoted in its entirety:

Schulmeister. Ist das Respect vor einen Unter-Schulmeister, daß er mit den Jungens solche Possen treibt, fort ihr Jungens, weil sich dieser Kerl so schlecht aufzuführen weiß, so prügelt ihn selbst zur Schule hinaus. (Sie prügeln sich einander herum, und ziehen zu.) (56)

The curtain closes on a scene of utter disorder and we are left asking what we should make of it all. In effect we have seen a failed attempt to integrate Arlequin into structured, practical, productive society which would require him to deny his essential nature, his exclusive concern for his immediate well-being, his abandonment to the pleasure of the moment, and refusal to become involved in anything structured by convention. The key to his person is freedom from all of this, and this freedom he has no intention of giving up. The work is indeed a raucous comedy, but beneath the surface it calls into question the values and structures of the society in which it is played – the prototypical happy shoemaker, the respected schoolmaster, the gentleman scholar, the woman married off to the highest bidder – and does so with characters and comic techniques that had been an essential part of the Nachspiel tradition since the beginning of the century.

Conclusion

Chapter 4 concluded with two central questions: What traditional Nachspiel elements are evident in each of the representative works to be analysed in detail? To what extent are these elements as strongly represented in the later group (after 1770) as in the earlier one? We can now begin to answer these questions. The six works just discussed show strong evidence of traditional Nachspiel elements. The main evidence is their inclusion of a central comic figure: four of them star Harlequin by name, the other two have similar persons under the names Johann and Trivelin. All of these comic figures have considerable licence to extemporize beyond the text, and are thereby responsible for much of the comic effect. Four of these six Nachspiele are also connected to a previous work, which is another characteristic of the early Nachspiel before 1770. Beyond this, three of the works have definite signs of serious thematics below the surface, but this characteristic on the whole is clearly secondary to the main purpose of entertainment and good fun. We move now to the second group, those appearing after 1770, which will provide the remaining answers.

The Nachspiel as Text after 1770

Krispin der geplagte Lehenbediente [1770]

As it is bound in a volume containing an unrelated selection of works with the title-page 'Deutsche Schaubühne, 124. Theil' and no other information, this work is difficult to date precisely. Meyer's *Bibliographia* lists the publication date of the collection from 1770 through the end of the century. The play's content provides no specific hints for dating, although its language suggests strongly that it is Viennese. We know further from analysis of the Viennese repertoires that Krispin became the leading comic figure in the Theater in der Leopoldstadt by the eighties, appearing on stage in almost every program.

The plot is a facile depiction of Krispin's brief attempt to serve two masters at once. He is the focus of every scene, producing a *Bravourstück* for this comic favourite. From the beginning, the physical set lays the groundwork for the comic situation and subsequent action: 'Das Theater stellet einen Wirtshaussaal vor, worinnen auf beyden Seiten zwey Nebenzimmer sind' (3). Krispin uses this spatial arrangement to induce a freewheeling, tumultuous action through the familiar slapstick routine of rushing in and out of doors, from one side to the other, hither and yon, pausing only on the neutral centre stage in between to gather his wits and consult with the audience. It is a set which demands rapid movement, hence offering great potential for the comic figure to extemporize and fully exploit the vehicles of gesture and mime. The play's effectiveness depends upon his actions in this frantic situation.

Having accepted the first position as servant to Scharffhau, then the second with Hanenkamp, Krispin recognizes at once his predicament

and foresees trouble: '[to Hanenkamp] Gut! Ihro Gnaden; (beyseit) das
würde jetzt ein verfluchter Streich seyn, wann die zwey Herrn etwan
just zugleich Speisen, Aufstehn und Schlafengehn thäten; ich wüßte mir
nicht zu helfen; hm! probieren will ichs doch, der G'späß ist mir mein
Lebtag nicht geschehen' (9f). This speech has the effect of a starter's gun
for the mad race to follow. It is significant that the words sealing the
impossible deal, 'Gut! Ihro Gnaden,' are followed immediately by
Krispin's '(beyseit)' and a statement of the predicament. Of course the
aside is meant for the audience; it acknowledges them as the only ones
besides the speaker who are fully aware of what is likely to happen,
and it serves as an invitation for them to join in the fun. The words
'verfluchter Streich' and 'G'späß' are vocabulary often used to signal
extemporized actions on the Viennese stage; the same terms are used
for example in *Der falsche Verdacht*.

So the race begins with Krispin on the track and the audience cheer-
ing him on. Called now by Scharffhau, Krispin responds: 'Ihro Gnaden,
ich werde gleich den Tisch decken, und mich zum Aufwarten an-
schicken. (beyseit) Wenn nur jetzt der Baron Hanenkamp ausbliebe, bis
der Baron Scharffhau gespeist hat, sonst wüßte ich wahrhaftig nicht,
wie ich zurecht käme – Fickerment! hier kömmt er just, das ist jetzt ein
verfluchter Streich' (10). The aside here reinforces Krispin's special
relationship with the audience, occurring as before in conjunction with
a perceived crisis. His repetition of the phrase 'verfluchter Streich' continues the notion of extemporized play, this time with an added dash of
spice through the exclamation 'Fickerment!' which in general connotation is equivalent to 'Sackerment!' or 'Sapperment!' but which had also
carried an obscene connotation since the sixteenth century (Grimm; as
today's 'ficken').

As suppertime approaches, tension mounts along with the frequency
of Krispin's consultations with the audience. When both masters suddenly call for their dinners at the same time, Krispin asks the audience
how on earth he will manage, in effect voicing their very thoughts, and
his actions '(lacht: hä! – hä! – hä! –)' (11) point to much more than just a
verbal outburst. If it were only that, why does it not appear as text instead of as a stage direction? 'Ha! – ha! – ha!' was a common signal for
extemporization. Krispin must now get down to serious business and
the rest of the play is a veritable whirlwind of action. There are constant
shouts from both sides for new courses, objections about the slow service, with Krispin dashing to and fro until finally

> (währenden Auftragen fällt Krispin nieder, wirft den Braten, samt Schüssel
> auf die Seite, klaubt ihn wieder in die Schüssel, und trägt ihn auf.)

Scharff. Krispin! den Sallat!
Krisp. Gleich, Ihro Gnaden! (trägt ihn auf, und kost vorhero davon.) (13f)

The scene offers fertile ground for improvisation with a culinary focus, mixing the comic figure's traditional love for food with an age-old restaurant gag. To the audience's delight, 'Ihro Gnaden' is forced to eat food from the floor, sampled in advance by his servant.

With dinner miraculously survived, Krispin must now perform other tasks, all the while emitting a steady stream of asides to his allies in the parterre. Simultaneous commands from his masters to clean the dust from their uniforms are met dutifully with

Gleich, Ihro Gnaden! (trägt eben das Kleid über dem Arm hangend zum Ausstauben heraus.)
(Krispin, welche von beyden Kleidern, wegen des Ausstäuben die Taschen ausräumt, und denn die Kleider ausstäubt, verwechselt die aus den Taschen geräumten Stücke.)
...
(steckt die Sachen so jenen zugehören, in des einen, und diesen seine verkehrt in des andern Tasche, und trägt die Kleider hinein). (15)

Again we witness a totally extemporized scene with only a scenario for structure, a mimic solo for Krispin. With the various activities of beating the coats (would he pretend to be beating his masters?), emptying and refilling the pockets (would he find titillating or incriminating articles to hold up to the audience?), he could make the solo last as long as he wished. The very act of going through someone's pockets and examining the contents with others is a mischievous business in itself, always with the potential to produce insights into the owner's character which he would much prefer undisclosed. After his duplicity has been discovered, Krispin turns as a penitent for the last time to the audience (with the specific stage direction 'Ad Auditorium'). He confesses his error, promises never to serve two masters again, and in a final gesture '(beugt sich und gehet ab)' (19), just as many comic figures before him. With this he takes official leave from those for whom, and with whom, he has played.

The text of this work is a mere nineteen pages, but it would be interesting to know just how long it took to perform. The spoken dialogue would certainly comprise the lesser part, the extemporized sections, largely without words, holding the upper hand by far. Most of the time Krispin is alone on stage, his masters appearing infrequently, and after the early scenes exclusively as voices from their separate rooms until the end when they reprimand him and magnanimously spare punishment. The work is thus essentially non-literary, a tour de force of extemporization for Krispin and a special treat for his doting audience. Opportunity for social commentary is also present, as in the scene of the pockets, but the magnanimity of both barons at the end suggests that any such commentary on the upper class was done in good fun without the bitterness or barbs that sometimes marked it in other works, for example *Das lustige Elendt*, also a Viennese product. Krispin was a character loved by all, not just a surrogate social critic for those who felt mistreated. He represents in this work, as he did in many others, pure joy in theatrical play, the primary source of enjoyment for audiences everywhere.

Die Melonen (1771)

Reading *Die Melonen*, one feels cast back to an era when theatre was at its crudest. The theme of a poor couple fantasizing about how they can make a fortune, very much limited in their vision by general misery and ignorance, is not original and had its voice in other eighteenth-century plays (viz. Johann Christian Krüger's *Herzog Michel*). It can be grounds for delightful fantasy, but not in this case. Any imagined release gained by Lise and Michel from their undesirable circumstances is overwhelmed by the crude brutality that mars their relationship. This is conveyed both through Michel's harsh language, and above all through his physical treatment of his wife, as indicated in the frequent stage directions. After a brief flight of fantasy together with Lise, Michel 'schlägt sie; der Nachbar will sie aus einander bringen, und bekommt einen Schlag ... Er schlägt sie; der Nachbar läuft davon' (83). This is followed soon after by Michel's second attack: 'Er wirft ihr die Schüssel an den Kopf' (85); and he continues to berate Lise as she lies prostrate before him, finally adding the *coup de grâce*: 'Er gibt ihr Stockschläge' (86).

On the basis of the text and Lise's character, it is hard for the reader to understand how Lise could have been thought to 'deserve' such punishment, and it is painful to imagine its depiction on stage. Naturally we expect Michel to receive some sort of well-deserved retribution, but this never happens. The work concludes with a connubial duet introduced by Michel directly 'an das Parterre':

Michel. Geplagte Männer, wollt ihr wissen,
      Was böse Weiber mürbe macht?
      Der Stock. Den brauchet Tag und Nacht!
   Sie werden endlich schweigen müssen.

Lise.   Wie sind wir Weiber zu beklagen!
             Der beste Mann
             Ist ein Tyrann;
             Sehn wir ihn einmal sauer an:
             So werden wir halb todt geschlagen.
Michel. Dir will ich deine Pflicht schon zeigen.
             Willst du in meiner Gnade stehn,
             Mit ganzer Haut zu Bette gehn:
             Was mußt du thun?
Lise.   Ach leider! schweigen. (86)

Justified and apparently harmless beatings had long been part of the comic genre. But just how would a contemporary audience react to the events portrayed here, which seem nothing more than the cruelty of a raging spouse against his defenceless partner? The vision of a better life for both is trodden to the ground with Lise and long forgotten by the end of the play. Michel's song, directed at the audience, and Lise's passive support of his self-asserted authority suggest that the song fell on receptive ears, for similar songs about the necessity for men to subjugate their wives were well known to audiences of the era (see, for example, the conclusion to *Eurydice*). But in other examples of this topos, the atmosphere is one of playful rivalry between the sexes and a vindication or reversal occurs (as in *Harlequin der ungedultig-hernach*), or there is an attempt at a balance between guilt and punishment. While such is more palatable, the underlying notion of female subjugation still grates on modern readers. Even in an age when suppression of women was very much part of the social structure, it is hard to accept this work as appealing to audiences of the day, for the same audiences were witness to more frequent and popular contemporary works which took the theme of women's rights seriously and depicted women as strong characters who act independently, or in fact control their partners, as in the Nachspiele *Friederike von Rosenhayn* (1783), 3.13.33 (1789), or C.F. Weiße's *Amalia* (1765) and Lessing's *Minna von Barnhelm* (1767). One explanation for the tonal and thematic inconsistency with its age is the fact that *Die Melonen* really had little connection with the German tradition. It is not only a very close adaptation of Linguet's *Intermède des melons et de la femme têtue* (published 1770), but that work itself is a translation of the Spanish *Entremes del melonar y la respondona*. The freedom to extemporize and the motif of beating are nevertheless integral to this work and set it within the Nachspiel tradition; but it lacks any of the merriment characteristic of the genre.

Die Aussteuer (1778)

The thematic substance of this work had been the subject of dramatic treatment from Roman times to the eighteenth century when Christian Friedrich Schwan published this version 'Nach dem Französischen einer noch ungedruckten Operette.' In 1774 J.M.R. Lenz had published Plautus's dramatization of the theme in *Lustspiele nach dem Plautus fürs deutsche Theater* (Frankfurt and Leipzig) and Iffland's later five-act *Aussteuer* of 1796 enjoyed immense popularity. Schwan's source, according to a handwritten entry in the copy examined, was Joseph Fiévée, but despite Schwan's subtitle the French writer never did publish an operetta on this theme. He did, however, author the short novel *La dot de Suzette*, but not until 1798. Evidence of Schwan's source thus remains inconclusive.

Two principal elements of the Nachspiel make it so effective and no doubt led to its contemporary popularity: witty dialogue and the wealth of gestures, extemporization, and pantomimic activity. Unlike any of the Nachspiele discussed to this point, this one rests as much on the dialogue as on physical movement, and it has no character who could be seen as central or a veiled successor of the *komische Figur*. It represents a higher level of dramatic sophistication than we have seen before.

The first half of the work relies on dialogue, but this is reversed after the mid-point where we find this general parenthetical direction for Margrethe: '(Die Alte muß ihre ganze Rolle mit vieler scheinbaren Unruhe spielen, als ob sie weder Zeit noch Geduld habe.)' (23). Then, in the key Scene 8 in which Sußchen and Jacob meet with the Amtmann and hear that they must sleep together, we read: '(Jacob und Sußchen müssen die ganze Scene hindurch eine gute Pantomime spielen.)' (33). These are in fact instructions to the play's director rather than the actors, suggesting that the author assumed a director's hand for production, expecting co-operation between the actors and him to produce the desired effect. Such general stage directions reflect a change in the way plays were produced after about 1770 when standing theatres became a more formal focus of dramatic activity.

The play also uses stage directions requiring much more characterization than in earlier works. Of Margrethe we are told: '(Sie läuft dem Amtmann entgegen und scheint in der Ferne mit ihm zu sprechen, nachdem sie viele lächerliche Vorbeugungen gemacht.)' (31). Similarly, Michel, when trying to impress the Amtmann and gain personal advantage, '(macht allerhand lächerliche Krazfüße' (48). Similar gestures were common in earlier Nachspiele, most frequently used by a central comic character to parody a person of authority or higher class, but now the actors use the gestures to make *themselves* look ridiculous, to define their own characters, an indication of growing attention to acting technique.

There is also much opportunity for gestural communication between characters as a complement to the dialogue. These gestures convey secret meanings shared only by those involved, and, of course, the audience. When Margrethe describes the marital plans for her daughter, Sußchen surreptitiously communicates her own opinion to her sweetheart: '(giebt durch Zeichen dem Jacob ihr Misvergnügen zu verstehen)' (23), a mode of communication which probably reached its height as Jacob and Sußchen prepared to bed down. Gestural language is also used by the less positive characters, as when Margrethe unhappily accepts the Amtmann's arrangement and '(... drückt durch ihre Gebehrden ihren äussersten Unwillen aus)' (41), the expression serving as a silent communication to the audience more than anyone else.

The play's conclusion underscores the importance of motion and position when, amid rapid witty dialogue, Margrethe and Rosine rush to protect their respective interests: '(die eine ergreift die rechte, die andere die linke Hand des Amtmanns und schreien beide zugleich.)' (51). This concluding image summarizes the theme of the play in physical terms: a love conflict between old and young. The work has developed from dialogue-based action at the start through increasing dependence on non-verbal communication to a conclusion stated by concrete visual means.

Die Aussteuer depends as heavily on gestures, mime, and extemporization as do many of the works previously discussed, but it shows a mixture of these devices with clever language to an extent not seen until now. It signals a new level in the sophistication of theatrical performance, but one which nevertheless still relies on techniques and devices important to the Nachspiel since the beginning of the century.

Die beiden Billets (1783)

This was beyond doubt the most popular Nachspiel published in the eighteenth century. There are hundreds of documented performances in Cologne, Frankfurt, Munich, Weimar, Vienna, and many other centres from as early as 1783 until far into the nineteenth century, and the play spawned a number of published continuations (*Der Stammbaum*, 1791; *Das Bauerngut*, 1798; and Goethe's *Der Bürgergeneral*, 1793).

Only twenty-seven pages of text, with a tiny cast of three and the simplest of plots, this work shows better than any other the lasting comic potential of certain devices and situations when they are well employed. As the subtitle indicates, *Die beiden Billets* was adapted from the French, which requires us to keep in mind the extent to which the play was a translation or an adaptation of Florian's original *Les deux billets*.

The play begins thus: 'Gürge (allein: springt hervor).' The opening is an immediate signal to the audience about the heritage of this character. Gürge does not just appear, he jumps out onto the stage, emitting a sudden energy that sets the rapidly paced work in motion. This opening recalls Joseph von Kurz/Bernardon's custom of making his grand entrance alone, immediately setting a tone of intimacy with the audience and extemporized play. It was common for central comic figures to enter first, and with a flurry, a convention appropriate in view of their primary importance. Suspicions about Gürge's heritage are reinforced by Florian's original. Here the main character is, as we might by now expect, Arlequin, his female counterpart Argentine instead of Heyne's Rösgen, his adversary the traditional rival Scapin instead of Schnapps. The characters are Germanized – Arlequin in name no longer acceptable to theatre reformers – but despite the change it is clear from the start where Gürge's roots lie. *Die beiden Billets* is founded on Florian's work, but is an adaptation rather than a translation, the differences extending to aspects of the structure (eleven scenes in *Billets* instead of twelve, for example) as well as to the content and theatrical devices used.

Both works contain a wealth of stage directions of several types which are applied throughout to all three characters. Short notes indicating changes in position or explicit actions (e.g. 'kehrt um'; 'klopft an die Hausthür'; 'weint') are common, as is the indication '(bey Seite)' which repeatedly sets up a double level of meaning on stage. Most important are directions involving mien or gesture, as when Gürge and Schnapps begin Scene 6 ('nach einer Stille, während Beyde einander angesehen, sehr wehmüthig,' 458). Such a pause required the actors to do more than stand and gaze wistfully at each other. It is a miniature extemporized scene before the dialogue begins. The comparable place in Florian's play reads 'Ils se regardent sans rien dire' (25; all Florian references are to *Oeuvres Complètes* [Leipzig: Fleischer, 1826]). Heyne's adoption of this and other stage directions from his source shows his awareness of their importance and potential for the work, but he has also added to the original by including an indication of disposition ('sehr wehmüthig'), placing even higher demands on the actors' expression. It is not just in distinct stage directions such as this that the gestural dimension of the work becomes apparent. The dialogue throughout is fast-paced and witty, providing much humour of language and rapid interchange, and very often the style in which passages are written suggests that a good deal of gestural activity was required along the way, even when explicit stage directions are lacking. Here Schnapps explains to the naive Gürge what he must do to collect the prize for his lottery ticket: 'seht Ihr – eh' Ihr in die Straße kommt – so rechter Hand – das ist ein grosser Thorweg – Seht Ihr – zum Exempel hier wäre die lange Strasse – so ist hier ein bißgen Rechts ein grosser Thorweg, mit Gänsekothfarbe angestrichen, nach der allerneuesten Mode – *Gürge.* Gut, gut, ein Thorweg mit Gänsekothe' (449f). The dashes interrupting Schnapps's description and the content of the speech itself indicate pauses during which he employs gestures to describe in visual terms what he is saying; word and actions are complementary. His unusual use of 'Gänsekothfarbe' to describe the correct entrance, the one point that attracts Gürge's notice in particular, injects a scatological note, and Schnapps's additional 'nach der allerneuesten Mode' should be understood as a local joke. In Florian's original, these lines read: 'il y a une porte cochère … jaune. / *Arlequin.* Une porte jaune?' (21). Heyne's faecal embellishment says something about his judgment of the taste of the German audience as opposed to the French who witnessed the original.

As Schnapps continues his instructions, a level of mime play is added to his gestures:

> Ihr klingelt, da kommt ein Bedienter, blau mit Silber. – 'Ich wollte gern mit Ihre Hochwürden, dem Herrn Lottodirektor sprechen.' – 'Kommt nur herein, guter Freund!' man führt Euch in die Expedition, Ihr zeigt Euer Billet – 'Geschwind, so und so viel tausend Dukaten für den ehrlichen Mann, und alle in Fleischergewichte!' (Er erwischt endlich das Billet) Man nimmt Euch euer Billet ab, und die ganze Freude hat ein Ende. (450)

The speech contains two concurrent levels of meaning. Beyond the immediate intention to communicate directions, Schnapps moves to role play, constructing a projected fictitious dialogue between Gürge and the lottery director's servant which, if effective, will result in Gürge's willing surrender of his ticket. Gürge is unaware of this level of meaning, but the audience, of course, has it very much in mind and watches in suspense to see the result. As Schnapps 'erwischt *endlich* das Billet,' we see the culmination of a sequence of movements introduced by this general stage direction earlier in the scene (there is a similar one in the source, p. 21): '[Schnapps] sucht Gürgen das Billet zu stehlen; dieser aber stört ihn immer durch seine Bewegungen' (449). Schnapps must thus make attempts to snatch the ticket from the beginning, probably whenever the text indicates pauses through punctuation, but the actual details of gestural play are left very much up to Schnapps and Gürge to develop themselves. When two characters are involved in a scene whose dramatic effectiveness depends on convincing gestures and mime, their timing in concert is crucial.

This scene is followed in both versions by a soliloquy with Schnapps (Scapin) alone on stage. Such situations always reinforce a character's intimacy with the audience and initiate or continue a double level of meaning. But we have seen initial signs of this intimacy between actor and audience in the character of Gürge, not Schnapps, and it is clearly Gürge who represents Florian's Arlequin in this work. Still, his rival now establishes his own clandestine relationship with the same audience, putting them in an ambivalent position toward the actors and action on stage. A device customarily employed by the central comic figure is here shared by another (as it was in *Die Bauren* where not only Görgel but also his rival Hiesel spoke directly to the audience); and the effect is a dramatic tension which forces the audience to be both participant and judge. In this case the audience realizes with Schnapps that he has stolen not the lottery ticket but Rösgen's love letter. We then hear his devilish plan to take both money and bride, and we are forced into an uncomfortable alliance with him, sharing full knowledge in contrast to Gürge's simple trust and ignorance of his precarious situation. This is a theatrically clever manipulation, for the audience would naturally sympathize with Gürge and want to warn him of the danger. It encourages us to project our involvement into the play, show our true colours as allies of the good Gürge, and perhaps if the actors are skilful enough in constructing the fiction, even shouting out our warnings and support. The audience receives opportunity to do so almost at once in Scene 5 with the full cast on stage, Gürge believing he still has Rösgen's note, Schnapps and the audience knowing he does not, and as he learns the awful truth and the disappointed Rösgen denounces him, we witness a sorry change in the young hero from jubilant lover to dejected outcast. What audience could not come to his aid?

Inevitably fortunes turn; Gürge sacrifices his lottery ticket for Rösgen's note and gives it then to her:

> *Gürge.* (Zeigt ihr den Brief.)
> *Rösgen.* 'Lieber Freund.'
> *Gürge.* Wie war's? Ich habs nicht recht verstanden.
> *Rösgen.* 'Lieber Freund.' (466)

Rösgen is reading her own words, but now they have deeper meaning for both the happy couple and the audience who has shared their trial. Gürge's pretence of not understanding – 'Wie war's?' – is merely a ruse to have Rösgen speak the deliciously endearing 'Lieber Freund' once again. It is a tender and satisfying little love scene cleverly based on the original document which started the entire intrigue. In the French version the scene reads:

(Il lui montre la lettre.)
Argentine (lit). 'Je t'aime.'
Arlequin. (lazzi.) Hé! comment dis-tu?
Argentine. 'Je t'aime.' (29)

Heyne modified Argentine's explicit 'Je t'aime' to 'Lieber Freund' and omitted a stage direction in the place of the original's 'lazzi.' With this word Florian signalled an extemporized interlude for Arlequin who no doubt did a little dance to show his bliss at the lady's words. Considering the wealth of gesture required in Heyne's version, it is unlikely that Gürge would let a similar opportunity pass unexploited.

The gestural requirements, alone and in concert, are very much intertwined with the dialogue and thematic development of this play. They place considerable demand on the actors' talents of invention throughout and spelled the reason for the work's ongoing success. Clearly Heyne had adapted Florian's original with a keen eye to preserving essential elements of the Arlequin tradition, although the skills of improvisation which earlier tended to concentrate on the single comic star are now spread over the entire cast. This greater balance is an indication that German writers were learning to use the best of the Nachspiel tradition to create effective theatre which was aesthetically acceptable and theatrically satisfying for their own times.

Plenty of contemporary evidence attests to the great popularity of *Die beiden Billets*. Iffland himself was impressive as Schnapps in Mannheim, as one critic wrote of his 1786 performance in the National-altheater: 'Herr Ifland als Schnapps, ein Dorfbarbier, verschaffte heute dem Publikum sehr grosses Vergnügen durch sein sehr gutes komisches Spiel' (*Tagebuch der Mannheimer Schaubühne*, 5 [1786], 73). The review of a 1789 performance in Mainz is representative of contemporary reaction to the work as a whole, calling it 'eine allerliebste Bagatelle, die man, wie sie hier gespielt wird, alle Woche einmal sehen könnte' (*Frankfurter Dramaturgische Blätter*, 2. Jg [1789], 165; quoted from *Sammlung Oskar Fambach* archives).

Other reports are helpful to establish a more precise picture of exactly how this Nachspiel was performed in its day. For example, much unintentional humour must have resulted from Henriette Beck's portrayal of the young Rösgen in Frankfurt (1789) according to Katharina Elisabeth Goethe (mother of J.W. von) in a letter of 24 April in that year:

'Muß es nicht alle Illusion stören, wenn Madam Beck[,] die wenig
Zähne mehr hat[,] in den Beyden Billiet das Rösgen macht – ich will
ihren sonstigen Talenten dadurch gar nicht zu nahe tretten – aber ein
Rösgen ist sie doch warlich nicht' (*Briefe*, 276). The published text on its
own would also not reveal much of the reason for laughing at a Dresden performance in 1785: 'Zum Nachspiele die beyden Billets. Hr.
Th[ering,] der die Lacher einmal auf seiner Seite hat, spielte schlecht
memorirt, und verwechselte daher, wie alle Kuhrkreißer, ungram-
matisch, das mir und mich. Grammat. Unrichtigkeiten sollte man auf
einem Hoftheater niemals hören, und es ist Ungerechtigkeit gegen den
Verfasser, wenn der zu beqveme Akteur sie ihm aufdringt' (*Magazin der
Sächsischen Geschichte*, 24. St.[1785], 706). So much for the primacy of the
literary text!

Just as hilarious was the occasional incongruity of costume, apparently still part of the Berlin theatrical scene in 1790, as this performance
in the Royal Theatre attests:

In den beyden Billets, welche am 17ten Novembr. gegeben wurden, und wo
Madam Baronius [=Baranius], der die Natur eine so herrliche Bildung und
Gestalt gab, das Röschen spielte, machte das Publikum eine Bemerkung, die
ich Ihnen mittheilen will. Madam Baronius hat im Anzuge Geschmack; daß
sie diesen aber bey jedem Bauermädchen und in andern Rollen, welche gar
keinen übertriebenen Putz erlauben, auf Unkosten der Wahrscheinlichkeit
zeigen will, verdient Tadel.* Wenn Madam Baronius als Bauermädchen im
schönsten Atlas, mit den neuesten Bändern und Blumen behangen auftritt,
was will sie dann anziehen, wenn sie als Dame erscheint? Solcher Putzunfug
wird über kurz oder lang der Ruin jeder teutschen Bühne seyn, und hat fast
schon alle Wahrheit im Kostume verscheucht. Es ist anjezt nichts baroker,
als in einem ländlichen Schauspiele die Frauenzimmer neben den
Mannspersonen zu sehn: jene in seidnen Anzügen nach neuester Mode und
Schnitt, diese in Kamisölern und Pumphosen von leinenen oder wollenen
Zeuchen.
* Dieß beweißt – mit Erlaubniß unsers Herrn Correspondenten sey es gesagt
– vielmehr, daß Madam Baronius sich zwar schön zu putzen versteht, aber
keinen Geschmack im Anzuge hat, denn wahrer guter Geschmack im
Anzuge, auf und außer dem Theater, gründet sich allzeit auf Raisonnement,
und verstößt nie gegen Zweck und Verhältniße. Indessen ist dieß ein Unfug
der auf mehreren teutschen Theatern getrieben wird, und den auch das liebe
gedultige Publikum nicht mißbilligt. d[er] H[erausgeber] (*Journal des Luxus
und der Moden*, V [1790], Feb, 114f; quoted from SOF archival materials)

The reviewer not only makes it evident that gross incongruities in costume were common, but the editor's inability to resist comment from

the point of view of fashion illustrates how much theatre was integrated into the trendy social scene. Later we will be considering developments in acting technique throughout the century, with reference as well to costume. These reviews serve as a warning. Published texts often fail to reveal the bizarre incongruities of language and costume that frequently accompanied performance.

Was ist's? (1786)

Was ist's? derives its theatrical effectiveness from a wealth of comic devices including eavesdropping, disguise, verbal misunderstanding, witty repartee, caricature, physical threats, and various types of pantomimic interplay. The action, in which an intelligent young woman relegates her pretentious suitor to the status of fool and overturns her father's design, reveals further a comic statement on social structures, masculine authority, and female emancipation. This combination of comic devices, clever language, and underlying serious thematics raises the play to a level of sophistication above any Nachspiel so far considered.

A host of stage directions show that the author had very much in mind how his work should be played. The directions place continuing demands on the actors to think beyond the script, making the work as a whole more a field for play than a literary-based text. While many examples could be cited, two stand out as certain comic highlights. The first sets up the character of the pretentious and pedantic suitor von Wendheim who enters 'mit einer weissen Neghaube [knitted cap], übrigens reisemässig mit Karrikatur gekleidet' (9). From the start his speech is full of exaggerated compliments and irrelevant or unnecessary foreign snatches, particularly Latin, as here to von Raden: 'ergo, muß ich Sie veneriren ... Ergo und ratione dessen, bleib ich hier' (9, 10), and to von Raden's daughter: 'Belobteste Fräulein Amalie! – Naturalia, freylich! non sunt turpia, aber doch pflegt mein gnädiger Herr Vater zu sagen, – in Gegenwart eines Frauenzimmers, läßt sich auch das Natürliche nicht schiklich bey Nahmen nennen' (13). And so he goes on and on until the young woman takes matters into her own hands. The initial description of von Wendheim's costume makes it clear what the effect should be, but the director and performer must decide on details, with the exception of his silly cap which is to stand in contrast to what would presumably be a familiar barrister's headpiece. Caricatures of lawyers are common in comedy, but this one provides not just the means to poke fun at the pedantry of some in that profession; it has a deeper significance for the underlying serious thematics. Von Wendheim is not just a lawyer – he stands for the law, society's official system of regulation and sanction which gives von Raden absolute authority over his daughter's future and which in cases of marriage pairing was a legal mechanism to maintain the class structure. Both von Raden and von Wendheim are noblemen, whereas Amalie's lover Streitberg is not, and she alone is unconcerned about their social difference. So the caricature of the law introduced through Wendheim's costume and language early in the work, and maintained throughout, is a steady signal for the audience that the theme of class restriction is on the agenda.

Von Wendheim's address to Amalie above, beyond its pretentious latinisms, probes this serious substratum of the work. With 'Naturalia … non sunt turpia' ('Natural things … are not ugly'), and 'aber doch … läßt sich auch das Natürliche nicht schiklich bey Nahmen nennen,' von Wendheim passes Amalie a veiled compliment but also makes an indirect statement on his concept of Nature and Natural Law. He is reluctant to say what is natural; his language and its content are as contorted as his appearance, and both betray a primacy of artificial structure and thought over natural inclination. Underlying this is a fundamental conflict between natural and social order, freedom and restriction, the essence of Amalie's predicament, and in theatrical terms it is von Wendheim's *unn*aturalness that makes him so ridiculous. The unnatural is always a focus for ridicule in comedy. Although he is not to be seen as a direct relative of the traditional comic figure, this unnaturalness reminds us of the importance of *natural* inclination for Hanswurst, Harlekin, and other comic types for whom the 'natural' is the basis of action and morality. They are not ridiculous like von Wendheim, they make us laugh about others while von Wendheim himself is the object of derision here. Von Wendheim's reference to his father in the speech ('pflegt mein gnädiger Herr Vater zu sagen') further signals something of his character. By repeating it frequently in the course of the play, he reveals a total ideological dependence on the older generation and accordingly his own intellectual and personal restriction.

This visual and linguistic groundwork leads directly to a crucial scene in which von Wendheim and von Radheim, in the presence of Amalie, discuss their notions of the role of husband and wife. Von Wendheim explains his understanding first:

Also, das Hauswesen, die Wäsche, die Kocherey, die Mägde, und die
Amme, das besorgen Sie alles, meine noble Fräulein Braut. Ich sehe denn
dem Ackerbau, der Vieh- und Schafszucht und den Waldungen nach.
Von Raden. (Etwas ungeduldig.) Vermehrt sich die Familie, sag ich, so ist es

des Mannes Pflicht, über eine gute Erziehung, vorzüglich der Söhne zu machen –
Von Wendheim. Richtig! das hat mir mein gnädiger Herr Vater auch gesagt. Um die Töchter, sagt er, soll ich mich nicht viel bekümmern; das ist der Frau Mama ihre Sorge, sagt er. – Die Mütter, sagt mein gnädiger Herr Vater, wissen aus eigener Erfahrung, daß es kützlich ist, ein Mädchen zu hüten –
Amalie. O schön! – (20f)

Von Wendheim's notion of wifely duties reflects the conservative position of his day (and, embarrassingly enough, even of our own to some extent); his idea of a husband's responsibilities comprises a mixture of masculine bias and aristocratic assumption. Comments on the education of sons and daughters are particularly jarring, for they too reflect the contemporary norm and point to one of the greatest impediments to woman's self-determination, the lack of educational opportunity. In all of these remarks on education sons are treated seriously while daughters are dismissed with condescension, the final blow coming in the words 'daß es kützlich ist, ein Mädchen zu hüten' which reduce females to sheltered playthings and elicit Amalie's exasperated gasp of disbelief 'O schön!'

Twice during this explanation does von Wendheim remind us that he is really a puppet speaking for 'mein gnädiger Herr Vater,' and it is Amalie's father whose interjection indicates that his opinion is not much different. Amalie's exclamation thus is a statement on that entire generation and the authority it holds. Fortunately, by the end of the play, her father at least surrenders this traditional ground.

The theme is continued soon after in a confrontation between the rivals for Amalie's hand. Defending himself against Streitberg's verbal attack, von Wendheim cries out:

Um aller Barmherzigkeit Willen – ich bin ja noch nicht emancipiert!
Streitberg. Emancipiert? Bauernschinder, sprich, daß Dich ehrliche Leute verstehen. Was heißt emancipiert?
Von Wendheim. Nicht emancipiert heißt, daß ich von der väterlichen Gewalt noch nicht entlassen, sondern noch eine res mancipi bin. Diese Entlassung wird im jure romano Emancipatio genannt, weil der filius familias und die filia familias, oder der Sohn und die Tochter vom Hause, in der Gewalt des Vaters, und also res mancipi sind. Eben so wie die Ehefrau in der Gewalt des Ehemanns, und Knecht, Magd, Pferd, Ochs, Esel, mit einem Worte, alle Bestiae, quae collo & dorso dormantur, das ist; alles Zug- und Lastvieh, als res mancipi in der Gewalt des Eigenthums Herrn sind, und für sich keinen Willen haben dürfen. (30f)

A greater insult to women than classifying them with horse, ox, ass, 'Zug- und Lastvieh' and 'alle Bestiae,' as chattels of their masters '[die] für sich keinen Willen haben dürfen' could scarcely be imagined. In this legal definition, von Wendheim supplies a concise summary of the servitude and inequity prevalent in that society. But while he does know the legal definition of emancipation very well indeed, it is questionable whether he understands what it really means. Streitberg's question was 'Was heißt emancipiert?' Von Wendheim's answer begins 'Nicht emancipiert heißt ...,' which demonstrates that he does not really know what it is to be emancipated, only what it is not to be. This is the greatest irony, for here is a man and a lawyer who has every advantage over women in his society, who could enjoy the benefits of social emancipation, but who really has no idea what it is – the most stunning indictment of men of his type in the play.

So much for the work's serious undertones. What makes it tick, however, is the dazzling array of comic techniques, particularly gesture and mime. One of the best scenes in this regard is the fifth (22-7) with von Wendheim and Amalie on stage alone for the first, and only, time. Only one confrontation is necessary to establish her superiority in intellect and maturity:

Amalie. (Geht in Gedanken vertieft, auf und ab; setzt sich, ohne Wendheim anzusehen, an den Tisch.)
Von Wendheim. (Folgt ihren Schritten in einiger Entfernung. Nach einer Pause, wenn Amalie sitzt.) Sie sind recht hübsch, meine noble Fräulein Amalie! –
Amalie. (Antwortet nicht.)
Von Wendheim. (Gaft einer Antwort entgegen; da keine erfolgt, setzt er sich in einiger Entfernung von Amalien denkend auf einem Stuhl, und zieht ein Ringfutteral aus der Tasche, das er öffnet. Da Amalie ihn nicht bemerken will, rückt er mit dem Stuhle, und zeigt ihr von weiten einen Ring. –)
Amalie. (Vor sich.) Ich rede das Schaaf gewiß nicht an. –
Von Wendheim. (Kurze Pause. Vor sich.) Wenn ich nur wüste, was ich ihr sagen soll! – (Er versucht mit Geräusch näher zu rücken, verliert das Gleichgewicht und fällt auf den Boden. Er bleibt liegen und sagt, halb weinend.) Gefallen bin ich! Es thut mir weh!

Although very little dialogue is exchanged, the scene depicts a pivotal reversal of power roles from the beginning when von Wendheim plays the generous benefactor to the end when he is reduced to physical prostration and whining supplication before his aloof bride. Amalie withdraws almost completely from the dialogue, saying only to herself, and with that to the audience, that she simply has no comment on such a fool. She is saying by this that no amount of dialogue or reasonable conversation can save this man from what he is or from his calcified standards. But even without dialogue, even without much action at all on her part, she towers over him – her very inaction, her very presence brings him to his knees. Von Wendheim's approach is conventional for his class: the compliment about her beauty; the reference to her nobility; the offering of the ring, symbol of the marital bond and expected to be an enticement she cannot resist. But she simply does not react. She says nothing to his compliments, her refusal even to look at him denies her interest in the visual world or in the attractive bauble in his hand; she remains entirely withdrawn. The beginning of the sequence emphasizes this dichotomy between the superficiality of the physical world to which von Wendheim is bound and the world of the mind and intellect into which Amalie withdraws and in which she maintains her strength. She 'geht in Gedancken vertieft' from the beginning, maintaining a contemplative pose while he does everything he can to attract her attention. It would be insufficient for the actress playing Amalie simply to do nothing but sit lost in thought throughout the scene. She must convey through subtleties of expression, gesture, and movement how serious she is in contrast to her empty-headed suitor; she must convey an air of strength and sovereignty to contrast with von Wendheim's subservience. His initial movements, following behind her as she paces, illustrate through pantomime their appropriate positions and roles. His 'Gaft einer Antwort entgegen' is a mimic depiction of an action which never occurs, underscoring the silence and his inability to come to terms with it. With no answer forthcoming, he resigns himself to silence as well, this time pantomiming her thoughtful pose – 'er setzt sich in einiger Entfernung von Anschein denkend auf einen Stuhl' – noticeably different from the way Amalie's introspection is expressed in the stage direction 'in Gedanken vertieft,' a difference which requires the actors to make the contrast clear through nuances of expression and gesture. Similarly, his exasperated 'Wenn ich nur wüste, was ich ihr sagen soll!' underscores his mental vacuousness as opposed to her inner strength. When his final attempt to command her attention ends in physical collapse, von Wendheim's total submission is sealed by the direction 'Er bleibt liegen,' whence 'halb weinend' he attempts the last resort of every child, 'Gefallen bin ich! Es thut mir weh!' It is obvious that this man needs a mother, not a wife.

As important as Amalie's part is in communicating meaning through expression and gesture, it is clear that the role of von Wendheim is more challenging. Three further entire scenes which set up the conclusion of the work belong almost completely to him and his talent for extemporization. To give an indication of just how important his actions here are, as opposed to the dialogue among the other characters on stage, Scenes 12 to 14 (44-52) can be quoted and fully understood solely through the stage directions which apply to him:

> *Von Wendheim.* (Hat die Weste über den Rock angezogen, und sich überhaupt gekleidet als ein Verwirrter. In einer Hand trägt er die Tatze, die Nannette vorhin in sein Zimmer trug, in der andern das Töpfgen.)
>
> …
>
> (Singt.)
> Wenn du mein Schätzgen willst seyn,
> Mußt du mich lieben allein u.
>
> …
>
> (Setzt sich auf einen Stuhl, und galoppirt.) Trap! Trap! Hott! Hott! Trap! Trap!
>
> …
>
> (Tanzt.)
>
> …
>
> (Kriecht unter den Tisch, bellt wie ein Hund.)
>
> …
>
> (Singt.) Wenn du mein Schätzgen u.
>
> …
>
> (Singt und tanzt.)
>
> …
>
> (Kniet.)
>
> …
>
> (Singt.) Wenn du mein Schätzgen u.
>
> …
>
> (Reitet.) Trap! Trap! Hott! Hott!
>
> …
>
> (Nimmt Winkeln und tanzt.)
>
> …
>
> (Läßt ihn los, singt und tanzt allein herum.)
>
> …
>
> (Kriecht unter den Tisch und bellt.)
>
> …
>
> *Winkel.* (Geht ab, bringt zwey Hausknechte die Stricke bey sich haben.)
>
> …
>
> (Die Hausknechte gehen furchtsam auf ihn zu.)
> *Von Wendheim.* (Der ihnen ausweicht.) … (Er schlendert den Hausknechten Stühle entgegen.) … (Er läuft in Amaliens Zimmer, die Hausknechte nach.)

Who needs dialogue to understand this scene? It represents a turning point in the action and at the same time allows an improvisational tour de force for the actor playing von Wendheim, a freedom and a challenge reminiscent of that taken on regularly by traditional comic figures. Clearly all depends on his ability to extemporize for maximal comic effect. His appearance is ridiculous, the reversed coat and vest an immediate sign of character inversion; the symbols of authority he holds, as the king of fools, are in one hand the 'Tatze,' a little tray on which Nannette has brought his cocoa-butter salve, in the other the 'Töpfgen' containing his medicinal warm wine, both of which signify not authority but infantile regression. His repeated song is indicated only by the first two lines plus 'u.,' a sign that it was likely a familiar one of the day, known to audiences and hence not necessary to quote in full. The galloping and accompanying horsy noises underscore his childishness, as does his doggie imitation under the table. Dancing throughout requires nimble celerity, reminding us of the extemporized ballet antics of Nachspiele in bygone days. And all this coming from a nobleman – the last straw in the ridicule of his class.

Was ist's? is a work with great potential on stage, primarily because of scenes like the one above and the sheer fun they generated for audiences. But beneath this surface of frenetic energy and extemporizational licence, serious questions about important social issues are put so that the work also stands as an indictment of contemporary sexual roles and authority. Increasingly the Nachspiel is becoming more serious and explicit in its social thematics despite a continued dependence on devices central to the genre since the early decades. The comic figure in his old identifiable form, or the comic servant as his replacement, is absent from this play, but much of the work's strength still rests largely on the same theatrical foundations.

Der Magnetismus (1787)

Iffland's place among the most popular German dramatists at the end of the century has long been recognized, but more attention has focused on his many full-length works than the shorter ones. *Der Magnetismus* remained a favourite on German stages from 1787 through the end of the century with some fifty documented performances in Frankfurt, Mannheim, Munich, Vienna, and many other centres, and has enjoyed numerous printings since. Magnetism was of considerable topical interest at the time. In broad terms, it is the scientific teaching of magnetic fields in vacuo and in solid materials, but in this case means the medical application of magnetic theory, which was purported to have various healing effects on body and mind, and which shows up in German lands as early as Paracelsus. In the final decades of the eighteenth century magnetism became popular through the work of Anton Mesmer, who began experimenting with magnetic cures in his Viennese, then Parisian, medical practice in the seventies. He soon became famous, but his ideas and their application were condemned by medical authorities of the day, which caused him to withdraw from society at century's end. Still, his work resulted in theories of animal magnetism and mesmerism still known today and which, along with his emphasis on the technique of suggestion, have earned him a place as one of the pioneers of hypnotic and group therapy. Mesmerism involves procedures of touching, stroking, and passing hands over the patient, which made it fertile ground for charlatans to engage in unprofessional fondling. In the late eighteenth century it was popular in a broad cross-section of German-speaking society.

In a Foreword to the work, Iffland makes his intentions clear:

> Aber die Charlatanerien der emigrirenden Lehrer, empören die gesunde Vernunft, und Gott gebe, daß ich die lächerlich gemacht habe. Forscher Blick, sah schnell den tragikomischen Tand, der hier die Stelle Arlequins wie bey jedem andern Marktschreier vertritt. Die, welche im ersten Eifer manches übersahen, allmälig sich überzeugen und mit That und Wort, weise innehalten, sind stillschweigend meiner Meinung, und so ist die gesunde Vernunft, und alle gute Menschen auf meiner Seite. (5)

While one of Iffland's primary objectives is clearly to expose and ridicule the charlatans involved in this pseudo-medical practice, further in the Foreword he makes it clear that he does not wish to exclude the possibility of the existence of positive effects of magnetism per se, though he remains sceptical that these can be proved: 'Ich schreibe nicht gegen die Möglichkeit der Erschütterung unserer feinen Maschine ... diese Möglichkeit bestreite ich nicht, aber da alle die seit Jahr und Tag dieses künstliche Fieber erregt haben, seinen Nutzen nicht bestimmen konnten: so steht seine Würde, für mich auf einer schlechten Stelle' (6). Underlying Iffland's remarks are his obvious faith in 'die gesunde Vernunft' which he sees as the best weapon to combat medical chicanery, and in empirical evidence, without which he cannot accept magnetism's purported effects. The work is an indirect praise of the rational method, intended by its author as a vehicle for education and social correction, enlightenment on the foundations of reason and good sense. This view sounds very much like Gottsched's own.

Most curious is Iffland's equation of such charlatans with Arlequin in the first quotation above. The convoluted prose of the passage makes it difficult to understand, yet it would seem that the author does not intend to deride Arlequin himself; rather, he sees medical charlatans as parallel to Arlequin figures in their propogation of an unproved fantasy as opposed to 'gesunde Vernunft.' Such mountebanks prey on others' delusions with their 'tragikomischen Tand,' but Iffland does not say that Arlequin is comparably destructive. Rather, it is their mutual manipulation of fantasy that joins Arlequin and the charlatan together. *Der Magnetismus* contains many comic devices that were part of Arlequin's standard repertoire, which suggests that Ifflands cursory comparison in the Foreword carried more significance for the construction of his play than the brief reference above would lead us to believe at first glance.

Most of the comic action focuses on Grundmann, who functions as Linden's servant. A good deal of the comic effect results from the fact that he is deaf, requiring Linden to shout at him much of the time, thus setting up many humorous interchanges based on verbal misunderstanding. In Scene 2 (12-16) alone the stage directions tell us six times that Linden speaks 'laut' to Grundmann, once 'halb ärgerlich ins Ohr.'

Of the numerous scenes in which Grundmann is the comic focus of the humour, this segment of Scene 5 is most illustrative:

Linden. Wir haben was vor!

Grundmann. Vor's Thor?

Linden. Wir haben einen Spaß vor.

Grundmann. Einen Spaß? ah – so – einen Spaß! das ist brav!

Linden. Du sollst einen Professor vorstellen.

Grundmann. Wie mache ich das?

Linden. Du ziehst einen schwarzen Rock an – und sagst zu allem, was gesagt wird: 'das weiß ich besser!'

Grundmann. Das ist nicht höflich.

Linden. Du bist ein Gelehrter; du mußt alles, und allem widersprechen.

Grundmann. Nichts sprechen?

Linden. Wenn das so viel als Nichts ist – gut. Du mußt widersprechen.

Grundmann. Aber man wird mir doch auch widersprechen.

Linden. Dann sey grob.

Grundmann. Aber wenn man mir beweißt, daß ich unrecht habe?

Linden. In diesem Falle mußt du, als Gelehrter, schimpfen.

Grundmann. Scharmant! und auch – (er macht die Pantomime von Schlägerey.)

Linden. Nicht! – bewahre aber grob bis zum prügeln; das ist hergebracht. Das heißt in den schönen Wissenschaften Freymüthigkeit. (21f)

As an exercise in verbal misunderstanding and satire on academics, the passage speaks for itself. The last exchange between the pair is less transparent, however. As his enthusiasm for the disguise mounts, Grundmann apparently goes too far in his pantomime with the threat to deal out some well-deserved beatings. Traditionally it is the servant figure who is the one beaten, and perhaps this opportunity to reverse roles is at the root of Grundmann's enthusiasm. The motif of beating was of course commonly connected with comic figures, and we are reminded of Iffland's link between medical charlatans and Arlequin in the Foreword. In checking Grundmann's impulse abruptly here, Linden shows that despite the smouldering inclination to continue traditional practices of early comedy, for Iffland and his dramatic sphere such devices were by 1787 out of the question.

Scene 11 depicts the actual attempt to cure Karoline by means of magnetic techniques. Posing as the expert, Grundmann oversees the operation, 'das weiß ich besser' standing as his constant claim to authority. As magnetism called for procedures of touching and stroking the subject, such is the activity here, and with a result we might expect:

> (Linden dirigirt, sagt Rendius leise, was Er thun soll; der berührt tölpisch Wange und Hände [von Karoline], grob)
>
> ...
>
> *Linden.* (sieht Sie starr an; führt seine Hand an ihrem Gesichte vorbey an den Hals, da er von der Schulter an den Busen kommen will.) (40f)

Soon after, the procedure has this dramatic effect: '*Karoline.* (steht auf und sagt mit Eckstase) Ich bin in himmlischer Freude' (43). By making the fondling of a female a public event, Iffland adds a generous dash of spice to a scene already containing great comic potential. The stage directions present the main thrust of the pantomime, but all characters involved would have to extend them considerably through improvisational skills to reap maximum effect. And while Iffland's primary purpose may have been to satirize medical charlatans, his use of sexual innuendo as a device to titillate his audience is in dramatic terms no different from the explicit sexuality common in earlier Nachspiele. Iffland knew what made audiences come to the theatre and he usually sent them home contented.

Beyond the general wealth of gestural and mimic action in the work, Grundmann is the strongest link with the Nachspiel tradition. Like Trivelin in *Die Aussteuer*, he is an impertinent and spirited servant who often defies his master, comments critically on decisions, and seems to enjoy a freedom and immunity from punishment which puts him outside the sphere of the rest on stage. Beyond these links, it is clear that this Nachspiel was primarily a satirical and correctional piece which smacks of rational enlightened philosophy. From such works the increasing use of the Nachspiel as an instrument of social education is evident.

Der kindische Vater (1788)

Although it appeared just one year after *Der Magnetismus*, this Nachspiel throws us back into the ribald tone of earlier works and carries little of the social pedagogy of Iffland's play. Juxtaposition of the two illustrates just how varied the theatre scene was at the time. While there is a clear message to parents about child-rearing, that theme is so coarsely handled as to be no more than an excuse for the wild activity on stage. The first part of the title to the volume in which this Nachspiel appeared, *Etwas wider die Mode*, points to Franz Jann's deliberate attempt to present works against the current grain, and in this case he is continuing a type of theatre which had long been popular before the impulse to moralize had drawn many playwrights into its clutches. The second half of his volume title, *Trauer und Lustspiele ohne ärgerliche Caressen, und Heurathen, für die studierende Jugend herausgegeben*, is a gibe at the growing number of dramatists who approached their work as a serious moral enterprise and locates his in the tradition of the school play written exclusively for the performance and enjoyment of young people. Indeed, they must have had a wonderful time producing and watching this play.

Scene 6, the longest in the work, depicts the schoolmaster's attempt to teach three intolerably misbehaved, stubborn, and stupid children. Like Scenes 12-14 of *Was ist's?* its content can be understood entirely by citing only the stage directions (516-21):

(Hiesel geht fort [zu lesen], Thomerl schlieft unbemerkt unter den Tisch.)

...

Tonel. (Bläßt Papierchen von der Hand weg.)

...

   (Bläßt wieder.)

...

(Der Tisch fängt an spazieren zu gehen.)
Schulmeister. (Giebt ihm [Thomerl] eine [Ohrfeige].)

...

Hiesel. (Angelt in der Stille dem Schulmeister die Perüque vom Kopf.)
Schulmeister. (Reißt ihm die Angel aus der Hand, klaubt seine Perüque auf, und setzt sie wieder auf den Kopf.)
... (Peitscht den Hiesel.)

As with von Wendheim's antics, who needs text to understand this scene? The dialogue is only a technical device for introducing a situation in which extemporized pranks are central, and is almost irrelevant for the effect. The scene of course is familiar to anyone who ever went to school, and while most of us never participated in rowdiness to this extent, what child never thought with glee of doing just what these children do? None of the gags is original; in fact it is their familiarity to the audience that makes them appealing – they are assured of vicarious pleasure through the antics of the boys, however nasty they actually are. These miscreants show blatant disrespect for the schoolmaster's position and task, an anti-authoritarian impudence sure to appeal to many on-lookers, particularly the young, but carried so outrageously far that it can only be seen as a flight of schoolboy fantasy. In the end, when the fun is over, the boys are forced by legal intervention to take lessons, conform, and show respect for the institution and its representatives. But not before they and the audience have their fun in strong doses.

Following the schoolroom scene, the boys complain to their father of the 'mistreatment' they have suffered, receiving his fullest sympathy. It is now his turn to show that blockheaded ignorance can also be characteristic of parents; before our eyes he regresses to childhood:

> *Hiesel.* Itzt wollen wir Galopp reiten, und trompeten dazu. (Sie thun es.)
> *Vater.* Die unschuldigen Närrlen! Was sie itzt für eine Freud haben! – Ich hätte schier selber Lust. – Ach, es siehts ja Niemand. (Nimmt seinen Stecken zwischen die Füße, und reitet auch.) (523)

The adult, sure that no one is looking, jubilantly becomes a child again. In the previous scene, the audience could relive their fantasies of schoolroom mischief and anti-authoritarianism; here, in private, they can shake off their bonds of social conformity and share the father's pleasure in regressing to a state of childlike innocence. Both final scenes of the play offer the audience a window of fantasy and escape from the problematic real world.

These scenes are highly reminiscent of both the conclusion to *Die neueste Verheyrathung* and von Wendheim's antics in *Was ist's?* The comic techniques are much the same, devices long central to the Nachspiel's effectiveness. While *Der kindische Vater* makes no pretensions to carry a serious social message, its sheer fun and flights into comic fantasy point to an alliance with earlier Nachspiele whose primary goals always included these.

Das Nachspiel zur berühmten Komödie, Erklärte Fehde oder List gegen List
(1789)

The presence of Pantalon, Brigella, Columbina, and the explicit equation of Frontin with Arlequin place this work firmly into the Italian/French comic tradition. Again, despite its date of appearance, it is far removed in tone and substance from other Nachspiele in the decade which had underlying social comment. It contains some satire on French manners and hence a socio-critical dimension, but foremost it is a unique commentary on the fate of the Nachspiel as genre itself, and what it stood for in the German theatrical tradition.

Early in the play, the Marquis, furious at having been manipulated by a disguised troupe of Italian comedians, consciously and explicity summarizes the stock *commedia dell'arte* scenario in which an old fool is duped of a young woman (342-3). He sees that his own situation with Rosaura is just that, so that his revenge, which takes up the rest of the play, is a retaliation on that comic tradition and the characters who gave it acclaim.

The clever comic servant Frontin is the engineer of this reprisal, but before it begins, he surprises his master by suggesting a personal link between himself and the stock characters from the theatrical tradition he now plans to debunk:

> *Frontin* ... Wenn Sie ja noch einen Schritt in dieser Sache thun wollten, gn. Herr, so wär es Der, meiner Columbina eine gute Aussteuer zu unserer Hochzeit zu geben, weil sie mir das Geheimniß noch zu rechter Zeit entdeckte.
> *Marquis.* Deiner Columbina? Wer ist diese?
> *Frontin.* Nu – die Jungfer Ihrer vermeinten Baroneße. Auch sie hat den Namen Lisette, erst hier angenommen.
> *Marquis.* Und du willst sie doch heyrathen?
> *Frontin.* Mehr als vormals. Columbina oder Lisette, bleibt mit jedem Nahmen und Prädikat, ein Kammermädchen, so das Glück hat mir zu gefallen. Meine Familie kann mir deswegen nicht den geringsten Vorwurf machen; und wegen ihrer Aufrichtigkeit, hat die Columbina, nach meiner Meinung, noch Vorzüge vor der Lisette. (336f)

Frontin is pleased to have been tipped off by the loquacious Columbina, traditionally a blabbermouth (see characteristics, p 89); but that is hardly motivation enough to marry her. A stronger link exists between the two, and he recognizes it instinctively. In effect Frontin sets himself up as her traditional partner – he is *Harlekin* in disguise. One wonders what costume he wore – perhaps it was reminiscent to some degree of

Harlequin's attire – and his choice of her over the French soubrette Lisette testifies to his true loyalties. Trivelin/Harlekin here is also the master-mind of the intrigue, but it is curious indeed to see that his every action works in fact to the detriment of his traditional comic colleagues. We suspect that the work is turning tradition inside out, using its own characters and devices to undermine it, an almost underhanded strategy to bring about its downfall, suggesting that the tradition carries with it the ingredients of its own destruction.

As Frontin takes control, he appears '(Als Gerichtskomißär in einer großen Parücke, schwarzem Rocke und Mantel ...)' (352). While his role and exaggerated costume provide humour through caricature, more important, they eventually show that not just those charged before him, but much more is being judged and finally condemned. He sentences Pantalon and Brigella to ninety-seven years at hard labour as galley slaves; and further they are commanded to remove the uniforms that have so far provided their disguises. On Frontin's order:

> (Ein Gerichtsdiener zieht ein Pantalons- und Brigella-Kleid unter dem Mantel hervor und nimmt dafür die Uniform[en] zu sich.)
> *Frontin.* Nur hurtig angezogen! – Diese Kleider passen [in original 'lassen'] solchen Schwänkmachern viel besser als Uniforme!
>
> ...
>
> Nun aber lass' ich euch so lang allein, bis eure Schandbühne aufgestellt ist. (355)

The new clothing produced is undoubtedly the recognizable costume of Pantalon, the Venetian merchant, and Brigella, Harlequin's customary cohort. Brigella's role was traditionally that of clever intrigant, and usually as confirmed opponent of Pantalon. Here, the situation seems doubly reversed as he becomes both Pantalon's colleague and victim to Harlekin.

Alone in their misery, Pantalon and Brigella come to a realization:

> *Brigella* ... im Grunde – wißt ihr, daß ihr mir in diesem Kleide recht wohl gefallt?
> *Pantalon.* Schicksamer wär' es wohl für den Streich gewesen, den ich heut gespielt habe als die Uniform; in so weit muß ich selbst dem Herrn Kommißär Recht geben. (356)

By disguising themselves in uniforms (Pantalon even as a nobleman), they have sacrificed the immunity from reprisals traditionally guaranteed comic figures in the real world, and so must face the consequences of their actions and the force of the law as citizens of society. While all this is carried off very much tongue-in-cheek, as the exorbitant severity of their penalty suggests, the message remains nevertheless that it is the denial of their true roles that has brought on their demise. If they had been all along in the costumes produced by the court clerk, recognizable immediately to those on stage as well as the audience, then their actions in deceiving the Marquis would truly have been a comic 'Streich' without such painful consequences. The truth of Frontin's comment 'Diese Kleider passen solchen Schwänkmachern viel besser als Uniforme!' is acknowledged by Pantalon's 'so weit muß ich selbst dem Herrn Kommißär Recht geben.' But keeping in mind Frontin's relation to the Harlekin type, should we understand his insight and enforced correction here to mean that he is in fact fighting to maintain the traditions of his clan, or is he condemning them forever? Is he their agent in disguise, or is he a Harlekin converted to social functionary? When he leaves them alone 'bis eure Schandbühne aufgestellt ist,' he seems to encourage Pantalon and Brigella to continue their acting tradition, but his choice of words accords that tradition little respect. Moreover, he plays an active part in tricking them now into an eventual beating. Once they are in their true attire, there is talk of a renewed danger at being seen in public, a comment on the status of the comedian in society in this era, and hence they agree to get into sacks to be shipped abroad. Once confined, they are delivered a thrashing by Momolo and the sailor who think they are sacks of contraband. Thus, even as the real Pantalon and Brigella, they cannot escape punishment, a final statement on the loss of status and freedom they had once enjoyed.

The final scene of the play lifts this clutch of motifs to a theoretical level:

Frontin ... ich werde ein Theaterstück daraus machen, und es [in original 'sie'] Euch auf dem ersten Jahrmarkt vorspielen lassen.
Marquis. Du – ein Theaterstück?
Frontin. Das gewiß allgemeinen Beyfall erhalten soll.
Marquis. Allgemeinen gar? darauf mache Verzicht, lieber Frontin!
Frontin. Warum? Ich bin wohl klug genug, kein Stück von der feinern Gattung, oder gar ein Trauerspiel in Versen daraus zu machen. Die werden hier sehr wenig verstanden, und immer schlecht vorgestellt. Mein Stück soll so Etwas – Etwas...
Marquis. Von der gröbern Gattung werden?
Frontin. Nicht doch! so Etwas – nach der Natur!
Marquis. Damit sagst du noch nichts Frontin. In der Natur gibt es Sonnen und Sterne, aber auch Wanzen und Kröten; unter den Menschen feine und plumpe; willst du für die letztern schreiben? Auch ein Nährvater des unechten, oder gar des pöbelhaften Geschmakes werden, wovon jetzt unsre

Theater die Lehrstühle sind?
Frontin. Das wäre mir eine schöne Ehre! Ich will mir das Lob der Kenner erwerben.
Marquis. In diesem Fall halte dich immer lieber an die feinere Natur! Vielleicht lernet Marseille sie dereinst besser kennen. Dann lobt es dich, daß dein
Gefühl feiner war als deine Zeit, und dankt dir, daß du diese zu bessern
suchtest. Nur hüthe dich, jemals der vortrefflichen Regel unsers Boileau zu
vergessen: Aux dépens du bon sens gardez de plaisanter! (365f)

This conclusion is a concise statement of tensions in German theatrical
production in the eighties. It also reveals the truth about Frontin – he is
a spokesman for traditional comedy, but he is very much aware of the
problems it faces now. By announcing that he will write a play about
this play, he elevates the previous action to the level of *Lehrstück.* His
play will be written for performance in the market-place, in other
words on the temporary stage of an itinerant acting troupe, not for one
of the new permanent theatres. His work will appeal to a cross-section
of society, not just the lower class, to achieve 'allgemeinen Beyfall.' This
is the crux of the issue for the Marquis and also for the aesthetics of the
age. To whom should theatre appeal, one segment of society or a broad
cross-section? Which theatres do hold the greatest general attraction,
the mushrooming so-called Nationaltheater or the hundreds of temporary stages that had carried the tradition until then? The Marquis is
startled at Frontin's intention to please the masses, and his admonition
reflects the snobbish theatre bias of his class as well as many others of
the day. 'Why shouldn't he write for the masses?' asks Frontin, it is a
waste of time to write plays 'von der feinern Gattung, oder gar ein
Trauerspiel in Versen' which are 'hier sehr wenig verstanden, und immer schlecht vorgestellt.'

   Frontin's critical sally at the elevated and respectable dramatic genres, especially tragedy, is meant for German actors, producers, and audiences alike. But when asked by the Marquis to describe just what
kind of play it will be, Frontin can only deny that it will be 'Von der
gröbern Gattung,' struggling to define it then as 'so Etwas – Etwas ... so
Etwas nach der Natur!' If it is neither fine nor coarse, and he cannot
find a term for it, then what genre does he mean? Through this inability
to define his idea within the customary terminology, Frontin is saying
that genre is irrelevant for what he has in mind. Contrary to theoretical
discussion on the aesthetics of the tragedy and comedy, for him it is not
the question of genre designation which should be foremost, but rather
the imitation of nature – he will write 'so Etwas – nach der Natur!' Of
course this word itself was subject to many contemporary understand-

ings and interpretations; some of the most artificial theatre of the age was produced by playwrights and theoreticians who believed that Nature was their first guide. The Marquis's subsequent disparagement of the ugly side of nature, his thorough disapproval of 'pöbelhaften Geschmack,' and his criticism of theatrical standards in general represent much of what the author of this work wants in the end to dispel. Frontin does not hold the same opinion as the Marquis. To write for those whom the Marquis dismisses so pompously is precisely what he has in mind with 'Das wäre mir eine schöne Ehre! Ich will mir den Lob der Kenner erwerben.' Who then are the 'Kenner'? – those who recognize what Nature can offer the theatre, whatever social class they may be. And how is Frontin's concept of Nature to be understood? Through the fates of Pantalon and Brigella in this work, we have seen evidence that he means by Nature the affirmation of true character, origin, and heritage. In previous works we have seen a repeated emphasis on the comic figure whose essence resides in his human instincts. This essential humanity in all its ugliness as well as its beauty is what Frontin means. The Marquis's last words finally acknowledge this position. 'Feinere Gattung' is now replaced with 'feinere Natur'; Marseille is cited but stands in fact for German cities; Frontin's understanding is seen as what is necessary for the healthy development of the stage, a task that can still be accomplished with some redefinition of the notions of decency and restraint that the arch-classicist Boileau had in mind. Hence, the play is dedicated in its sub-title not to the aesthetic legislator of French classicism, but rather, mischievously, 'seinem Schatten.'

Die Tugend auf der Schaubühne oder Harlekins Heirath (1798)

Although Justus Möser's play was written in 1763, its publication was delayed until the end of the century. We know of one performance in 1765, and Nicolai tells of an unfulfilled intention by Döbbelin to produce it. The play has an unusual place in the development of the Nachspiel, for any dramatic characteristics it has went largely undiscovered until the end of the century. Although Nicolai expresses reservations about the intrinsic quality of the work (an assessment which belies his own bias for what makes a play good, and with which one might disagree), his notes as editor and his account of Möser's life make it clear that for him at least the work had much to say about the contemporary theatre scene (his focus was Berlin). Nicolai refers us in particular to Möser's essay 'Den alten Geckorden sollte man wieder erneuern' (*Phantasien* II), the thrust of which is to advocate revitalizing the practice of drawing together persons of all classes to play dramatic roles, thus breaking down social barriers at least temporarily. In the mind of Nicolai, this work contained ideas for social improvement through the medium of the stage despite the fact that in content and character it is very much in the mould of the early Nachspiel. It should be understood in conjunction with Möser's well-known defence of Harlekin in 1761, a period classic in its own right. My analysis of the work concentrates on its place within the Nachspiel tradition. Readers are also referred to Ulrich Lochter's enlightening treatment which emphasizes the play's position within Möser's literary development and its connection to the author's experiences in London (Lochter, 204-15).

Several indicators place *Die Tugend auf der Schaubühne* into a specific context before the play begins. Three of the central characters are obviously meant to be understood as representatives of the *commedia dell'arte / Théâtre Italien* tradition by their very names: Harlekin, his customary partner Kolombine, and Scapin, Harlekin's rival. 'Der Schauplatz ist auf dem Schauplatze' and Herr Berthold (often Barthold) is identified as the 'Principal der Bühne,' both of which tell us immediately that the play will operate on two levels. An ambivalent world of concurrent fictional spheres is constructed, alerting the imagination to interpret everything from now on in a double sense. This is not just a play, it is a play-within-a-play, and since the players are by profession actors, it is also a play about the theatre itself. These characters and Berthold's professional position suggest further that the actors are members of an itinerant company.

The action begins thus:

Harlekin. (macht drey tiefe Verbeugungen).
Barthold. Was will Er, mein guter Freund?
Harlekin. (Macht wieder einige Verbeugungen).
Barthold. Bücke Er sich so lange bis Er müde wird, und dann kann Er mir sagen was Er zu sagen hat. Die jungen Leute gewöhnen sich das itzt so an, daß sie einem die Zeit mit tausend Komplimenten verderben ...
Harlekin. (in fremdem Ton) Hochedelgeborner und Gestrenger –
...
Harlekin. Sie erlauben großgünstig –
Barthold. Noch ein Wort von solchem Schlage, und ich prügle Dich zum Dinge hinaus.
Harlekin. (im gewöhnlichen Ton) Ich komme Herr Barthold, wegen Ihrer jüngsten Tochter Kolombine ... (3f)

Harlekin's initial entrance to begin the action is by now recognizable common fare (viz. *Harlequin der ungedultig-hernach*). His 'drey tiefe Verbeugungen' here again announce a reappearance before his old friends and allies in the audience – not just one bow but three, a gesture of considerable ceremony – and assert his role in the spotlight. Harlekin's gestures here are already ambivalent. On the one hand he is taking his traditional introductory bow; on the other, by continuing with 'Macht wieder einige Verbeugungen' he exaggerates the gesture into a parody of courtly formality which invokes Barthold's irate reaction to contemporary affectation. On a second level then, Harlekin's gestures are a mimed parody of courtly convention, and we can expect that the rest of his actions continue this motif. He soon complements this gesture with a similar parody in language by addressing Berthold with exaggerated politeness, the stage direction 'in fremdem Ton' contrasting with the 'gewöhnlichen Ton' to which he quickly reverts when threatened with punishment. Through distortion of his natural voice, Harlekin conveys parody not just by what he says, but also by his method of delivery. Like Pantalon and Brigella in *Das Nachspiel zur berühmten Komödie … List gegen List*, when Harlekin falls out of his natural role he is subject to punishment. He must remain natural to maintain his integrity and immunity.

The ensuing conversation on the subject of Kolombine reveals Harlekin's thoroughly simplistic view of life and marriage. But true to his fundamental character he has an acute sense of what theatre is all about. Explaining to Berthold his reluctance to marry, he says, 'Sie wissen, mein werthester Herr Berthold, daß man von den Comödiantinnen mancherley sagt' (6). Beneath the literal meaning of this statement for the immediate dramatic action is a direct commentary on contemporary attitudes toward theatre folk, and actresses in particular. The general assumption that actors and actresses, especially those of itinerant companies, were an immoral lot had long plagued their lives, kept them in constant tension with local and church officials throughout the century, and contributed to the prevailing notion that theatre was immoral. Only in the last decades of the century did this bias soften into gradual acceptance and respect, then even into admiration and acclaim. Of course there was some justification for thinking such things of theatre folk (e.g. Eckenberg's antics in the early decades), and it was true that members of itinerant companies – in fact actors throughout the ages – did not conform to general patterns of bourgeois respectability. Moreover, the common use of sexual allusions in comedy naively led many to assume that such fictions reflected personal conduct. Like any other group, actors no doubt enjoyed their share of moral digression, but not necessarily more than social groups with the advantage of anonymity. That Harlekin's doubts about Kolombine's virtue are a

comment on the public attitude toward actresses is further evidenced as
he turns his remarks directly to the audience:

> Aber sehen Sie einmal Selbst, Herr Barthold, alle diese schönen Herrn,
> welche hier vor unsrer Bühne sitzen. Ihre Augen scheinen meinem lieben
> Kolombinchen das Mark aus den Knochen zu ziehen; und wenn sie tanzt;
> ach, wenn sie tanzt: so – so – tanzen alle Herzen mit ihr.
>
> ...
>
> Denen Mädchen, die so hoch springen wenn sie tanzen, kann leicht ein
> Blümchen entfallen; und wenn das auch nicht wäre: so rühmt sich doch ein
> jeder, vielleicht selten mit Recht, daß er eines aufgenommen habe. Herr
> Barthold, Herr Barthold! eine hübsche Comödiantinn ist wohl selten, selten,
> selten eine Kirsche woran nicht schon ein Vogel gebissen hat. (7f)

Now this was a spicy little titbit for the gentlemen in the parterre, but
every morsel of vicarious pleasure they might have derived from it
only underscored their own guilt. By addressing them directly, Harlekin exposes their intentions in coming to the theatre. In graphic terms
he mixes natural and even oral/sexual images ('Blümchen,' 'Kirsche ...
gebissen') to describe the actress's effect and the way her entranced
public virtually undresses and deflowers her with their eyes. The high
point is clearly her dancing, and in conjunction with his captivating
description 'so – so – ' he obviously performs a mime of her dance himself – who knows with what emphasis on delicacy, grace, or sexuality.
We are reminded of how important ballet was for itinerant troupes
such as Schuch's, Schönemann's, and Ackermann's, and know that
there too physical and sexual elements likely played an important part.
In the end Harlekin's speech here is foremost an accusation, for whatever Kolombine or any other actress does on stage is simply a fantasy
which it is her job to produce. When the gentlemen of the parterre 'vielleicht selten mit Recht' claim to have personally enjoyed her favours,
they are contributing to the long-standing bias from which actresses
suffered.

Berthold argues against this point of view, in effect presenting the
counter-position of the parterre (which the men would no doubt
adopt), turning the scene into a debate, and thus the play-within-a-play
is set up as a test of Kolombine's virtue.

As she and Harlekin begin to rehearse their roles as 'Braut' and
'Freyer,' her enthusiasm and considerable knowledge of the part immediately suggest that Harlekin's concerns are well-founded, but this sug-
gestiveness again is simply a good actress at work. He, by contrast,
plays his role as an affected fop, continuing the parody of manners

which began with his entrance in the first scene of the play. The rehearsal ends in dispute.

A further layer is added to the fiction before the climactic scene is played. Using a technique common to modern film, we digress suddenly to Isabelle and Valer concurrently rehearsing a scene of a count and an actress in love; the theme: the impossibility of love between classes. They too are rehearsing, so we now have in effect a play-within-a-play-within-a-play. What they depict adds depth to what has gone before and the resolution to follow. It further reminds us and the parterre that the relationship between Harlekin and Kolombine is meant to have broader significance for contemporary mores. Isabelle addresses her lover: 'Nein, mein werthester Graf, so schmeichelhaft es mir auch ist von Ihnen geliebt zu werden, und so sehr ich von Ihren rechtschaffenen Absichten überzeuget bin, so wenig finde ich mich vermögend Ihnen meine Hand zu geben' (17). The suitor's pompous language betrays his insincerity, so that Isabelle's polite refusal carries an underlying ironic comment on the integrity of the class her suitor represents. The scene may also be meant as a parody of other works of the time which tried to treat this theme seriously, usually resulting in unconvincing melodrama.

Isabelle upbraids Harlekin for his lack of confidence in Kolombine and his mistrust of the integrity of actresses in general: 'Ich glaube, Harlekin, Du dächtest besser von unsrer Schaubühne. Wenn man alle diejenigen von uns verurtheilen wollte, welche etwa einen freundlichen Blick regelten, oder sich eine Versuchung zuziehen, so würde man sehr ungerecht gegen uns seyn' (22). The test of Kolombine's virtue begins as Harlekin reappears disguised in a captain's uniform: '*Harlekin*. (Zieht das Kleid über das seinige, und macht dabey ein Theaterspiel).' The levels of meaning are deepened again as Harlekin changes costume and role before our eyes, not off-stage. Harlekin disguised? – we remember the consequences of this for Pantalon and Brigella in *Das Nachspiel zur berühmten Komödie ... List gegen List*. Here too there is an immediate flaw. Peter and Scapin inspect Harlekin's uniform:

Peter. Aber die Hosen?
Scapin. O! die kann man bey jedem Kleide tragen, und ein Witwer mag sie so gar in der Trauer anziehn.
Peter. Bey uns sagt man, es ist kein Herr so groß, oder der Narr blickt irgendwo hervor. (23)

Harlekin's identifiable chequered trousers obviously show from beneath his tunic, but his rival Scapin, who has wagered with him about the outcome and stands to give Harlekin a beating if he wins, is just as happy that the disguise is ridiculously incomplete. It shows us, however, that Harlekin's true identity cannot be hidden, and Peter's remark lifts the entire scene to a general level of social commentary. The 'Narr' here is the fool in all of us. That is why the comic fool on stage has always enjoyed identification with and loyalty from the public.

Then comes the conclusive meeting between Kolombine and Harlekin as half-disguised captain:

> (Er nimmt sie bey der Hand, und stellet sie so daß sie ihm nicht entgehen kann.)
>
> ...
>
> (Er will sie küssen, und sie wehret sich.)
>
> ...
>
> (Er dringt ihr solche [Ohrringe] auf, sie fallen aber auf die Erde.)
>
> ...
>
> (wie vorher [mit Dukaten].)
>
> *Harlekin.* und nun gehts auf die Bresche los.
>
> (Er umarmt sie auf seine Art.)

As she screams, others rush in to help: '(Kolombine hebt inzwischen das Kästchen [mit Schmuck] auf und sieht aus Vorwitz hinein.)'; and the scuffle concludes as Berthold steps in: '(Er prügelt ihn zur Schaubühne herunter. Scapin und Peter halten ihm überall wo er hin läuft, die Hände vor, um ihr Geld zu empfangen. Harlekin entfleiht endlich.)' (28f).

The scene is strongly reminiscent of the conclusion of *Was ist's?* and of von Wendheim's misguided overture to Amalie as well as his idiotic antics at the end. Here, similarly, Harlekin is afforded limitless opportunity to extemporize. His coarse licentiousness belongs to the character of the officer he is playing, a further comment on this social type, and with it an extension of the scene played moments before by Isabelle and Valer. After failing to impress Kolombine with the usual baubles, the traditional tactics of the wealthy gentleman in search of a poor girl's favours, he reveals his true character, finally attempting to take her by force. Kolombine's dallying interest in the jewel box while her oppressor is being brought under control provides an ironic twist, but is not enough to place in question the moral victory she has won. The final beating, so common in the traditional Nachspiel, is thus directed two ways: to all those of the upper class bent on seduction; and to the real Harlekin for his disloyalty to the troupe and his natural partner by doubting Kolombine's virtue.

Although this scene in effect ends the play, a final scene is devoted to unravelling the internal fictional construct, bringing us back to the level of meaning with which the opening scene began. Harlekin returns, cap in hand, and wants to play bride and groom once again, but this time as himself, and a duplication of his misguided rehearsal with Kolombine in Scene 3 occurs. But now that he has reassumed his natural role and true identity, Kolombine cheerfully takes him back.

Conclusion

We can now return to the two central questions posed at the end of Chapter 4: What traditional Nachspiel elements are evident in each of the representative works to be analysed in detail? To what extent are these elements as strongly represented in the later group (after 1770) as in the earlier one? Chapter 5 showed that Nachspiele published before 1770 gave prominence to the comic figure by name and afforded him considerable licence to extemporize, in effect making him responsible for much of the comedy. The majority of those early Nachspiele were also connected to a previous work. Finally, the early group showed signs of serious thematics below the surface, but this remained clearly secondary to the purpose of entertainment and good fun.

The Nachspiele published after 1770 show a continuation of these traditional elements to some extent, but an evolution as well. The central comic figure by name has lost his predominant position (he is present in only two of the nine works considered), yet the extemporized comedy which was the trademark of his performance is still very much alive. Now extemporization has become dispersed among the performances of many characters, and the comic effect results more from shared comic situations than from the antics of one character. These later Nachspiele also show little dependence on other works – only one of the nine considered was connected to a previous work – and hence suggest a growing independence for the genre. Finally, as was the case with the earlier group, the later Nachspiele also show signs of serious thematics beneath the surface, but once again these are subordinate to the comic fun. In the end, it is the talent of the actors, either as individuals playing identifiable comic figures by name or in concert with others in the cast, that made these Nachspiele successful throughout both periods examined. Technique was as important as, perhaps even more important than, text. With this in mind we turn to an examination of acting technique, as the raw talent of the comic actor meets with a new emphasis on controlled acting at the end of the century.

Acting:
Talent and Rules

The foregoing analyses have attempted in part to find out something about the nature of performances; concurrent developments in the acting profession must be kept in mind. A relatively sudden change in the venue of theatre from the temporary stages of itinerant troupes to the dominant position of standing theatres had major consequences for performance style. The change resulted in large measure from the shift from performance based mainly on fragmentary scenarios to increasing dependence on a fixed text base. Working from scenarios, actors had to improvise almost everything except the basic idea and plot line. With a full, and as the century progressed, published script, their task was primarily to say and do what the author presented in written dialogue and stage directions, only secondarily to create characters and dramatic interplay from scratch. The change from scant scenario to text-based production naturally bore consequences for acting style and technique, an aspect of eighteenth century theatre that has recently drawn scholars' renewed attention. For helpful overviews, see Maurer-Schmoock, *Deutsches Theater*, 149-99 and Simon Williams, *German Actors*. Readers may also wish to consult Dene Barnett's outstanding work on *The Art of Gesture* in the European eighteenth century.

We know that itinerant troupes performed wherever they could, from hastily constructed open-air stages to inns, halls, and, if they were lucky, formal theatres. Needing to carry all costumes and props from place to place, these were restricted drastically to skeletal needs; there could be no thought of maintaining a wardrobe realistically suited to all roles and characters, so that bizarre combinations, anachronisms, and misfits were common. At least the itinerant troupes had a logical excuse, but such incongruities were still evident at the end of the century even in standing theatres, as we saw in the reception of *Die beiden Billets*. Small temporary stages in public places such as market squares meant that audiences were often very close to the action and could see nuances of expression and gesture much more easily than could later visitors to larger theatres. Without a fixed text base, and with little time to prepare for performances, there was rarely a question of rehearsal, let alone direction from an authoritative person. How were actors to act? In the absence of a formal method or training, they were left largely to their own inventiveness and what they knew would gain audience response. Any models they could follow were foreign, particularly those set by the many French companies who provided their foremost competition and who brought to German territory a cultivated classicist style of acting and costume from the *Comédie Française* in Paris. But German actors lacked the professional training and experience of their rivals and thus provided essentially an inadvertent caricature of the French manner. Their strength and popularity resulted not from their imitation of the French, but rather from their natural talent for improvising; indeed, it was this talent that remained the key to the actor's craft even as the century progressed and schools of acting technique developed. An ability to improvise may well be essential to good comic acting in all cultures and times.

In plain terms, however, the spectator of German theatre in the early eighteenth century saw a kaleidoscope of individual talent with an abysmally low standard of ensemble coherence. The first to address this situation seriously with concrete suggestions for improvement was Gottsched in his *Ausführliche Redekunst* (1. Aufl., 1728; [5]1759), a work primarily intended to correct what the author saw as the deplorable state of written and spoken German and the inability of citizens to communicate effectively in the public domain. Written to be 'ein beständiges Lehrbuch auf Universitäten' (7), the *Redekunst* is an exhaustive presentation of good examples in the art of rhetoric starting from a firm base in classical antiquity. While the work was not written primarily with the stage in mind, its emphasis on the importance of verbal communication is fundamental to effective theatre, and Gottsched does not fail to address this realm directly. In the chapter 'Vom guten Vortrage einer Rede überhaupt, und im Absehen auf die Aussprache insbesondere' (1. Theil, 415-33) he draws a distinction that remained central to discussions of acting for the rest of the century: 'Ein Redner ... muß mit gleichem Fleiße darauf denken, wie er seine

Rede wohl halten, als wie er sie wohl ausarbeiten wolle. Mit dem bloßen Naturelle, darauf man es gemeiniglich allein ankommen läßt, ist es gewiß nicht ausgerichtet. Es thut zwar bey einigen viel, allein es muß auch durch die Regeln geleitet, und durch die Nachahmung guter Muster gebessert werden' (416). The crucial distinction is between natural talent and rules. For Gottsched, the former is important, but not enough in itself. This talent must be cultivated and developed by the observation of rhetorical principles and imitation of good examples.

Specific directions for improving natural deficiencies follow this statement, including detailed prescriptions for the vocal expression of particular feelings and moods, such as hate, anger, and sympathy, as well as rhetorical techniques to achieve desired effects (424-31). Gottsched continues exploring the duality of nature and rules soon after in 'Von guten Stellungen und Bewegungen eines Redners' (I, 434-43), which concentrates on gesture and body movement. He holds it to be true that every good speaker accompanies his vocal projection with complementary facial expressions and movements, which also serve to influence his listener, especially in the case of actors: 'Er folget also billig seinem Naturelle, und suchet selbiges, so viel ihm möglich ist, aufzuwecken und zu verbessern. Ich rede hier von dem Naturelle, und zwar nicht ohne Grund: denn die natürlichen Gaben thun auch in diesem Stücke sehr viel' (435f). Again Gottsched pays homage to natural, instinctive ability; yet in describing how the actor is to enhance this natural talent, he betrays an underlying prejudice that colours the entire work. Of 'die Beredsamkeit des Leibes' in general he writes: 'In neueren Zeiten ist diese Kunst sehr in Verfall gerathen, und in einigen Ländern fast gar aus der Beredsamkeit verbannet worden ... die Italiener treiben dieselbe mit so vielen Ausschweifungen, daß sie einen Ausländer oft zum Lachen zwingen. Nur die Franzosen haben durch Regeln und Exempel gewiesen, wie man das rechte Mittel darinn halten müsse' (434f). Despite Gottsched's heavy emphasis on Greek and Roman examples, he saw France as the mecca of modern rhetoricians and actors. His disparaging comments about the state of rhetorics in his own land and in Italy are based in part on his observation of itinerant theatre performance and the unharnessed, uncontrolled, and unregulated style of improvised gesture and mime. In the end he places much more emphasis on the support of proscribed and learned rules for expression and movement than on natural talent and instinct.

In practical terms Gottsched looked upon Caroline Neuber's troupe to set an example in the German theatre world according to his ideas, but when the principles of his *Redekunst* and encouragement of French models were applied by her company, the results hardly dignified the theory behind them. As Reden-Esbeck describes, French plays in stultifying alexandrines were the rule for Neuber:

Die französische Declamation, ihr outrirtes Pathos mit den lange vibrirenden Achs und Oh's ... Die Grazie wellenförmiger Bewegungen, Erhabenheit des Anstandes, Großartigkeit der leidenschaftlichen Gestikulation lag in der Intention, aber es war Alles, wie vom Balletmeister zugestutzt, Alles geziert und aufs äußerste übertrieben. Der Schritt war taktmäßig. Nur ein Fuß trug die stehende Gestalt, der andere war im coupepied mit der Spitze nur aufgestellt. Arme und Hände machten keine andere als gewundene Bogenbewegungen und fuhren mit Pathos völlig aus dem Gleise der Natur. Die Arme sägten durch die Luft, die Hände wurden wild geschüttelt, der Schritt spreitzte sich und der Oberkörper wand sich vorn und hinten über. (73)

To make matters worse, the cast was of course subject to the usual costume restrictions of itinerant troupes, in this case with emphasis on French courtly attire, often with absurd results: 'Die Helden oder Heldinnen mochten nun einen Brutus, einen Cato oder eine Phädra, eine Alzire vorstellen; der Galanteriedegen in der Hand, der dreieckige Hut unter dem Arme, oder, wenn der Fächer gegen die allzutragische Situation verstieß, doch ein wehendes Schnupftuch in der Hand der reifröckigen Heldin, konnten und durften nicht fehlen' (74). In practice, virtually nothing natural was left, and the rules Gottsched prescribed to enhance instinctive talent in the end served to stifle it.

Typical for the time, members of the Neuber troupe were subject to the *Fach-system* of role distribution, a practice which remained part of the theatre scene even to the end of the century (see Williams, 9f). Plays were divided up by character types to produce a generic list including kings, queens, tyrants, courtiers, servants, lovers, and old men. Actors were identified with these types and hired to play them in whatever works were performed. This type-casting of actors resulted naturally in stock character depiction and understanding, which contributed to caricature rather than the fresh exploration and depiction of the characters.

Schönemann's troupe was more successful in combining instinct and regulation, and largely because of a single member's contribution. Conrad Ekhof, sometimes called the 'father of German acting,' begins a meagre line of distinguished German actors in the eighteenth century. Here is an example of some of the instructions typically given to Schönemann's actors before Ekhof's influence became apparent:

Ein Drittheil des Gesichts müsse allemal gegen den Mitspielenden und zwei
Drittheil gegen die Zuschauer gerichtet seyn; bey Hebung der rechten
Hand, müsse der linke Fuß; und bei Hebung der linken Hand, der rechte
Fuß, vorgesetzt werden; bei einer solchen Bewegung der Hände müsse sich
erst der obere Theil des Arms vom Körper lösen, bis zu einer gleichen Linie
langsam erheben, und dann in der Mitte sanft biegen; hierauf würde der
untere Theil, und endlich die Hand in Bewegung gesetzt, welche nun, mit
leicht gesenkten Fingern, den Inhalt des vorzutragenden Textes andeuten
müsse ... (Maurer-Schmoock, 153)

To test how constricting these instructions are, the reader might try to
follow them before a mirror, preferably wearing a large helmet
adorned with a spray of feathers and as cumbersome a costume as the
attic will yield.

Ekhof started his career in extemporized parts, joined Schönemann's
troupe and stayed with them for seventeen years. After Schönemann's
departure he remained with the troupe under Koch before joining the
company of the Hamburg Nationaltheater with Ackermann in 1767
and ending his career as the director of the Gotha court theatre from
1774 to his death in 1778. He was often praised and admired as the best
actor of his age, Lessing being just one of the many who raved:
'Welcher Reichtum von mahlenden Gesten, durch die er allgemeinen
Betrachtungen gleichsam Figur und Körper giebt, und seine innersten
Empfindungen in sichtbare Gegenstände verwandelt! Welcher fortreis-
sende Ton der Ueberzeugung!' (*Werke*, Hanser edition, IV, 309).

Ekhof was a small man of unimposing physical attributes, which did
not make him a natural for stardom; yet he nevertheless gained fame
and became a model for others to emulate. Although he matured at a
time when Gottsched's emphasis on French models was powerful, he is
said to have overcome these restrictions to develop his own technique.
Ekhof believed that the art of acting was to imitate nature – Gottsched's
claimed source of wisdom too (as well as of virtually every other dramatic theorist through the end of the century) – but to do so in such a
way that truth could be seen through the performance. Ekhof was
aware that while taking nature as his guide, the actor had to be aware
that the stage was not life, and thus by definition unnatural, artificial.
He saw it as a danger, one too often prevalent in the acting style of his
contemporaries, to abandon oneself completely to the role or character
portrayed. The actor needed principles, rules, a methodology to govern
his interpretation, and then, as Ekhof put it in 1753, it was the actor's
task, 'die Gramatik der Schauspielkunst [zu] studieren' (Kindermann,
CE, 21). But this grammar, this methodology for German actors, did

not as yet exist despite resources such as Gottsched's *Redekunst* and its models.

Ekhof's call for a fixed set of guidelines for actors was not to be answered for several decades, but he himself tried to make a start with the Schönemann troupe in 1753. He proposed and inaugurated the Academie der Schönemannischen Gesellschaft whose purpose it was to bring company members together every two weeks, on Saturdays from two to four o'clock to discuss the repertoire, their artistic objectives, and their method of acting and performing plays (see a good account of the academy in Devrient, 206-40 and Kindermann's full documentation of it in his *CE*). To this point Schönemann as principal had carried the burden of direction, but now the troupe was to share the responsibility, an important development for the history of acting in the century, for in effect Ekhof had introduced the notion of the actor's own internal direction as opposed to external direction through the director as an omnipotent observer. This idea would lead to similar experiments and successes in Mannheim and other theatres, and in general terms bring to the foreground the necessity for actors to think of their place in an ensemble, not just as individuals on stage.

Ekhof wrote a constitution of twenty-four articles for the academy, presenting them for discussion at committee meetings. In the assembly of 2 June 1753 he presented a full outline of their deliberations ahead:

> Die Schauspielkunst ist: durch Kunst der Natur nachahmen, und ihr so nahe kommen, daß Wahrscheinlichkeiten für Wahrheiten angenommen werden müssen, oder geschehene Dinge so natürlich wieder vorstellen, als wenn sie jetzt erst geschehen. Um in dieser Kunst zu einer Fertigkeit zu gelangen, wird eine lebhafte Einbildungskraft, eine männliche Beurteilungskraft, ein unermüdeter Fleiß, und eine nimmermüßige Uebung erfordert. Dies sind die sicheren Mittel, wodurch alle Abwege vermieden werden und alle Schauspieler das Ziel ihrer Bemühungen erreichen können. Der Zweck unserer Sitzungen ist, diese Mittel so viel als möglich auseinander zu setzen, und zu erleichtern. Bevor wir aber die Seelenkräfte eines Schauspielers in Erwegung ziehen, wird es nöthig seyn, Betrachtungen über die mechanischen Theile der Schauspielkunst anzustellen, und in den künftigen Sitzungen unser Augenmerk auf folgende Dinge zu richten, nemlich: (a) auf die Schauspiele, (b) auf das Theater und dahin gehörigen Theile, (c) auf die Schauspieler, und endlich (d) auf die Vorstellungskunst.
> (Kindermann, *CE*, 17f)

The undertaking was immensely ambitious. Ekhof understood the full extent of the problems faced by the stage in his time, and was prescribing diagnosis and treatment from the ground up. Striking in the statement above is the order in which the problems were to be discussed and tackled. Although in principle he saw nature as the ultimate guide, it was art that could make it work, and this must be learned through hard work and practice. Before 'Seelenkräfte' can play their part, full attention must be paid to 'die mechanischen Theile der Schauspielkunst.' These mechanical parts are things that could be learned: appropriate expression, pose, gesture, movement, and voice control.

We know from the last assembly of the academy, just thirteen months later on 15 June 1754, that the guidebook used to discuss these mechanics had been Lessing's 1750 translation of Francesco Riccoboni's *L'art du théâtre* (*Die Schauspielkunst*), soon after the original appeared (Kindermann, *CE*, 40). It is a detailed set of instructions for actors and one somewhat removed from the tendency of French classicist style. In fact Riccoboni distanced himself diplomatically from his father who had previously published an influential treatise on declamation, which was more in line with the French tradition (Lessing, *Die Schauspielkunst*, *Werke*, Bong edition, X, 79). Riccoboni's work treats movement, voice, declamation, expression, character portrayal, the concept of the ensemble, and many other aspects of performance, often in minute detail (see full list, Lessing, *Werke*, X, 78). In a blunt assessment of the French declamatory style, Riccoboni shows himself to be a true maverick:

> Die Heftigkeit und Monotonie zusammen sind es, welche die Deklamation ausmachen. Sachte anfangen, mit einer gezwungenen Langsamkeit aussprechen, die Töne dehnen, ohne sie zu verändern, plötzlich einen davon mitten im Verstande erheben und schleunig wieder in den Ton, den man verlassen hat, fallen; in den Augenblicken, da sich die Leidenschaften äußern, sich mit einer übermäßigen Stärke ausdrücken, ohne jemals die Art der Tonfügung zu ändern; das heißt deklamieren. Das wunderbarste ist, daß diese Art zu reden in Frankreich aufgekommen ist und sich auch beständig daselbst erhalten hat. Diejenige Nation, die am meisten das Angenehme, Liebliche und Ungezwungene sucht, und die auch die meiste Fähigkeit darzu hat, ist gleich diejenige, bei welcher auf dem Theater zu allen Zeiten die Monotonie, das Schwerfällige und das Gezwungene geherrscht hat. (*Werke*, Bong edition, X, 85)

Thus from France came this important articulation of the weakness of declamatory style, which was then adopted by Ekhof, Lessing, and others. Obviously that style ran counter to any sense of naturalism or realism on stage. It was also an expression of preconceived ideas of what theatre rhetoric should be. In contrast to this, Riccoboni suggests where the essence of good acting should lie. In the section 'Die Einsicht,' he writes:

> Das, was in der Tat den Namen Einsicht verdienet, ist die vorzüglichste theatralische Gabe. Sie allein macht große Schauspieler; und ohne sie kann man niemals was anders als einer von den mittelmäßigen Leuten werden, welchen gewisse Annehmlicheiten des Körpers oder der Stimme dann und wann einigen Glanz geben, mit denen aber ein Kenner unmöglich gänzlich zufrieden sein kann. Das ist nicht genug, daß man die Rede, welche uns der Dichter in Mund gelegt, versteht und sie nicht widersinnisch ausdruckt: man muß alle Augenblicke das Verhältnis einsehen, welches das, was wir sagen, mit dem Charakter unserer Rolle, mit der Stellung, in welche uns die Bühne setzt, und mit der Wirkung, die es in der Haupthandlung hervorbringen soll, hat. (*Werke*, Bong edition, X, 88f)

For Riccoboni, 'Einsicht' – understanding or insight – is the actor's most valuable asset, indispensable for excellence. What he means by this is not exactly intuitive genius, but rather sensitivity to the needs of the role and ensemble. Put another way, Riccoboni wants the actor to think, to combine the technical skills in his command with a sensitive reaction to the dramatic situation in which he is performing. More is demanded of him than a pure projection of the text, less than total abandonment to the resources of his own inventive genius. Riccoboni felt too that it was impossible for an actor to identify precisely with each character he played. The actor must therefore explore each character within the terms of the text delivered by the playwright and try to abstract and portray the character's feelings broadly and convincingly to convey a sense of what he is like. The stage for Riccoboni was not reality but rather a medium for realistic impression (see Williams, 15).

Riccoboni also says in his treatise that actors must progress through the instructions contained in his work in the order set out. In that order, movement is first, then voice, declamation, and 'Einsicht.' Only much later, toward the end of the work, come the more sophisticated considerations of 'Theaterspiel,' 'Übereinstimmung,' and 'Ton' which relate to the overall harmony and impression of the ensemble. It is significant that immediately before his discussion of this concept, Riccoboni placed 'Das stumme Spiel' – one of the last things an actor should attempt to learn, only after all rudimentary elements had been studied:

> Das allerachtungswürdigste Stück bei einem Schauspieler ist das stumme
> Spiel, und nur wenige besitzen es wohl. Es müssen sich alle Leidenschaften,
> alle Bewegungen der Seele, alle Veränderungen der Gedanken auf seinem
> Gesichte abmalen, wenn er will, daß die Zuschauer einen lebhaften Anteil
> an der Vorstellung nehmen sollen ... Der Leib bewegt sich bei diesen
> Gelegenheiten auch und trägt das Seine zum Ausdrucke sowohl als das
> Gesichte bei. (*Werke*, Bong edition, X, 104)

With this statement Riccoboni pays homage to gesture and mime, and in doing so to the backbone of extemporized theatre. While he does serve a broad caveat that excess in expression and gesture is unacceptable to ensemble harmony, he nevertheless recognizes this aspect of the actor's craft as the most difficult to master.

It is meaningful that both Ekhof and Lessing regarded Riccoboni's treatise so highly. Both believed in nature as the ultimate guide and instinctive genius as the most essential attribute of a good actor. But both saw the study and perfection of regulated technique as the first thing to be mastered. Underlying their thoughts is the division between two types of actor, the purely intuitive and the technically competent. Ideally the poles would be combined, as they probably were in Ekhof himself. Failing this, the technically correct actor had the advantage over the other in that his performance would at least be acceptable and professional, if not inspired. Conversely, without regard for formal technique, there were no limits to be observed at all, no standards against which to measure professionalism and quality – the way would be free for unbridled charlatanism on the stage. This is what Ekhof and Lessing both saw as characteristic of the past decades and the main reason for the disrepute of the acting profession. Unfortunately, that period of charlatanism had also been a heyday of improvisational genius. With the growing emphasis on rules for actors, the cultivation of instinct and spontaneity was being pushed to the background in favour of uniformity and professional respectability.

One of the few contemporaries who thought little of Ekhof's acting or approach was his arch-rival Friedrich Ludwig Schröder. Born of the well-known actress Sophie Schröder and Konrad Ernst Ackermann (though his fathership was uncertain), Schröder was a child of the theatre to which he devoted his life. Although Ekhof is called the father of German acting, Schröder rivalled him in renown, but for entirely different reasons. He was stunning in improvisation, acrobatics, and pure innovative comic genius. He thought Ekhof stiff and talentless, often mocking his serious approach, and when Ackermann took the great opportunity to play in the Hamburg Nationaltheater in 1767

Schröder refused to go, preferring instead to join Joseph von Kurz to tour in Vienna, Frankfurt, and Mainz – two kindred spirits, perhaps the last of the great improvisational talents. Later Schröder assumed leadership of Ackermann's company upon the latter's death in 1771 and thereafter devoted himself more to text-based roles, but he never abandoned his belief in the fundamental power of improvisation. Schröder insisted that freedom, not restriction, was the essence of effective acting, as his contemporary Friedrich Ludwig Schmidt recorded in this conversation:

> Sie thun sehr wohl daran [sagte Schröder], die Affen- und Afterkunst des Copirens schlechthin zu verwerfen; Ein selbständiger Schritt vorwärts ist mehr werth, als meilenweit auf fremden Krücken zu hinken. Die Schauspielkunst wird sehr herabgewürdigt, wenn man nur den Begriff der Nachahmung vorhandener Muster damit verbindet. Allenfalls staunt man den Fleiß des Copisten an, aber auf den Namen eines Künstlers darf nur Derjenige Anspruch machen, der aus der Fülle seiner Phantasie eigene Gebilde frei erschafft. Ein Schauspieler sei kein Antiquar, der seine Gestalten durch Tradition empfängt und wiedergibt! (Schmidt, *Denkwürdigkeiten*, 206f)

Central to Schröder's concept of the actor as artist is the ability to create through fantasy and intuitive genius instead of slavishly copying models adhering to prescribed technique. While Ekhof and Lessing may well have agreed, unlike Schröder they would not have been willing to take the risk he accepts by encouraging the actor first and foremost to create something new each time he performs. This freedom was of course common in the extemporized theatre tradition which retained Schröder's allegiance, but in the sixties and seventies, with complete texts forming the basis of most performances, such freedom was more difficult to maintain. Still, even within this mode, Schröder defended his position, and despite his own evolution toward text-based performance, he tirelessly rejected its primacy over the actor:

> Selbst den Dichter muß der Schauspieler überwinden; je größer jener, um so schwerer der Kampf, um so glorreicher der Sieg. Wehe der Kunst, wenn der Herausgehende sagt: 'Wie schön war die Decoration und wie trefflich das Costüm!' Wehe dem Schauspieler, wenn, statt mit Thränen im Auge oder mit Lächeln auf den Lippen wortlos das Theater zu verlassen, der Zuschauer laut sagt: 'Das Stück ist schön geschrieben!' Dann war es eine Lesegesellschaft, die er verlassen hat. (Schmidt, *Denkwürdigkeiten*, 136)

The last sentence says it all. What counts for Schröder, what counts for true theatre, is not costume, not props, not scenery, not text – what counts, the only thing that counts, is the actor's ability to move the audience. That is his genius. How he does it is irrelevant. Failure to do it is fatal. The position is extreme, but in the face of a wave of fashion in the opposite direction, understandable. And while Schröder, Kurz, and their school were to be the losers by the end of the century, what Schröder says here was picked up, modified, and reiterated by others who were more influential in directing the course of the theatre in coming decades.

Critics and advocates like Lessing, while leaning much more toward regulation than Schröder and Kurz, nevertheless retained the highest regard for intuitive genius. Lessing himself felt he learned most about the theatre from Ekhof, and of course during the years of the Hamburg Nationaltheater experiment they were in constant partnership. Setting out from Riccoboni's *Schauspielkunst*, Lessing began to refine his thoughts on theatre and acting by attempting to write an instruction book for actors himself (*Der Schauspieler*, 1754-5), by translating Diderot (*Das Theater des Herrn Diderot*, 2 vols., 1760), and through the *Hamburgische Dramaturgie* (1767-8).

In *Der Schauspieler*, Lessing tried to set down for German actors what he had recently seen Riccoboni do for the French. The fact that the attempt was published only posthumously shows that he believed he had failed, and indeed he had. There are two versions of the fragmentary work, the second even less complete than the first, with both subtitled 'Ein Werk worinne die Grundsätze der ganzen körperlichen Beredsamkeit entwickelt werden.' 'Körperliche Beredsamkeit' is divided into various forms of expression, body movement, gestures, voice tones, posture, and position. Some of these subcategories are accompanied by directions to achieve desired effects in tragedy or comedy or to depict certain character types such as the 'Stutzer,' 'Alten,' or 'Bedienten.' This underlying principle for all movement on stage guides his observations: 'Bewegungen aus *graden* Linien. Diese gehören für alles das was unter der *schönen* Natur ist, z.E. für das bäurische etc. und zugleich für heftige Leidenschaften, weil diese den kürzesten Weg gehen. Bewegungen aus unangenehmen krummen Linien. Diese gehören für alles das, was über der schönen Natur sein will; für das affektierte zum Exempel' (*Werke*, Hanser edition, IV, 729). In this assessment of the effect of curved and straight lines of movement, Lessing shows that he was already forging a path in a different direction from the French tradition which would have reversed the two effects. He stresses the beauty of nature as a guide and associates this beauty with direct movement, affectation with indirect movement or what he calls 'curves.' His argument is pragmatic, realistic – 'weil diese den kürzesten Weg gehen' – and points to his growing sense of realism in acting technique. But the work on the whole does little more than make a start toward the objective set in its subtitle. Lessing evidently abandoned it for more pressing concerns.

In 1760 he published a translation of some Diderot works, *Das Theater des Herrn Diderot*, clearly because he saw in Diderot a kindred spirit to Riccoboni and himself, all three rebels against the French style. In his foreword Lessing describes the reason for his admiration:

> Daher sieht er [Diderot] auch die Bühne seiner Nation bei weitem auf der Stufe der Vollkommenheit nicht, auf welcher sie unter uns die schalen Köpfe erblicken, an deren Spitze der Prof. Gottsched ist. Er gestehet, daß ihre Dichter und Schauspieler noch weit von der Natur und Wahrheit entfernet sind; daß beider ihre Talente, guten Teils, auf kleine Anständigkeiten, auf handwerksmäßigen Zwang, auf kalte Etiquette hinauslaufen etc. (*Werke*, Hanser edition, IV, 148)

Of Diderot's *Der Hausvater*, which follows in translation, Lessing adds: 'Selbst unsere Schauspieler fingen an dem "Hausvater" zuerst an, sich selbst zu übertreffen. Denn der Hausvater war weder Französisch, noch deutsch: er war bloß menschlich. Er hatte nichts auszudrücken, als was jeder ausdrücken konnte, der es verstand und fühlte' (*Werke*, Hanser edition, IV, 150). These two quotations illustrate an important duality in Lessing's thoughts on acting and theatre. The first emphasizes once again the role of nature as the means to depict truth, and Lessing's belief that the French style was not the way to achieve it. The second does not address acting but rather text. He praises Diderot's play and its central character for their universality, their humanness. As he moved towards his most important dramatic enterprise in Hamburg and his most significant writing on the subjects of theatre and acting, Lessing had begun to distil a concept that would be central to the most positive developments in German acting and performance for the rest of the century: 'theatre, in text base as well as execution on stage, must be humanizing; it must relate to contemporary audiences; it must thus be natural and realistic. Until this time, the stage was a vehicle to portray *exceptional* humanity, kings and courtiers, heroes and heroines, and this was done in exceptional ways, through artificial verse, costume, and movement. Hereafter, the German stage should endeavour to present *average* humanity, the bourgeoisie, in their own natural setting and language, in a theatrically effective way' (Williams, 14).

Das Theater des Herrn Diderot also contains translated discussions of some Diderot plays. In the one on *Der natürliche Sohn*, one conversant observes: 'Wir reden in unsern Schauspielen zu viel, und folglich spielen unsere Akteurs nicht genug. Wir haben die Kunst, welche die Alten so vortrefflich zu nutzen wußten, ganz verloren' (*Werke*, Bong edition, IX, 109); and further:

> Was ich bei dieser Szene sonst noch anmerkte, war dieses, daß es Stellen gibt, die man fast ganz und gar dem Schauspieler überlassen sollte ... Was rührt uns bei dem Anblicke eines Menschen, der von gewaltigen Leidenschaften bestürmet wird, am meisten? Sind es seine Reden? Zuweilen. Aber das, was allezeit rühret, sind Schreie, unartikulierte Töne, abgebrochene Worte, einzelne Silben, die ihm dann und wann entfahren, und ich weiß selbst nicht, was für ein Murmeln in der Kehle und zwischen den Zähnen. (110)

Both of these observations emphasize the importance of the actor's freedom to explore his innovative genius in ways that go beyond the text. It is impossible for a playwright to tell the actor precisely how to achieve the most convincing effects; as the conversant observes: 'Sie [Künstler von der ersten Klasse] werden nicht durch Regeln, sondern durch etwas ganz anders, das weit unmittelbarer, weit inniger, weit dunkler und weit gewisser ist, geführet und erleuchtet' (112). So Lessing approached his grand plans for Hamburg with an unsystematic mixture of growing convictions: that theatre should be natural, realistic, and human; that actors needed systematic direction in their craft; that movement and gesture were the most difficult and most important to master; nevertheless, that no system of rules could replace innovative genius on the stage. The *Hamburgische Dramaturgie* (1767-8) reflects this mélange.

Lessing began the enterprise with great optimism. Already in the 'Ankündigung,' he gives enormous freedom and commensurate responsibility to the actor: 'Er muß überall mit dem Dichter denken; er muß da, wo dem Dichter etwas Menschliches widerfahren ist, für ihn denken' (*Werke*, Hanser edition, IV, 234). In pursuing the highest goal of humanized theatre, the actor must indeed correct and improve the text delivered by his playwright. The statement, right at the beginning of the *Dramaturgie*, recalls Schröder's statement to the same effect and testifies to Lessing's belief in the power of acting genius and to the primacy of performance over text. His belief in this genius carries through to the end, where in article 96 he holds up this notion against those who only pretend to respect it:

> Wir haben, dem Himmel sei Dank, itzt ein Geschlecht selbst von Kritikern, deren beste Kritik darin besteht, – alle Kritik verdächtig zu machen. 'Genie! Genie! schreien sie. Das Genie setzt sich über alle Regeln hinweg! Was das Genie macht, ist Regel!' So schmeicheln sie dem Genie: ich glaube, damit wir sie auch für Genies halten sollen. Doch sie verraten zu sehr, daß sie nicht einen Funken davon in sich spüren, wenn sie in einem und eben demselben Atem hinzusetzen: 'die Regeln unterdrücken das Genie!' – Als ob sich Genie durch etwas in der Welt unterdrücken ließe! Und noch dazu durch etwas, das, wie sie selbst gestehen, aus ihm hergeleitet ist. Nicht jeder Kunstrichter ist Genie: aber jedes Genie ist ein geborner Kunstrichter. Es hat die Probe aller Regeln in sich. Es begreift und behält und befolgt nur die, die ihm seine Empfindung in Worten ausdrücken. (*Werke*, Hanser edition, IV, 673)

By the end of the experience with the Hamburg Nationaltheater Lessing was clearly as convinced as ever of the singular importance of 'Genie' and of the fact that it overrides all rules for actors that could possibly be formulated. Still, by then he despaired that this quality was not sufficiently present in the present stock of German actors to carry the stage through to the goals he had in mind when the enterprise began. In the concluding articles 101-4, this disappointment sets the tone as the *Dramaturgie* concludes:

> Wir haben Schauspieler, aber keine Schauspielkunst. Wenn es vor Alters eine solche Kunst gegeben hat: so haben wir sie nicht mehr; sie ist verloren; sie muß ganz von neuem wieder erfunden werden. Allgemeines Geschwätze darüber, hat man in verschiedenen Sprachen genug: aber spezielle, von jedermann erkannte, mit Deutlichkeit und Präzision abgefaßte Regeln, nach welchen der Tadel oder das Lob des Akteurs in einem besondern Falle zu bestimmen sei, deren wüßte ich kaum zwei oder drei. (697)

Presumably one of the existing guides for actors he had in mind was Riccoboni's; perhaps another consisted of Ekhof's academy articles. But there was certainly still no complete guide written for German actors, including Lessing's own *Schauspieler* and the scattered attempts within the *Dramaturgie* to address the problem. His call for a set of rules confirms what he learned from his association with Ekhof, that while genius is the root of excellence in acting, technical perfection was the next best thing and would always guarantee acceptable standards at the very least.

Ekhof's and Lessing's call was finally answered by Johann Jakob Engel in his *Ideen zu einer Mimik*, first published in 1785, numerous times thereafter, and soon translated into both French and Dutch. Engel's extensive work was a conscious and direct answer to Lessing's plea (Engel, *Ideen*, I, 4). He shared Lessing's admiration of Ekhof's greatness as an actor (Engel, *Ideen*, I, 18), seeing his strength in the ability to blend his sense (*Empfindung*) of what a character was like with constant reflection (*Besonnenheit*) on his own portrayal of that character. This passage points to the fundamental principle of Engel's approach:

> Das Höchste, was ein Künstler herausbringen kann, der sich bloss seiner Empfindung überlässt, ist denn doch immer nur das: dass er die Leidenschaften, die ihm der Dichter in die Imagination legt, getreu so darstelle, wie sie in der Wirklichkeit selbst sich an den Personen äussern würden; mit einem Worte: dass er die *Natur* völlig erreiche. Aber Nachahmung, Darstellung der Natur ist, wie man schon oft erinnert hat, und noch immer von neuem zu erinnern Ursache findet, ein Grundsatz der nirgend hinreicht. Der Natur gelingt Manches in einer Vollkommenheit, dass die Kunst nicht weiter thun kann, als es sorgfältig aufzufassen und getreu wieder darzustellen; aber Manches erreicht bei jener, auch wo sie am besten wirkt, den Grad der Vollkommenheit nicht, den es sollte; Manches geräth ihr falsch, Manches zu schwach oder zu stark: und da erfordert denn die Pflicht der Kunst, aus einer gesammelten Menge von Beobachtungen, oder nach Grundsätzen die aus diesen Beobachtungen gezogen sind, die Fehler der Natur zu verbessern, das Falsche zu berichtigen, das zu Starke auf den gehörigen Grad herabzusetzen, das zu Schwache bis zur gehörigen Kraft zu verstärken. (*Ideen*, I, 18-20)

Engel's goal for actors is to depict not just nature but harmony. It is not the actor's business to portray disharmony, imperfection, or aberration, despite the fact that they do indeed exist. Unreflective imitation of nature is insufficient; rather, the actor must consciously manipulate his depiction of nature to approach its harmonious perfection, and this he can do 'aus einer gesammelten Menge von Beobachtungen, oder nach Grundsätzen die aus diesen Beobachtungen gezogen sind.' Engel actually uses the terms 'Instinct' and 'Genie,' but to these he adds the 'deutlich gedachte Regel' (*Ideen*, I, 23, 24f, 29f). Such a collection of rules Engel then presents in the following two volumes' eight hundred pages. Lessing could hardly have asked for more had he been alive to read the extended descriptions of movement and voice control, many accompanied by illustrative engravings and copious examples from specific plays and roles. German theatre now had its guidebook, and indeed Engel's work had enormous influence and became widely known, respected, and used, although it must have been impossible for any actor to master consciously all of its directions. Still, the authoritative primer was now there as a constant source of advice. Those who followed it could be sure that their performances would be at least respectable, even if they did not possess the genius and insight for excellence. As Lessing foresaw, the general standard of acting on German stages was on the road to steady improvement.

All credit, of course, could hardly be given to one man or one work. At the same time in Mannheim a new approach to acting and production was emerging under Heribert von Dalberg and one of his most important company members Iffland, who had served apprenticeship under Ekhof in Gotha before coming to Mannheim in 1779 for a decade which would establish him as the most famous German actor of his time. Dalberg's leadership of the Nationaltheater in Mannheim was enlightened to say the least (see Koffka's full account of the Dalberg/Iffland years). His institution of a committee in 1781, consisting mainly of actors, to discuss regularly the repertoire and their performance is strongly reminiscent of Ekhof's academy three decades earlier. Dalberg's committee lasted not one year but eight, the seriousness of its discussions well recorded in Martersteig's *Protokolle*. Committee members were often given questions to which they responded in written essays, as Iffland did to the question 'Können französische Trauerspiele auf der deutschen Bühne gefallen, und wie müssen sie vorgestellt werden, wenn sie allgemeinen Beifall erhalten sollen?' (Koffka, 471). Iffland's response is as follows:

Die Franzosen haben Hang zu Ostentation und Enthusiasmus. Das verursacht bei ihren Dichtern Tiraden, deren glänzende Recitirung, vereinigt mit jenem berühmten Tragödien-Schritt, den Kothurn der französischen Bühne ausmachen. Ihre Sprache gleicht einer Grazie, welche über blumigte Wiesen hüpft; Sprache und Sitten sind aber im nothwendigen Verhältnisse; nach der Wahrheit von der Wirkung der Contraste sollen daher die Franzosen diesen erhöheten Kothurn auf ihrer Bühne haben. Wir auch? – Durchaus nicht!

Die deutsche Sprache gleicht einem großen wohlgeordneten Körper, der mit Majestät einherschreitet. Der Kothurn der französischen Bühne muß daher bei dieser Sprache ein kaltes, ermüdendes Einerlei wirken. Der deutsche

> Schauspieler darf nichts von der Art des Französischen haben, dieser nichts
> von jenem.
>> Die Franzosen geben Vorstellungen.
>> Die Deutschen Darstellungen.
>> Ihre Gemälde der Leidenschaften sind prächtig; unsere wahr. ...
> Die mehresten der alten deutschen Schauspieler aber waren eine glückliche
> Mischung von Eigenheit und Copie französischer Schauspieler; viele der
> späteren sind Copien dieser Copien. Diese dritte Verpflanzung ausländ-
> ischen Kothurns – was kann sie wirken?
>> 'Staatsaction auf der Bühne; Gähnen oder Spott im Amphitheater.' ...
>> Die deutschen Schauspieler sollen daher mit Gefühl für Rhythmus und
> Harmonie überhaupt einen Kothurn wählen, welcher der Sprache und den
> Sitten der Deutschen angemessen ist. (Koffka, 472-4)

Still in the eighties the starting point for Iffland's observations is the
French style – it was clearly still prevalent on German stages, in repertoires, and in the actors who were mere copies or copies of copies of
the French actors rather than originals. While many before Iffland had
decried German imitation of that tradition, none had in the same
breath lauded the German language and dramatic style in its face. Instead of the artificiality of French 'Vorstellungen,' Iffland hoists German 'Darstellungen' which alone, he claims, are 'wahr.' If truth is indeed the highest goal of theatrical presentation, then Iffland could af-
ford his compatriots no greater compliment. Speaking in the eighties,
he was surely overstating his case, but it is nevertheless refreshing to
read such a bold confirmation of German drama instead of yet another
expression of disappointment and inferiority. Iffland insists that German theatre have a style commensurate with its unique language, cultural background, and interests, and that speeches be delivered 'mit
Gefühl für Rhythmus und Harmonie überhaupt.' The representation of
truth on stage involved for him a conscious artistic process. Truth necessitated realism, but the impression of reality could not be achieved
by pure imitation – actors must learn to accomplish that end.

By the time he left Mannheim Iffland was renowned as an actor and
could bask in the limelight for the next several decades in many German theatres. His most important post after Mannheim was as director
of the Königliches Theater in Berlin, and it was there that he began
writing and publishing his own detailed guidelines for actors. Published first in the *Berliner Almanachen* from 1807 to 1812, many such
guidelines can be read in Iffland's *Theorie der Schauspielkunst*, collected
and published by Christian Gottfried Flitner in 1815, just after Iffland's
death (1814).

The two volumes of the *Theorie* include many plates depicting scenes from contemporary plays with comments on the acting technique; biographies and laudatory assessments of the acting careers of Conrad Ekhof and Johann David Beil; and numerous essays on performance and the theatre in general. Iffland recalls how so many of Ekhof's contemporaries praised his work – 'Er war Naturalist,' they said (Iffland, *Theorie*, I, 7) – but Iffland goes on to enlarge upon this by comparing Ekhof's talent to a 'Nachtwandler angewandt auf die zarte Spur, wo bei dem Schauspieler Natur und Kunst sich vereinen, um von Allen gesehen, doch unbewußt daß es Zuseher gibt, die Wahrheit in Fülle und Schönheit darzustellen ...' (*Theorie*, I, 9f). This quality, Iffland claims, is the same as that central to Schiller's idea of performance. As others before him, Iffland stresses the depiction of truth as the highest goal of performance, and in Ekhof this was achieved through a delicate, even unconscious combination of natural instinctive talent and artistry. But Iffland's goal is not just truth, it is 'Schönheit,' hence an idealized impression of truth which depicts the rounded fullness of life, not aberration or incompleteness. At the end of his tribute, he resorts to the word 'Genius' to describe Ekhof's innate talent (*Theorie*, I, 29f), adding: 'Eckhof hat festgegründet, Schröder hat in edlem großen Sinne herauf gebauet' (I, 30). Despite his characterization of Ekhof's balance between natural instinct and artistry, Iffland's linking of Ekhof with Schröder – the epitome of the natural actor – shows that he saw instinct and genius in the end as the keys to excellence.

Among the other essays in the *Theorie*, 'Ueber die Bildung der Künstler zur Menschen-Darstellung auf der Bühne' and 'Ueber körperliche Beredsamkeit' are the most illuminating. The title of the first recalls a crucial distinction already made in his essay written for Dalberg in Mannheim, 'Darstellung' as opposed to 'Vorstellung.' Continuing here, he argues that the word 'Schauspiel' to refer to dramatic works should be replaced with the term 'Menschendarstellung' (*Theorie*, II, 37f). 'Schauspiel' belies the same theatrical approach as 'Vorstellung,' which he insists merely represents 'Äußeres' – it 'kann durch konventionelle Regeln erlernt und fertig geübt werden' (*Theorie*, II, 38). By contrast, 'Die Darstellung des Menschen betrifft das Innere desselben, den Gang der Leidenschaften, die hohe, einfache, starke Wahrheit im Ausdruck – die lebendige Hingebung der Uebergänge, welche in der Seele wechseln und allmälig zum Ziele führen. – Das ist Kunst' (*Theorie*, II, 38). Iffland certainly had a high regard for rules and guidelines in acting, and indeed in the remainder of this essay and in 'Ueber körperliche Beredsamkeit' he writes many of his own. But he knew that rules could lead only to competent depiction of the external, to 'Vorstellung' or 'Schauspiel,' not to revelations of character. While warning against the danger of too much 'Phantasie' (*Theorie*, II, 50), and emphasizing the importance of practising language, articulation, and gesture, he nevertheless emphasizes again and again the goal of reflecting 'den Seelenzustand' in every expression and movement (*Theorie*, II, 77). It is striking how much attention Iffland gives in the lengthy 'Ueber körperliche Beredsamkeit' (*Theorie*, II, 65-91) to 'Augensprache' (82-5) and minutiae of facial and muscular nuance. He obviously has in mind a highly controlled, reflective actor and believes that through tightly directed language, a character's inner 'Seelenzustand' could be revealed. While instinct and genius are acknowledged by Iffland to be the essence of excellence in acting, control and mastery of regulated technique were evidently just as important for him.

While Engel was writing his *Mimik* and Iffland his essays, Goethe in Weimar was refining his ideas through active involvement in the *Liebhabertheater* and then as director of the court theatre. Iffland's tendency toward idealization, and his comment on Ekhof as a forerunner of Schiller, flow naturally into Goethe's theatrical concept, much of which is reflected in his *Regeln für Schauspieler* (written 1803; first published 1824). Beyond the many detailed instructions on aspects of gesture, movement, voice, and delivery, several sections of the *Regeln* illustrate an underlying philosophy beneath all that the rules advocate. A group of guidelines subtitled 'Stellung und Bewegung des Körpers auf der Bühne' shows Goethe's overriding concern for idealized harmony in the performance of both individual actors and the ensemble: 'Zunächst bedenke der Schauspieler, daß er nicht allein die Natur nachahmen, sondern sie auch idealisch vorstellen solle, und er also in seiner Darstellung das Wahre mit dem Schönen zu vereinigen habe. Jeder Theil des Körpers stehe daher ganz in seiner Gewalt, so daß er jedes Glied gemäß dem zu erzielenden Ausdruck frei, harmonisch und mit Grazie gebrauchen könne' (*Regeln*, 153f). Despite the fact that Goethe insisted repeatedly that nature was the primary guide, the desired effect of harmonious, idealized truth was really the same as advocating artificiality. While he too stressed the importance of individual gesture, instructing actors to rehearse every speech and accompanying movement before a mirror and to use their imagination to develop a convincing mix of spoken and silent expression – we recall his praise of extemporization as the best school for actors in the *Theatralische Sendung* – still, the predominant factor was the overall sense of harmonious beauty projected by the entire cast. Goethe's idea of theatre is not much different from the living depiction of a beautiful painting: 'Das Theater ist als ein figurloses Tableau anzusehen, worin der Schauspieler die Staffage macht.' Accordingly, 'Man spiele daher niemals zu nahe an den Coulissen. Eben so wenig trete man in's Proscenium. Dieß ist der größte Mißstand; denn die Figur tritt aus dem Raume heraus, innerhalb dessen sie mit dem Scenengemählde und den Mitspielenden ein Ganzes macht' (*Regeln*, 166f). This conception of the stage is a very long way from the stages of the itinerant troupes which usually had no wings or proscenium at all. But even if they had, these certainly did not prevent the actors, especially the comic figure, from penetrating the framework of the stage to step out into the audience directly. Goethe's notion of acting in his *Regeln* is like a hybrid blossom in a greenhouse; that of the itinerant troupes a wildflower on a dung heap.

Goethe has been called the first real director (*Regisseur*) of the German stage (Winds, 65). He ruled with an iron hand over his actors, confident in his vision of the harmony he wished to achieve. He placed a premium on rhythmic ensemble expression, gave precise directions for group positioning on stage, and his attention to details of lighting and costume as well as his insistence on repeated rehearsal, especially *Leseproben*, are legendary (see Winds, 65-8). Goethe was an autocratic dictator with complete responsibility for the product, the epitome of what is sometimes called *äußere Regie*. If we trace the history of acting from Goethe back to the beginnings of the century once again, we see that the opposite – *innere Regie* – was more characteristic of the eighteenth century as a whole. Dalberg's meetings with actors such as Iffland, when repertoires and details of performance were discussed and implemented, is a grand example of the success of *innere Regie*, that is, democratic or collective self-direction formulated by the participants themselves. Dalberg and his colleagues were also concerned with a certain overall harmony, but certainly not to the extent that Goethe was, and without a complete and overriding sense of the impression the repertoire as a whole was to make. Going back further, the Mannheim school leads to Ekhof and the Schöneman troupe which again through their discussions in the academy practised *innere Regie*. They also had rehearsals and *Leseproben*, but by no means as stringent as Goethe's. The actors themselves were all-important, not the director, and hence, as in Mannheim, they enjoyed greater freedom than in Weimar. And when it comes to internal direction to produce a co-ordinated, unified presentation, what better example could there be than the actors of Vienna's Kärntnertortheater in the forties and fifties who worked from scenarios to produce brilliant gems of extemporized comedy night after night? Or the harmony described by the contemporary theatre historian Friedrich Ludwig Schmid in an account of Schröder's company: 'Das Zusammenspiel bei Schröders Gesellschaft war mustergiltig; kein Wunder, denn viele der Mitglieder hatten noch in der Stegreifkomödie mitgewirkt' (Schmidt, *Denkwürdigkeiten*, 12). Among the less respected and no doubt bawdier troupes, actors enjoyed almost total freedom, aspiring to individual stardom at the expense of others. This chaotic world nevertheless produced some magnificent extemporaneous actors, players who had nothing to resort to but their own genius and instinctive talent. Despite the fact that standing theatres gained the upper hand in German territory after 1770, many itinerant troupes remained active through the end of the century, and many actors employed by the standing theatres had also learned their craft initially as members of such troupes. How much of that apprenticeship remained with them in the formalized setting of the Nationaltheater? In a 1786 performance of Lessing's tragedy *Emilia Galotti* in the Viennese Burgtheater, Stephanie the Elder no doubt riveted the crowd as he 'sein ohnedem großes Maul bis an die Ohren aufzureißen schien und die Zunge langmächtig aus dem Halse streckte, um das Blut von dem Dolche Odoardos aufzuschlecken' (Niessen, 57). The more sophisticated itinerant troupes and most permanent theatres levied fines against actors who took too much liberty, but anecdotes such as this suggest that flashes of the unbridled Haupt- und Staatsactionen were still common at the end of the century, even in tragedy. One suspects such flashes even more in comedy despite the apparent disappearance of the traditional comic figure in most repertoires. While treatises on acting in the century paid relatively little attention to comedy, focusing rather on tragedy and serious character depiction, the fact was that in the repertoires of the age, be they of standing theatres or of itinerant troupes, much more comedy was played than tragedy. Where then was the guidebook for comic actors? It is as if those concerned with these problems recognized that no such primer was possible, for more than any other characters, comic figures rely on instinct, innovation, and genius. Our analysis of individual Nachspiele demonstrated the extent to which these qualities continued to assert themselves beyond the heyday of the itinerant troupes into the period of text-based theatre. In the last decades of the century, however, Nachspiele with serious themes and characters began to predominate and with this there was a shift in the way they were performed. The actors who performed them were most likely influenced by the theories, rules, and guidelines discussed above.

❧ *8* ❧

The Socio-Critical Nachspiel: Text and Performance

As Appendix 1 shows, published Nachspiele were much more likely to contain serious thematics as the century advanced. Of the forty-one Nachspiele listed before 1770, nineteen show serious thematics (46 per cent) while fifty of the seventy-one published later have strong socio-critical themes (70 per cent). This makes it clear that the genre was undergoing a change in function to become principally a vehicle for social commentary, criticism, and education. The change requires careful analysis, however: first because the range of serious thematics after 1769 was very broad; second because it is difficult to estimate the extent of social criticism and commentary contained in the Nachspiele performed by itinerant troupes earlier in the century, of which we have no published record. The very nature of comedy is to poke fun at the human being in society; the relationship between the two and the individual's ability to function alongside his fellow man are always central to the comic situation. While social commentary and criticism were doubtless part of the Nachspiel's effectiveness for early itinerant troupes, it can hardly be claimed that deliberate pedagogy and planned social reform were as alive in the earlier decades as they were by mid-century when the notion of the stage as a tool for enlightenment became entrenched. The focus of this study must turn now away from elements of theatrical performance critical for the success of the comic Nachspiel to questions of theme and literary style. Text gains primacy over performance; the *literarisches Sprechstück* is now at the centre. In this context reference should be made to Markus Krause's excellent book *Das Trivialdrama der Goethezeit 1780-1805* (1982) which investigates the themes and social dynamics of popular drama in a way similar to the treatment of the Nachspiel in this study. While Krause focuses on longer works, his methodological approach and the wealth of material he brings are of great value for an understanding of the age.

The sixty-seven Nachspiele in question here contain a great number of themes among which these predominate: Enlightenment and Pedagogy, with the sub-themes Self-Discovery and Correction, In Praise of Virtue, Patriotism, Religious Fanaticism, and Gambling; Money and Class, with the sub-themes Class and Money; Sentimentality and Melodrama; and Reflections of the Literary Scene, with the sub-themes Directions for Actors and Cultural Debate. The discussion in this chapter is organized by these themes and sub-themes. It will provide a range of examples from the Bibliography to which readers are referred for persona lists and plot summaries.

Another socio-critical aspect of the Nachspiel will be discussed in the following chapter. There, *Die Martinsgänse* will be dealt with on its own. Not only does this Nachspiel contain an unusually wide range of socio-critical themes, but the copy examined is a censored prompter's version which offers unique insights into the work's performance. Accordingly, the analysis of *Die Martinsgänse* is preceded by some general observations on theatre censorship in the century.

Enlightenment and Pedagogy

One is reluctant to classify a body of dramatic works as literature of Enlightenment since by doing so an analytical assumption or prejudice is established at the outset. The term 'Enlightenment' immediately evokes certain philosophical, social, and literary notions bound with scholarly and historical concepts, and there is a danger in associating the second half of the eighteenth century too closely with these notions and what they usually imply: the triumph of reason, social progress, and liberalization, for example. However many social, historical, and literary examples one can find to give evidence of 'Enlightenment,' one can find even more from the same time which stand in contradiction. 'Enlightenment' can be traced in formal philosophy throughout the century from Leibniz and Wolff to Kant, but then one must contend with such influential figures as Francke, Hamann, and the early Romantics who saw man and society in a very different light. One can cite liberalization in education and in women's roles and the rise of the bourgeoisie; but at the same time vast disparities in economic and social opportunity, a privileged position for the aristocracy, and the despotic absolutism of rulers still characterized daily life. To use the term 'Enlightenment' as if it were a clear, homogeneous concept would be to distort the age and our understanding of it. Nevertheless, the moral and social tone of many of the works before us now is so consistently didactic that they must be described as having the direct intention of educating the audience and improving contemporary society. Eternal truths are rare in these works, which is perhaps one reason why they are almost all forgotten today. They address themselves to a limited social milieu and its citizens, again and again drawing firm lines for personal and social improvement. Essentially moralists using the stage for social reform, their authors appear confident that they know what should be improved and how it can be done.

Self-Discovery and Correction

Discovery and awareness of individual and collective folly are the first steps toward learning and improvement. While others can facilitate this process, the individual must in the end pass through a process of self-discovery to reach the desired goal of truthful insight into himself and the situation, and thereafter of behavioural adjustment. In the very titles of *Der sehende Blinde* (1752), *Der Blinde aus Leichtgläubigkeit* (1780), and *Blind und lahm* (ca 1800), this process of illumination is underscored. Feigned physical blindness has metaphoric meaning for the characters who initially fail to see the truth of their circumstances and in the course of the play gain insight. *Der sehende Blinde* was among the most popular Nachspiele performed in the last decades of the century, and *Der Blinde aus Leichtgläubigkeit* was well known at least on the Viennese stage, which attests to the public's attraction to the message they conveyed. They are essentially corrections of an individual's misunderstanding of his place in relation to others about whom he cares, and thus speak for the importance of sensitivity and honesty in human relationships. *Der sehende Blinde* and *Der Blinde aus Leichtgläubigkeit* bury this message in a light comic structure and tone, which no doubt also contributed to their popularity, while *Blind und lahm* is ponderous and much more direct in its instructive component. Hence, the uncle's final words in *Blind und Lahm* leave no mistaking the lesson we are intended to take home. After ushering the united lovers from the scene, he returns to the audience, remembering 'Doch die Moral!...Zum Publikum':

Sie heißt: Du sollst die Menschen in ihrem Wahn nicht stören,
Wenn er sie nur zufrieden und schuldlos glücklich macht. –

Zwar schöner ist die Wahrheit in ihrer Strahlenpracht;
Doch will man selbst in unseren hochaufgeklärten Tagen
Noch in gar vielen Stücken die Wahrheit nicht ertragen;
Noch preiset man die Dämmerung. – Ja und ich tadl' es nicht:
Kommt doch erst Morgenschimmer, und dann erst volles Licht.
Drum wollt' ich jenen Beiden auch den schönen Wahn nicht rauben,
Daß sie sich gegenseitig recht edelmüthig glauben.
Ich seh' in diesem Irrthum der Wahrheit Dämmerschein:
Wofür sie jetzt sich halten, bald werden sie es seyn. (142f)

The optimism of such a speech and the outcome of the play reflect compassion for others and also the belief that human beings, given direction, will learn from their errors and find greater harmony in society. The speech and outcome also suggest that there is indeed a sensible order of things which must emerge in the end and which we would do well to recognize and accept if we are to live happily.

In Praise of Virtue

The lesson that virtue will conquer vice in human relations is further evidence of such optimism. By mid-century the concept of virtue became linked in drama so closely to its counterpart vice that one is apt to forget the long-standing religious tradition that advocated virtue for its own sake, with chastity a major part. So in the earliest published Nachspiel of the eighteenth century, *Die verachtete Eitelkeit der Welt* (1702), the central message of virtue and chastity is linked with the way of life in religious orders. This example relates more to the Baroque world of the century preceding than to the increasingly secular decades to come and their broad depiction of virtue in relation to specific social vices or foibles.

Uffenbach's *Haß und Neid* (1733) is remarkable as another early Nachspiel on this theme. It lacks any semblance of moral shading, presenting the utterly cynical Neidhart in contrast to the euphoric optimist Reinhold. Here, the lesson is primitive – death to the cynic Neidhart, a penalty that recalls Old Testament judgment on the deadly sins of hatred and envy, and felicitous reward to the optimist Reinhold. Considering the play's date, Wanfried's final words also stand out as an unusual plea for the use of tragedy set among the lower class as an instructive medium for education:

Wer sich bespiegeln will, braucht große Gläser nicht,
Als in Pallästen stehen,

Wo falscher Schein und offt ein trüglich Licht
Uns pflegt zu hintergehen.
Ein kleines zeiget sich allhier
In einer niederen und engen Hütten,
Das stelle man sich lehrbegierig für,
So strahlen ihm die tugendhaffte Sitten
Zum folgen an, da schaut hinein,
Und achtet solches nicht für niederträchtig,
Auch wärt ihr noch so groß und mächtig,
So wird es euch doch nicht zu klein
Für einen guten Spiegel seyn.
Von Grossen schildert man offt Helden-Thaten,
Und lässt die Mängel drauf in gleicher Gröss' errathen,
Hier ist am Niedrigen ein klein Exempel werth,
Daß ihm' ins Groß gebracht ein gleiches wiederfährt. (318f)

This position stands in contradiction to Gottsched's view that the milieu of tragedy should be restricted to the upper class, which appeared almost concurrently in the *Critische Dichtkunst* (1730).

While the social stratum and characters in *Mis Jenny* (1771) are elevated considerably from the level of Uffenbach's play, it is not much different in its stark juxtaposition of virtue and vice, or in the death of Jenny at its conclusion. One of the few Nachspiele designated on its title-page as 'tragisch,' the English personae and bourgeois milieu reveal an attempt to take advantage of the popular new genre of middle-class tragedy, growing since Lessing's *Miß Sara Sampson* (1755), and often based on English models. Unlike Lessing's play, however, this Nachspiel is a ludicrously contrived juxtaposition of goodness and evil with a dramatically incongruous conclusion. No wonder the author decided on anonymity. Brief casual contact with Jenny has left no doubt in the minds of her defenders in the play that her virtue is exemplary, and this is their sole motivation for championing her cause. Unlike the conclusion of *Haß und Neid*, her death is a temporal victory for the forces of vice over virtue, and hence carries the implicit suggestion that something is wrong in the society which allowed such a tragedy to occur. The four decades dividing *Haß und Neid* and *Mis Jenny* seem to have dissolved a simplistic view of good and evil into a much more complicated moral dilemma.

Less problematic are the Nachspiele that simply hold up to public view paragons of virtue and honesty. *Adel des Herzens* (1770), also frequently performed, is set among simple folk, and is really no more than an illustration of good conduct from the beginning. The one aristocratic character in the end proposes to a simple virtuous girl, thus ignoring realistic limitations and bridging contemporary class barriers. Virtue is an ideal, as are the characters who convey it here on stage. As the ambivalent reference to nobility in the title reflects, the play is also a praise of virtue over class and hence a statement on basic human values. By contrast, some criticism of aristocratic moral standards is present, but this is so subdued that the work could not offend audiences of mixed class.

Similarly, *Der Neujahrstag* (1779) holds up for admiration a young lad who is both sensitive to the needs of others and modest to the point of absurdity. Its subtitle 'Nachspiel für Kinder' shows that the author was in essence a pedagogue who wanted to convey lessons in behaviour and morality, which the play does. It not only advocates honesty and caring for one's fellow man, but also gives some tangential instruction for parents in the correct raising of children.

Patriotism

Exemplary behaviour is also at the core of *Verlobung bei Kaiserslautern* (1795), but here reflected against a society embroiled in the revolutionary atmosphere of its time. It is a dramatically exciting work, capturing the terror and tension of the age in France (as does the Nachspiel *Die arme Frau*), and the central character François de Bercheau suffers truly under the dichotomy between his intense sense of duty to France and his horror of recent political events. His patriotic loyalty is admirable, underscored by the contrasting Kommissarius, who is an embodiment of evil and vice. Bercheau is an interesting dramatic figure, and it is significant that these exemplary actions in dire circumstances are associated with a Frenchman in a German play of the time. But then, more precisely, Bercheau is a French *nobleman*, while the bloodthirsty representatives of the revolution are commoners. The colour of blood – blue in this case – is what is being held up as synonymous with integrity here. The work is also a praise of German society and political order in contrast to those of France. Liberation comes in the end through the valiant Prussian Hussars, and Bercheau's grateful adoption of Germany as his new home is a strong statement of nationalism from one whose honour and patriotism make him a man to be respected: 'Auf, fort zu den braven Teutschen! Beim deutschen Becher wollen wir der Liebenden Gesundheit und uns Vergessenheit der traurigen Vergangenheit trinken. – Es lebe unser Retter von Linkheim hoch! – Nun fort ins teutsche Lager! – ' (78). The model Bercheau provides calls for both patriotism and duty, convinced that these are possible only on German soil.

One year earlier (1794) another Nachspiel thematically related to the French Revolution had expressed similar patriotism. *Die Jacobiner* contrasts two forces, the German sympathizers, the Sansculotes, as opposed to representatives of the establishment, the ruling lord and the pastor. Speaking for his Sansculotes (the only one of their number articulate enough to do so) is Secretair Neuwing who greets the visiting Jacobins with: 'Ich bin glüklich Ihre Bekanntschaft zu machen. Die Deutschen sind bis jetzt in der Aufklärung noch etwas zurük' (13). Coming early in the work this statement suggests that the play's intention is to advocate reform in Germany, but this is not the case. Neuwing continues:

> Es ist nur ein Unglük, daß der grosse Haufe in Deutschland so am alten Herkommen hängt, an seinen Fürsten[,] nicht, so wie in Frankreich, gleich jeden Fehler rügt, und überhaupt einen so hohen Werth auf Treue und Anhänglichkeit sezt. Was die Sache vollends erschwert, ist, daß unsere Schriftsteller in den Hauptpunkten selbst noch nicht unter einander eins werden konnten, als wenn die gute Sache nicht in Ausübung der Rechte bestünde, die Freiheit und Gleichheit allen Menschen zusichern. (13f)

Even the Jacobins themselves sense that a revolution in Germany is impossible: '*de Vie.* Und dennoch besorg' ich, daß es uns in Deutschland nicht so gelingen wird, alles untere zu oberst zu kehren, und den Haß der verschiedenen Stände unter einander so zu unserm Vortheil zu benutzen wie in Frankreich' (18). Not long after, the two Jacobins are jailed and sentenced. Their accusations against the aristocracy ring hollow in the mouths of those who have contributed to a reign of terror in their own country and who would bring the same on their neighbours. Moreover, the German Sansculotes comprise a pitiful band of misguided simpletons. What stands out in the end is the conservative stabilizing counter-force contained in the pastor's admonition to them:

> Unter dem Vorwand, Rechte zu vertheidigen, die ihr nicht kennt, zieht ihr aus, andern Menschen ihr ererbtes Eigenthum zu entreißen. Glaubt mir, Kinder! Freiheit besteht nicht in dem Vermögen, die Neigungen zu befriedigen, zu denen Leidenschaft und Verderbtheit uns antreiben, sondern in der Selbstgewalt von dem Guten nichts ungethan zu lassen, was Pflicht und Beruf von uns fordern. Sucht erst selbst besser zu werden, eh ihr darauf ausgeht, die Weltordnung verbessern zu wollen. (60f)

'Pflicht … Beruf … Weltordnung,' these must be protected in the face of the 'Leidenschaft und Verderbtheit' that revolution brings. The pastor's condescending summation may grate on the modern reader, but it was obviously what this Nachspiel's author wanted to impress: a conservative reinforcement and moral justification of the contemporary hierarchy.

Religious Fanaticism

A further group of Nachspiele recalls strongly Gottsched's formula for the *Lustspiel* decades earlier in their exposure and correction of folly. Their message of enlightenment couples satire on characters and beliefs detrimental to rational harmonious society with a final realization and correction of attitude or behaviour. In *Die Gespenster* (1757), *Hochzeittag* (1789), and *Die Christen in Abyssinien* [1780] the objects of attack are human gullibility and intolerance in religion. *Die Gespenster* is foremost a comic work which makes extended effective use of such traditional techniques as disguise, transformation, and even direct comment 'ad spectatores,' but beneath the mirth lies a serious conflict between rampant spiritualism and sensible faith, as the protagonists' names themselves succinctly reflect – Herr Afterglaube versus Magister Leberecht. The work belongs thus to the same thematic continuum as Luise Gottsched's *Pietisterey im Fischbein-Rocke* (1736) and Johann Christian Krüger's *Die Geistlichen auf dem Lande* (1743). The play's unmistakeable lesson is that exaggerated superstition and spirituality destabilize social order, in this case particularly the institution of marriage, and that a rational philosophy of life should predominate instead. As chief spokesman of this school, Magister Leberecht advocates a 'Mittelweg' between religious belief and reason: 'So schwer er zu finden ist, so ist es doch keine wahre Unmöglichkeit ihn zu treffen. Man muß nur die Religion zur Handleiterinn der Vernunft annehmen' (320). The Magister's choice of words in the play often encourages us to go beyond the immediate context to think of the general philosophical debate between Pietist theologians and philosophers such as Lange and Francke in Halle and their counterpart Christian Wolff and his practical reworking of Leibniz's principles for application in daily life. Although the most heated battles had been fought well before 1757 when *Die Gespenster* appeared, with Wolff ousted from the University of Halle in 1723, and Lange and Francke dead by 1744, Wolff's practical philosophy had by 1757 gained wide acceptance, and the debate between religious spiritualists and rationalists was as alive as ever.

In the same year the Nachspiel *Der fromme Stutzer* appeared, worth mentioning here because it also treats the theme of religious hypocrisy, but without the comfortable resolution of *Die Gespenster*. A nasty conclusion leaves the religious fanatics still in control at the expense of a person with less power who suffers humiliation and rejection.

Hochzeittag sets its sights more sharply on one target, the false piety and avarice of the country clergy. Criticism of the clergy was still a daring undertaking at the time, their social power usually granting them immunity, as many censor's deletions in *Die Martinsgänse* will demonstrate. In *Hochzeittag* Pastor Mehzeg's grasping, calculating motivation is despicable; Frau Willmer's realization and correction of her folly at the end are as predictable as any Gottschedian model.

Lenz's *Christen in Abyssinien* is a work of quite different mettle. Except for one somewhat incongruous stage direction calling for 'einen Lazzi' (231), which traditionally meant a scene of comic extemporization, hard to imagine in this play, *Christen in Abyssinien* is foremost a serious discussion of world religions and a call for tolerance, especially to Christians, as summarized in these strophes from the closing song:

> Der Türke wie der Katholik,
> Der Mohr wie die Manzuren –
> Es findet jeder seinen Strick
> Auch auf der Weisheit Spuren.
>
> Doch kennt er ihn und geht vorbei
> Und hofft auf Gottes Gnade,
> So findt er oft ein großes Ei!
> Geduld – und Ackolade.
>
> Der Menschen Zungen sind so spitz,
> Der Menschen Witz so feindlich;
> Doch durch Geduld wird Zung' und Witz
> Und Schadenkitzel freundlich. (238f)

The distant place of action and exotic personae of the work were the author's way of providing direct comment on religious intolerance in his own time with impunity from the ire of church officials.

Gambling

Ernst Heydevogel's *Das Trentleva* (1774) appeared among the nineteen volumes of *Theater der Deutschen* (1768-83), one of the earliest and best-known collections of dramatic literature at the time, thus ensuring its widespread circulation. It can hardly be praised for its intrinsic dramatic merits, but its theme is one which reflects an obvious fascination of the period. The vice of gambling was central to a significant group of plays including the other Nachspiele *Das Lotto* (1779) and *3.13.33* (1789), and even to some extent *Die beiden Billets* (1783). Gambling is presented as an aberration which threatens individual and social stability, and Leander's addiction to it in *Das Trentleva* is so overpowering that not even correction in his own milieu is possible. He is banished to Peru to make a new start, and in this way is given a pariah status which suggests how seriously contemporaries must have regarded the problem. Gambling is taken to be more than a folly, it is an addictive sickness, at the root of which is the drive for money, and it reflects a society in which wealth was becoming central to happiness. While in virtually all societies money is essential for survival and comfort, there are times when the materialistic impulse seems to drive spiritual values underground. *Das Trentleva* and other gambling plays at the time point to a shift in the value system of the society in which they appeared. This value shift gives a focus of exploration for the following group of works.

Money and Class

Money and class, class and money, it is difficult to know which should be set first in the final decades of the century. In terms of rising power, wealth prevailed; in terms of traditional superiority, class. The Nachspiele in this group testify to tensions and fluctuations between the two as aristocratic privilege remained entrenched in social intercourse while signs of a power transfer from that class to the bourgeoisie were becoming increasingly prevalent. Central to this shift was an overall change in civic and economic structures; ever more authority was flowing into the hands of the wealthy citizenry.

Class

Many Nachspiele underscore a continuing respect for the privilege of the upper class and even confirm their right to that advantage. This is particularly evident in works that have marriage as their central complication, understandably so since the blindness of love often plays havoc with social structures. Lovers of different classes present a social problem, a potential dilution of the aristocracy which maintains its strength through guarded, exclusive inbreeding under the pretence of defending certain personal and social characteristics. When a representative of the nobility falls in love with and wishes to marry someone of lower class, an insidious rot begins to infest his hybrid roots, usually to his peers' alarm. The situation is most complicated when the aristocratic lover is female, for by law and custom of the time her marriage meant the automatic transfer of her wealth and indeed much of her personal liberty to her spouse, resulting in a betrayal of her class and a threat to its very existence. A common dramatic device for introducing this problem, without going so far as to offer a solution, is to construct a social mismatch, move toward the logical conclusion of inter-class marriage, then obviate the problem by introducing new and surprising evidence late in the play to reveal that the identity of the lower-class partner is in fact mistaken, and that he/she is in truth aristocratic as well. Although the problem is finally avoided in such works, its introduction suggests that it was a live social issue which needed more time to be resolved.

Several Nachspiele represent unquestioning reinforcement of the current class structure. The tragic *Mis Jenny* (1771), just discussed in terms of its praise of virtue, is such a case. Mylord Gordon's negative reaction to his son's marital intentions is founded on Jenny's doubtful heritage first, only second on her poverty. His attitude is reversed when her true identity, bloodline, and wealth are revealed. The title of *Die glückliche Entdeckung* (1806) refers to the same type of discovery, but in double measure and with considerably more dramatic spirit. It is a clever comic work above all, with the serious social problem underlying. Two couples are involved, and a recognition of double mistaken identity provides the vent for an uncomplicated solution, in this case a conclusion which not only evades the social problem but also underscores the attitude that aristocratic stock is of finer stuff than socially inferior material. A motif throughout, for example, is Aglaja's aesthetic insensitivity as opposed to Marie's active intellect. When it is discovered that the women were exchanged at birth, each of them nestles comfortably into her appropriate role and the play ends on a note of 'all's well.'

The social hierarchy always carried a certain religious aura about its head, for historically many believed it to be a temporal expression of God's will. Thus the ruler, absolute in his power, was for many godlike, and his deistic presence at the pinnacle was the ultimate reinforcement of aristocratic right. Several Nachspiele bow to the authority and almost magical beneficence of this figure, using what God represents to resolve a dramatic entanglement and at the same time casting their lot directly on the side of the entrenched social structure. In Eckardt's *Der Landprediger* (1778) a pitifully destitute pastor and his family are saved from the clutches of an avaricious official through the direct intervention of a distant, unnamed monarch, a mysterious, omnipotent guardian angel. In Sander's *Der Sohn* (1783), the dramatic problem is resolved through the ruler's (King Frederick II of Prussia's) sudden beneficence which provides a pension for a stalwart loyalist in need; similarly, in Decker's *Die Brandschatzung* (1806) the king (of Prussia) offsets a financial injustice and brings happiness to valiant and honourable subjects in desperate circumstances. Not to be outdone, Austrian works show the same veneration, such as *Kaiser Joseph auf der Reise im Amthause* (1799), which even features the emperor himself personally rooting out a nest of civic corruption and ensuring justice for the peasants whose faith in their monarch remains unshaken. Of the four works cited, only the last gives any real indication of addressing the question why these people are in such need at all. To the modern reader, such plights point to systemic problems in the socio-economic structure, but the message prevailing in these Nachspiele is that where injustice exists a supreme temporal authority will intervene.

There are at the same time Nachspiele that draw attention to the cracks across this façade. No clearer statement of aristocratic privilege can be found than in *Der Weihnachtabend* (1803), but privilege here is accompanied by deep reservations about its continuing justification and practicality. The hackneyed device of discovered mistaken identity ensures an uncomplicated dénouement when Braun is revealed as von Sindel's *illegitimate* son, hence diluting his pedigree and responsibility for maintaining the purity of his line. His father can now endorse a marriage with Hannchen without taking a revolutionary social stand, and the withdrawal of her aristocratic suitor Fritz is all for the best. There is even a backhanded compliment to Braun's profession as a painter. Nevertheless, von Sindel is an uneasy representative of aristocratic tradition. He begins by taking the hard line with his nephew Fritz, in the customary fighting stance of his class:

Ich wünschte doch, Du schlügst Dir diese Heirath aus dem Sinn. Wäre sie von Adel, ich würde Deiner Wahl mich herzlich freuen, statt daß sie mir jetzt Kummer macht. Du kennst mich, ich bin nicht stolz auf den Adel. Aber die Erfahrung hat mich belehrt, daß dieser Stand durch eine Menge Vorrechte ausgezeichnet wird, die sehr richtig sind. Ich glaube, daß man das Verdienst nicht darum geadelt habe, weil vom edlen Stamm edle Reiser sprossen, sondern weil ein altes Sprichwort, welches von Heldensöhnen nicht gar zu ehrenvoll spricht, Recht hat. Fast scheint es, als hätte man den

Nachkommen Brief und Siegel darüber gegeben, von ihnen weniger Verdienste zu fordern, weil ihr Ahnherr für sie gethan hat, was sie selbst thun sollten. Nicht, als ob das Absicht gewesen wäre, und es so seyn sollte, aber die Erfahrung zeigts, und es ist nun einmal nicht anders. (10)

In this second scene of the play, von Sindel sets out the difficult problematics as well as the quandary of enlightened aristocrats of his type. He enjoys his privilege, but suspects that for the young generation of his day it is an undeserved luxury that encourages indolence. Between the lines he also questions where there is justice at all in the class structure, but knows that this structure remains formidable and that aberrations, such as that imminent in his nephew's proposal, cause heartache for all involved. Thus his strategy is first to test Fritz's resolve in the hope that the problem can be avoided. With this attempt made, we learn in the subsequent soliloquy von Sindel's real position:

Die Tochter meines verstorbenen Freundes [Hannchen Ludolph] liegt mir freilich näher am Herzen, als die Enkel oder Urenkel meines Neffen [Fritz], und das Glück der Familie Ludolph näher, als die Wohlfahrt des Adels ... Warum sollen die Sindels des künftigen Jahrhunderts etwas vor andern ehelichen Kindern voraus haben? Möglich auch, daß bis dahin manche Veränderung vorgegangen ist! (13)

Spoken in 1803, von Sindel's words are a remarkable forecast of the European hierarchy's dissolution over the next hundred years, his questioning of social privilege being extremely bold for its time. What von Sindel says here he would not say in public, but of course he is saying it to the audience; and we must assume that at least some of them were receptive and, like him, ready to join in the dismantling of the hierarchy in which they lived. As an enlightened and caring human being, von Sindel wants in the end to judge with his head and his heart, without the blinders of class. He continues:

Wenn er [Fritz] ohne sie [Hannchen], und sie ohne ihm, wie man zu sagen pflegt, nicht leben, das heißt, nicht glücklich seyn kann, so muß er sie freilich haben. Er ist erwachsen genug, um das zu überlegen ... Sie ist nicht reich, aber sparsam, weiß mit Wenigem auszukommen, und kennt die Eitelkeit nicht, um deren willen so mancher Edelmann, der ein reiches Mädchen erkohr, nur allzugern ihr ganzes Vermögen als Reukauf zurückgäbe. Sie hat keine Ahnen, aber Tugend ist in ihrer Familie zu Hause. (13f)

Von Sindel in the end denies his class and gives priority to his instincts. He recognizes qualities in Hannchen that are superior to lineage when it comes to that highest of goals, happiness. True enough, the play's conclusion avoids the inevitable consequence of rupturing convention by in fact celebrating a mixed marriage, but von Sindel and his anonymous playwright make a large stride in that direction.

One of the greatest problems faced by the fading aristocracy was economic, as seen as early as 1771 in *Die Chymici*. Here the debt-ridden Marquis, seeing economic ruin ahead and powerless to stop it unless friends bail him out, is eventually forced to take the humiliating step of hiding to escape his creditors. At the same time, he falls prey to charlatans, vultures circling in anticipation of a good feed. This Marquis stands for a class in decline, helpless to reverse the trend, gradually losing honour and status. He is portrayed with sympathy, whereas the survivors are not; but, one suspects, it is those who forage for money rather than status who will eventually rise to the top in a newly structured economic system. In the face of his creditors, the Marquis's good name and title count for nothing.

Contrasting this sympathetic portrayal is a group of Nachspiele that stridently expose some of the moral decay which contributed to aristocratic decline. *Die eheliche Versöhnung* (1795) serves as just one example of the many negative depictions of noble characters and interrelationships at the end of the century. Any sense of fidelity or moral conscience is lacking in Count von Rosenhain at centre stage as he flaunts his marital vows of just six months to pursue his passion for a beautiful stranger. The comic action uses devices such as disguise and misunderstanding to channel his ardour back to its appropriate subject, but not before a licentious display by the count and a wealthy crony smudges the reputation of their class in the audience's mind. Another work, *Der Finanzbediente* (French original 1761, German 1789), is a devastating attack on aristocratic arrogance. Von Courville, described as 'ein französischer Markis,' is a thoroughly unscrupulous cynic, his moral vacuousness set directly against the integrity of Baron von Edelmann, 'ein deutscher Edelmann.' In Scene 9 of the play, the Baron strips bare the Marquis's licentiousness and duplicity in this heated exchange:

Baron. Verweilen sie noch einen Augenblick, Markis.
Markis. Was ist dir? Du siehst ja ganz zornig aus. Hat dich jemand beleidigt?
Baron. Ja, auf das empfindlichste beleidigt.
Markis. Wer denn?
Baron. Sie selbst —
Markis. Ich?
Baron. Ja, sie. Und ich will es ihnen nur gerade heraussagen: Sie sind der niederträchtigste boshafteste Mensch, der —

Markis. Was fehlt dir? Bist du verrückt – Herr! ich verbitte mir dergleichen
Beschimpfungen, oder –
Baron. O ich beschimpfe sie nicht, ich rede die Wahrheit. Beweisen will ich
es ihnen, durch Thatsachen beweisen, daß sie der niederträchtigste, ab-
scheulichste Mensch unter der Sonne sind.
Markis. Und ich, daß ichs nicht bin. (Er zieht den Degen.) Ziehen sie Herr,
oder –
Baron. Oh laßen sie doch ihren Degen in Ruhe, der kann ihren Frevel nicht
wieder gut machen. Oder wollen sie auf Niederträchtigkeit noch Thorheit
häufen? – Wissen sie, Herr, ich bin über diese lächerlichen Vorurtheile unsers Standes längst weg. In meinen Augen kann ihnen kein Zweikampf die
einmal verlohrne Ehre wiedergeben. Und Schande ist es für unsern Stand,
daß dem größten Haufen desselben, bei so vielen andern Thorheiten, auch
dieses barbarische Vorurtheil anklebt, und daß ihres Gleichen sogar eine
Ehre in der Ausübung einer Handlung setzen, die in den Augen aller
Vernünftigdenkenden die Menschheit erniedriget. – Stecken sie ihren Degen
in die Scheide, denn, ich wiederhol' es noch einmal: er kann das Brandmal,
daß sie ihrer Seele, durch ihr frevelhaftes Betragen, eingedrückt haben,
nicht wieder ausmärzen –
Markis. (Geht wüthend auf ihn los) Ah! Feiger! vertheidige dich, oder ich
durchbore dich auf der Stelle –
Baron. (Zieht den Degen, vertheidigt sich aber bloß.) Sie zwingen mich
dazu. – Wohlan dann, kühlen sie ihren Muth! (Er parirt die Stöße des
Markis eine Zeitlang aus und entwaffnet ihn zulezt) So – Nun will ich's ihnen sonnenklar beweisen, daß ich sie vorhin nicht beschimpft habe –
Markis. Herr, sie sehen, ich habe keinen Degen –
Baron. Nur Geduld, den sollen sie gleich wieder haben. Nur hören sie mich
erst gelassen an. – Sie hatten mir auf das feierlichste versprochen, daß sie
sich des unglücklichen Greises und seiner Tochter mit Nachdruck annehmen wollten. Weit entfernt, ihr Versprechen zu erfüllen, haben sie sogar
den Hrn. von Vallebois gegen die Unglücklichen zu erbittern gesucht. –
Und in welcher Absicht verübten sie diesen Gräuel? – Nicht wahr? blos
deswegen, weil das Mädchen ihnen gefiel, weil sie dieselbe als eine Beute
betrachteten, die sich ihren schändlichen Lüsten zufälligerweise darbot.
Zwar zeugten die Mienen des Mädchens von der Ehrbarkeit ihrer Seele:
Aber, dachten sie in ihrem schnöden Herzen: – welche Seele läßt sich nicht,
wenn Unglück und Kummer sie dazu zwingen, ihrer schönsten Zierde be-
rauben? Wohlan, dachten sie ferner, ich will damit beginnen, daß ich sie
vollends niederbeuge, ihr alle Rettungsmittel raube und auch den kleinsten
Funken von Hoffnung in ihrer Seele auslösche; mit den lebhaftesten Farben
will ich ihr den seelenerschütternden Auftritt vormahlen, wie ihr alter Vater
von Schergen in das Gefängniß geschleppt wird, und dann will ich aus ihrer

> Angst, aus ihrem Kummer meinen Vortheil ziehen, dann sollen ihre Leiden die Waffen seyn, durch die ich über ihre Tugend triumphiren will. – Ah Markis, ihre Handlung war eben so niederträchtig, eben so abscheulich, als wenn ein verruchter Mädchenschänder ihr den Dolch auf die Kehle gesezt und so den Versuch gemacht hätte, sie zu entehren. – Dies ist's, was ich ihnen sagen wollte, und nun nehmen sie ihren Degen zurück. (149-52)

It is doubtful that words stronger than these were spoken in any play of the era. Not many would dare to write or deliver a speech that concludes by equating a nobleman with a rapist. The speech is so highly charged that we can understand the author's reluctance to have anyone but a peer to the Marquis deliver it. In the original, a French nobleman says this to one of his own countrymen; the play's adapter was not so daring – or foolhardy – as to have one of his compatriots do the same. By making the Baron a German instead of a French Chevalier, the adapter defused the salvo somewhat, but at the same time set his sights on a broader target, the German aristocracy. What the Baron objects to first is the insult this man has brought to his peers – he feels 'auf das empfindlichste beleidigt' – for as a nobleman himself he is forced to share the presence of such a despicable equal. The Marquis's immorality is a reflection on all nobility in the Baron's eyes, but he himself is clearly a man of different ilk. When the Marquis resorts to the traditional method of defending his honour by combat, the Baron can only heap derision on 'diese lächerlichen Vorurtheile unseres Standes,' yet must acknowledge that most, 'den größten Haufen unseres Standes,' still solve questions of honour by the sword, a practice which 'in den Augen aller Vernünftigdenkenden die Menschheit erniedriget.' He himself belongs to a new class of aristocrats, one which puts more faith in reason than rank or tradition. No audience or reader of the day was so naive as to believe that only French aristocrats acted with the Marquis's complete disregard for people of lower class and for moral principle; they were likely aware of enough examples closer to home to transfer this indictment quietly in their minds to targets whose identities they knew. The Marquis and the Baron represent both poles of a fading class: corruption born of privilege and a true sense of human values. They point to the fact that society's entire conception of value and worth was very much in flux at the time.

Money

Thus one arrives at the importance of wealth as a major theme in the Nachspiel of the last three decades of the century. A curious and to some extent amusing parallel exists on this count between the era under discussion and our own. Today much is said and written of rampant materialism, particularly in the Western democracies. In these countries there are basically three legal ways to amass wealth: by inheritance, by work, and by luck. Many have no chance via the first avenue, only faint hope by the second, but long to grasp the brass ring by the third. The materialistic drive and the avenues to satisfy it seem to have been not much different at the end of the eighteenth century. Today, in many Western nations, there is an insatiable appetite for lotteries and their accompanying 'get rich quick' mentality. There is also an outspoken minority against them, but this group seems to be fighting a losing battle. In the Nachspiel of the late eighteenth century the theme of happiness through the sudden amassing of a fortune through lottery winnings is striking, and it reflects an attitude similar to today's that instant wealth will bring just as immediate happiness. In *Das Unerwartete im Heyrathen* (1765), *Das Lotto* (1779), *3.13.33* (1789), and *Der fromme Betrug* (1789) sudden lottery winnings trigger the dramatic action. The social backdrop of these and several other Nachspiele stressing the importance of money is almost exclusively the world of the wealthy or petite bourgeoisie, and happiness was ensured by the windfall usually associated with marriage. Rarely are details given about the steady means of income of wealthy bourgeois figures, with the exception of the occupation of *Kaufmann* – merchant – which is more frequently associated with the middle class than any other.

Das Unerwartete im Heyrathen (1765) shows a family with a daughter to marry off and a hopeful suitor who wins a lottery, which suddenly makes the match attractive. To this plot it adds the figure of a failed and hence banished businessman who subsequently succeeds, returning in triumph to reclaim his wife and place in society. The improbability of events is unimportant for the lively comic action, but beneath this lightheartedness stands the inescapable economic fact that all of the happiness in the end is made possible by money. In *Der fromme Betrug* the backdrop and criteria for success are almost identical. Again a marriage is made possible only by a sudden injection of funds through lottery winnings; a niggardly bourgeois mother, resolutely opposed to the match, reverses her position to welcome her new son-in-law (and his fortune) into the family. In *Juliane Dürrbach* (1783) happiness in the world of the petite bourgeoisie is hinged completely on finances, but this time a marriage is made possible by the contrived mechanism of inheritance. We see the extent to which monetary power was becoming the primary delineator of social status in *3.13.33* where the fact that the hopeful suitor is a nobleman seems to count for nothing in his quest for a bride of equal status. Penniless, he despairs of his chances, but again a financial windfall in the form of a lottery prize changes his circumstances abruptly and ensures a future with a suitable wife.

The negative consequences of such rising materialism were not left unexplored. Then, as now, the growing wealth of one segment of a capitalistic society led inevitably to economic imbalances and took its toll on another less fortunate group. Wezel's *Der erste Dank* (1784) presents a melodramatic and bitter picture of a family stripped of their last possessions and home, finally disappearing into a life of destitute poverty as their thoroughly sympathetic merchant father sinks helplessly into bankruptcy. As disturbing as this picture may be, the social consequences of the invigorated capitalistic drive are even more drastically presented in *Das Lotto*, which depicts an entire town that has gone mad in its avaricious compulsion to gain instant wealth through lottery winnings. Here legal and civic officials, the representative of education (schoolmaster), and all citizens but two are consumed by the obsession, and the sole resisters are faced in the end by an armed insurrection. Only external intervention from a supreme authority can correct the situation – in fact a completely undemocratic means to solve the problem and one that fails to offset the dark picture of human nature presented in the play.

While some playwrights clearly believed that materialism and avarice among the bourgeoisie represented a growing social problem and saw the stage as a means to expose and correct it, there is no evidence to show that any of them seriously called into question the wisdom of the capitalistic system. Problems like the above are presented as correctable aberrations rather than symptoms of systemic disease. Two means recur frequently by which correction can occur: through the reform of individuals themselves, and through increased moral responsibility of public officials. An example of the first can be seen in *Der Versuch* (1806), the title itself suggesting that the play is intended as an experiment with a progressive goal. Here we witness a sympathetic merchant on the verge of financial ruin because of the unrelenting compulsion of his family to spend and enjoy materialistic pleasures to excess. They have the same spirit as do recklessly irresponsible credit-card toters two centuries removed. Only through the intervention of his brother is the merchant's ruin averted, and the family's reluctant agreement to change their attitudes and reform their ways according to a rigid budgetary plan is what saves them from penury. Here it is not a lottery prize, or an inheritance, or even intervention from an external saviour that remedies the situation; it is self-correction brought on by the diagnosis and prescription of a professional – a fully qualified 'Ökonom' indeed! – surely a sign of changing times.

The other means to correction, reform of civic officials, is more extensively represented in Nachspiele of the period. While the exposure of social aberration is an extension of the comedy type initiated by Gottsched, the broad criticism of officialdom at the end of the century is something new, a product of a changing social and economic structure. Really the term 'moral indictment' would be more appropriate than social criticism, for these plays place the blame for individual and collective ills squarely on the shoulders of those holding public posts, and underpinning them all is the motif of financial injustice. The plays represent a moral indictment in civic terms equivalent to that levelled against the decaying aristocracy. The extensive fragment *Jedem sein Lohn* (1779) is one of the sharpest such charges, portraying a conscientious clergyman struggling to repay the debts of his ancestors, a situation that calls into question the entire concept of inherited debt, guilt, or privilege. In contrast to the clergyman stands a woefully corrupt public inspector who represents the worst in civic officials. Rounding out the picture are another official and a representative of the professional class (the doctor) whose moral sense prevails in the end. Justice is achieved as the inspector is legally indicted and stripped of authority while the suffering pastor is relieved of debt. Similarly in *Der Landprediger* and *Kaiser Joseph auf der Reise im Amthause*, heartless, irresponsible, and corrupt officials who bring misery to the economically vulnerable are rooted out and punished, though in these cases the means to that end lies in the authority of enlightened monarchs.

One of the sub-themes that becomes evident in these Nachspiele, and one of interest to many in today's society, is the emancipation of woman. Love and marriage are probably the most frequent themes of comedy, and when combined with tensions of class and financial status lead often to the problem of a woman's freedom in influencing her marital course. In the discussion above, the focus has been on wealth and class, but most of the works considered have at their centre a woman whose future will be determined by the play's outcome. In the majority of cases, the question of her right to play an active part in the selection of her spouse is either never asked, or is treated superficially. But there are enough examples to show that many authors were genuinely concerned about the right of a woman to choose. This meant at the same time some adjustment to the legal and conventional codes of material possession as well as to conceptions of familial authority. Toward the end of the century, father and guardian figures, who had legal authority over the future of their daughters, show increasing consideration for their wishes, even to the extent that they make the final decision contingent upon the daughter's agreement. So, for example, Sophie in the lottery play *3.13.33* has the freedom to select her spouse from the start and Caroline's personal inclination in *Heyrath aus Liebe* (1781) carries more weight than her guardian's authority. Some playwrights even spoke out boldly for a woman's right to complete and independent self-determination. For example, in *Friederike von Rosenhayn* (1783), the bluntest illustration of this position, the entire action consists of a young woman reviewing aspiring suitors before selecting a partner on her own. Friederike, however, unlike most of the women depicted in the age, is independently wealthy and of equally independent mind. Her refreshing choice is not one of the noble pretenders, but rather the honest, sincere, penniless, and untitled Wahrmann, whose name tells it all.

Sentimentality and Melodrama

Thematically serious Nachspiele offer a broad impression of stylistic trends in their time. In terms of literary history, the years 1770 to 1810 include the periods often designated as Sentimentality, Storm and Stress, Classicism and Romanticism, classifications useful for the delineation of literary trends but at the same time dangerous if understood to refer to a precisely defined time frame or set of structural, stylistic, and thematic characteristics. The task of sorting them out here is simplified by the fact that one would be hard pressed indeed to find a single Nachspiel that would fit obviously under the general rubric Classicism or Romanticism. Conversely, Nachspiele showing strong characteristics of Sentimentality and the Storm and Stress abound.

Sentimentality is a very broad term indeed. One of its strongest associations is with dramatic literature of the middle class, and it is on audiences from this class that the later Nachspiel concentrated. In terms of performance opportunities this emphasis is not surprising since the many standing theatres after 1770 catered principally to the bourgeoisie as their largest clientele; the works performed were selected, even written, with this audience very much in mind, and the sense of theatre as an instructive social institution prevailed. Classical works of tragedy that had held full sway in earlier decades were forced to share the spotlight with, and even be eclipsed by, bourgeois tragedy as it rose to prominence, steered by the aesthetic treatises of Nicolai,

Lessing, and Mendelssohn in the foreground (viz. Nicolai's 'Abhandlung vom Trauerspiele,' 1756 and the ensuing written correspondence among the three; Lessing, *Werke*, Hanser edition, IV, 155-227). This lowering of the class milieu in the tragic genre necessitated reconsideration of the aesthetics of drama, for now, instead of elevated kings and sovereign queens in their courts, bourgeois homes, merchants, and pregnant daughters were becoming the focus of tragedy.

A convincing tragic action on stage has a number of requirements, as theorists such as Lessing and Nicolai pointed out, the most important being the evocation of sympathy (*Mitleid*) for the tragic hero(ine), his or her growing stature and dignity in the face of a tragic end, and the protagonist's inescapable tragic flaw. Lessing insisted that the tragic action must move in stages, the tragic hero(ine) through waves of fear and relapse, then confidence and spiritual domination, all of which would gradually build sympathy in the audience and evoke their emotions, leaving them satisfied at the end. But this process takes time on stage. The Nachspiel is characteristically a one-act work, and despite obvious attempts by some authors to extend Nachspiele to two acts or more, they are structurally ineffective for projecting a tragic action. The half-dozen Nachspiele in the Bibliography designated 'tragisch' in their subtitles represent a tiny minority and none stands out as a particularly striking dramatic work. The serious Nachspiel, and the serious one-act Lustspiel for that matter, was a new genre that tried to fill the gap between tragedy and comedy in the bourgeois sphere, as a result often turning into sentimental melodrama, melodrama in the broad sense of the word: tragic potential without convincing development and depth; primal emotions and close audience identification; extremes of mood based on a universal sense of the forces of right and wrong. This negative statement on the aesthetic properties of such Nachspiele must be taken with caution, however, for it betrays a modern perspective which may be inconsistent with the tastes and expectations of theatre-goers two centuries ago. The fact stands that many of these sentimental pieces were very popular at the time, as witnessed by their repeated production and success. The theatrical novelty of seeing bourgeois characters and problems, the binding effect of personal identification with the characters on stage, offered a distinct advantage over the distant classical tragedy. These sentimental Nachspiele were a vehicle by which citizens could vicariously analyse and come to terms with themselves and the society in which they lived. Yet all theatre-goers and critics were not completely enamoured with this new type of drama. In a review of theatrical developments in the last decades of the century, an anonymous critic writes this assessment of 'Die sogenannten Familien-Gemählde, eigentlich bürgerliche Dramen':

> Diese Gattung wird sich am längsten halten. Sie ist fühlbar und verständlich allen Ständen; zeigt der Tugend und dem Laster ihre wahre Gestalt, und läßt jene triumphiren. Iffland, Gemmingen, wurden Lieblings-Dichter in dieser Manier, und außerdem erschien darinn noch manch sehr vorzügliches Stück, z.E. von Schröder, F L u.s.w. aber – leider! auch eine Menge Schofel! Ein ermüdendes Gewinsel vertrat die Stelle wahrer Leidenschaft und tragischer Situationen, und bürgerliche Karaktere wurden zur leibhaften Crapule; es entstanden weinerliche Stadt- Dorf- Bauernweiber-Wachtstuben und Handwerker-Sitten-Gemählde. (*Journal des Luxus*, 351f)

All of the most illustrative examples of this Nachspiel type are set in the bourgeois milieu. The two earliest, *Mis Jenny* (1771) and *Fanny* (1772), are among that handful bearing the pretentious subtitle 'tragisch,' and they are similar, both pointing consciously through their personae to English sentimental prototypes, both highly dependent in problems and themes on German plays with serious bourgeois themes or undertones (e.g. Lessing's *Miß Sara Sampson*, 1755 and Weiße's *Amalia*, 1765). Both Nachspiele depict virtuous women who are manipulated and deceived by men, who withdraw stoically to accept their fate, and who by a sudden unexpected (and improbable) turn of events are stabbed to death in the end. Virtually all of the action is described retrospectively, the works themselves containing little dramatic development. This combination of features, added to their brevity, leaves little opportunity for the heroines' stature or audiences' sympathy to build, and their deaths are more unfortunate flukes than tragic inevitabilities. The emotions nevertheless run strong, for the playwrights tug at public heart-strings by offering heroines of impeccable morals whose fates the audience would be ashamed not to lament; the tragedy, if it can be truly called that, does not lie in the death of a heroine, but in the triumph of corruption over the virtue she represents. It is a message with social rather than personal dimension, a general tragedy rather than an individual one.

When works are subtitled tragedies, we know that we will likely face death at the end and are supposed to be moved. Despite the fact that they do not share this subtitle, and even eventually have happy endings, many other Nachspiele from the time are essentially melodramas. *Cangé* [1795], for example, draws on the contemporary horrors of the French Revolution by citing actual dated documents from the National Convention as its starting point and claim to veracity, thereafter painting a dramatic picture of exemplary virtue in the face of monstrous vice: an innocent father's imprisonment, a starving family, a despicable seducer, and all with a backdrop of terror. With little actual dramatic action or development on stage, the play is more of a titillating peep-show than a drama, an emotional stimulation for the audience on the pretence of championing a moral cause.

Whether designated specifically as tragic or not, all of these works are filled with highly charged emotional dialogue. *Liebe und Vaterland* (1789) compares with many others in its lack of action, excessive use of retrospectives, contrived revelations to bring on a surprise conclusion, and generally melodramatic atmosphere; and it offers some exemplary passages of dialogue to illustrate the emotional language of these plays. Scene 13 between Steinberg and Karl is dramatically central, revealing all hitherto unknown relationships among the characters and making the conclusion possible. It presents a climax of the emotional patriotism suggested in the title of the play. Karl begins:

> Ja mein Herr! mein eifrigster, mein einziger Wunsch, das Ziel aller meiner Begierde wäre nun, diesen für mich so unglücklichen Aufenthalt verlassen zu können, und in fremden Gegenden ein günstigeres Schicksal oder mein Grab zu finden – Sie scheinen ein edler, wohldenkender Mann zu seyn; denken Sie sich zurück in die Zeiten, wo Ihr Zustand dem meinigen gleich war – auch Sie hatte Unmuth und Unglück einst tief gebeugt – auch Sie haben Ihr Vaterland verlassen?
> *Steinberg.* Nicht verlassen! – aber mich einige Zeit aus seinem väterlichen Schoos losgerissen – junger Mann! das Vaterland hat ein heiliges, ein unverbrüchliches Recht auf unsere Dienste, auf unser Leben; seine Wohlfahrt ist unsere erste Pflicht, es verleiht uns Sicherheit und Ruhe, dafür sind wir ihm Unterstützung schuldig – Vaterlandsliebe und Vaterliebe haben gleiche Rechte auf uns – beyde dürfen wir ohne Frevel nicht verlassen –
> *Karl.* Auch nicht verlassen will ich mein Vaterland – Ach! wenn ichs auch wollte! – und doch! ... doch! ... (56f)

The atmosphere is one of high melodrama as the choice, in Karl's mind at least, is 'ein günstigeres Schicksal oder mein Grab zu finden,' extremes of happiness or sorrow that discount the possibility of a more realistic middle ground. The pathos-ridden nature of his language, as that of Steinberg – a series of exclamations, protestations, lamentations, and meaningful pauses – serves as a linguistic vehicle to dramatize these emotions. As well, Steinberg's impassioned equation of paternal love with love for one's country and the responsibilites bound thereto heightens Karl's romantic predicament, expanding it by intertwining personal goals with familial and patriotic responsibilites so that failure on one count becomes symptomatic of deficiency on another. Thus his precious little business becomes a matter for all, and his singular fate supposedly meaningful for his country. Such unrestricted expansion of what is essentially a private tribulation to national proportions is typical of many of these melodramatic works. They try to capitalize on an intense public interest to see socially relevant thematics on the stage, dipping into a shallow pool of public emotion instead of sinking new wells of socio-critical drama.

The tangential themes of paternal love and patriotism here are thus developed to bizarre proportions. As a contrast to life at home, Steinberg describes to Karl what it will be like to live abroad:

> ... wissen Sie wohl, was das heißt: seinen Freund, seine Bekannte, Vater und
> Mutter, alles was man liebt und ehrt, auf einmal zu verlassen – sich unter
> fremde Menschen zu schleichen, die durch gleiche Absichten beseelt mit
> dem unbarmherzigsten Egoismus, mit Hinansetzung aller Menschenliebe, ja
> oft durch das Verderben von tausenden ihrer Mitbrüder, das gemein-
> schaftliche, das blutige Ziel zu erreichen suchen – eine halbe Welt zwischen
> sich und seinem Vaterland zu haben – unaufhörlich zwischen Leben und
> Tod zu schweben – alle Gefühle einer sanften Seele zu unterdrücken, um
> nicht in die Gefahr zu laufen, durch List und Ränke seines sauer erworbe-
> nen Guts beraubt zu werden – Gefahren aller Art zu trotzen – Krankheiten
> ohne Zahl auszustehen – und am Ende noch es für den glücklichsten Zufall
> zu halten, wenn Sie ja wieder Ihre Heimath zu sehen bekommen – wenn Sie
> das können – gut – so reisen Sie nach Ostindien – ich war auch dort, habe
> Gold gesammelt – Gold die Menge – komme wieder in mein Vaterland
> zurück – und bin dennoch unglücklich.
> *Karl.* Welches Bild! – ich träumte so süsse, das Erwachen ist schrecklich – ja
> mein Herr, ich traue Ihnen Erfahrung zu – ich glaube Ihnen – aber fort muß
> ich – o Arabiens Wüsten sind nicht schrecklicher in meinen Augen, als
> dieser Aufenthalt – (58f)

Karl's knowledge of geography is feeble to say the least, but that is irrelevant for what is conveyed. The point is here that he must go as far away as possible – 'eine halbe Welt zwischen sich und seinem Vater- land' – to make the contrast beween life there and at home dramatically striking. Steinberg's description deals only with extremes: 'un- barmherzigster Egoismus ... Hinansetzung aller Menschenliebe ... Verderben von tausenden ihrer Mitbrüder ... unaufhörlich zwischen

Leben und Tod zu schweben ... Gefahren aller Art zu trotzen ... Krankheiten ohne Zahl auszustehen.' In the face of this hyperbolic flood, who wouldn't shudder at the prospect and appreciate the German home and hearth all the more?

The motif of paternal love is handled with similar excess as the scene concludes with the revelation that Steinberg is Karl's uncle, Steinberg's offer to be surrogate father, and Karl's impassioned response:

> *Steinberg.* Thränen des Sohns auf das Grab seines Vaters sind heilige Thrä-
> nen – lass sie fliessen, mein Sohn! – dein zweiter Vater, – ich will sie von
> deinen Wangen abküssen. (küßt ihn, kleine Pause) Aber nun hat mir die
> Natur ein feierliches Recht auf dein Vertrauen gegeben – ...
> *Karl.* Gütiger Himmel! wie kann ich dir genug danken, für diese so grosse,
> so sehr unerwartete Wohlthat – bester Mann! die Natur gebietet mir, Sie zu
> lieben, Sie zu verehren – aber mein Herz liebte Sie, eh' ich noch wußte, daß
> es Pflicht war, Sie zu lieben – nicht also dem Bruder meiner Mutter, nicht
> meinem Oheim, will ich mein Leiden erzählen – sondern dem Menschen-
> freund, dem edlen grosmüthigen Mann will ich mein Herz eröfnen – (62f)

The gush of tears, the primacy of 'Herz' over 'Pflicht,' these signal a triumph of sentiment over the cold reason commonly associated with the Enlightenment. The language and sentiment evident here are typical of the Storm and Stress, and indeed, many Nachspiele of the eighties reflect this literary movement.

Two other Nachspiele from the same time show this influence further, but go beyond the characteristics of high emotion and charged language to give evidence of structural affinity with the Storm and Stress drama. We saw in *Der erste Dank* (1789) a depiction of financial and social downfall. This play ends in a human catastrophe without sign of hope or resolution, a problematic open-ended conclusion, as opposed to the happy, if transparently contrived ends of most Nachspiele with underlying serious themes. A further case in point is *Am Ende eine Betschwester* (1783), which brings us full circle from the first Nachspiele discussed in this chapter, all of which depicted the process of recognition, enlightenment, and subsequent happy union. In *Am Ende eine Betschwester* the scene is set for exactly the same process to occur. It begins and proceeds amid an exaggerated flood of emotion and impassioned rhetoric, but this time the impeccably virtuous heroine is not vindicated of the charges of immorality laid against her. Innocent, she is abandoned in the end, utterly bewildered, as must have been the audience, for this play offered them neither the finality of death nor the satisfaction of a reversal. It is an example of unresolved dramatic conflict and points to a more realistic and sophisticated handling of the question of social relations on the stage.

Reflections of the Literary Scene

Directions for Actors

In considering developments among Nachspiele with strong elements of traditional comedy, opportunities for extemporization were seen as a primary characteristic. Through these the life-blood of the traditional Nachspiel continued to flow. At the same time, it is undeniable that Nachspiele of that type became less and less frequent toward century's end, and that short works with increasingly serious themes became dominant. What Goethe wrote about extemporization as the best school of acting, and the numerous initiatives to improve acting (by Ekhof, Lessing, Engel), should be remembered as we consider the production of these serious works. Literary reviews of performances had also begun to play a major part in the critical reception of drama, and theatre journals proliferated. Commentaries on theatrical productions often included an appraisal of the acting, something largely absent from theatre reception before about 1765.

By the 1780s there is a noticeable tendency among authors of Nachspiele to show in their published texts concern for the way in which the actors would perform their roles. This concern was expressed either in the frequent use of stage directions to instruct and influence performance or in direct notes to actors and directors indicating how a particular scene was to be conveyed. Three examples will illustrate this tendency.

Juliane Dürrbach (1783) contains many stage directions applying to several characters requiring them to go well beyond the text. Their gestures are employed on one level as a complement to the dialogue, expressing opinions and moods that underscore or enhance it, on another as extensions of the text which develop the characters' stage personalities beyond the use of words. Here is a sampling:

> *Juliane.* ... (fällt in Nachdenken) ...; (5)
> *Juliane.* ... (sucht sich in ruhigere Fassung zu setzen); (11)
> *Jakob.* (im Abgehn vor sich zitternd) ...; (17)
> *Franz.* (unwillig.) ...; (19)
> *Meister Elis.* (aufbrausend.) ...; (19)
> *Jakob.* (mit bejaenden Blicken) ...; (28)

Marie. (Marie Dürrbach wirft auf Grünwald verächtliche Blicke, und geht zur Seitenthür hinaus.); (29)
Grünwald. (mit edeln selbst bewußt seyn.); (31)
Juliane. ... (fällt in Nachdenken) ...; (5)
Franz. (voll innigen Entzückens sie anblickend). (38)

It is possible to predict what the actors would do to follow some of these directions; in other cases, however, we only know the effect that is to be produced. There are many ways to evoke these effects, perhaps as many as actors to play the parts. Although guidance could be given, no author or director could tell an actor precisely how the instructions were to be carried out well. The days when stock movements and gestures signified certain emotions and reactions were at an end; instead, with the rise of acting academies and theoretical interest, the goal was increasingly to present natural characters and emotions on stage, in other words, as wide a range of unique personages as could be imagined in the theatrical pieces the characters inhabited. Thus Juliane or Franz or Marie was each unique, and each time they were played they were created anew as the actor interpreted the role. Little room for such interpretation was presented in the dialogue itself, but it was in the tone and pace of delivery, and foremost in the gestures.

As the central character, Juliane is called upon more than any other to provide character development and depth through her gestures. She is alone on stage for the first and third scenes of the play, during which time the nature of her character and her motivation for the rest of the action are set. Scene 3 contains the following:

(Man sieht deutliche Spuren ihrer Unruhe, sie setzt sich an den Flügel, der Affekt steigt – sie greift in den Flügel – und singt aus Kleists und Bendas Elegie. Sie fliehet fort u. die Strophe:)
Nur einen Druck der Hand, nur halbe Blicke
Ach einen Kuß, wie er mir vormals gab
Vergönne mir von ihm; dann stürz Geschicke!
Mich, wenn du wilst, ins Grab.
(Nach Vollendung sinkt sie von Wehmuth ergriffen in den Stuhl zurück.)*
(10)

'Sie fliehet fort' is the first phrase of Christian Ewald von Kleist's poem 'Amynt' (1751) in which a man mourns the loss of his beloved. The perspective has been altered here to a woman mourning the loss of her beloved. 'Nur einen Druck ... Grab' is the second-last strophe of the poem (see Kleist, 62f). The prominent musician and composer Georg Benda published his cantata *Amynts Klage* in 1774, which presumably provided the basis for the melody intended. Benda was a leading proponent of the contemporary 'Melodrama,' a recitative form which combined rhythmic dramatic delivery with musical accompaniment. In the footnote indicated (*) the author adds this: 'Die Schauspielerin sey hier nicht Sängerin, verläugne gern ihre Kunst, und stelle lieber das liebe, schmachtende, sanfte, gute duldende Mädchen dar.' Despite the musical text, the actress is reminded that not her singing talents are to shine here but her ability to evoke pathos – 'Affekt.' If the audience is really to witness 'deutliche Spuren ihrer Unruhe,' then she has a vocal and gestural task to make this occur, a challenge to her improvisational skills. This vocal and gestural communication presumably would continue throughout her melodic delivery, at the end of which she collapses into a wave of melancholy. While such a scene is potentially rife with melodramatic pathos, it also presents a talented actress with the freedom to explore a vast range of vocal and gestural potential; indeed, it demands that range.

Also from the eighties, *Liebe und Vaterland* (1789) places similar demands on its actors, as for example in the climactic scene between Karl and Steinberg discussed above, in which all concealed relationships are revealed and the resolution made possible. Supporting the passionate dialogue is a network of gestures cued by the author's stage directions. The author makes it clear that performance was very much in his mind when he provided this introductory directive to the scene: 'Dieser Auftritt muß nicht wild, sondern bald mit verbissenem, bald mit geäussertem Affekt von Karls Seite gespielt werden' (54). The key word, as it was in the author's note in *Juliane Dürrbach*, is 'Affekt.' In both cases the term is a challenge to the actor to stimulate the audience's emotion. We have seen examples of the charged dialogue in this scene which contributed to that pathos; here are the stage directions accompanying those passages:

> *Karl.* (leise und bebend)
> *Steinberg.* (faßt ihn bei der Hand)
> *Steinberg.* (mit Nachdruck)
> *Karl.* (fällt ihm um den Hals)
> *Karl.* (Pause) ... (weint)
> *Steinberg.* (küßt ihn. kleine Pause)
> *Steinberg.* (lächelnd)
> *Karl.* (küßt ihm die Hand)
> *Steinberg.* (bei Seite) ... (laut) ... (umarmt ihn) ... (umarmt ihn)
> *Karl.* (tief gerührt) ... (zeiget auf sein Herz) ... (ab). (55-66)

As was the case with some stage directions in comic Nachspiele, those above on their own, without benefit of the dialogue, are enough to tell us what happens in the scene. In a sense they are more important than the dialogue and its revelations since that information is only an artificial means to engineer the play's neat conclusion, whereas a primary intention of both this scene and the entire work is to evoke enough 'Affekt' to move the audience. The emphases, movements, and gestures above cover a considerable range of emotions in the space of twelve pages of text, a scene of perhaps fifteen minutes. Although both actors must depict this emotional flux, Karl's role is particularly demanding as he moves from quivering uncertainty to explosive affection, to pregnant silence, to tears, to humble gratitude, and finally to the greatest depth of feeling, as signalled by the final gesture to his heart. This range risks melodramatic exaggeration as a likely result, but the result would depend very much on the intentions and skills of the actor performing this role. There is no doubt that the role was demanding or that it allowed considerable freedom for his personal interpretation through extra-textual means.

The third example comes from the scene between Rittmeister von Sindel and Hannchen in *Der Weihnachtabend* (1803). From the point of view of interplay between dialogue and gesture it is unusual, since one character, von Sindel, does all the speaking, while Hannchen utters not a word. She communicates her wishes nevertheless, although our understanding of them and that of von Sindel are different. As von Sindel carries on what is essentially a monologue in her presence, this is how she communicates:

(in ihrer Verlegenheit sieht stumm und verschämt vor sich nieder.)

...

(zittert und kann noch immer keine Worte finden.)

...

(zittert heftiger, und immer unmöglicher wirds ihr zu reden.)

...

(zwingt sich zu lächeln.)

...

(schaudert zusammen und zittert heftiger.)

...

(sucht sich loszuwinden.)

...

(weint.)

...

(wirft sich mit heftigen Thränen an seinen Hals.)

...
    (verläßt schluchzend das Zimmer.) (27-9)

It is a contradiction in terms that a central character in a text-based drama cannot speak. Hannchen pays dearly for this failing as the well-intentioned von Sinden misinterprets her wishes to assume that she is prepared to enter into marriage with his nephew. The audience knows, however, that her loyalty is to the painter Braun and that her silence is evidence only of the quandary that binds her. The scene thus has potential to draw the audience into partnership with Hannchen's suffering silence, for they alone can provide the answers she should be giving, and as she struggles to say what is on their minds – and fails – a stimulating tension is created which heightens interest in the remaining action and culminates in a satisfying release at the end when the problem is resolved. So much depends here on Hannchen's ability to convey meaning and emotion through gesture and movement. It is the type of scene that a gifted actress can explore, mould, and relish as an opportunity to let her own creativity shine through. Except that the content here is serious, the principle is no different from the one driving central figures in comic works who so often carried the plays with their talent.

Cultural Debate

Developments in acting technique were only part of the growing reassessment of theatre and society in general. The Nachspiel also reflects something of the public debate about literature and the arts directly. We can reach back to as early as Luise Gottsched's *Herr Witzling* (1745) to see a Nachspiel with the clear intention of commenting on the contemporary intellectual scene. The plot here is little more than an excuse to discuss current trends in philosophy, poetics, mathematics, and language with the intention of publicizing J.C. Gottsched's views. At the same time, in keeping with his idea of the theatre's function, the play ridicules and corrects those whose attitudes and actions run contrary to what J.C. Gottsched considered progressively constructive for society. While *Herr Witzling* uses the stage as a medium to express this position without commenting directly on the state of theatre in its time, some later Nachspiele do make the contemporary state of theatre their critical focus.

Die frohe Frau (1775), for example, has a cast comprised of professional actors and a theatre critic as well as students. The action is a post-mortem of their performance of Klinger's tragedy *Die leidende Frau* (more commonly entitled *Das leidende Weib*, 1775), including its relations to contemporary influences such as Richardson's *Clarissa* and Goethe's *Werther*. Recently, renewed scholarly attention has been drawn to Klinger's play (see Klinger, *Gesamtausgabe*, XII-XVII). Klinger's tragedy itself was an overt example of Storm and Stress writing, solidifying his position alongside Goethe with his *Werther* (1774) and J.M.R. Lenz (*Anmerkungen über das Theater*, 1774; *Der Hofmeister*, 1774; and *Der neue Menoza*, 1776); it joined these works in the newest publications of the Weygand house in Leipzig and thus closely associated itself with their literary style and socio-critical intention. Weygand was aware of the stir it might raise, so the publisher's advertisement of *Das leidende Weib* rings very much like an apologia, calling upon readers to resist attacking the play's imitative character and dramatic weaknesseses:

> Wenn ich meinen Lesern sage, daß dieses Stück in der Göthischen-Lenzischen Manier abgefaßt ist: so werden sie mir einräumen, daß hier kein Platz ist, die Verdienste desselben zu entwickeln. Nur dies einzige bitte ich, es nicht sogleich Nachahmung zu schelten, wenn im Durchblättern Regellosigkeit sichtbar ist, wenn Spott über die Belletristen, Eifer über die Schädlichkeit der Romane, ein humoristischer Schulmeister, und ein verführtes Frauenzimmer, ein Geheimderath, verschiedne Schwärmereien und verschiedne Paradoxa, wie im Hofmeister vorkommen. Nur dies bemerke ich, daß der Verfasser mehr Skizzen von Charakteren giebt, als sie, wie Lenz, mit starken Farben darstellt. (*Gesamtausgabe*, XIV)

Nevertheless, the play was the object of much more critical invective than kindness (examples cited by Harris, *Gesamtausgabe*, XIVf). Weygand's apologia serves as a general summary of the work to which the Nachspiel *Die frohe Frau* reacts. *Die frohe Frau* is in essence an entirely literary reaction, for the suggestion in the Nachspiel's subtitle that it be performed after Klinger's tragedy is more facetious than anything else, and there is no evidence that it in fact ever crossed the boards. After *Die frohe Frau* was published, Klinger responded to its author Johann Gottlieb Gönten by means of an open letter in the *Frankfurter gelehrten Anzeigen*, 11 August 1775, in which he defended himself against the attack: 'Ich habe die von Ihnen mir überschickte, und auf meinen Karakter gemachte Pasquil erhalten. Ich hielte es, als ich den Titel ansah, für eine Witzeley über mein Drama, und fing ganz gelassen zu lesen an. Aber wie sehr erstaunt ich, als ich sah, daß ein feindlicher Mensch unter diesem Deckmantel meinen moralischen Charakter und mein Herz auf die unfreundlichste und unedelste Art durch Lügen vor der

Welt zu schänden suchte ...' (Rieger, I, 377). And so he goes on for some two dense pages, lamenting the attack and wishing he had the financial means to begin legal procedures against his oppressor. Klinger's impassioned reaction shows just how offended he was, and examples from *Die frohe Frau* make it understandable, for instance the personal invective of one of the actresses:

> Was weiß so ein junger Mensch, wie der Verfaßer ist, viel von Staat, von Republik. Kaum schlupft er des Tags einmal aus seinem engen Gäsgen. Dann steken ihm seine Charactere noch wie ein Rausch im Kopf, die er in seinem Kämmergen hin und wieder las. Sein junges unstätiges Gehirn, macht tausend Zusäze, die nicht hingehören. Nun glaubt er, alle Personen die ihm auf der Straße begegnen, wären solche Leute, und wenn er schreibt, ist's die ganze Welt. Dem Edelmann gibt er des Bauern Brodmesser, und dem Bauern die Sprache des Degenmannes, mit dem er spricht. Ich bin doch begierig zu hören, was die Kunstrichter darüber sagen. (5)

Beyond the personal disparagements, the objects of her criticism are Klinger's fragmentary style, his attempt to reflect broad society all at once, and his inaccurate portrayal of social types. These accusations are rooted in her own confident bias of what makes drama good, and she has no room for such an unconventional and disrespectful free-spirit as Klinger. But finally she defers to the professional critics, a sign of the growing importance of this caste. Her apparent confidence in them is not shared by all on stage, however; the leading actor's immediate rejoinder is: 'Die Kunstrichter? Ja das sind mir die rechten. Die meisten gehören samt unserm Trauerspielschreiber ins Tollhaus. Da zupfen und schnizen sie wo nichts ist, verderben das Bild zum Jammern, und bessern um kein Haar' (6). The triangular tension between author, actor, and critic, part of the stage scene ever since, emerges from this comment, and despite Göntgen's primary intention to attack Klinger, the Nachspiel's reflection of the contemporary theatrical climate remains more important today. In a small way it encapsulates the energy of a medium that was being taken more and more seriously and becoming increasingly important in its time. The triangle of judgment, as set up here, has author on one side as defendant, and actors and critics facing as prosecutors; the general public, the audience, however, are merely invisible observers with no official place in the process. When the critic finally speaks, we understand their role better:

> ... Doch muß man Leute belehren, die noch nicht Festigkeit genug haben, das blendende Flitterwerk einer übertriebenen Schreibart zu verachten.

...
für dem Verfasser der leidenden Frau, muß man ehrliche Leute warnen. (17)

The theatre critic sees the general public as an object of education, his and the theatre's responsibility to teach them, to guide them in their aesthetic judgment and appreciation. While in 1775 we are almost a half-century removed from Gottsched's didactic prescriptions, the critic's point of view above continues in the same vein.

Although this didactic function doubtless continued to carry weight through century's end, the pendulum was swinging away from direct pedagogy toward broad social criticism as well as pure enjoyment through theatrical experience. As drama matured toward 1800, it gained increasing credibility as a pure art form, playwrights and actors both enjoying a rise in status and esteem. The final word is best given to one of the greatest contributors to this change. Kotzebue's Nachspiel *Das Liebhabertheater vor dem Parlament* (1790) points in its title to the two main forces in deciding the success of theatre in society in the coming years. The *Liebhabertheater* itself is a telling cultural invention of the period – we saw how the one in Weimar spawned the famous Nationaltheater there. *Liebhabertheater* were active and central to the cultural lives of many educated groups, a natural outgrowth of the rising interest in the arts in general, the stage in particular. They were private expressions of cultural interest, initially informal gatherings of acquaintances with a common interest in theatre who performed primarily for their own amusement and pleasure, only secondarily for others in a more formal setting. The other force in the title, the *Parlament*, represents all that opposes this free cultural expression. Here are the philistines with civic authority, incapable of understanding or appreciating the initiative of the *Liebhaber*, spoiled and fat, prejudiced against actors and their work, ignoring pleas for the cultural development of society. At the end of the Nachspiel they pronounce a judgment rooted in ignorance: victory for the philistines; triumph for myopic officialdom. The debate, even the conclusion, could easily be set in many different countries today with little adjustment. But ignorant judgment is not the end of the work, for it concludes with a magical transformation as the heavens open, supernatural patrons of the arts appear, and the judgment is overturned. This is Kotzebue's final message: on its own terms, in the world of illusion, allegory, and theatrical magic, the victory is won nevertheless. The stage goes on. Higher values and justice prevail. But that is the ephemeral world of theatrical illusion. Just outside the stage doors stood contemporary reality: the state and all its authority. This was a world in which theatre-goers were again public citizens, where victory through the stage's illusion had to yield to the very real power of the state. It is on this power that we shall concentrate as we turn to the question of censorship.

9
Between Text and Performance: Censorship

The question of theatre censorship in the eighteenth century must have a double focus, the church and the state, for the two worked hand in hand to control both performance and dissemination of dramatic works. A long-standing antagonism between church and stage lay at the foundation of theatre censorship, which in the decades before the widespread publication of plays naturally focused on performance, but also affected the daily lives of actors and actresses in itinerant troupes. One must almost write 'actors' alone here, for the church generally condemned the profession for women outright. On the surface, ecclesiastical objections to actors and their craft were based on conceptions of morality and were expressed in regular denunciations from the pulpit, particularly when troupes set up their stages nearby. A more severe censure was the refusal of the sacraments, even of Christian burial, to members of acting companies. Theatre people were denounced as immoral, lascivious creatures who exercised a corrupting force on Christian society. But the argument of moral turpitude had deeper roots which stretched very much into the realms of politics and economics as well, leading to a complex antagonism summarized by Hilde Haider-Pregler in *Des sittlichen Bürgers Abendschule* (131-3). Theatre stood in direct competition with the church in more than a moral sense (if it ever really did that). It competed for citizens' leisure time as well as their money; it offered the enticement of vicariously enjoying love intrigues with underlying sexual connotation, of watching actresses 'displaying' themselves on stage, not to mention the ribald antics of the comic figure, sinful recreations indeed; it propagated the world of illusion, a distraction from the reality of daily life to which the good citizen should be bound in regular labour and devotion; it was, historically, a relic of heathen practice and ritual. The church joined with the state in its discouragement or censorship of theatre. After mid-century, theorists in increasing numbers propagated the idea that the stage could be used to exert moral influence on the populace; indeed, this should be its primary function, making it a potential moral force in society, whereas that role had always been carried by the church. Thus, the Enlightenment drama emerged as a secular competition for the church in the moral education of the people and the two found themselves on a direct collision course in the quest for authority and power.

In analysing Nachspiele we have seen frequent evidence of satire on various representatives and aspects of society. Otto Rommel expresses the view that such satire performed an important function as a release for theatre-goers in an essentially restrictive society. The satire was often recognized and indeed condoned by rulers and government officials, even enjoyed by them, as long as it was kept within acceptable limits (*Altwiener*, 18). Evidence of this tolerance can be seen in Vienna's Kärntnertortheater which in mid-century enjoyed a clientele from all classes. Rommel suggests that in fact censorship was less vigorous in larger centres such as Vienna than in smaller ones where petty-minded despots were more likely to undermine any suggestion of criticism.

The question of censorship has attracted scholars increasingly over the last decade. A helpful overview of the climate that produced it in German territory and of those who carried it out is provided by Wolfgang Martens's 'Obrigkeitliche Sicht ...' (1981). Theatre and literature represented a relatively minor focus for the activities of police and state authorities (Martens, 20), and in the early decades occurred mostly in connection with restricted performance on religious days and other special occasions. The overall purpose of the state representatives of 'Policey und Cameralistik' was to uphold and reinforce the general peace, order, and propriety of society. But these offices also represented the financial arm of the state, and indeed it was on financial grounds that theatre received most attention from them. Martens stresses the fact that entrepreneurial theatre (itinerant troupes, later standing theatres) was always seen as a separate entity from Hoftheater (and Nationaltheater) which were largely under court control; these needed no police supervision, being under the direct authority of the ruler. Beyond that, the state interest in entrepreneurial theatre concentrated primarily not on morals but on finances, particularly the potential flow of resources through the hands of itinerant troupes out of the state; it became a civic responsibility to place strictures on this drain. At the same time, the theatre was regarded more and more as an acceptable social institution, the state having indeed a responsibility to provide citizens with appropriate outlets for amusement and leisure, as long as their proper social roles and their productivity were not endangered. Drama should encourage good morals, behaviour, and virtue among the populace but not interfere with their work.

Gottlob von Justi in the north (active in Saxony and Prussia) and Joseph von Sonnenfels in Vienna were two of the most influential monitors of social and theatrical activity in the age. Justi's *Die Grundfeste zu der Macht und Glückseligkeit der Staaten; oder ausführliche Vorstellung der gesammten Policey-Wissenschaft* (1760-1) represents the culmination of a series of writings on state order and controls. In this statement, Justi summarizes his notion of the state's role in the activities of the theatre:

> Die Comödie ist unstreitig eine der erlaubtesten und angenehmsten
> Vergnügungen vor das Volk; und es soll so leicht kein ansehnlicher Staat
> seyn, der nicht in seiner Hauptstadt und andern ansehnlichen Städten des
> Landes, dem Volke diese Ergetzlichkeit durch sehr geschickte Schauspieler
> verschaffet. Die Comödie bey einer guten Einrichtung ist vortreflich
> geschickt, die Tugend und guten Sitten zu befördern ... Die Regierung
> sollte zum Aufseher über die zu spielende Stücke einen Mann setzen, der
> sowohl von guter Einsicht und Geschmack wäre, als ein edles Herz hätte,
> welcher sowohl die Regeln des Theaters, als den Geschmack der meisten
> Zuschauer verstünde, beyde mit einander zu vereinigen suchte, und
> welcher den Endzweck der Comödie, die Tugend und guten Sitten zu
> befördern, auch bey denen lustigen Stücken nicht außer Augen verlöhre.
>
> Wenn die Comödie die Tugend und guten Sitten zu befördern im Stande
> ist; so können schöne Trauerspiele gewiß viel beytragen, edle Grundsätze
> dem Volke einzudrücken, dessen Caracter und Genie vortreflich zu bilden,
> und dasselbe zu großen bürgerlichen Tugenden aufzumuntern. (*Grundfeste*,
> II, 375-7)

The statement confirms the moral value of both comedy and tragedy, but also says in effect that a state censor should be appointed to control all works and performances. It also reflects an honest sensitivity to the aesthetic needs and values of the theatre. Numerous other prominent officials later published similar views, but the enactment of these opinions naturally varied greatly from state to state, from reactionary sanctioning of anything smacking of social satire or infelicitous comedy to liberal acceptance of the stage as a special zone which required a certain degree of tolerance.

Lest it be thought that all officials and censors were as mature in their thinking as Justi, attention must be drawn to the mighty and ongoing pressure in some places to stifle all theatrical activity. This was exerted by Roman Catholics and Protestants alike, and in one of its most virulent forms by the Pietists. As late as 1788 Johann Heinrich Jung contributed this fanatical tirade to the debate in his *Lehrbuch der Staats-Polizey-Wissenschaft*:

> Schauspieler von allerhand Art, Gaukler, Taschenspieler, Seiltänzer u.d.g. sind ein Gift für die Gewerb-Stände, alles lauft hinzu, verschleudert Geld und Zeit, und jene brodlose Künstler verschwenden den Gewinn wieder, oder schleppen ihn auser Land. Ueberall also wo Industrie und Fleis die Mittel zur Glückseeligkeit und Pflicht sind, da müssen Schauspiele von jeder Art nicht gedultet werden. Folglich ist es ganz recht, wenn man sie in commerzirenden Städten und auf Universitäten durchaus nicht erlaubt. (304)

As Martens points out (35), such a statement could well have been written sixty years earlier, perhaps then with some greater degree of accuracy. Jung seemed quite unaware, or at least unwilling to acknowledge, that the theatre had undergone considerable change since the days when rag-tag itinerant troupes had dominated the scene.

In Vienna, with wider influence over all of Austria, stood Joseph von Sonnenfels as the champion of state censorship with his comprehensive work *Grundsätze der Polizey, Handlung und Finanzwissenschaft* (1770), the first volume of which was revised and republished as *Handbuch der inneren Staatsverwaltung mit Rücksicht auf die Umstände und Begriffe der Zeit* (1798), coincidentally the same year as the Nachspiel *Die Martinsgänse* appeared. Although his attitude toward the stage was less liberal than Justi's, Sonnenfels expressed the same sense of state responsibility to provide such entertainment for the populace:

> Gemeinschaftliche Ergetzlichkeiten, wo sich die Menge versammelt, sind hauptsächlich für die Hauptstädte unentbehrlich, in denen es so viele unbeschäftigte Menschen von allem Alter, Range und Stande gibt, die ihre Zeit nicht auszufüllen wissen, und in die verderblichsten Arten von Ausschweifungen verfallen würden, an deren statt ihnen die Schaubühne die Leichtigkeit anbietet, einige müßige Stunden hinzubringen. (*Handbuch*, 406)

Like Justi, Sonnenfels had a good idea of what type of theatre was acceptable to perform this function:

> Hierunter sind die Schauspiele, vorzüglich seiner [des Gesetzgebers]
> Aufmerksamkeit würdig, die, woferne sie ihre gehörige Einrichtung
> empfangen, das Ergötzende mit dem Nutzbaren vereinigen, und ... eine
> Schule der Sitten, der Höflichkeit und Sprache werden können.
>
> Wenn die Schauspiele eine Schule der Sitten werden sollen, so ist es
> darauf zu sehen, daß solche Stücke aufgeführet werden, die diesem
> Endzwecke zusagen. Das Laster muß also in seiner scheuslichen Gestalt
> und mit der Strafe als einer unabsönderlichen Folge, die Tugend mit allen
> ihren Reizungen, und in ihrer liebeswürdigsten Gestalt, und wenigstens am
> Ende siegend, erscheinen. (*Grundsätze*, I, 138f)

Thus the overall impact of dramatic works was to be in the end a moral one and an instructional focus for the good behaviour and social values of its audience. With such emphasis on the clear delineation of virtue and vice by Sonnenfels and Justi, as well as by the many other less prominent officials who voiced similar views, it is easy to understand that infuriating tendency of serious Nachspiele to arrange persistently an artificial reversal at the conclusion, ensuring the triumph of virtue over vice. Moreover, while the discussion above creates the impression that censorship was foremost an expression of state force against the public will, in fact many citizens agreed with the necessity for such restrictions and saw the police simply as the executive arm of the people. Citizens too, especially playwrights in this case, must also do their part, as this critic declares:

> Es war vorauszusehen, daß die Schriftsteller-Freyheit sich auch auf die
> Bühne erstrecken würde. Hier aber muß sie durchaus ihre bestimmten
> Gränzen haben. Wenn auf der Bühne vieles gesagt werden darf, und gesagt
> werden soll, so behalten doch Moral und Policey sich das Wann und Wie
> bevor. Nicht alle Augen vertragen moralische Nuditäten aller Art. Der
> Dramatische Dichter wirkt im weitesten Felde, und zwar doppelt stark, da
> mehrere Sinnen zugleich seine Bilder genießen. Desto strenger ist seine
> Rechenschaft! Der Staat schützt Leben und Eigenthum, warum nicht auch
> Grundsätze und – Sitten seiner Bürger? (*Journal des Luxus*, repr. 1967, 352f)

In Austria during Empress Maria Theresia's reign (1740-80), the censorship of all books was pursued with a fanatical vigour, power resting in the hands of the Bücher-Censors-Hofcommission from 1751, i.e. the Jesuits, with tremendous influence and their monarch's blessing. Heinrich Houben's pithy and amusing account of these practices in mid-century is an eye-opener for anyone interested in the literature of the age. He recounts regular practices such as confiscation of all foreign books at the border, screening them by a committee of censors controlled by Jesuits, encouraging citizens through financial rewards to denounce others in possession of forbidden works, and enticing booksellers to order contraband literature, then exposing and prosecuting them (Houben, 22f). As far as theatre was concerned, the first major battle of censorship was fought against the beloved institution of extemporization, because of its penchant for crudity. The struggle ended in 1752 with an edict from the empress banning extemporization on stage entirely, a command which actually had little effect in the short run on the resilient improvisational spirit of the stages in her capital (Haider-Pregler, 270). Enter Sonnenfels. Named official theatre censor in 1770, charged with reorganizing the practices of theatre censorship in Vienna, he took up the cause against extemporization with a passion (see Haider-Pregler, 345-50) and succeeded in gaining imperial sanction for his suggested restrictions. They included these points:

— Daß derselbe [Sonnenfels] bey der Censur nichts zulassen solle, was die Religion, den Staat oder die guten Sitten im mindesten beleidiget, oder auch offenbarer Unsinn, und Grobheit, folglich des Theaters einer Haupt- und Residenz-Stadt unwürdig ist.

— Sind sothaner Censur nicht nur alle neue hergebende sondern auch die schon vormals aufgeführte Stücke, sie seyen zum Druck, oder zur blossen Vorstellung bestimmt ohne Ausnahme zu unterwerfen, weilen, besonders in älteren Zeiten, aus Übersehen, verschiedenes eingeschlichen, welches mit der fürs künftige ohnveränderlich festgesetzten Regul nicht bestehen kann.

— Hat der Impresa, oder wer sonsten ein Stück auf das Theater geben will, solches jederzeit wenigstens 14. Tage vor deren Druck oder Aufführung dem Censori in duplo zu überreichen, damit dieser es neben seinen übrigen Amtsverrichtungen mit dem behörigen Fleiß durchgehen, und ein exemplar davon zu seiner Legitimation für sich behalten, das ander aber mit dem admittatur hinausgeben könne.

— Ist, nachdeme ohnehin schon, das extemporiren verbotten worden, den Schauspielern in der Vorstellung alles geflissentliche Zusetzen, Abändern, oder aus dem Stegreif, ohne vorgängige gleichmässige Billigung der Censur, an das publicum stellende Anreden, auf das schärfeste, und mit der Bedrohung zu untersagen, daß auf den ersten Übertrettungsfall ein dergleichen acteur oder actrice ohne Unterschied, wer es seye, also gleich nach geendigtem Schauspiel auf 24. Stunden in Arrest gebracht, bey dem zweyten Übertrettungsfall aber, der oder dieselbe, ohnnachsichtlich vom Theater abgeschaffet werden solle. (Haider-Pregler, 346)

By 1782, two years after the ascension of Joseph II, this edict applied to the entire territory of the Austrian monarchy. It was clearly comprehensive and severe, not only for published works but indeed for every performance. Thus the theatrical climate in Vienna changed abruptly in the seventies and the heyday of unrestricted extemporization was over. These laws of censorship established in 1770 remained the backbone of literary restriction there until 1848; Maria Theresia's successor Joseph II (1780-90) liberalized them somewhat, but Leopold II (1790-2) strengthened them again and his successor Franz I (1792-1835) even more in the wake of the French Revolution.

Any thought of relaxing the censorship laws was put aside in panic in reaction to events in France. The experience of the revolution was a clear signal to despotic monarchs in other lands not to liberalize their states but rather to clamp down more securely to prevent similar insurrection in their own territory. Hence on 16 Jan 1795, the theatre censorship laws of Austria were reinforced, as these excerpts demonstrate:

- Es können in einem monarchistischen Staate keine Stücke aufgeführt werden, deren Inhalt auf die Abänderung der monarchischen Regierungsform abzielt, oder der demokratischen oder einer anderen Vorzug vor der monarchischen einräumt, oder auch die ständische Verfassung eines Landes herabsetzt.
- Die Gesetzgebung eines Staates oder dessen bestehende Gesetze können überhaupt in keinem Stoffe mit Tadel aufgeführt werden.
- Die Ausdrücke: Tyrann, Tyranney, Despotismus, Unterdrückung der Untergebenen müssen auf dem Theater soviel wie möglich vermieden werden.
- Von dem Worte 'Aufklärung' ist auf dem Theater ebenso wenig Erwähnung zu machen, als von der Freyheit und Gleichheit. (Alth/Obzyna, 68)

There was a host of further incredible restrictions, including the prohibition of figures representing the clergy (Catholic or Protestant) on stage. (See further details in Hadamowsky, 'Ein Jahrhundert,' 293.) From 1772 until 1804 Regierungsrat Franz Karl Hägelin was in charge of theatre censorship in the city. He delivered to the monarch detailed analyses of every play performed along with the censors' judgment; in every theatre a censorship commissioner sat through rehearsals and performances with emended text in hand; contraventions were prosecuted by the police. Oddly enough, in many cases complete uncut texts of the works could be bought and read by citizens, but not seen on stage in that form, a testimony to the ruler's belief that theatrical performance was much more likely than passive reading to incite strong and undesirable reactions (Hadamowsky, 'Ein Jahrhundert,' 292, 304; Hadamowsky's assiduous and concise account of censorship in Vienna from 1751 to 1848 is the best available).

Keeping in mind these guidelines as well as the role of the church in state affairs, the censored copy of *Die Martinsgänse* below can well be understood, as can the fact that it did not appear on stage in Vienna until 1815, having been performed widely by then in many German centres since 1798. It is just one of the many censor's copies resting in the stacks of the theatre collection of the Austrian National Library. And while the following is just one example of theatre censorship at the end of the eighteenth century, it is likely that every Nachspiel in the Bibliography published and performed after about 1770 was similarly touched by censorship in some form. Moreover, amid this climate of restriction and reprisal, it is impossible to estimate the degree to which playwrights and actors engaged in a continuous process of self-censorship so that they might continue their work.

Die Martinsgänse [1798]: A Censored Version

Gustav Hagemann (b. 1760, Oranienbaum in Brandenburg, d. between 1829 and 1835 in Breslau) was in his time a prolific playwright and a well-known actor. He performed with several companies in northern locations such as Altona, Bremen, Hamburg, and Stralsund, and also gained reputation as a director. This triple talent as playwright, actor, and director contributed to the theatrical effectiveness and popularity of many of his works, among them *Die Martinsgänse* which was performed widely throughout German territory.

The play's title and action focus on the religious festival of St Martin, held annually on 11 November. Martin von Tours (b. 316, d. 397), son of a Roman tribune, became a cavalryman in Gall, was christened at age eighteen and then left the army. After service as a missionary and a monk, he founded the first Gallic monastery soon after 360 and was named Bishop of Tours in 371. The rest of his life he spent in proselytizing and tireless missionary work, and after his death he was canonized to become the patron saint of the Merovingian-Frankish kingdom. The cloak and the goose are associated with St Martin, the former likely because of the legend that as a soldier he shared his own garment with a freezing beggar at the gates of Amiens, the goose being the traditional festive roast on his day. St Martin's Day is celebrated foremost in Holland, Flanders, Luxemburg, and the Lower Rhine re-

80

aber ich will euch erzählen, wie mir Gott einen
Freund sandte. —

Marthe.

Einen Engel, einen Habakuk!

(Während dieser Reden ist Jeder an seinem Stuhl.)

Kühnow.

Setzt euch jetzt. —   (Sie setzen sich.)

Groß ist der brave Mensch in jedem Stande,
In jedem Stande trift den Schurken Schand'
O, Vorsicht! Seegne jeden braven Mann,
Man treff' ihn nun im Schauspielhaus, man
      treff ihn in der Kirche an.

(Der Vorhang fällt.

Ende.

Gustav Hagemann, *Die Martinsgänse* [1798]
Final Page of Censored Prompter's Copy
Österreichische Nationalbibliothek, Sig. 626301 ATh.

gion, but also elsewhere, although more in Protestant than in Roman Catholic circles. (I cannot resist adding the personal note that the censored prompter's text of the play discussed below in fact came into my hands precisely on the eleventh day of the eleventh month, which made me think I should do something about it – one of those ironic quirks that brings a smile when digging in the dusty stacks.)

Hagemann's choice of this background suits his purpose of describing and lauding the virtue of human charity as practised by Pastor Kühnow in his own modest way. In the face of this background the play is loaded with reflections on a society that makes such generosity difficult and brings suffering on its proponent. Criticism of this society is stated most sharply by Kühnow's old student chum Friderici, now an actor and troupe principal, so that whenever he speaks he brings a dual perspective: the private citizen and the proponent of theatre as a tool for social comment. Many of the themes discussed above, from enlightenment to class, wealth, and social injustice, are strongly represented in this play, but what makes it even more valuable as a reflection of the period is the fact that the text at hand was used as the basis for a performance. Thus we have not just Hagemann's published text but also the censor's and director's deletions and insertions which give us a fuller picture of the taboos and restrictions affecting its performance at the time.

On the title-page is written 'Soufflierbuch Ulbrichs' but the nature of the markings (ink, pencil colour, handwriting style) suggests that three different persons amended the text. One set of corrections comprises only minor and insignificant stylistic alterations. Another is likely the hand of the director, or the prompter Ulbrich. It consists of deletions and alterations that generally improve the dramatic flow and also tamper with the content. These changes were likely made after the censor had done his job, to bridge the lacunae his deletions had caused in the dialogue; they give evidence of some self-censorship as well. At times it is difficult to tell the difference among hands in the markings since most consist simply of lines that strike through text, but the overall effect of the emendations is clear.

Handwritten on the final page of the text is the following, a summary of the third set of emendations which came from the censor's hand: 'Darf mit den Aenderungen S. 7, 18, 22, 24, 37, 40 [or] 48 [the second digit is illegible, and both pages contain markings], 49, 51, 56, 57, 65, 68, 74, 80, aufgeführt werden. 22 Juny 1800. Meyer.' With one exception, these pages all bear witness to the censor's cuts. Oddly, p 37 contains no markings, although pp 36 and 38 do – pp 36 and 38 may in fact have been meant. Further, some pages with markings that seem to have been made by the same hand as the censor's are not among those listed above, indicating that the list may be incomplete. This is particularly noticeable on pp 46 and 47 which belong in context to p 48 and whose markings I assume stem from the censor as well. The deletions are extensive, some a sentence or two, others entire paragraphs of dialogue. 'Meyer' was no doubt one of the censors under Regierungsrat Hägelin's supervision, although I have not discovered further details about him. In addition to the censor's marks, at least as many more on the same and other pages come presumably from the director's pen. It is also possible that some of the markings were added later than the initial ones in 1800, and it remains a mystery why these changes were recorded as undertaken in 1800 when the first documented performance of the play in Vienna was in 1815. Possibly this copy was used elsewhere. Despite these difficulties, the sum of the emendations to the text for performance is clear. Glued to the last page of the text is also a small folded sheet of paper which blocks the final passages of the play and adds a handwritten replacement for them.

It would not be worthwhile to reproduce all the emended portions of the text here, for the following extensive examples illustrate sufficiently the nature of the changes made. The deletions concentrate on four broad areas of thematic content: the nature and situation of the clergy; progressive thinking as opposed to traditional customs; comment on the nobility; and the role of actors and the theatre. Through the use of italics and symbols the passages reproduced below show which parts of Hagemann's original text were deleted or added by censor or director in the following manner:

[x censor's deletion x];
[^ censor's addition ^];
{x director's/prompter's deletion x};
{^ director's/prompter's addition ^};
<--> illegible letters;
[my addition].

Kühnow is a member of the small town or rural Protestant clergy. In his own character and actions one could hardly imagine a more positive representative, and while the virtues of such figures in dramas of the time were often so exaggerated as to lose all credibility, Hagemann's depiction of Kühnow is more rounded, and despite some excess of patience and goodwill the character comes across sympathetically. What we learn about other members of his profession is somewhat different. Peter, the waiter at the local inn, tells us how he knew Kühnow's predecessor in the parish: '... er liebte Bier und Wein, denn der Wein, sagt' er, erfreuet des Menschen Herz, und vom Biere bekommt man eine angenehme {x *geistliche* x} Baßstimme' (4).

The director's deletion here is but the first gentle sign in the text of a general taboo on clerical criticism. A second occurs shortly afterward as the farmer lad Hans completes the picture for Kühnow: 'Alle waren gegen Sie. {^ *Sogar* ^} Der Bierbrauer {^ *denn er* ^} hatte gehört, Sie seyn nur ein sehr mäßiger Trinker, {x *und schüttelte mit dem Kopf; denn er sagte: Ein Geistlicher muß ein Pfeiler seyn, und eine Bierschenke ist einem Pfeiler zu vergleichen.* x}' (17). The clergy's reputation for drinking is expanded to general slothfulness with this comment from Kühnow's spouse:

[x *Betrachte deine Amtsbrüder in der ganzen Gegend gegen dich; der Pastor Ambrosius ist in den Waden so dick, als du im Leibe: das ist Wohlstand.*
Kühnow. *Das ist nur Fett, Mama.* x] (24)

These sets of emendations are small compared with a major censor's deletion early in the play. Friderici arrives and finds his way into the absent pastor's house:

Friderici. (Nach einigen Gängen durchs Zimmer.)
Noch gerade wird mir die Zeit lang! – Sonderbar! – So was ist mir noch nie vorgekommen. Eine Pfarrwohnung, und alle Thüren offen! – [x *Eine Pfarrwohnung, und kein Kindergeschrei! – Eine Pastorwohnung, und kein Joli* [Hund] *bellt mich an! – Nicht einmal eine alte Haushälterin mit einer gelbgeräucherten Haube und einer schmutzigen Küchenschurze schnarrt mir entgegen: Zu wem will der Herr –* x] Daraus erkenn' ich das Haus meines Kühnow, still und offen, wie er selbst. Wie er als Student war, wird er als Pastor noch seyn. [x *Bei einem Manne von Grundsätzen bleiben Herz und Geist sich immer gleich, und kein Stand kann ihnen andere Form geben. Wehe der Gemeine, wo man den Seelsorger nur am schwarzen Kleide, und an der runden Perücke erkennt!* x] – (Pause.) Reinlich, aber dürftig! (Er öfnet eine Kammerthür.) Wie sieht es denn hier aus? – Ein Spinnrad! – Ein Korb voll Obst! – Etwas Flachs! – Der Schein deutet auf Armuth, und doch wollte der gute Mann Leuten, die noch ärmer sind, einen vergnügten Tag machen; [x *und böse Menschen verderben ihm die Freude, und bestehlen ihn. – Werde nur kein Menschenhasser, guter Kühnow, du sollst auch wieder gute Menschen kennen lernen.* x] Ich glaub', er kommt. Aber nicht allein. Ich bin doch neugierig, was er – wenn ich da einträte und lauschte? Geschwind Friderici, ohne dich lange zu besinnen: er ist da!
(In die Kammer ab.) (6-8)

What is left of the scene after the censor's purge is an idyllic picture of a poor and simple pastor, tidy, frugal, and generous to those in need. Gone are the satire on country clergymen with their excessive drinking, their large noisy families, and slovenly household help; gone the recollections of Kühnow's character strength which distinguishes him from his pompous colleagues; gone the reference to the thieves who victimize him and represent a dark side of their society. The dialogue has been neutralized to exclude any sense of the contentious or critical, be it directed toward the clergy or other elements of society; what is left is merely stereotypical pap.

Further changes show a general sensitivity to Christian and folk traditions. Kühnow explains to Hans: 'Ich esse selbst gern Gänsebraten, warum sollt' ich meiner Frau die kleine Freude nicht gönnen! {x *Auch hat es sein Gutes, wenn man auf alte unschädliche Gewohnheiten hält; nur müssen wir Neueren nicht vergessen, etwas Gutes hinzuzufügen, wenn wir können.* x}' (10). Is the deletion a sign of sensitivity to the cultivation of religious traditions – perhaps a reaction of Roman Catholic Vienna to a predominantly Protestant festival; or simply a conservative reaction to Kühnow's progressive suggestion that even when traditions are maintained, they should be subject to ongoing reappraisal and revision? Similar sentiments from Kühnow after the goose is stolen are also expurgated:

> ... Da haben wir wieder reinen Tisch! War so nahe an der Martinsgans, so ganz nahe, und ist doch wieder verschwunden, wie [x *das* x] [^ *nur* ^] Traumbild [x *eines Propheten* x]. – Marthe wird sich schwer zufrieden geben. [x *Die denkt, es sei Pflicht eines guten Christen, am grünen Donnerstag braunen Kohl, am Osterabend frische bunte Eier, am Weihnachtabend einen Karpfen, und am Martinstag einen Gänsebraten in frommer Einfalt des Herzens zu verzehren.* x] Indeß, wenn ich ihr sage, wie es gekommen ist, giebt sie sich zufrieden; ...
> (18f)

Even this brief exclamation by Friderici is struck: 'Lebt wohl, denkt an mich, trinkt auf meine Gesundheit, ich werde Acht geben, ob mir heut' Abend die Ohren klingen, wenn – {x *Ist das, so soll dieser alte Volksglaube Orakel seyn.* x} – Adieu! – Geseegnete Mahlzeit!' (60). It would seem that both censor and director were intent on removing all signs of folk belief, even in the slightest turn of phrase.

It is more easily understandable why the censor and director adjusted speeches with direct reference to contemporary social conditions. We learn that Kühnow was in the past a rebel bent on avenging injustice and changing society, and thus posed a threat to the social order as conservatives would like to maintain it. Reminiscing with his old friend, the admiring Kühnow recalls that fighting spirit when Friderici once returned after successfully championing the rights of a mistreated Jew:

> Ich sehe dich immer noch wie du zurückkamst! – Stolz, als hättest du eine Schlacht gewonnen, gallopirtest du über den Marktplatz, und {x *stimmest* x} {^ *riefst* ^} voll hoher Gefühle {x *ein: Landesvater! u. an.* x} {^ *Gott erhalte den guten Landesvater.* ^}
> *Friderici.* Ach, damals war ich ein dummer Junge! (32)

It is interesting to note that the reference to the Jew's victory remains, while the horseman's greeting is tempered from a single jubilant exclamation to an endorsement of good citizenship sanctioned by God; his final expression of embarrassment at his own youthful extravagance is left as appropriate comment on such excess.

The targets are more sensitive as Friderici comments on Marthe's pride with this parallel: '{x *Das ist viel unschuldiger, als wenn ein vornehmer Schurke seine Bubereien mit der Maske bürgerlicher Ehrlichkeit zudeckt. –* x}' (35); and expounds at length along the same lines when recounting the early events of his career which led him in the end to reject conventional society in favour of the asocial realm of the stage:

> Meldet' ich mich zu einem Amte. Nur einen einzigen Mitwerber hatt' ich, [x *weil es ein Jeder für eine ausgemachte Sach' ansah, daß meines angesehenen Vaters Sohn die Stelle erhalten solle, müße und würde. – Mein Mitwerber war* x] eines Handwerkers Sohn, ein hoffnungsvoller junger Mensch. Aber Kenner hatten schon seinen Repuls geweissaget, als sie ihn mit wollenen Strümpfen und einem abgetragenen Rock zum Examen wandern sahn. Er bestand vortreflich. [x *Ich wüßt' auch nicht ein einziges Fach, in welchem er mich nicht überflügelt hätte. Auch war er ein halbes Dutzend Jahre älter als ich.* x] Aber sein Vater war Schneider. {x *Der meine Kammerrath, drum wurd' er abgewiesen, und ich sollte das Amt erhalten.* x} Das kannst du dir wohl vorstellen, daß ich den Herren auf Studentenmanier den Text las, und das Amt verbat. Vier Monate drauf starb mein Vater, {x *und von allen meinen übrigen Verwandten war Niemand wichtig genug, mein Talisman zu seyn. Ich war diese Zeit für vier Jahre fleißig gewesen, um mich von dem Schneidersohn nicht wieder überwinden zu lassen, und* x} {^ *ich* ^}meldete mich abermals zu einem Amte. Jetzt hatt' ich mehrere Nebenbuhler, aber elende Stümper, die ich ohne Pralerei weit übersah, allein just der dümmste erhielt das Amt, weil seine Schwester [x *Maitresse des* x] [^ *beim* ^] Präsidenten war. Ich trieb mich noch eine Zeitlang unter Halbmenschen umher, {x *und fand, daß unter ihnen mein System nicht realisirt werden konnte. Entweder ich mußte mich dem Strudel*

überlassen: oder gerade auf Klippen steuern. – Was am meisten mich ärgerte, ich konnte keinem recht derb die Wahrheit sagen, und du weißt, wie gern ich immer meinem Herzen Luft gemacht habe. x} {x *Drum* x} {^ *Dann* ^} ergriff ich meinen jetzigen Stand, und befinde mich wohl dabei. – [x *Hier kann ich selbst Serenissimo Dinge sagen, die ihm so leicht kein Hofschranz sagt!* x] Hier hab' ich freies Feld, Misbräuche anzutasten und Narren zu verspotten, sie mögen in {x *schwarzen oder bunten Livreen gehn.* x} {^ *einem Kleid erscheinen, in welchen sie wollen.* ^} (46-8)

What is left of this tirade after major surgery is an uncritical account of an everyday job competition. Friderici was simply a candidate whose one opponent, because of his appearance, bearing, and family background, was unsuitable for the job. Hence it was offered to Friderici. Here his character first showed true colours as he rejected the advantage. Soon after, without the benefit of influential backers, the roles were reversed and he was the loser, but because of the censor's change from 'weil seine Schwester Maitresse des Präsidenten war' to 'weil seine Schwester beim Präsidenten war,' the thoroughly scurrilous nature of the process is obfuscated. The same can be said of the previous deletions concerning Friderici's own father and the outstanding superiority of his first opponent, both of which blunt a sharply pointed attack on the practice of patronage. The deletions in the second half of this speech serve to eradicate the credo of a potential anarchist who rejects the hierarchy and seeks to put into practice 'mein System'; a man who wishes only the freedom to say what he thinks, to speak the truth – even to 'Serenissimo' (the ruler) – to expose injustice and to ridicule ecclesiastical or aristocratic fools ('in schwarzen oder bunten Livreen'). To allow these statements public voice was to admit their validity, too much indeed for the censor to accept. In the end, from our perspective, the emendations to the speech make it an even more damning comment on the social restrictions of the time than before. Any negative remark about the wealthy or socially elite and any admission of social corruption in the prevailing system was clearly taboo.

Some of the most comprehensive and at the same time most fascinating deletions have to do with the subject of actors and the theatre. When Friderici finally explains to the pastor and his wife that he is 'Prinzipal einer eigenen Bande,' this is how they react:

Marthe. (für sich.) Hauptmann einer Zigeunerbande, o ich verstehe!
Kühnow. Vergieb mir mein bedenkliches Kopfschütteln. Zwar der Himmel führt die Seinen wunderlich. – Befindest du dich denn wohl dabei?
Friderici. Ich habe die Guillotine aufs Theater gebracht, und viel Geld damit verdient.

Marthe. (für sich.) Ach du Mordbrenner! – Das ist ja die französische Kopfmaschine!
Friderici. Wenn heut ein Lessingisches Stück meine Kasse leer läßt, geb ich morgen ein {x *altdeutsches Trauer* x} {^ *Lust* ^} spiel {x, *wo die Helden wie besoffene Grenadiere sich schimpfen, schlagen und prügeln, wo bald einer aus dem Fenster hundert Klafter hoch springt, ohne den Hals zu brechen, bald eine Dame in einem Gottesgericht ein glühendes Eisen in die Hand nimmt, ohne sich weh zu thun.*
Marthe. *(bei Seite.)* Ich sags ja: ein Zigeuner, ein Hexenmeister!
Friderici. *Der große Haufe sieht auch wohl in den Raritätenkasten.* x} – Oder, ich lasse Burg' und Schlösser zerstören, Städte verbrennen, Weiber einmauern, {x *Männer spießen, köpfen, rädern.* x} Ich lasse würgen und massakriren, denn solche {x *Henkers* x} arbeit wird {^ *zum Publikum* ^} treflich bezahlt, {x *besonders, wenn Hanswurst mit einer modernen Maske seine Zweideutigkeiten dabei anbringt.* x}
Marthe. Papa, Papa! (40f)

Their initial shock at hearing of his profession, intensified as he recounts the gory details, encapsulates the attitude of many even as late as 1798 toward the itinerant actor and his craft. Friderici's account hardly serves to dispel this notion; he seems to relish the thought of blood and thunder, death and destruction – the old Haupt- und Staatsaktion – through which his cashbox is filled. Still in 1798, when so many permanent theatres had been established and so much attention given to so-called theatre reform, Friderici's account makes it clear that the old tastes remained strong. The deletions here are from the director's pen – perhaps a matter of honour, for his was surely a company with higher principles than this! The deletions curb the excesses of Friderici's description, extricate the pretentious Trauerspiel from this bawdy context, and notably eliminate reference to Hanswurst at the end. This last deletion is particularly revealing. Even Friderici does not put the old Hanswurst on stage in his traditional attire, but conceals him in 'einer modernen Maske' to inject 'seine Zweideutigkeiten' into the action. Clearly the traditional comic figure lived on in disguise with the age-old function to comment on and add ironic depth to the main action. We recall the several comic Nachspiele discussed earlier which had no traditional comic figure by name, but did by nature.

Just as the comic figure always served to comment critically on central events and characters, so is this function one of Friderici's two chief purposes in theatrical productions, and while he does paint a garish picture of his company, it also clearly had a more serious side:

*{x Das war nur halber Scherz; so arg mach ich es nicht, und wenn ich es thue, so
thu' ichs aus Satyre, wenn mir Abends vorher einige Hofrathsweiber bei Babo's
Bürgerglück die Nase gerümpft haben.*

...

*Kurz; ich glaube ohn' all dies Wesen meinen Zweck eher erreichen zu können,
nehmlich zu belustigen, und zugleich zu belehren. Freilich giebt es Bälge, die nur
die Peitsche fühlen, und jedem feineren Gefühle zu stumpf und zu hart sind, da ist
alles umsonst, Satyre und Moral, da arbeiten Schauspieler vergebens, und – sans
comparaison Pastoren. – x}* (48-50)

Friderici's objectives are the same as those emphasized by Johann Elias
Schlegel a half-century before and had been part of theatre since
Aristotle's time. Obviously Friderici is prepared to spend a good deal
of time on pure entertainment, a practical necessity for financial viabil-
ity, but his more serious intention beyond that is to educate. In this regard, his final comparison between the traditional arch-enemies of
stage and pulpit comes as a revelation, though one that obviously un-
earths a taboo for Kühnow who at that point interjects '*{x Laß uns ab-
brechen. x}*.' But Friderici is not to be denied now:

*[x {x Noch nicht: x} {^ höre ^} ich will dir {x erst x} einen Vorschlag thun,
{^ <--> ^} daß du in die Residenz versetzt wirst, ich werde dort vermuthlich das
Theater übernehmen. Dann sag mir immer den Inhalt deiner jedesmaligen Predigt
vorher. Sprichst du Sonntags von den Pflichten der Kinder gegen ihre Eltern, so
geb ich den Montag drauf den Edelknaben oder den dankbaren Sohn, und zum
Gegenstück am folgenden Abend Shakespears Lear. – O, das soll herrliche Wirkung
machen! Menschen, denen du die schrecklichen Folgen des Spiels vorhieltest, sollen
aus der Kirch' in die Komödie gehen, wo ich Verbrechen aus Ehrsucht geben werde.
– Wohl gemerkt: du mußt sie mir selbst hinschicken. – Bei dir werden sie glauben;
bei mir sehen und fühlen – und – vielleicht – nun erst glauben, nachdem sie
gesehen haben. – O, Pastor, die Verbrüderung unserer Stände scheint mir schön,
und wäre so leicht zu bewürken!*
Kühnow. *Ich erwiedere: Wenn Theater und Kanzel Brüder sind, so sind sie Stief-
brüder, und die sind selten eins, zanken sich gern.*
Friderici. *Die Regierung muß nur keine Stiefmutter gegen einen der beiden Stände
seyn, nicht dem einen Alles, dem andern Nichts geben. Sind nicht meistentheils die
Eltern Schuld, wenn Geschwister nicht friedlich mit einander leben? Und unsere
Censoren – diese müssen so gut reformirt werden, als der Stand selbst. Kein Censor
müßte ein Stück verbieten, wo den Grossen gelegentlich eine gute Dosis Wahrheit
gegeben wird – denn nur das Theater ist die einzige ächte Hofapotheke der Fürsten
– und o, gesegnetes Theater, wo der Fürst selbst Dinge hören kann, die keiner*

seiner ganz unterthänigsten Schmeichler das Herz hat, seiner Durchlaucht in aller-
tiefster Ehrfurcht sterbend vorzutragen! – x] (50f)

The emperor was certainly not ready for this medicine! But what an innovative and potent duo, church and stage hand in hand, both with the same purpose of moral and social improvement! For Friderici, the greatest impediment to this felicitous union is the state, which in the end must bear full responsibility for the rift between the two. And in his business it is the censor who is the arm of authority that stifles potential. One can imagine the expression on Censor Meyer's face as he struck out this speech with three bold black strokes! The time was not ripe for Friderici's ideas, the church was not ready to enter into this illegitimate union, the court certainly not prepared to stand up and be criticized in public. Still, Friderici's statement stood as a vision of the future for readers of the text at least, and as an ultimately optimistic expression of the power of his profession. The final lines of the play were rewritten by Censor Meyer, no doubt still smoking from the previous exchange, so that

[x Seegne jeden braven Mann,
Man treff' ihn nun im Schauspielhaus, man
treff ihn in der Kirche an. x]
becomes
[^ Man treff' ihn nun im Schauspielhaus, man
treffe ihn wo immer an. ^] (80)

With that, Friderici's explosive idea is firmly stamped out.

The text and performance history of *Die Martinsgänse*, along with the wealth of socio-critical themes central to the many Nachspiele discussed earlier in this chapter, recall two of Yüksel Pazarkaya's statements in his *Einakter* book: 'Es gibt im 18. Jahrhundert kaum Einakter politischen Inhaltes' (115) and 'Die Zeit- und Gesellschaftskritik kommt … im Einakter nur am Rande vor, nicht als Stoff oder gar zur Handlung ausgebaut' (120). It is doubtful that these views can still be supported.

This chapter demonstrates one fact above all: what we might read today in published texts or even manuscripts tells us only part of the story of dramatic works two centuries ago. Previous chapters showed that the actor's own freedom to interpret a role, be it through extemporization, external direction, or individual technique, in many cases carried that role far beyond what stood in the script. Now the act of censorship must be added as a second major influence on text. Clearly, for these two reasons, the modern reader must always be vigilant against interpretation and understanding based solely on the written word. In theatre, not just for the eighteenth century but for all ages, what could be captured in text tells just part of the story. Only through an understanding of the performance of that text, and the conditions under which each performance took place, can we gain a reasonably accurate picture of any dramatic work. In this study I have attempted to take account of performance when discussing individual Nachspiele, but one could do far more in this regard. Appendix 2 provides the reader with specific information on performance dates and places of many of the Nachspiele discussed, and many others just mentioned and listed. Thus the groundwork has been laid for a more detailed investigation of them by anyone so inclined.

CONCLUSION

In light of this investigation it is time to reassess the lexical definitions of the Nachspiel summarized at the outset. The German Nachspiel was a principally comic form only in the first two-thirds of the century, thereafter changing its general tone to become a predominantly serious dramatic work. It was most frequently performed in conjunction with a preceding longer play, but often with more than one shorter piece. There is little evidence to show that the Nachspiel was linked regularly with tragedy; in fact, it appeared most often alongside comedy, bearing little or no relationship to the other work(s) on the program, except in the early decades when the central comic figure often appeared in both the principal work and the Nachspiel. A marked division must be made between the undocumented, non-literary, extemporized Nachspiel and the literary one for which many texts have survived. Of the former, repertoires tell us that there were a great number performed and that they were overwhelmingly comical; of the latter we know that while the comic Nachspiel continued to be well represented, the serious, socio-critically oriented Nachspiel became dominant toward the end of the century, though these works often show evidence of comic personages and devices as well. Despite considerable influence from France and Italy, most of these eighteenth-century Nachspiele were distinctively German in their content and thematics. Translations and adaptations represent only about a quarter of the total volume of extant works, a figure which was on the decline in the later decades. With regard to its length, it is too simple to assume that the Nachspiel was typically a one-act form; this is true with very few exceptions after

1770, but is not a valid assumption before that time when more than a quarter of the literary Nachspiele examined had a multi-act structure. With regard to its nature, throughout the century the Nachspiel made frequent use of artistic forms other than the strictly dramatic, for music, song, and dance played important roles.

Most important for our understanding is the division between the traditional comic and serious Nachspiel. Until 1770, 41 per cent of literary Nachspiele showed strong characteristics of traditional comedy, thereafter only 21 per cent. Conversely, before 1770, 46 per cent contained strong serious thematics, compared with 70 per cent thereafter. These percentages show that the Nachspiel, despite its traditional comic and extemporized nature, always contained strong elements of social thematics and criticism, but that the comic elements were diluted in later decades in favour of intensified serious themes, including questions about moral issues and the social, economic, and cultural structures of the age. As the extemporized comic Nachspiel satisfied one need of its public, the serious Nachspiel addressed another as it developed after mid-century. This was the need to explore publicly the problems arising from rapid social change caused principally by the inversion of authority, power, and wealth from aristocracy to bourgeoisie. Theatres became permanent social fixtures with deliberate social functions, and the Nachspiel a convenient vehicle to address the problems in a form recognized for decades as one that would bring pleasure to its audience. The Nachspiel's traditional popularity as genre was utilized as a vehicle for a new trend in social analysis and awareness.

The Nachspiel as genre obviously changed in structure, content, and function throughout the century. For contemporaries, the word also changed in meaning, or carried various connotations. In the first two-thirds of the century, the term 'Nachspiel' was understood largely within its comic sense, which continued later on but became mixed with vague and conflicting notions of the Nachspiel as any short work to complete the dramatic program, but most commonly one that was light in tone. This vague understanding continued into the nineteenth century and even to our own time, as can be seen in the loose classification of works as Nachspiele by such as Goedeke, when some of the texts themselves never bore this designation.

The Nachspiel in its pure form was cultivated by the itinerant troupes before 1770. Their repertoires show that it was an indispensable part of the performance, highlighted by the *lustige Person*, who in turn derived his strength from his powers of improvisation, both in the spoken word and in movement. This Nachspiel is thus often closely linked with extensive gestural and mime play, with acrobatics and with rudimentary ballet. When the *lustige Person* and the Nachspiel in general encountered opposition from theorists and officials in mid-century, some troupes clearly tried to modify the Nachspiel into other forms such as the ballet, and to disguise the *lustige Person* behind various names and costumes. My analyses of individual Nachspiele to the end of the century show that key comic personages, elements, and devices from the early Nachspiel were carried forward in a somewhat sanitized or refined form. Most important among these is the tradition of extemporization which contributed greatly to the fundamental skills of actors in the latter part of the century and to developments in acting technique.

In the end, our understanding of the importance of the Nachspiel for German-speaking theatre in the eighteenth century must go far beyond the common belief that it was just a trifle, a throw-away piece of farce to entertain the lowest representatives of society. In many ways the Nachspiel serves as a microcosm of German drama in the eighteenth century. In miniature it depicts the passing of influence from itinerant troupes to permanent theatres; from extemporized performance to controlled acting; from improvised scenario to text-based drama; from unrestricted expression to censorship and control.

APPENDIX 1.
OVERVIEW OF PRIMARY WORKS

The following chart contains all 136 titles listed in the Nachspiel Bibliography at the end of this volume. Classification categories reflect significant common elements among the works.

CLARIFICATION OF CATEGORIES AND ABBREVIATIONS

Author: This category includes single as well as joint authors, translators, and adapters of works. In the case of a translation or adaptation, the author of the original work appears first, followed by a slash (/), followed by the name of the German translator or adapter. Surmised authors or authors identified through sources other than the work's title-page appear in square parentheses. A hyphen mark (-) indicates that the author is unknown.

YP = year published: The year of publication (in the case of manuscripts noted 'Ms', date of authorship) according to the title-page of the copy examined for this study. Surmised dates appear in square parentheses. Hyphen marks (-) indicate that the year of publication is unknown.

FR = French or other foreign: As far as their origins can be determined, Nachspiele translated or adapted from the French as indicated either on the title-page or through other means. Also included is the handful of works based on other foreign originals (Dutch, English, Spanish).

2-3 = Nachspiele in two or three acts: As indicated on the title-page or deduced from the work's internal divisions. (All others are one act.)

CP = connected to a preceding work: Nachspiele published with and bound to another play.

MSD = music, songs, dance: Nachspiele containing these elements.

TC = traditional comedy: Nachspiele containing a strong component of traditional comic elements such as identifiable comic figures (Hanswurst, Harlekin, Bernardon, Crispin, etc) or comic devices, particularly those requiring extensive gestural or mime play, and comic improvisation. Works actually containing one of the traditional comic figures by name are designated by the figure O instead of X.

SC = social criticism: Nachspiele containing serious themes, social commentary, or contemporary social criticism. Nachspiele specifically called 'tragisch' on their title-pages are designated by the figure O instead of X.

If a work does not exhibit a strong component of any of the elements above, then its category fields are blank. Titles of the 22 works unavailable for inspection are preceded by an asterisk (*).

TITLE	AUTHOR	YP	FR	2-3	CP	MSD	TC	SC
Abschied, Der	A Kotzebue	1804						X
Adel des Herzens	J C Bock	1770						X
alte Bekantschaft, Die	-	1773						X
Am Ende eine Betschwester	-	1783						X
arme Frau, Die	Marsollier/-	[1797]	X					X
Aussteuer, Die	J Févée/ C F Schwan	1778	X				X	
Austern, Die	T J Quistorp	1748					X	
Bauern vom Stande, Die	J A Romagnesi, P F Biancolleli/	1756	X				X	X
Bauren, Die (Ms)	-	-					X	X
beiden Billets, Die	J P C Florian/ C L Heyne	1783	X				X	
belebte Statua, Die	-	1769						
*beschaemte Geizhals, Der	Wagenseil	1787						
bestrafte Hochmuth, Der	-	1751					X	
betrogene Alte, Der	-/-	1747	X	X	X		O	
*betrogene Betrüger, Der	B Mottoni/-	1797						
betrogene Kadi, Der	P R LeMonnier/ [J André]	1749	X					
beyden Portraits, Die	J H F Jünger	1784						
bezauberte Gürtel, Der	J B Rousseau/-	1748	X			X		

TITLE	AUTHOR	YP	FR	2-3	CP	MSD	TC	SC
Bildsäule, Die	L C Carmontelle/							
	C L Heyne	1782	X			X		
Blinde aus Leicht-								
glaübigkeit, Der	-/-	1780	X				X	X
Blind und lahm	L Robert	[1800]						X
Brandschatzung, Die	J H Decker	1806						X
Calliste	E T J Brückner	1772						
Cangé	A. Goufflé/-	1795	X					X
Caroline	-	1777						X
Christen in Abyssinien, Die	J M R Lenz	[1780]				X	X	X
Chymici, Die	-	1771		X				X
Comödie ohne Tittel	-	1759			X		O	X
Drei. Dreizehn.								
Dreiunddreißig	C L Seipp	1789						X
Drei Stockwerk hoch	-/K G T Winkler	-		X				
Dreßdner Frauen Schlend-								
rian, Der	J U König	1742					X	
*edelmütige Bauer, Der	-	1771						
eheliche Versöhunug, Die	-/-	1795	X					X
Enterbte, Der	[E T J Brückner]	1772					X	
entführte Dose, Die	J E Schlegel	[1747]						
*erfüllten Wünsche, Die	A G Hartmann	1777						
Er ist es selbst	K G T Winkler	1808				X		X
erste Dank, Der	J K Wezel	1784						X
Eurydice	H. Fielding/-	1759	X		X	X		X
falsche verdacht, Der (Ms)	[J Kurz or							
	F L Weiskern]	[1745]					O	
Fanny	-	1772				X		O
faule Bauer, Der	A G Uhlich	1745						
Finanzbediente, Der	G F P Saintfoix/-	1789	X				X	
*Freiheitsbaum, Der	N. Müller	1794						
Friederike von Rosenhayn	-	1783						X
frohe Frau, Die	J G Göntgen	1775			X			X
*frohe Tag, Der	J W Heuberger	1798						
fromme Betrug, Der	C A Seidel	1789						X
fromme Stutzer, Der	-	1757						X
Gärtnerkönig, Der	J E Schlegel	[1747]						
*Geburtstag, Der	A G Hartmann	1776						
*Geisterbanner, Der	-	-						

TITLE	AUTHOR	YP	FR	2-3	CP	MSD	TC	SC
geraubte Dose, Die	H C H Trautzschen	1772					X	
Gespenster, Die	J C Ast	1757		X			X	X
glückliche Entdeckung, Die	K G T Winkler	1806						X
Glycine	-	1756						O
Harlequin, Der ungedultig...	-	1743			X	X	O	X
Haß und Neid	-/J F Uffenbach	1733	X				X	X
Heirathslustigen, Die	E Bürger	1801				X		
Herr Habicht	K G T Winkler	1809	X					
Herrschaft der Weiber	S I Mathesius	1768					X	
Herr Witzling	L A V Gottsched	1745					X	
Heyrath aus Liebe	[S H Ewald]	1781		X		X		X
Heyrath der Thorheit, Die	J F Regnard	1757	X		X	X	O	
hinkende Bothe, Der	[J H G Justi]	1758			X			X
Hirten der Alpen, Die	Marmontel/ [D C Seybold]	1777	X					
Hochzeittag	-t-	1789		X				X
*Hypochondrist, Der	J C Brandes	1767						
Instinkt, Der	C du Fresny/ J F Jünger	1785	X					
Isaac und Rebecca	Jodocus	1722			X	X	O	
Jacobiner, Die	-/-	1794	X					X
Jedem sein Lohn	[H L Wagner]	1779						X
Juliane Dürrbach	Sprickmann/-	1783				X		X
jungen Rekruten, Die	J Lederer	1781		X	X	X		
Kaiser Joseph ...	-	1799		X				X
kindische Vater, Der	F Jann	1788					X	
Kirschen, Die	[J B Hirschfeld]	[1783]				X	X	
Klatschen, Die	-	1757			X			
Klätscher, Der	Voltaire/-	1746	X					
kleinste Lüge, Die	A Kotzebue/-	1800		X				X
kranke Frau, Die	C F Gellert	1747						
Krispin ...	-	[1770]					O	
Landprediger, Der	F S L Eckhardt	1778						X
*Liebe im Sommer	-	1790						
Liebe und Vaterland	L F Bilderbeck	1789						X
Liebhabertheater ...	A Kotzebue	1790				X		X
Lotto, Das	J L Huber	1779						X
lustige Elendt, das (Ms)	[F A Nuth]	[1741]				X	O	X
Magnetismus, Der	W A Iffland	1787					X	X

TITLE	AUTHOR	YP	FR	2-3	CP	MSD	TC	SC
Martinsgänse, Die	G Hagemann	[1798]						X
Maskerade, Die	P N Destouches/							
	F W Gotter	1773	X					
Matrone v Ephesus	-	1764				X		X
Melonen, Die	-/S H Linguet	1771	X			X	X	
Minna	-	1799				X		
Mis Jenny	[J F Behr]	1771						O
*Mißtrauen u Neckerei	H G Schmieder	1804						
Mündel, Das	B C Fagan/-	1746	X					
Nachspiel zur berühmten								
Komödie	C H Ayrenhoff	1789			X		O	
*Naturaliensammler	C F Weiße	1771						
Neueste Verheyrathung, Die								
	-	1759			X		O	X
Neujahrstag, Der	[F K A Trützschler]	1779					X	
Nur ein Stündchen ...	Loraux/							
	K G T Winkler	1805	X					
Officier, Der	J B Bergobzoom	1769					X	
*ohnmächtige Wolke, Die	H W Seyfried	1783						
*Perücke, Die	L Huber	1791						
Perücken, 2.Th.	L Huber	1791				X	X	X
*Phlegmatikus, Der	-	1799						
Portrait, Das	Beauchamps/-	[1778]	X				X	X
Prahler, Der	-	1761				X	X	
*redliche Betrüger, Der	-	1797						
Rekreation, Die	-	1766				X		
*Rendez-vous, Das	K H Röpe	1789						
Rosalia	Schinck	1777				X		
*Schatzgräber, Der	-	1799						
Schimpf und Ernst	-	[1760]					X	X
Schleppen, Die	-	1797						X
sehende Blinde, Der	Le Grand/-	1752	X					X
sich selbst Betrügende, Der	J B Rousseau/							
	D G H Behr	1754	X					
Sohn, Der	C F Sander	1783						X
Trentleva, Das	[E Heydevogel]	1774					X	
Tugend auf der Schau-								
bühne	J Möser	1798					O	
Unerwartete im Heyrathen	J H Steffens	1765						X

TITLE	AUTHOR	YP	FR	2-3	CP	MSD	TC	SC
*Vater in Cadix, Der	-/K H Röpe	1788						
verachtete Eitelkeit der Welt, Die	-	1702				X		X
Verbesserungen und Zusätze	-	1744			X			X
Verlobung bei Kaiserslautern	-	1795						X
vermeynten Nebenbuhler, Die	-	1754						
Versuch, Der	J H Decker	1806						X
Verwechselung, Die	K G T Winkler	1808					X	
*Vetterschaft, Die	F W Gotter	1784						
*Virtuoso und Irena	-	-						
Was ist's?	J F H Müller	1786					X	X
Weihnachtabend, Der	A K Walder	1803	X					X
Wildheit u Großmuth	J K Wezel	1784	X					X
*Witwe, Die	J B Bergobzoom	1772						
Wolken, Die	-	1782				X		

APPENDIX 2.
DOCUMENTED
PERFORMANCES
OF EXTANT NACHSPIELE

The Nachspiele from the Bibliography for which performances could be documented are listed below. Each entry includes the Nachspiel title, followed by a list of the troupe principals who performed it, then the cities in which it was performed, each in alphabetical order. Beneath each principal or city listed is given the total number of performances in brackets (round if known, square if surmised), the name of the stage on which the performance took place, if known, and finally an abbreviated reference to my source of information for that particular entry. Here is an example:

Portrait, Das	Title of Nachspiel
Ackermann	Performed by the Ackermann troupe
5 (1766-70) EI	Performed by Ackermann five times between 1766 and 1770. My source of information is EI = Eichhorn.
Koch	Performed by the Koch troupe
1 (1758) PR	Performed by Koch once in 1758. My source of information is PR = Prick.
Schönemann	Performed by the Schönemann troupe
8 (1751-6) DE	Performed by Schönemann eight times between 1751 and 1756. My source of information is DE = Devrient.
Gotha	Performed in Gotha
3 (1777 Hofth) HO, S/H	Performed there three times in 1777 at the Hoftheater. My sources of information are HO = Hodermann and S/H = Schäffer/Hartman.

Vienna   Performed in Vienna
11 (1779-82 Burgth) AL   Performed there eleven times between 1779 and
                                                1782 at the Burgtheater. My source of information
                                                is AL = Alth.
10 (1779-82 Burgth) HW   Performed there ten times between 1779 and 1782 at
                                                the Burgtheater. My source of information is HW
                                                = Hadamowsky, *Die Wiener Hoftheater*.
                                                Hadamowsky and Alth differ on this point.

The abbreviated references to my sources of information refer to the authors
and studies listed below. Full details on each are available in the list of secondary works at the end of the volume.

AL	Alth	LE	Legband
BA	Bauer	LI	Liss
BL	Blümml	LO	Lochter
BR	Brenner, *Possenspiele*	MA	Martersteig
BU	Burkhardt	ME	Mentzel
DE	Devrient	PR	Prick
EI	Eichhorn	RA	Raab
FZ	Frankfurt, Theater-zettelsammlung der Universitätsbibliothek	RE	Reden-Esbeck
		SC	Schlösser
		SCH	Schindler
		S/H	Schäffer/Hartmann
HL	Hadamowsky, *Leopoldstadt*	SI	Sichardt
HO	Hodermann	SOF	Sammlung Oskar Fambach
HW	Hadamowsky, *Die Wiener Hoftheater*	TP	Title-page of Nachspiel
		WA	Walter
JES	Johann Elias Schlegel, *Werke*	ZE	Zechmeister

**Adel des Herzens/ Die aus-
geschlagene Erbschaft**
Ackermann
   1 (1770) EI
Hamburg
   ? [1770] TP
Munich
   2 (1776 Nat Schaub) LE
Vienna
   1 (1771 Burgth) HW
   1 (1776 Kärntnertor) HW
   2 (1771-6 Kärntnertor) ZE

   1 (1776 Burgth) AL

alte Bekantschaft, Die
Munich
   ? [1773] TP

arme Frau, Die
Mannheim
   1 (1797) TP, WA

beiden Billets, Die
Großmann
   7 (1783-5) SOF

Altona
    3 (1797-9) SOF
Berlin
    20 (1784-5) SOF
    36 (1787-94) SOF
    4 (1831 Königstadt Th) SOF
    82 (1786-1828) S/H
Braunschweig
    1 (1788) SOF
Darmstadt
    10 (1813-29 Hofth) SOF
Dresden
    9 (1785-1831 Kön Th) SOF
Frankfurt
    22 (1785-1800 Fra/Mainz Nat
       Th) FZ
Hamburg
    9 (1786-90) SOF
Hannover
    1 (1787) SOF
Leipzig
    12 (1785-1824 Stadtth) SOF
Königsberg
    1 (1786) SOF
Mannheim
    32 (1783-1802 Nat Th) WA
    52 (1783-1821 Nat Th) SOF
Munich
    11 (1787-98 Nat Schaub) LE
Ofen
    1 (1793) SOF
Riga
    4 (1785) SOF
Schleswig
    1 (1793 Hofth) SOF
Stuttgart
    1 (1787 Hofth) SOF
Vienna
    16 (1788-1804 Burgth) HW
    1 (1790 Landstr) BL
    11 (1798-1804 Kärntnertor) HW

    4 (1807 Th a d Wien) SOF
    9 (1803-38 Leopoldst) HL
    43 (1788-1842 Burgth) AL
Weimar
    15 (1791-1815) SOF
    11 (1791-1805 Hofth) BU
    3 (1791-1803 Lauchstadt) BU
    1 (1803 Rudolstadt) BU
Würzburg
    20 (1804-31) SOF

**bestrafte Hochmuth, Der / Johann
    Scherenschleifer**
Ackermann
    27 (1754-70) EI
Schönemann
    1 (1751) DE
Berlin
    1 (1788) S/H
Munich
    1 (1783 Nat Schaub) LE
Vienna
    3 (1783 Leopoldst) HL

betrogene Betrüger, Der
Schönemann
    1 (1747) DE
Vienna
    1 (1763 Kärntnertor) ZE

betrogene Kadi, Der
Ackermann
    1 (1764) EI
Schönemann
    3 (1750-1) DE

beyden Portraits, Die
Vienna
    1 (1784 Burgth) AL, HW

Bildsäule, Die
Munich
    6 (1775-87) LE

Blinde aus Leichtgläubigkeit, Der
Vienna
    3 (1780 Burgth) HW
    4 (1780 Burgth) AL

Dreßdner Frauen Schlendrian,
   Der
Neuber
    2 (1735) RE
Schönemann
    1 (1747) DE
Frankfurt
    1 (1741 Bockenheimer-Gass) ME

entführte Dose, Die
Leipzig
    ? (?) JES

Eurydice
London
    ? [1759] TP

falsche verdacht, Der
Nürnberg
    1 (1766) RA
Vienna
    ? (1753-4 Kärntnertor) SCH
    1 [1765] (Kärntnertor) BA
    1 (1767 Brünn) BL
    1 (1769 Leopoldstadt) BL

faule Bauer, Der
Ackermann
    7 (1754-64) EI
Schönemann
    5 (1747-51) DE

Friederike von Rosenhayn
Vienna
    1 (1783 Burgth) AL, HW

fromme Betrug, Der
Munich
    7 (1789-96 Nat Schaub) LE

Instinkt, Der
Berlin
    3 (1786-7) S/H
Mannheim
    1 (1787 Nat Th) WA
Munich
    1 (1787 Nat Schaub) LE
    1 (1795 Faberbräu) LE
Vienna
    5 (1785-6 Leopoldst) HL
    2 (1785 Burgth) AL, HW

jungen Rekruten, Die
Ulm
    3 (1781) TP

Kirschen, Die
Vienna
    15 (1806-11 Leopoldst) HL

Klätscher, Der
Neuber
    1 (1735) RE

kranke Frau, Die
Ackermann
    ? (?) EI
Koch
    1 (1752) PR
Schönemann
    8 (1750-1) DE
Schuch
    5 (1755-8) LI
Hamburg
    3 (1767-8 Nat Th) SC

Liebe und Vaterland
Dürkheim
    1 (1788) (Gesellschaftsbühne)
      TP

Liebhabertheater vor dem Parlament, Das
Reval
    1 [1790] (Liebhaberth) TP

lustige Elendt, Das
Frankfurt
    2 (1741) ME
    1 (1742) FZ, ME
    1 (1755) ME
Vienna
    2 (1767-9) BL

Magnetismus, Der
Altona
    2 (1796-7) SOF
Berlin
    3 (1798) SOF
    2 (1786-98) S/H
Darmstadt
    1 (1813) SOF
Frankfurt
    7 (1787-90) FZ
Mainz
    3 (1788-92) SOF
Mannheim
    24 (1787-1802 Nat Th) WA
    25 (1787-1818 Nat Th) SOF
Munich
    3 (1789-97 Nat Schaub) LE
Vienna
    2 (1792 Landstr) BL
    2 (1814 Burgth) AL
Weimar
    2 (1788) SOF
Würzburg
    3 (1805-11) SOF

Martinsgänse, Die
Altona
    1 (1798) SOF
Berlin
    6 (1827-8 Königst Th) SOF

Breslau
    7 (1800 Königl Th) SOF
Darmstadt
    1 (1812 Hofth) SOF
Dresden
    1 (1799) SOF
    3 (1817-22 Königl Th) SOF
Hannover
    1 (1800) SOF
Lübeck
    1 (1799) SOF
Mannheim
    2 (1802-3 Nat Th) WA
    9 (1802-16 Nat Th) SOF
Vienna
    3 (1815 Th a d Wien) SOF
Weimar
    7 (1800-6 Hofth) SOF
    1 (1800 Hofth) BU
Würzburg
    5 (1804-28) SOF

Maskerade, Die / Die dreyfache Heirath
Ackermann
    6 (1761-5) EI
Hamburg
    1 (1767 Nat Th) SC
Munich
    3 (1780 Nat Schaub) LE
Vienna
    2 (1776 Burgth) AL,HW

Matrone von Ephesus, Die
Schuch
    5 (1750-65) LI

Mündel, Das
Ackermann
    2 (1760) EI
Koch
    1 (1754) PR

Neuber
   12 (1735) RE
Schönemann
   16 (1751-4) DE
Vienna
   1 (1769 Kärntnertor) HW
   2 (1783 Burgth) AL,HW

Naturaliensammler, Der
Ackermann
   ? (?) EI

Nur ein Stündchen war er fort
Place unknown
   2 (1806-7) SOF
Vienna
   3 (1806-7 Burgth) HW
   2 (1806 Kärntnertor) HW
   5 (1806-7 Burgth) AL

Perücke, Die
Berlin
   1 (1791) S/H

Perücke, Die, 2. Theil
Vienna
   1 (1786-7) BL

Portrait, Das
Ackermann
   5 (1766-70) EI
Koch
   1 (1758) PR
Schönemann
   8 (1751-6) DE
Gotha
   3 (1777 Hofth) HO, SC
Vienna
   11 (1779-82 Burgth) AL
   10 (1779-82 Burgth) HW

Rekreation, Die
Vienna
   ? [1766] TP

Rosalia
Place unknown
   4 (?) SOF

Schatzgräber, Der
Place unknown
   2 (?) SOF
Vienna
   1 (1769 Käntnertor) ZE

Schimpf und Ernst
Dachau
   ? [1760ff.] BR

sehende Blinde, Der
Ackermann
   15 (1754-66) EI, SOF
Koch
   1 (1752) PR
Schönemann
   5 (1756) DE
Schuch
   4 (1754-62) LI
Gotha
   4 (1777 Hofth) HO, SC
Hamburg
   5 (1767-9 Nat Th) SC
Hannover
   1 (1769) SOF
Mannheim
   7 (1781-2 Nat Th) WA
Munich
   2 (1783-4 Faberbräu) LE
Vienna
   15 (1764-83 Burgth) HW
   14 (1776-83 Burgth) AL
Weimar
   1 (1777 Liebhaberth) SI

**Tugend auf der Schaubühne oder
   Harlekins Heirath, Die**
Osnabrück
   1 (1765) LO

verachtete Eitelkeit der Welt, Die
Merseburg
    1 (1702) TP

Was ist's?
Vienna
    1 (1786 Burgth) AL, HW

Wildheit und Großmuth
Place unknown
    5 (?) SOF

Wolken, Die
Frankfurt/M
    1 (1782) FZ, TP

ANNOTATED BIBLIOGRAPHY OF THE GERMAN NACHSPIEL 1702–1810

FORMAT OF ENTRIES

Titles are listed in alphabetical order according to their first word, excluding definite and indefinite articles. Each entry contains the following information, with the exception of entries unavailable for inspection which contain only fields A and C.

A Title and subtitles according to title-page with minor orthographic editing for consistency. Author. Series or volume. Place of publication: Publisher, Date of publication. Pagination. Internal division. Verse form (otherwise prose). [Information in square brackets taken from sources other than copy of primary work itself.]

B Personae. Place of action. [Each in square brackets if deduced from text.] Plot outline.

C Location in parentheses (keyed to the catalogue below) and call number of copy used for this study. In case of entries unavailable for inspection, the documented reference appears here.

D Comments. Many of the Nachspiele in the Bibliography are discussed at length in the preceding study; if so, a page reference appears here, as 'see analysis p 000.'

See 'Introduction' to this volume for further information on the sources and construction of the Bibliography.

CATALOGUE OF LOCATIONS

Code numbers for German libraries follow the *Sigelverzeichnis des deutschen Bibliotheksinstituts* (BRD) and the *Sigel-Liste der Bibliotheken der DDR.*

Austria

ÖNB   Österreichische Nationalbibliothek, 1015 Wien
P   Palffy collection, Institut für Theaterwissenschaft, Universität Wien, 1010 Wien

Denmark

COP   Det Kongelige Bibliotek, 1219 København

Federal Republic of Germany

1   Deutsche Staatsbibliothek, 1086 Berlin
1a   Staatsbibliothek Preußischer Kulturbesitz, 1000 Berlin 30
6   Universitätsbibliothek, 4400 Münster
7   Niedersächsische Staats- und Universitätsbibliothek, 3400 Göttingen
12   Bayerische Staatsbibliothek, 8000 München
16   Universitätsbibliothek, 6900 Heidelberg
17   Hessische Landes- und Hochschulbibliothek, 6100 Darmstadt
21   Universitätsbibliothek, 7400 Tübingen
23   Herzog August Bibliothek, 3340 Wolfenbüttel
24   Württembergische Landesbibliothek, 7000 Stuttgart
25   Universitätsbibliothek, 7800 Freiburg i. B.
25*   Universität Freiburg, Bibliothek des Instituts für neuere deutsche Literatur, 7800 Freiburg i. B.
26   Universitätsbibliothek, 6300 Gießen
32   Nationale Forschungs- und Gedenkstätten der Klassischen Deutschen Literatur in Weimar, 5300 Weimar
33   Wissenschaftliche Allgemein-Bibliothek, Schwerin, 2750 Schwerin
38   Universitäts- und Stadtbibliothek, 5000 Köln 41
59   Fürstlich Fürstenbergische Hofbibliothek, 7710 Donaueschingen
70   Landesbibliothek Coburg, 8630 Coburg
385   Universitätsbibliothek Trier, 5500 Trier
122   Stadtbibliothek Ulm/Donau, 7900 Ulm/Donau
DI1   Studienbibliothek, 8880 Dillingen
Mh28   Bibliothek des Städtischen Reiß-Museums, 6800 Mannheim

United States

CRL   Center for Research Libraries, 6050 S. Kenwood Ave., Chicago 60637

CWR   Case Western Reserve University, 11161 East Blvd., Cleveland 44106
GMC   General Microfilm Co., Watertown, Mass. 02172-5097
H   German and Austrian Drama. Viennese Theatre 1740 to 1790. Microfilmed holdings of the Houghton Library at Harvard University (with reel and item number). Cambridge, Mass. 02138

Aberglauben und Unglauben, see **Gespenster**

A **Abschied, Der.** Ein Nachspiel für das Wiener Hof-Theater verfertigt. 1804. Theater von August v. Kotzebue. Bd. 18. Wien: Klang; Leipzig: Kummer, 1841. [145]-154. Vorbericht + 4 Scenen.

B Die Fürstin, das Publikum. Madame Selten, Sie! Babet, ihre Tochter. Der Czaar, aus dem Mädchen von Marienburg. Der Baron, aus Maske für Maske. Der Advokat, aus dem Jurist und Bauer. Mistreß Smith, aus den Indianern in England. Sekretär Willnang, aus Selbstbeherrschung. Der alte Klingsberg, aus den beiden Klingsbergen. Der Ritter, aus Liebhaber und Nebenbuhler in Einer Person. (Sämmtlich Mitglieder des Haus-Theaters der Fürstin.) Zwei Bediente. Der Schauplatz ist ein geschmückter Garten.

In the Foreword the author introduces his Nachspiel as a tribute to Madame Adamberger (Madame Selten), a favourite of the Viennese stage who is retiring after thirty-six years. With great affection and sincerity her talents and personality are described. The Nachspiel consists of a gathering of personae from some of the works in which she gained fame, as they bid her reluctant farewell. She introduces Babet as her successor to them and the Fürstin. Babet then performs several scenes from Kotzebue's works in concert with the assembled characters.

C (25) E 6649, y/18

D A touching tribute to a famous actress, serious and elevated in tone.

A **Adel des Herzens, Der, oder die ausgeschlagne Erbschaft.** Ein Nachspiel in einem Aufzuge. (Zum Behuf des Hamburgischen Theaters.) [Joh. Chr. Bock.] Hamburg u. Bremen: Cramer, 1770. [1]-30. 8 Auftritte.

B Jürgen, ein Bauer. Hannchen, seine Tochter. Herr von Rosendorf. Der Prokurator. Der Schauplatz ist zu Wien im Hause von Jürgens verstorbner Schwester.

The simple farmer and his daughter rejoice in immense riches left to them by his sister, but on learning that she herself inherited the fortune as a mistress, they are appalled and reject it absolutely. Two nephews of her benefactor, rightful heirs, had been ignored, so now Jürgen and Hannchen insist that these nephews assume the fortune. Rosendorf, one of the heirs, equally honest and upright, refuses resolutely, and much time is spent by each party trying to convince the other of their claim. Finally Rosendorf proposes marriage to the delightful Hannchen and the problem is resolved.

C (ÖNB) 625576 ATh

D Far-fetched but charming. A triumph of honesty and virtue. Some satire on the loose morals of Viennese high society. See analysis p 239.

A **alte Bekantschaft, Die.** Ein Nachspiel von einem DIALOG. Geschrieben für das churfürstl. deutsche Theater in München von G.M. Zu finden in der vötterischen Hof- und Landschaftsbuchdruckerey. 1773. [1]-19. 9 Auftritte.

B Herr v. Rheindorf. La chaudronière de Candillac. Jakob, Friseur des H. v. Rheindorfs. Friederich, Bedienter. Die Handlung geht vor in dem Wohn-zimmer des Herrn v. Rheindorfs.
   Jakob urges the reclusive Rheindorf to make and receive more visits, as Friederich anounces the arrival of a stranger who refuses to give his name but claims to be an old friend. Reluctantly, Rheindorf allows him in, where-upon the visitor Candillac acts as if they were dear old friends, but in truth they have only spent a few evenings together at a gaming table twenty-five years ago. His real purpose is to borrow money. The sceptical Rheindorf sees this from the start, gives him a verbal redressing, and sends him off with a meagre booty.

C (ÖNB) 1686 A

D After the list of personae, the author inserts an 'Erinnerung' in which he de-scribes his intention to write a theatrical dialogue in the Greek mode, disre-garding the usual requisites for dramatic writing; and as this foreword sug-gests, the work is in essence a dramatic dialogue on the subjects of friend-ship and honesty.

A **Am Ende eine Betschwester.** Nachspiel in einem Aufzuge. Berlin: Wever, 1783. [1]-35. 12 Auftritte.

B Raimund, Rath. Wille, sein Freund. Kleffer. Johann, Raimunds Bedienter. Sophie Kummer. Ein Gelehrten-Zimmer.
   After a year's absence and correspondence with his beloved Sophie, the proud and mercurial Raimund has returned to assume his new post. He has

heard rumours of Sophie's infidelity, of which we see signs in her conversation with Wille and coquettish behaviour. Yet she gives no ground to the womanizing Kleffer. Despite her earnest vow of love and fidelity, and his own feeling for her, Raimund remains sceptical, even brutal, in his investigation of her background and intentions. Finally, he chooses to believe Wille's report of her morals and rejects her forever. Sophie is left bewildered. The loquacious Johann serves to confuse matters throughout.

C (H) 23/1024

D Exaggerated emotions bordering at times on melodrama, often in language reminiscent of Storm and Stress. Interesting female protagonist, not conventionally virtuous, multi-dimensional, human and more appealing than the rigid Raimund. Shades of social criticism in master-servant relationship (Raimund-Johann) and woman's predicament. See analysis p 259.

A **arme Frau, Die.** Ein Nachspiel in einem Aufzuge nach dem Französischen von [Benoît-Joseph] Marsollier [des Vivitières. *La pauvre femme.* Comédie en 1 acte, en prose, mêlée de musique, paroles du citoyen Marsollier, musique du citoyen Dalayrac. Paris: Barba, an III (=1795)]. Manuscript, [ca 1797]. Paginated [1-4], 5-106. 15 Auftritte.

B Frau Armand. Julie. Germain, Juliens Schwager. Jacques, Wasserträger. Dermont. [Briefträger. Juliens Säugling.] Scene, Paris, Zeit, kurz nach Robespierre's Sturz. Das Theater stellt ein reinliches Dachstübchen vor. Man sieht darinn ein kleines Bett, einen Wasserständer auf einem Stein, einen kleinen Verschlag im Hintergrund, wo man auf einer Leiter hinaufsteigt. Künstlich gestellte Reisebündel verbergen den Eingang eines kleinen Holzschuppens, in welchem Germain versteckt ist.

In the days of terror after Robespierre's fall, the dispossessed Julie and her brother-in-law Germain, a writer, along with her infant, have been taken into hiding by the good and pious Frau Armand. They have lost husband and brother during the bloody revolution, and Frau Armand has suffered through the loss of her family. She has lived a life of simplicity for seventeen years, her generosity and charity to others a shining example for all. A strong devotion binds the three now and they lift each other's spirits in this dreadful time while reviewing events of the recent past (20-6). Only the trusted water carrier Jacques shares their secret. A mysterious letter arrives, dated 20 Thermidor [= July 1794], announcing a stranger's visit. He is seeking a valuable possession left with Frau Armand some time ago, but she cannot remember the event, and thus all fear that a plot is at hand to discover them. The visitor is Dermont, whom Frau Armand then recognizes

as a man who left with her for safekeeping a packet of papers, but she has
forgotten where and is beside herself at the thought that her honesty might
be impugned. After a thorough search the packet is found before the
stranger returns. Briefly, Frau Armand ponders stealing some of the bonds
in the packet, not for herself, but to enable her charges to escape and live a
good life again. But she does not, and returns the stranger's property intact
and with pride. He in turn cannot bring himself to offer her a reward, fearing offence, but he sends back Jacques with a generous gift. Frau Armand
rejoices in the good fortune, insisting that Julie and Germain take the gift for
themselves, and they all thank God for His goodness. Suddenly Dermont
returns and is recognized as Julie's husband and Germain's brother. All rejoice in the reunion.

C   (Mh28) M 249

D   The manuscript is an adaptation of Marsollier's published work, the only
significant difference lying in the omission of the twelve lengthy musical
pieces (solos, duets, ensemble) which lighten the tone of Marsollier's play
considerably.
    Pencil entry on title-page: 'Premiere (und einzige Vorstellung) 6.10.1797.'
The manuscript is clean and regular, which indicates the work of a copyist
rather than a playwright. According to Kurt Sommerfeld (64), such
manuscripts at the time were likely written out by the souffleur and copyist
J D Trinkle. The manuscript also contains a few corrections by a second
hand. There is no evidence that the play was ever published in German (viz
Goedeke, Heinsius, Kayser, *Gesamtverzeichnis*).
    While somewhat melodramatic, the play captures the mood of Paris
during the time of persecution in the days between Robespierre's fall and
his execution (27.7.1794). The few handwritten emendations to the
manuscript are for the most part unremarkable, but clearly serve to dampen
any sense of revolutionary fervour. The most striking is the change in Germain's final speech from 'Das ist das Volk – das wahre Volk!' to 'Das ist der
Bürger – der wahre Bürger' (106).

aufgehobene Belagerung von Neiß, Die, see **hinkende Bothe**

ausgeschlagne Erbschaft, Die, see **Adel des Herzens**

A   **Aussteuer, Die.** Ein Nachspiel in einem Aufzuge. Nach dem Französischen
einer noch ungedruckten Operette. [Verfasser Joseph Fiévée, Übersetzer
Chr. Fr. Schwan.] Mannheim: Schwan, 1778. [1]-54. 15 Auftritte.

B   Margrethe, eine alte Bäurin. Sußchen, ihre Tochter. Michel, Sußchens
Bräutigam. Jacob, ein junger Bauernbursche. Frau Rosine, eines reichen
Pachters Wittwe. Der Amtmann. Martin, der Schulz im Dorfe. Der Schau-
platz ist in einem Dorfe. Das Theater stellt einen mit Bäumen besetzten
Platz vor. Auf der einen Seite das Haus des Amtmanns, und auf der andern
Seite Bauernhäuser.

Framing the action is Frau Rosine's desire to remarry; Martin is interested, but she is attracted to the youthful Jacob and tricks him into betrothal. Central is Margrethe's effort to marry off Sußchen to the stupid and
grasping Michel in order to gain the 100 Thaler dowry left for village girls
by a deceased benefactor. They go to the Amtmann to collect, only to find
that the groom's presence is necessary. Jacob, Sußchen's former and still
true sweetheart, agrees to impersonate the absent Michel, but as the hour is
late the Amtmann insists they sleep the night. When they protest that they
are not yet married he calls for the clergyman to put things right. When
Michel and Frau Rosine appear, true identities are revealed and the right
couples joined: Sußchen with Jacob, Frau Rosine with Martin.

C   (Mh28) Mh 1681

D   Interesting use of conventional comic love triangles. Lively dialogue and
resolution at conclusion. Numerous stage directions indicating and requiring pantomimic improvisation.

The operetta referred to in the subtitle seems never to have appeared in
print, at least not in that form. Fiévée did, however, publish a longer prose
tale *La dot de Suzette, Ou Histoire de Mme. de Senneterre, racontée par elle-même*
(Paris: Marodon, an sixième [=1798]), xii + 233 pp. See analysis p 184.

A   **Austern, Die.** Ein Nachspiel. [Th. Joh. Quistorp.] Joh. Chr. Gottsched, Hrsg.
Die deutsche Schaubühne. Neue verbesserte Auflage, Bd. 4. Leipzig: Breitkopf, 1748. [463]-520. 27 Auftritte.

B   Herr Liebegern, ein Student. Peter, dessen Diener. Jungfer Gretchen und
Jungfer Fiekchen, zwo Schwestern. Lehnchen, deren Jungemagd. Brüller,
Feind und Gleichgut, drey Studenten. Hr. Krummfuß, Schmausefrey, u.
Freundlich, Liebegerns drey gute Freunde. Johann, ein Weinschenkenjunge.
Die Handlung fängt sich an um halb 5 Uhr und dauret bis um bald sieben.
Der Schauplatz ist zu Rostock in einem Weinhause.

Weak and indecisive Liebegern plots to impress the two sisters by ac-
quiring oysters for a communal feast. Peter delivers the invitation after
much practice and prompting, but the gathering is delayed by obnoxious
students who begin to devour the intended treat, then by the skinflint

Krummfuß who spies on the girls. A private party arranged by Johann is disturbed finally by Liebegern's old friends who are then invited to join in. But the oysters are discovered to be bad, so all agree that Fiekchen serve them in a special dish to old Krummfuß, who consumes the lot greedily to the mirth of all.

C   (25) E4246a/4

D   Lively and entertaining comic dialogue and action with interesting characters. Peter, Fiekchen, and Johann especially spirited and entertaining. Some comedy reminiscent of traditional farce: comic master-servant relationship of Liebegern and Peter; threats of beating; verbal misunderstandings; exaggerated gestures and language. Despite Gottsched's praise of this along with other plays in the volume, no direct correction of social vice, no clear didactic message.

Bauer-Arzt, see neueste Verheyrathung

A   **Bauern vom Stande, Die.** Ein Nachspiel. Aus dem Französischen. Breßlau, 1756. [Jean Antoine Romagnesi and Pierre-François-Dominique Biancolleli, *Les paysans de qualité*, Paris: Briasson, 1729.] [1]-40. 16 Auftritte.

B   Herr Orontes, Vater der Collette, Versprochene des (Bauern) Maturin [Bruder des Erast]. Erast, Bräutigam der Lucinde, geglaubte Tochter des Orontes. Ein Notar. Trivelin, Erasts Bedienter. Ein Bauer. Babet, eine junge Bäuerin. Die Vorstellung ist auf dem Lande in Orontes Garten.

   A confusion of lineage, in which the grumpy Orontes learns that his natural daughter is Collette for whom the gardener's wife had exchanged Lucinde at birth. Orontes thus commands Collette to abandon Maturin and marry Erast. But all four young lovers remain steadfast and indeed gain their wish when it is revealed by the notary that Maturin is Erast's older brother, hence wealthy. Marriage for love is now possible for both couples at the happy end.

C   (H) 15/634

D   Conventional yet amusing. Trivelin an impudent and entertaining comic servant. Freedom for comic improvisation clear from several stage directions. Contemporary gibes at gallant Parisian life and class-conscious petty nobility. See analysis p 172.

A   **Bauren, Die.** Ein Nachspill. 9 folio Manuskriptseiten. 9 Auftritte.

B   Görgel, liebhaber der urschel. Bartel, Vetter des görgel. Jockerl, Vatter der
urschel. Hiesel, liebhaber der urschel. Urschel, tochter des jockerls.
Achewettl, eine alte kuplerin. Wilhelm, pfleger. Lorenz, sein trabant. Cunz,
sein trabant.

   Görgel laments the fact that his love for Urschel seems hopeless because
of the bitter feud between his cousin and her father. We soon witness the
severity of this disagreement as the two meet, Bartel bewailing the violence
done to his rooster, Jockerl the mistreatment of his dog, along with a host of
other complaints against the other. Görgel's plea for their support is met
with rudeness and enmity. Meanwhile Hiesel makes a play for Urschel, intending to take her by force if necessary, and moves in before being driven
off by Görgel. In desperation Görgel turns to Aschewettl for advice but she
tells him to forget Urschel, who thinks he is a fool, and to marry her instead.
In the final scene the cast gathers before Wilhelm to air their complaints. He
pronounces severe sentences on all but Görgel and Urschel, granting them
instead permission to marry. The others, suitably frightened, are offered
clemency if they promise to reform their ways.

C   (ÖNB) Handschriftensammlung, Cod. 13.193 fol.

D   Lively, crude, rough and full of potential for improvising for a talented cast.
Colourful dialect adds to humour. See analysis p 133.

A   **beiden Billets, Die.** Nachspiel in einem Aufzuge. Nach dem Französischen
bearbeitet [Jean-Pierre Claris de Florian, 1755-1794, *Les deux billets*, 1780]
von Anton Wall [=Christian Leberecht Heyne]. *Deutsche Schaubüne*, 2. Jg,
Bd. 3. Augsburg, 1790. [443]-470. 11 Auftritte.

B   Gürge. Rösgen. Schnapps, ein Dorfbalbier. Die Szene ist auf einem freyen
Plaze vor Rösgens Hause.

   Rösgen is to choose a husband from her two suitors, the honest Gürge
and the cynical Schnapps. To his joy, she has sent Gürge a note indicating
her preference for him, but Gürge has no means and thus buys a lottery
ticket. When Schnapps reports the lucky numbers, Gürge discovers that he
holds the winner, which Schnapps attempts to steal by sleight of hand,
snatching the note from Rösgen by mistake. With it, he pretends to her that
Gürge is insincere and making a public display of her preference. Rösgen is
taken in, rejects Gürge, and promises to marry the bearer of the note. Unwilling to lose her, Gürge exchanges his lottery ticket for the note, where-
upon Rösgen not only pledges her love to him but also manages to trick
Schnapps into handing over the winning lottery ticket as well.

C   (ÖNB) 621763 ATh

D Spirited dialogue and action with clever reversals. Comic improvisation demanded through text.

Although the work was performed in German as early as 1783, I have found no evidence of an earlier printing than that above (viz Goedeke, Heinsius, Kayser, *Gesamtverzeichnis*).

Benoît-Joseph Marsollier des Vivetières is also credited with a comedy of the same title. His *Les billets nuls ou les deux billets*, comédie en 1 acte, was performed on 17 May 1784, but I have found no evidence that it was ever published (Brenner, 98). See analysis p 185.

A **belebte Statua, Die.** Ein Nachspiel in ungebundener Rede. Münster: Perrenon, 1769. [1]-23. 8 Auftritte.

B Eine Fee. Lucinde, ihre Tochter. Alidor, die belebte Statua. Der Schauplatz ist am Ufer des Meeres / ohnweit dem Pallast der Fee in einer grünen Gegend.

Lucinde has been kept ignorant of all humans since birth, her mother fearing the corruption of men. A statue in man's form has washed ashore and captured the girl's affections. When the Fee brings the statue to life it is Alidor, son of the sorcerer Marmindo, who transfigured his son for rejecting his father's choice of bride. For love of her daughter, the Fee allows the two to meet, warning Lucinde first against this dangerous basilisk whose very glance can mean death. Still, the girl falls in love and is finally allowed her mate, but only after a stern concluding warning to beware of the vice of all men.

C (H) 16/699

D A simple piece, not without charm.

A **beschaemte Geizhals, Der.** Gesaenge in dem nachspiel Der beschaemte geizhals. Verfertigt und in musik gesetzt von herrn Wagenseil. [Kaufbeuren]: Dorn, 1787. 12S.

C Binger, 178

A **bestrafte Hochmuth, Der** [oder **Johann Scherenschleifer**], ein Nachspiel von einer Handlung. 1751. [Steiner.] [1]-24. 11 Auftritte. Rhymed alexandrines.

B Herr Anselmo, ein wohlhabender Kaufmann. Jungfer Charlotte, dessen Tochter. Herr Leander, ein junger reicher Kaufmann, und Liebhaber der

Charlotte. Johann Scherenschleifer, ein loser Vogel. Der Schauplatz ist in
einer Allee vor dem Hause des Anselmo.

Charlotte's beauty has led to vanity. She rejects Leander and dreams of
marrying a count.The jilted lover engages Johann to impersonate a count
and ask for Charlotte's hand. This Johann does so convincingly that a marriage contract is his prize. Leander makes the ruse public, Lotte is humiliated, casts off her pride, and gratefully accepts Leander's attentions.

C (ÖNB) 819608 BTh

D Unexceptional. Johann's dual role offers improvisational potential. See
analysis p 171.

A **betrogene Alte, Der.** Nach-Spiel. Kyck in de Pot: no pub., 1747. 79-90. 3 Acti
(3 + 2 + 3 Scenae).

B Herr Truglieb, ein Liebhaber. Jungfer Wahr-Ehr, dessen Liebste. Charlotte,
ihr Aufwart-Mädgen. Herr Saur-Aug, der Vatter der Jungfer. Herr Spitz-
Sinn, ein Freund des Trugliebs. Harlequin, der Diener des Trugliebs. Die
Vorstellung ist das ordentliche Kupffer-Blat.

Truglieb enlists the help of Harlequin, Spitz-Sinn, and Charlotte to trick
Saur-Aug into giving him the hand of his daughter. To add insult to injury,
Charlotte changes loyalties as well, announcing that she will marry
Harlequin.

C (1a) Yr 1816

D Bound and published following *Der verlohrne Cranz der gewesenen Jungfer
Berg op Zoom. Ein Lustspiel. Nebst einem Nach-Spiel [Der betrogene Alte].*
Darinnen in dem ersten Die Belagerung dieser Stadt / in dem andern Ihre
unvermuthete Uebergabe vorgestellet wird. In the *Vorrede* to the volume
([3]-9), the author describes in general terms the strife between Holland and
France, concentrating on the town of Berg op Zoom which is allegorized as
a female figure. The town (Bergen op Zoom), with its extraordinary
fortifications, was in fact besieged in 1747 and surrendered, suffering extensive damage; history places responsibility for the defeat on the neg-
ligence of the eighty-six-year-old General Isaac Kock Baron Cronström. As
the work's subtitle indicates, *Der verlohrene Cranz* describes the siege, *Der betrogene Alte* the resolution, both in a humorous way. The *Vorrede* emphasizes the power of comedy to depict reality and truth, and particularly the
role of harlequin in doing so.

Another printing of *Der betrogene Alte* is bound to and published with
Die verlohrne Jungfershaft, ein Lustspiel (Frankfurt u. Leipzig: publisher un-

known, 1752) [(1a) Yr 2071]. With the exception of the title of the first work, this is a reprint of the 1747 edition, including the *Vorrede*.

The action of *Der betrogene Alte* occurs against a background of war, with reference to hostile French and Dutch troops. The vocabulary and imagery of war are transferred to the lover's campaign, which provides witty dialogue and often crude comic allusions. Harlequin's role is key in achieving the resolution. Stage directions frequently require players to address the audience or to play out what were likely extemporized scenes. See analysis p 168.

A **betrogene Betrüger, Der.** Nachspiel von B v. Mottoni. Leipzig: Köhler, 1797.

C Heinsius, IV, 257

A **betrogene Kadi, Der.** Ein Nachspiel von einer Handlung von T. [Johann André.] [Pierre-René Le Monnier, *Le Cadi dupé*, 1761.] *Schauspiele, welche auf der vom Könige von Preußen ... privilegirten Schönemannischen Schaubühne aufgeführt worden*, 4. Th. Braunschweig u. Leipzig, 1749. [1]-48. 28 Auftritte.

B Der Kadi. Rahel, dessen einzige Tochter, an Mulei versprochen. Nerine, ihre Sklavin und Vertraute. Mulei, ein alter reicher Seeräuber, Bräutigam der Rahel. Samsam, ein iunger Persianer, in Rahel verliebt. Lolo, dessen Sklav. Ein Gerichtsdiener. Die übrigen Gerichtsdiener. [Bediente des Mulei.] Der Schauplatz ist zu Constantinopel vor des Kadi Behausung. Die Begebenheit ist in der Demmerung, und dauret so lange als das Nachspiel.

The greedy Kadi has promised his daughter to old Mulei solely to gain the latter's fortune when he dies. Samsam and Nerine long to be united, and are assisted by the clever Lolo whose secret plan, if successful, will gain him both freedom from slavery and a healthy fee. He succeeds in bribing the servants to allow Samsam access to Nerine, in tricking the Kadi into leaving his daughter unprotected and granting formal permission to abduct her.

C (1a) Yr 1907

D An unimaginative and cumbersome work.

A **beyden Portraits, Die, oder Er ist schwer zu befriedigen.** Ein Nachspiel von J[ohann Heinrich] F[riedrich] Jünger. Aufgeführt im k.k. National-Hoftheater. Wien: Edlen von Kurzbek, 1784. [1]-39. 16 Auftritte.

B   Fräulein Althaus. Luise, ihre Nichte. Graf Rosenbach, Luisens Liebhaber.
Baron von Berg. Hauptmann Brav, ein abgedankter Offizier. [Johann, Be-
dienter]. Die Szene ist auf dem Fräulein Althaus Landgut.

Sheltered and admonished by her imperious guardian Fräulein Althaus,
who herself has a keen eye for the attentions of gentlemen, the reticent
Luise is reluctant to express her love to Rosenbach. He despairs and is aided
by the loyal and inventive Berg who manipulates guardian and charge to
bring the couple together. Rosenbach is finally convinced of Luise's love
when she reveals a portrait of him she has secretly painted while preparing
for her guardian a portrait of Berg. His job done, Berg escapes Fräulein Althaus's clutches, forcing her to accept the rough but honest Brav instead.

C   (ÖNB) 847800 ATh

D   Conventional, unexceptional.

A   **bezauberte Gürtel, Der.** Ein Nachspiel, aus dem Französischen des Herrn
[Jean Baptiste] Roußeau übersetzt. [*La ceinture magique*, 1702.] Berlin: Rüdiger, 1748. [1]-31. 13 Auftritte.

B   Frau Scabelle, eine Alte. Henriette, Amalie, ihre Muhmen. Leander, Antonius, deren Liebhaber. Harpax [und] Der Hauptmann Cannibal, zween verliebte Vormünder. Frantz, ein listiger Kopf. Die Schaubühne stellt einen öffentlichen Platz vor.

Frau Scabelle takes the young women under her wing to help them
evade marriage with the aging and foolish Harpax and Cannibal, but the
men resist and are determined to marry their charges, keeping them under
close guard. Leander and Antonius then enlist Frantz's aid. Posing as a
soothsayer, he dupes the two codgers with all manner of hocus pocus, finally tying them together with a magic band. This enables Leander and
Antonius to move in quickly and carry off their brides.

C   (32) 0,9:407

D   Agreeable suspension of reality in this theatrical trifle with plenty of potential for laughter. At the conclusion, a dance with Frantz and seven figures
representing the planets is announced.

A   **Bildsäule, Die.** Nachspiel in einem Aufzuge. Nach dem Französischen
[Louis-Carrogis Carmontelle, *La Statue*, 1768/69] bearbeitet von Anton Wall
[=Christian Leberecht Heyne]. Leipzig: Dyk [sic], 1782. [45]-80. 11 Auftritte.

B   Gräfin von Holm. Fräulein von Wirliz, ihre Nichte. Graf von Forster.
    Obrister von Teich. Rittmeister von Alberg. Verwalter des Grafen. Ein Zug
    Mädchen und jungen Burschen aus dem Dorfe. Die Szene ist in einem
    Bosket, auf dem Landgute des Grafen, nicht weit von Wien.

    Thinking his beloved countess has turned her favours to Alberg, the de-
    spondent count has resolved to direct his love to a statue of her erected in a
    secret grotto. The countess, likewise, thinks he has lost interest in her, and
    has appeared in Alberg's company to stimulate his jealousy. In fact, Alberg
    is devoted to her niece. The countess discovers the statue, takes its place,
    and surprises the count. Both pledge their love and celebrate to a parade,
    song, and dance of local village youth.

C   (ÖNB) 845000/34 ATh

D   Picture showing the climactic scene of the 'live' statue included in the text (p
    74).

A   **Blinde aus Leichtgläubigkeit, Der.** Ein Nachspiel in einem Aufzuge. Aus
    dem Französischen. Aufgeführt im k. k. Nationaltheater. Wien: beym Lo-
    genmeister, 1780. [1]-50. 19 Auftritte.

B   Orgon, Vormund der Julie, Geliebte des Valer, Juliens Liebhaber. Johann,
    Orgons Diener. Lisette, Juliens Mädchen. Ein Briefträger. Die Handlung
    geht im Hause des Orgons vor. Ein Saal mit einer Pendeluhr; an den Fen-
    stern sind Vorhänge und Fensterläden angebracht.

    At sixty-seven, Orgon controls Julie's fortune and intends to marry her
    himself. She enlists Johann's help to divert him, which the servant accom-
    plishes by tricking Orgon into believing he is going blind, impersonating an
    Italian doctor who heals him, then forbidding him to marry if he is to retain
    his sight. Orgon withdraws his intention and allows Julie freedom to select
    Valer. Upon learning that he has been duped, Orgon stands by his word
    and is glad of the lesson learned: he is no longer blind to his own foolish-
    ness.

C   (ÖNB) 626752 ATh

D   Johann is the engineer of all action, a clever comic role. Excellent stage po-
    tential: the comic fumbling of all characters on a darkened stage; Johann's
    impersonation of the doctor and particularly his mixture of German and
    Italian, no doubt effective on a Viennese audience, many of whom knew
    both languages. See analysis p 237.

A **Blind und lahm.** Nachspiel in einem Aufzuge von Ludwig Robert. *Jahrbuch deutscher Nachspiele,* hrsg. v. Karl v. Holtei, 3. Jg. 1824. Breslau: Graß, Barth u. Co. u. Leipzig: Barth. [71]-143. 7 Auftritte. Rhymed alexandrines. [Also as manuscript: title and author as above. 22 unpaginated leaves.]

B Der Oheim. Die Nichte. Der Oberst. [Ein Bedienter.] Ein kleines, aber modern und reich möblirtes Zimmer mit Fußteppich, Sopha, Blumengefäß u. dgl., mit einer großen Mittelthüre und einer kleinen zur Seite.

  The young woman laments the Oberst's intense attraction to her beauty, doubts his love, and feigns blindness to test him. He returns from battle, much decorated, and learns of her ruse from her uncle. Fearing his own dashing appearance is too important to his lady, the Oberst pretends to have lost a leg. This the uncle in turn reports to her. Thus the two lovers are reunited, each playing roles of infirmity, each knowing that the other is acting. They re-pledge eternal devotion. In his closing words to the audience, the uncle provides a moral: self-deception and discovery are necessary stages in enlightenment.

C (ÖNB) 620167/3 BTh. [Manuscript (Mh28) M945]

D In a preceding 'Vorbericht über das Metrum des folgenden Lustspiels,' signed 'Berlin im März 1823. Ludwig Robert' (73-8), the author discusses various metrical forms with examples from contemporary dramatic literature and argues for alexandrine verse with variants. The effect in this work is, however, stiflingly formal, unnatural and inappropriate for the simple content, which itself is verbose and altogether too drawn out.

  The Mannheim manuscript [ca 1800] carries the pencil notation 'In Mannheim nicht aufgeführt' above the title. It is a scribe's, not an author's manuscript, and also contains a few minor, mostly orthographic, alterations stemming from a second hand. Beyond minor differences, this manuscript is identical with the published version except that it does not include the 'Vorbericht.' See analysis p 237.

A **Brandschatzung, Die, oder Das Wiederfinden der Tochter.** [Johann Heinrich] Decker. *Neueste deutsche Schaubühne für 1806,* Bd. 4. Frankfurt u. Leipzig, 1806. [55]-96. 22 Scenen.

B Von Querfeldt, Gutsherr. Emilie, dessen Tochter. Von Wildenstein, feindlicher General, bey von Querfeldt im Quartier liegend. Gustav von Stein, Adjutant. Rappel, vormals Gefreyter, jetzt Invalide und zur Aufwartung des Generals. Clas, Aufwärter im Schlosse. Ein Adjutant. Die Handlung geht auf dem Schlosse des Gutsherrn vor.

It is wartime and properties are unstable. Querfeldt learns that he and
those on his estate must pay an enormous indemnity to the new king for
past damages despite the fact that not Querfeldt but his predecessor was at
fault. Emilie, we learn, is in fact a foundling who has been raised by Querfeldt and his late wife since infancy. Hearing this, Wildenstein reveals that
he is her true father and recounts at length why circumstances forced him
to abandon his young wife and their child years ago. Father and daughter
rejoice in their reunion. A joyful resolution is assured as word comes from
the king that the financial penalty has been removed. Consistent with her
wishes, Emilie's hand is given by her father to the trusty Gustav von Stein.

C (59) I Fr 11a7

D Table of contents: 'Deckers Nachspiele: Der Versuch. Die Brandschatzung.'
A long-winded and melodramatic work composed of ponderous recollections with virtually no dramatic action. See analysis p 246.

A **Calliste.** Ein Nachspiel. [Ernst Theodor Johann Brückner.] *Etwas für die
deutsche Schaubühne.* Brandenburg: Halle, 1772. [203]-260. 9 Auftritte.

B Damon, Erast, Arist, junge Edelleute. Louise, eine Aufwärterinn. Ein Wirth.
Johann, Damons Diener. Die Scene ist in Damons Zimmer.
   Until recently, Damon has led an irresponsible life, but since coming under Arist's influence he has been transformed into a virtuous and reasonable man. He now scorns the popinjay Erast and is full of praise for Arist's
gentility and values. But Arist suddenly announces that their close friend-
ship must end, refusing to say why, and leaves immediately. A note arrives
soon after, explaining the mysterious rupture: Arist is really the Countess
Calliste whose reputation and virtue are renowned; she could no longer live
a deception with her friend. Damon is jubilant, setting out at once to claim
Calliste once and for all.

C (ÖNB) 392620/91 A

D Despite its repetitious dialogue, its precious tone, and its artificial exaggeration of virtue, the work is saved by a novel and surprising dénouement.

A **Cangé, oder der wohlthätige Kommissionär.** Ein Nachspiel in einem Akte.
[Armand Goufflé. *Cangé, ou le commissionnaire bienfaisant,* traité historique
en un acte. Paris, 1795.] Straßburg: Treuttel, Im dritten Jahre der Franken-
Republik [1795]. [I]-VIII, [1]-42. Prologue + 13 Auftritte.

B Georges. Seine Gattin. August, Sophie, Georges Kinder. Basset, genant
   Scävola, ein gewesener Edelmann. Rollot, ein gewesener Priester. Cangé,
   ein Kommissionär. Gefangene. Thürschliesser. Bürger und Bürgerinnen.
   Die Scene ist in Paris.

   In the Prologue, entitled 'Auszug aus dem Journal des Débats et des
   Décrets de la Convention nationale. Sitzung vom drey und zwanzigsten
   Vendemiaire, im dritten Jahre der Republik,' citizen Desaudray presents
   Cangé and asks permission to tell of his good deeds. This he does by citing
   a poem (in alexandrines) by J.M. Sedaine in which Cangé's generosity and
   humanity are praised, as opposed to the barbarism of the revolutionaries.
   The assembly offers generous applause. In the Nachspiel, Cangé, once a
   man of wealth, has been imprisoned without just cause by Robespierre's
   regime. His loyal wife and children starve while he awaits death. The
   bloodthirsty Rollot, reponsible for announcing the names next to mount the
   scaffold, taunts him in prison, while Basset offers help through his influence, but only in exchange for favours from Georges's virtuous wife, a
   suggestion she rejects vehemently. Cangé is a constant source of support
   and strength for the family, anonymously supporting them financially as
   well. Their fear and misery are finally dispelled as Georges is released from
   prison.

C (6) AC 54405 Sondermagazin

D A weak and inconsistent dramatic structure with most action off-stage.
   Melodramatic sentimentality. Some insight into the atmosphere of terror
   during the French Revolution. See analysis p 256.

A **Caroline.** Ein Nachspiel. *Früchte der ländlichen Muse.* Leipzig: Holle, 1777.
   [100]-141. 10 Auftritte.

B Herr von Thalheim, ein junger Edelmann, der sich den Sommer über auf
   dem Gute seines Vetters aufhält. Frau von Treuberg. Caroline, Aufseherin
   auf dem Schlosse. Friedrich, ein alter Bedienter des Herrn von Thalheim.
   Marie, Carolinens Mutter. Ein andrer Bedienter. [Zimmer im Schloß.
   Schloßgarten.] Directions for set change from room to garden (121f).

   Thalheim and Caroline are in love but each is afraid to tell the other.
   Thalheim cannot bring himself to ignore their difference in social class.
   Friedrich also has eyes for her, but his clumsy overture is rejected. Frau v.
   Treuberg's chance visit after a carriage accident provides a solution when
   she recognizes Caroline as her missing niece. Caroline and Thalheim are
   thus free to marry.

C (23) Wa 868

D Highly artificial and tediously transparent with strong doses of sentimentality before the resolution. Thematic reinforcement of class barriers.

A **Christen in Abyssinien, Die, oder Die neue Schätzung**. Divertissement
zum Nachspiel. Johann Michael Reinhold Lenz, *Gesammelte Schriften*, hrsg.
v. Franz Blei. Bd. 5. München u. Leipzig: Müller, 1913. [223]-240. 2 Szenen.
[Written in or before 1780, the year of Lenz's death.]

B [Tintrong. Yarmund. Kaufleute. Ein preßhafter Mann. Alfaddin.
Schachspieler. Bedienter. Ein Tabaksraucher. Ein Betrunkener. Wirt.
Markör. Babelmansor. Alvarez (Scheik Daher verkleidet).]
   A dramatic discussion of the nature and merits of various world re-
ligions with a message (especially to Christians) of tolerance and accep-
tance, as summarized in a closing song.

C (25) E 6694,ak-5

D A philosophical rather than dramatic work, with odd remnants of improvised comedy (disguise, stage direction calling for 'Lazzi,' closing song). See
analysis p 243.

A **Chymici [Chemiker], Die.** Eine Comödie in zwey Aufzügen als ein Nachspiel. Leipzig: Müller, 1771. [1]-54. 9 + 14 Auftritte.

B Der Marquis. Die Marquise. Ein abgedankter Officier [Der Major]. Ein Doc-
ter. Ein Chymicus. Eine Wahrsagerin. Friedrich, ein Bedienter. Bernhard,
ein guter Freund des Marquis. Der Schauplatz ist in Paris, in des Marquis
Garten.
   Penniless and in debt despite his appearance and bearing, the Marquis is
desperately delaying his creditors while awaiting income from benevolent
sources. Believing the Marquis to be wealthy, the unscrupulous major, assisted by the doctor (whose credentials are forged) and chemist, endeavours
to deceive him of funds. A point of attraction is the Marquis's interest in
smelting, and both doctor and chemist, through the major's manipulation,
are called in to serve as instructors, for a fee. All changes when the intrigu-
ing triumvirate learns that their prey is bankrupt. Abruptly they depart,
followed by the Marquis who goes into hiding to escape his creditors.

C (ÖNB) 392620 A

D A vaporous plot almost devoid of dramatic merit. The financial plight of the
nobleman is of contemporary thematic interest. See analysis p 248.

A **Comödie ohne Tittel, Die.** Ein Nachspiel. 1759. [1]-12. 5 Auftritte.

B [Pantalon. Harlekin. Der Wirth. Brighella. Colombine. Florindo.]

   War times have caused a troupe of Itàlian comedians to fall into disarray, resulting in the loss of their leader Brighella and most of the female players. The innkeeper wants them to play in his hall nevertheless. To the joy of his colleagues, Brighella returns with tales of adventure in the war. They discuss the future, and despite their low opinion of the manners and dialect of German girls, decide to train them to act and to continue their work on the stage.

C (1a) Yr 3116

D Bound and published after *Der Krieg der Götter*. Ein Schauspiel von drey Aufzügen. Place of publication and publisher unknown, 1759, 64 pp, an allegorical work on the subject of war; preliminary material to the volume tells us that 'Der Schauplatz ist in Deutschland' [6].

   Comödie is an unusual piece in perspective and content. A satirical look at religious and political strife in German territory. Protestant and Catholic, Prussian and Austrian conflicts are likened to role playing on the stage. The innkeeper's language suggests Bavarian or Austrian dialect.

A **3.13.33. [Drei. Dreizehn. Dreiunddreißig.]** Ein Nachspiel. [Christoph Ludwig Seipp.] *Theaterstückchen zu betrachten als eine Zugabe zu den Hauptstücken der Ostermesse*, Bd. 2. Preßburg: Mahler, 1789. [231]-264. Anfang + 17 Fortschritte.

B Obrist von Werthen. Sophie, seine Tochter. Ludwig von Werthen, weitläuftiger Anverwandter des Oberst. Karl von Diesen, Lieutenant. Christian, Bedienter des Oberst. Die Handlung im Hause des Obristen.

   Diesen has loved Sophie since her childhood and the two have shared many happy hours of reading and discussion. He confesses his love and asks for her hand, confident now that he also has means in the form of a winning lottery ticket. Sophie is surprised as she has always thought to marry poor Ludwig Werthen, her motive being to bring him a healthy dowry, a position, and thus happiness. A demoralized pessimist, Werthen fails to respond as hoped, even when Diesen offers to donate his lottery winnings. To her father's relief, Sophie finally comes to her senses and accepts the lieutenant.

C (ÖNB) 844993 ATh

D An odd mixture of confused motives. Some thematic reference to the social position of women (Sophie is free to choose her partner) and the military (the lieutenant's honour). See analysis p 251.

dreifache Heirath, Die, see **Maskerade**

A **Drei Stockwerk hoch, oder das Lustspiel auf der Treppe.** Nachspiel in einem Akte nach dem Französischen bearbeitet v. Theodor Hell [Karl Gottfried Theodor Winkler]. Aus dessen Lustspiele vierter Band. Leipzig: Hinrichs, no date. [i-ii], [1]-78. 30 Scenen.

B Dünnebier, Hausbesitzer, wohnt in der ersten Etage links. Stempler, Advokat, wohnt in der ersten Etage rechts. [Zweite Etage links ist zu vermieten.] Sterblich, Arzt, wohnt in der zweiten Etage rechts. Streckvers, ein Dichter, wohnt in der dritten Etage links. Ein Kranker, wohnt in der dritten Etage rechts. Röschen, Dünnebiers Nichte. Mastmann, Röschens Bestimmter. Wilhelm, ein Haarkräusler. Feld [called Frank], Röschens Liebhaber. Peter, Portier und Schuster. Ein Lohnbedienter. Scene: Das Hinterhaus Dünnebiers. [Description of stage sets.]

By her uncle's arrangement, Röschen is to be married the following day to Mastmann whom she has never met. Time is thus quickly running out for her and Frank, who visits her disguised as a blind musician, evoking a stream of complaints from the other tenants. Frank enlists the help of Peter and Wilhelm to dissuade the eager groom upon his arrival. Already reeling from the effects of a bad storm and thieves during his travels, Mastmann arrives in disarray, is misguided into taking a nasty fall in the cellar, and told that Röschen has already had three previous husbands, all of whom died mysteriously on the same day of the year. This suffices to scare off the skittish groom, so Frank and Röschen realize their dream to be together.

C (ÖNB) 846829 ATh

D A work with light comic potential. Brief satirical comment on contemporary hack writers and the lowering of literary quality to suit mass taste. Streckvers serves as a humorous example of this hack writing with his own recited dramatic verses. Numerous stage directions linked to initial description of sets.

A **Dreßdner Frauen Schlendrian, Der.** In einem Nachspiel verfertiget von Herrn J[ohann] U[lrich] von König. Place of publication and publisher unknown, 1742. [1]-31. 12 Auftritte.

B Frau Rechts und Links, eine galante Wittwe. Herr Ohnesorge, ihr Bruder.
   Herr Bedachtsam, ein Wittwer und Hofbedienter. Jungfer Sittsam, seine
   Schwester. Valentin, der Frau Rechts und Links und Herr Ohnesorgens Be-
   dienter.

   Set in Dresden, the action depicts the socially conscious Frau Rechts und
   Links and her brother Ohnesorge's campaign to win Jungfer Sittsam as his
   bride. She is guarded closely by Bedachtsam who suspects the intentions of
   every suitor since the town is full of fashionable but insincere seducers
   ('Schlendrian'-figures). Valentin, disguised as one of the female cosmetics
   pedlars then common in Dresden, attempts to smuggle his master's love
   note to Jungfer Sittsam but is foiled by her obtuseness and sent home with a
   beating by Bedachtsam. Ohnesorge begs his sister to look favourably on
   Bedachtsam's romantic overtures, believing that this will aid his own cause.
   This she does and both couples are joined in the end.

C (33) Ob V 1020 (6. Bd)

D A comic view of contemporary Dresden, particularly the pretentious bourgeoisie. Local colour, reference to social conventions, and satire on the superficiality of the stylish middle class and its imitation of aristocratic and
   foreign (particularly French) manners. Valer is a traditional comic servant
   figure central to the intrigue and the focus of much humour through coarse
   language, word-plays, misunderstandings, exaggerated costume, disguise,
   and beatings.

A **edelmütige Bauer, Der.** Nachspiel. Halle: Hemmerde, 1771.

C Heinsius, IV, 255

A **eheliche Versöhnung, Die.** Ein Nachspiel in einer Handlung nach dem
   Französischen. Mannheim: Neuer Kunstverlag, 1795. [i-ii, 1-]72. 24
   Auftritte.

B Der Graf von Rosenhain. Die Gräfin, seine Gemahlin. Emilie, seine
   Schwester. Der Baron von Lilienthal. Der Baron von Wienburg. Herr von
   Hornstein, ein alter geadelter Wechsler. Joseph, des Grafen Kammerdiener.
   Klary, der Gräfin Kammermädchen. Ein Notar.

   Married just six months, the playboy count is already tired of his wife
   and has fallen passionately in love with a masked Venetian at a ball. In parallel fashion, Joseph has fallen for her Tyrolean servant. The objects of their
   desire, however, are in fact the countess and Klary who are attempting the
   masquerade to win back their love. Aided by Wienburg they succeed, and

in the bargain ensure the betrothal of Emilie and Lilienthal, to which the lovesick count agrees as a condition to meeting the mysterious Venetian again. The wealthy old Hornstein, previous claimant to Emilie, is left out in the cold.

C   (Mh28) Mh 1546

D   Satire on infidelity in aristocratic marriages and on French affectation (Hornstein). Transparent from the outset, largely uninteresting, and uninspired. See analysis p 248.

Eitelkeit und Herzensgüte, see **Versuch**

A   **Enterbte, Der.** Nachspiel. [Ernst Theodor Johann Brückner.] *Etwas für die deutsche Schaubühne.* Brandenburg: Halle, 1772. [261]-349. 7 Auftritte.

B   Damis, ein Major. Der Graf. Der Baron. Wilhelmine, des Grafen Tochter. Charlotte, des Barons Tochter. Christian, des Grafen Bedienter. Henrich, Damis Bedienter. Ein Bauer. Der Schauplatz ist ein Zimmer in des Grafen Hause.

   The count is a man who loves a joke. From his dear friend the baron and from Damis himself, he hides the fact that he knows Damis's true identity – he is the baron's son, disinherited a decade ago for despicable behaviour. Now Damis is a paragon of virtue, loved and admired by everyone, including the farmer who recounts tales of his generosity and concern for others. Wilhelmine and Damis are in love and he asks the count for her hand. At first agreement is given, but then the count withdraws permission, saying that Wilhelmine must marry the baron's son. To the others this reversal is incomprehensible; they urge him to reconsider, but to no avail. When Damis's true identity is revealed, the lovers are reunited, the baron content, and the joker apparently satisfied.

C   (ÖNB) 392620 A

D   A tiresome work of a length far exceeding the needs of this facile plot. As we suspect Damis's identity early in the work, there is little surprise at the final reversal or interest in reaching it. The dutiful Wilhelmine is of doubtful credibility as is Damis's anonymity.

A   **entführte Dose, Die, und der Gärtnerkönig.** Johann Elias Schlegel. *Werke,* hrsg. v. Johann Heinrich Schlegel. 5 Bde. Kopenhagen u. Leipzig: Verlag der Mummischen Buchhandlung, 1764-73. Bd. 2 (1773). Nachdruck Frankfurt:

Athenäum, 1971. [619]-638, including introduction and comments by editor. [*Dose*: 9 Auftritte. Alexandrines. *Gärntnerkönig*: alexandrines.]

B   [*Dose*: Foppendorf, Charlottes Liebhaber. Glocke. Charlotte. Christine, ihre Schwester. Dratmann, Charlottes ehemaliger Liebhaber; *Gärtnerkönig*: Hephästion. Abdolonimus.]

   Dose: Only the first and last two scenes are printed here, with editor's comments summarizing those omitted. They are in unrhymed alexandrine verse with many irregularities. The elated Foppendorf tells Glocke that he has stolen Charlotte's snuff box. Charlotte shows no displeasure but her sister is angered at the thought of a man taking such liberties and showing his prize in public, not to mention the loss of their snuff. The box had been a gift from the faint-hearted Dratmann who now resolves to get it back, even suggesting a modified duel to his contemptuous rival. Christine smashes the snuff box to end the dispute.

   Gärtnerkönig: The brief printed fragment extends just seventeen lines and includes a speech by Hephästion praising Abdolonim's qualities as ruler of Sidon despite, and partly because of, his humble background as a gardener. Written in unrhymed alexandrines.

C   (25) GE 71 6711/2

D   In the table of contents and his introduction to these fragments, the editor (JHS) identifies *Dose* as a Nachspiel and sets it within the tradition of the 'Nachcomödie' (621f). *Gärtnerkönig* is called a 'Fragment eines tragi-komischen Nachspiels.' We are told further that *Dose* was performed and warmly received in Leipzig before his brother (JES) had finished *Der geschäftige Müßiggänger* [1741]. JHS reports that JES in later years had criticized the work severely and even resisted attempts to improve it; because of this, JHS did not reprint it entirely here. He claims that its principal importance lies in the author's use of alexandrine verse. JHS has published here all that is extant of the *Gärtnerkönig*, a tragi-comic heroic piece despite its Nachspiel designation, and also of interest chiefly for its use of alexandrines, on which the editor comments in detail. Both works reflect JES's interest in the use of verse in comedy and the contemporary debate on that subject.

A   **erfüllten Wünsche, Die.** Kleines Nachspiel. Andreas Gottlieb Hartmann. 1777.

C   Goedeke, IV[1], 667

A **Er ist es selbst.** Ein Nachspiel von Theodor Hell [Karl Gottfried Theodor Winkler]. Leipzig: Hinrichs, 1808. [ii, 1-3], 4-55. 17 Scenen. Intermittent songs in short irregular verses.

B Donna Lopez, Französin, vermählt an Don Lopez, Hauptmann in spanischen Diensten. Emil, Donna Lopez Bruder. Pedro, Don Lopez Bedienter. Donna Lopez geht in französischer, Don Lopez in spanisch-militärischer, Emil in französischer, Pedro in spanischer Tracht. Die Scene ist in Madrid.

  Though only recently married, Don Lopez has left his wife at home alone. His trip, however, is a pretence; in fact he has remained nearby to serenade her nightly as an anonymous stranger below her window in order to test her fidelity. Pedro collaborates by delivering mail from him, purportedly from distant places. Donna Lopez has been amusing herself in his absence by painting a portrait, the subject of which she will not reveal to the curious Pedro who is convinced it is her lover, and informs his master. But Emil tells his sister of the plot and they engineer a revenge. She accepts a rendezvous with the anonymous Romeo, but when he and Pedro enter, Don Pedro is confronted with his own picture – the completed portrait – and his wife's charges of mistrust. Pedro too is taught a lesson, as they trick him into believing his beloved Jacinthe is untrue. Convinced now of his wife's fidelity, Don Lopez asks forgiveness and re-pledges his love.

C (38) ST Hell 2110

D Comment on Spanish bias against moral standards of the French. Interesting early scene in which Donna Lopez, alone, plays roles of both herself and her husband in fictitious dialogue, including voice changes ('mit Männerstimme') (10f).

Er ist schwer zu befriedigen, see **beyden Portraits, Die**

erste Dank, Der, see **Wildheit**

erste Liebe, see **Liebe und Vaterland**

A **Eurydice.** Ein Nachspiel. So, wie es ist ausgepfiffen worden auf dem Königlichen Theater in Drury-Lane. [1759]. [143]-180. No internal divisions. 8 arias. Largely prose with some recitatives in rhymed alexandrines.

B Pluto. Orpheus, Proserpine. Eurydice. Charon. Einige Geister etc. [Der Autor. Der Criticus. Captain Weazel. Mr. Spindle. Ihr Diener. Mr. Maccahour.

Ein irrländischer Bauer.] Places of action: [Theatre backstage.] Des Pluto Hofstatt. Am Ufer des Flußes Styx.

The action begins behind the scenes as author and critic discuss the play. The author dismisses the critic's suggestion that the classical myth of Orpheus and Eurydice is unsuitable for a common audience. They are joined by Weazel and Spindle, deceased contemporaries familiar with Pluto's underworld after lives of mortal licentiousness. These characters continue to be present throughout the classical action, providing comment and criticism, often related to their own contemporary world. The classical action focuses on the myth of Orpheus who journeys to the underworld to reclaim his lost wife Eurydice and bring her back to life. True to the myth, Pluto is overcome by Orpheus's song and allows this exception on condition that Orpheus does not look back in the course of his return journey. The classical legend is twisted with irony, however, as Eurydice is anything but a willing companion. She would prefer to stay where she is, for marriage holds no attraction for her. Proserpine is equally jaded about matrimony as a result of her relationship with Pluto. Nevertheless, Orpheus and Eurydice begin their journey, but she tricks him into looking back, thus dashing his hopes for a mortal reunion. The cynical Eurydice returns with pleasure to the underworld where she becomes Proserpine's closest confidante.

C (ÖNB) 819608 BTh

D Bound to and published with *Der Hochzeitstag, ein Lustspiel, wie es auf dem königlichen Theater in Drury-Lane ist aufgeführet worden. Beyde aus dem Englischen des Herrn Henry Fielding übersetzt.* Kopenhagen: Rothe, 1759. No direct connection between the two works.

Eurydice is a loosely structured and irreverent travesty of the classical myth with secondary references to contemporary mores, especially marital roles. Concluding ballet indicated.

A **falsche verdacht, Der.** ein nachspill. [1745.] [Johann Joseph Felix von Kurz or Friedrich Wilhelm Weiskern.] 7 folio Manuskriptseiten. 10 Scenae.

B Odoardo, gerhab der colombina. Celio, des odoardo Schwester-Sohn, ein ausgelaßener mensch. Bernardon, des odoardo bruders Sohn, ein armer einfältiger tropff. Colombina, ein ungehorsame pupillin des odoardo. Hanswurst, des odoardo gewesener diener, amant der colombina.

Bernardon appears in rags after a long journey from Linz. Penniless, he asks for employment at the house of the wealthy Odoardo who recognizes him as his cousin and employs him as *Hausmeister* to keep an eye on Colombina and Celio. The latter, along with Hanswurst, resent his presence as he interferes with their thievery; they try to gain his support and then to trick him into situations of guilt. Fooled at first, Odoardo maintains faith in Bernardon's innocence and finally catches the dishonest Colombina and Hanswurst, throws Colombina out to fend for herself, and rewards Bernardon.

C (ÖNB) Handschriftensammlung, Cod. 13.193 fol.

D No dialogue, just a sketch of the action in each scene. Typical *commedia dell'arte* characters and techniques (constellation of plot, beatings, eavesdropping, improvisation). See analysis p 88.

A **Fanny, ein tragisches Nachspiel in einem Aufzuge,** dem Herrn Hofrath Uber gewidmet. Breslau: Gutsch, 1772. [1]-40. 5 Auftritte. Rhymed alexandrines; aria in short rhymed iambs.

B Fanny, die Mutter. Lucia, ihre Tochter. Martha, ihre Begleiterin. Lentley, Gemahl der Fanny. Reevens, Freund des Lentley. Die Handlung ist in einem Walde in einem dicht mit Bäumen besetzten Orte. [P.(3) a dedication to Hofrath Uber.]

   Years ago, while her husband was away, Lord Briton had attempted to seduce the virtuous Fanny, then defamed her. Since then she has lived alone with Lucia and Martha, mourning her fate and the loss of a beloved husband. Meanwhile, the dying Briton has confessed to Lentley who has now come to reclaim his wife and child. He employs a lover's ruse by leaving Fanny a note, ostensibly from Briton, begging forgiveness and urging a reunion with her husband; Lentley then appears to Fanny disguised as her former seducer. The ruse backfires tragically as Fanny stabs him and then dies at his side.

C (H) 46/1829

D A ponderous, melodramatic, and unlikely tragedy, charged with effusive sentimentality. An almost entirely retrospective account through dialogue, the only action confined to the end of the last scene. One brief aria by Lucia. See analysis p 256.

A **faule Bauer, Der.** Ein Nachspiel. A[dam] [Gottfried] Uhlich. Hamburg u. Leipzig, 1745. [1-31 unpaginated.] 5 Auftritte. Rhymed alexandrines.

B Nickel Clas, der faule Bauer. Hänsgen, dessen jüngster Bruder. Stephen, in Trinen verliebt. Trine, in Nickel verliebt. Lise, eine junge Bäuerinn.

The action consists chiefly of playful dialogues (Trine/Lise, Stephen/ Hänsgen, Hänsgen/Lise) about the nature and techniques of love. Lise's father has promised her to Nickel, despite her distaste for the lazy farmer. She loves Hänsgen and in the end is released from her obligation by Nickel himself when he hears of her preference. Trine's eager offer to replace her is greeted without enthusiasm by the sleepy Nickel who prefers his bed to thoughts of marriage.

C (7) Poet dram III, 1722

D P[3]: Foreword to reader in which author claims to have first called the work a 'Schäferspiel,' but finding himself too unfamiliar with such persons changed his characters to farmers. He gives no rationale for the designation Nachspiel. A simple rural work with little dramatic invention.

A **Finanzbediente, Der.** Ein Nachspiel. Nach dem Financier [1761] des Herrn [Germain François Poullain] de Saintfoix. *Nachspiele, für Schauspielergesellschaften, die keine Operetten und Ballette aufführen können, oder wollen.* Wesel u. Leipzig: Röder u. Heinsius, 1789. [125]-160. 13 Auftritte.

B Herr von Vallebois, ein französischer Finanzbedienter. Baron von Biederwald, ein deutscher Edelmann. Herr von Courville, ein französischer Markis. Dumat, Vater des Hrn. von Vallebois. Henriette, Dumats Tochter. Ferdinand, Bedienter des Markis von Courville. Der Schauplatz ist auf Vallebois Landgut [in der Nähe von Paris].

The wealthy and hard-hearted Vallebois has ordered reconstruction of the road near his new estate, which has caused Biederwald's and Dumat's coaches to overturn. The former he has treated with generosity, the latter, a commoner, with disdain. Biederwald is incensed at such disregard for human need. Courville meets Henriette and, taken by her beauty, resolves to make her his. She and her father have come for Vallebois's help, he being the authority to whom Dumat must answer for the loss of treasury funds recently stolen. The cunning and hypocritical Courville promises assistance, but in fact misrepresents their case to Vallebois, reports his refusal, and offers to clear their debt himself and take them to live with him. But Henriette sees through his guile and rejects the offer. Biederwald has overheard all this and denounces Courville in a heated diatribe. The marquis draws his sword, but is disarmed and exits. In a startling conclusion, Henriette reveals past events to discover that Vallebois is their lost brother and son. His heart changes abruptly, he assures their safety and security, and matches Henriette with Biederwald as a sign of his esteem.

C (ÖNB) 2416 A

D Striking contrast between French and German nobility, a tribute to the latter. Biederwald's indictment of the immorality and cowardice of the upper class as represented by the marquis is powerful and unusually direct (pp 152f). Dramatically intense, but artificial resolution through rapid revelations and reversals in final scene.

Beyond the above adaptation, a translation of Saint-Foix's play into German appeared in 1762: *Der Finanzpächter, ein Lustspiel in einem Aufzuge, von den französischen Comödianten zu Paris im Jahr 1761 zu verschiedenenmalen aufgeführt.* Leipzig: Lankisch. The Nachspiel adaptation maintained much of the original, with the most striking exception in the role of Biederwald. Saint-Foix depicted this person as a French chevalier, the Nachspiel's author made him a German nobleman, thus shipping the credit for such honest gallantry across the Rhine. See analysis p 248.

Frau mit zwenen Männern zugleich, Die, see **Unerwartete**

A **Freiheitsbaum, Der.** Nachspiel. Nikolaus Müller. Straßburg: Specht, 1794.

C Goedeke, VII, 237

Freyer, Die, see **Friederike**

A **Friederike von Rosenhayn, oder die Freyer.** Ein Nachspiel. Augsburg: Stage, 1783. [4]-62. 18 Auftritte.

B Baron von Mayendorf. Friederike von Rosenhayn. Catharine, ihr Mädchen. Graf Farell, Rittmeister. Baron von Wolfszahn. Kammerherr von Tannfeld. Wahrmann. von Zuckermantel. Carl, Bedienter des Mayendorfs. Johann, Bedienter des von Zuckermantels. Heinrich, Bedienter des Grafen. Die Scene ist in einem Landhause des Baron Mayendorfs.

The well-meaning baron has called together suitors so that his niece Friederike may choose a husband on this her eighteenth birthday. Farell, Wolfszahn, and Zuckermantel are the chief contenders, each ridiculous or scheming in his own way. A woman of independent means and mind, Friederike chooses the honest, penniless, but sincere Wahrmann, disappointing the rest.

C (H) 24/1038

D Enlightened praise of a young woman's independence and the virtues of honesty and sincerity, unimaginatively cast in dramatic form. See analysis p 254.

A **frohe Frau, Die.** Ein Nachspiel, schicklich aufzuführen nach der Leidenden Frau. [Johann Gottlieb Göntgen.] Offenbach u. Frankfurt: Weiß, 1775. [1]-23. 4 Scenen.

B Frau Hilaria. Sophie, ihre Tochter. Ein Kritiker. Zween Studenten. Zween Bedienten. Komödianten. Der Schauplatz ist auf dem Theater. Der Innhalt blos Dialog.
   The actors have just finished performing [Friedrich Maximilian] Klinger's *Die leidende Frau* [more commonly *Das leidende Weib*, 1775] and with the others now discuss that play, their roles, its author, and the main influences, *Werther* and Richardson's *Clarissa*. Except for one of the students, they uniformly condemn both work and author.

C (H) 46/1824

D An unusual critical commentary on the contemporary theatre scene. See analysis p 264.

A **frohe Tag, Der.** Ein Nachspiel. [Johann Wilhelm Heuberger.] Wesel, 1798.

C Goedeke, VII, 322

A **fromme Betrug, Der.** Ein Nachspiel in einem Aufzuge von C[arl] A[ugust] Seidel. Leipzig: Fleischer, 1789. [1]-48. 11 Auftritte.

B Frau Rambek. Ludwig Rambek, ihr Sohn. Julie, ihre Tochter. Baumann, Rambeks Freund.
   Penniless Baumann lives with the Rambeks, spending his days in depressed self-pity with no hope of fulfilling his secret love for Julie. Her private feeling for him is as fervent, but she fears the reaction of her dominating and niggardly mother who has forbidden her any contact with him. Ludwig, a happy-go-lucky, generous soul, wins a huge lottery and gives the prize to his moody friend, assuring his wealth and acceptance into the family. Now Frau Rambek sees Baumann quite differently and blesses his union with her daughter.

C (ÖNB) 698427 ATh

D   A testimony to the importance of money in bourgeois society. See analysis p
251.

A   **fromme Stutzer, Der.** Ein Nachspiel in Versen. Frankfurt u. Leipzig, 1757.
[1]-28. 18 Auftritte. Rhymed alexandrines.

B   Frau Wunderbar. Charlottchen, ihre Tochter. Magister Scheinhold, ihr
Bruder. Lorchen, ihre Hausjungfer. Johann, ihr Bedienter. Der Schauplatz
ist in dem Hause der Frau Wunderbar. Einige Stühle nebst einem Tischgen
mit einem Schreibzeuge, und Nähgeräthe sind auf demselben nöthig. Die
Handlung tauret von Mittag bis gegen Abend.
   The tyrannical Frau Wunderbar rules the household with hypocritical
piety, making Lorchen the object of her cruelty. She vows to dismiss the
servant, and does so in cruel fashion by having Scheinhold feign love for
her, opening the path to a new life, then only to renounce his promise bru-
tally. The injured Lorchen summons her pride and virtue once again in the
face of such mistreatment and leaves with dignity.

C   (ÖNB) 845000/326 ATh

D   A black picture of the hypocritical tyranny of the powerful and wealthy
over the servant class.

Gärtnerkönig, Der, see **entführte Dose, Die**

A   **Geburtstag, Der.** Ein Nachspiel. Andreas Gottlieb Hartmann. 1776.

C   Goedeke, IV^1, 667

A   **Geisterbanner, Der.** Nachspiel. Breslau: Meyer.

C   Heinsius, IV, 286

geprellte Geizhals, Der, see **Schatzgräber**

A   **geraubte Dose, Die.** Ein Nachspiel in einem Aufzuge. *Deutsches Theater von
H.C.H. von Trautzschen*, [1. Theil], Leipzig: Jacobäer, 1772. [275]-312. 23
Auftritte.

B   Der Präsident. Lottgen, dessen Tochter. Der alte Herr von Ehrenwald. Der
junge Herr von Ehrenwald, dessen Sohn. Der Herr von Reichenstein, ihr

Vetter. Julie, Lottgens Kammerjungfer. Johann, Bedienter des Herrn von Ehrenwald. Der Schauplatz ist in einem Zimmer des Präsidenten, welches an den Speisesaal stößt.

Financially desperate and struggling to feed his old father, the honest Ehrenwald is suspected of stealing a gold case at the President's dinner party. The other guests agree to be searched, but Ehrenwald refuses. Reichenstein takes steps to offset a family disgrace by calling in the authorities before a servant confesses the theft and clears the accused. He had refused the search, ashamed that his pockets contained leftovers meant for his father. The old man rejoices in his beloved son's devotion, Lottgen pledges her love, Ehrenwald receives her hand and a promised income from Reichenstein.

C (1a) Yr 4356

D Highly sentimental and improbable.

A **Gespenster, Die, oder Aberglauben und Unglauben.** Ein Nachspiel in drey Aufzügen. [Johann Christian Ast.] *Neue Theatralische Versuche entworfen von einem Verehrer der Schaubühne.* Breßlau u. Leipzig: Pietsch, 1757. [285]-330, 8+9+4 Auftritte.

B Herr Afterglaube, ein Bürger zu Schilde. Babchen, seine Tochter. Mag. Leberecht, sein Sohn. Marqvis de Rien. Mons. de la Sage. Crispin, des letztern Diener. Merlin, Diener des Marqvis. Herr Ehrlich, Küster in Schilde. Falentine, der Babchen Bedientinn. Giruntie, ein altes Weib. Der Schauplatz ist theils die öffentliche Straße, theils das Haus des Herrn Afterglaubes.

On her deathbed, Babchen's mother has promised her to Ehrlich but the cynical and unscrupulous Marquis seeks her too and must overcome Herr Afterglaube's religious superstitions and fear of contradicting the deceased's last wish. He uses Merlin and Giruntie as a disguised soothsayer and ghost to convince Afterglaube to relent and make him Babchen's suitor. De la Sage has come to avenge the Marquis's earlier mistreatment of his sister and with Crispin's help also uses disguise and superstition to frighten the Marquis and Merlin into admitting their deception. The Marquis agrees to make amends to Mlle de la Sage and Babchen is promised to de la Sage after Ehrlich withdraws his claim.

C (H) 19/798

D Although a comic action, serious social thematics: superstition versus genuine spirituality; religion guided by reason; contemporary references to dispute beween rational philosophy and Pietism; the institution of marriage as social stabilizer and the threat to society from those who undermine it.

The Magister and Merlin are *raisonneurs*, the former representing sound rational philosophy with respect for religious spirituality. Many traditional comic techniques: song, statement 'ad spectatores,' ghost effects, disguise, and transformations. See analysis p 242.

A **glückliche Entdeckung, Die.** Ein Nachspiel von Theodor Hell [Karl Gottfried Theodor Winkler]. Leipzig: Weigel, 1806. [1]-94. 19 Scenen.

B Herr von Klingenthal, ein Landedelmann. Fritz sein Sohn, Offizier. Frau von Feldheim. Aglaja, ihre [Stief-]Tochter. Blatzmann, Verwalter des Klingenthalischen Guthes. Marie, seine Tochter. Erdmann, Dorfrichter. Christian, sein Sohn. Die Scene spielt im Park des Klingenthalischen Guthes.

   Two young couples are in love, Fritz and Marie, Aglaja and Christian. The former are refined, with a sense for literature, the latter delightfully simple, with a love of rural life. Socially, each is a mismatch. Fritz will defy convention, but Marie refuses. Christian and Aglaja plan to break social barriers by eloping. The inclinations of each directly contradict parents' intentions, especially those of Frau v. Feldheim who is determined to educate Aglaja in the arts, despite the girl's disinterest. Blatzmann, good-natured but ignorant, has no understanding of Marie's intellect. A happy resolution is assured for all when it is discovered that the two young women were exchanged as infants, so in fact each can now marry the partner appropriate in birth and disposition.

C (ÖNB) 626440 ATh

D An interesting and lively plot, often clever language. Underlying thematics encompass serious analysis and criticism of contemporary society and the arts: marriage and social class, aesthetic sensitivity, naive simplicity vs. pretended sophistication. Comedy through dialogue and situation, as well as devices of eavesdropping, mistaken identity, and seduction. See analysis p 245.

A **Glycine,** ein tragisches Nachspiel. *Neue Erweiterungen der Erkenntnis u. des Vergnügens,* Bd. 7. Frankfurt u. Leipzig: Lankisch, 1756. 54-73. 11 Auftritte. Rhymed alexandrines.

B Nicer. Glycine, seine Gemahlinn. Eurot. Timav, Freund des Eurot. Hormine, Schwester der Glycine. Ein Bedienter. Der Schauplatz ist in Nicers Hause.

   Having had his advances rejected by Glycine, the villainous Eurot seeks revenge by convincing Nicer that she has been unfaithful with Timav, whom he blackmails into collaboration. Timav, racked with guilt, seeks

Glycine's forgiveness and is discovered with her by Nicer who takes this as
final evidence of her infidelity. He forces her to take poison before a note arrives from Eurot revealing the truth, but not soon enough to prevent her
death. Her last words are an expression of joy at having been exonerated.

C (21) Kb 80 a.80

D High tragic tone and black conclusion unusual in Nachspiel genre. Verbose
heroic pomposity reminiscent of Baroque tragedy.

Harlekins Heirath, see **Tugend**

A **Harlequin, der ungedultig-hernach aber mit Gewalt gedultig gemachte
Hahnrey.** In einem Sing-Spiel als eine lustige Nach-Comödie vorgestellt.
[Frankfurt a. M.], 1743. [i], 101-20. X Scenae. Verse (rhymed iambic trimeter,
tetrameter, and pentameter).

B Harlequin, der geplagte Hahnrey. Columbina, seine schöne junge Frau, und
Amantin der Franzosen. Monsieur Partout, ein Französischer Domestique,
der bey der verkehrten Regierung als Richter zu befehlen hat, und der
Columbinae Liebhaber ist. Monsieur Charle, auch ein Französischer Domestique, der in dem Orte plagen und schinden hilfft, gleichfalls der
Columbinae Liebster. Frau Liese, der Columbinae getreue Nachbarin, die
zu der Hahnreyschafft des Harlequins Viel beyträgt. Krips, Kraps, zwey
Häscher. Das Theatrum ist Häuser und Gasse.
   With the help of Partout, the unfaithful Columbina resists Harlequin's
attempts to bring her to justice and with her neighbour's assistance also foils
his plan to catch her with Charle. The final scene presents him defeated
with babies and cuckold's horns.

C (H) 2/53

D Bound and published with *Franzosen in Böhmen*, als eine theatralische
Comödie mit allen zu der Zeit geschehenen Begebenheiten lächerlich
vorgestellet von einem dabey gewesenen Teutschen. Nebst einem lustigen
Sing-Spiel zu einer Nach-Comödie / genannt: *Harlequin* ... 1743. *Franzosen*,
[1]-100; *Harlequin*, [i], 101-20.
   A brief Foreword to the work describes it as a 'Nachspiel' and refers indirectly to the reader: 'durchlaufft die paar Blätter zu einer kurzen Zeit'
(102). The work contains a host of traditional comic devices including well-
known character types, beatings, comments to the audience, asides, disguises, and stage directions indicating extemporization. See analysis p 162.

A **Haß und Neid.** In einem Nach-Spiele, aus dem Holländischen, mit einiger Veränderung. Joh[ann] Fr[iedrich] v. Uffenbach. *Gesammelte Neben-Arbeit in gebundenen Reden.* Hamburg: König u. Richter, 1733. [257]-320. 20 Auftritte. Alexandrine verses with frequent variation.

B Neidhart, ein Schuhflicker. Hedwig, dessen Weib. Reinhold, ein Schuh-flicker und Nachbar des vorigen. Wanfried, ein Wirth. Judith, dessen Weib. Grete, deren Magd und Braut des Reinhold. Werner, Haus-Knecht. Vait, Wendel, Zween Spitzbuben. Ein Reffträger. Ein Notarius. Der Schauplatz stellet eine Strasse von einer Stadt vor, an deren beyden Ecken zwo Werck-stätte oder Winckel für Schuhflicker sich befinden.

The two cobblers represent opposite human types, Neidhart a whining pessimist, Reinhold a cheerful optimist, which irritates his neighbour who takes every opportunity to slander Reinhold's character. His wife Hedwig's honest objections are silenced by means of verbal and physical abuse. A notary appears with news that Reinhold has inherited a large sum. This heightens Neidhart's jealousy and he convinces Grete that Reinhold is a thief, almost destroying their engagement before she comes to her senses with encouragement from Wanfried and Judith. Events take a sudden turn after Reinhold's inheritance arrives in sacks and the thieves Vait and Wendel close in to steal it. They are accidentally disturbed by Neidhart and Hedwig, and they stab the surly shoemaker while making their escape. Help arrives, but too late to prevent Neidhart's death. Little sympathy is expressed for the deceased and no tears are shed. We are left with the lesson that hate and envy will receive their just rewards.

C (ÖNB) *38.Z.16

D Below title: 'Rerum magnarum parva potest res / Exemplare dare & vestigia notitiai.' ['The small thing can give the pattern of the large, and a clue to its understanding,' from Lucretius 2, 123-4; but in the original Lucretius is explaining that one can get an idea of the activity of molecules/atoms in the primeval void by observing the behaviour of dust in a sunbeam.]

A long-winded work with an unusually harsh moral lesson. Rough manners and language; violent actions. Neidhart's death is a rare exception among Nachspiele. Curious speech by Wanfried in final pages (318f) in which a case is made for instructive tragic drama set among the common folk. See analysis p 238.

Hauswirth unter Siegel, Der, see **Herr Habicht**

A **Heirathslustigen, Die.** Nachspiel in einem Aufzuge. Elise Bürger. *Sämmtliche theatralische Werke von Elise Bürger, geb. Hahn,* Bd. 1. Lemgo: Meyer, 1801. [63]-130. 18 Scenen.

B Lord Henry Sieber, ein reicher Engländer. Wilhelm, sein Bedienter. Peter Veit, ein Pachter. Baron von Zierlich, ein alter Landedelmann. Magister Beißan, Candidatus Philosophiae. Monsieur Poltron, Fechtmeister. Herr Mondschein. Niklas Rebensaft, Barbier. François sans Chagrin, ein Schneider. Susanna Geldlieb, eine alte Kammerjungfer. Frau von Lieblich, eine Betschwester. Frau Grimmig, Wirthin zum goldnen Schwan. Madame Ricobert, Gouvernante. Mamsell Springinsfeld, Tänzerin. Signora Zechini, Opernsängerin. Mamsell Joli, Putzmacherin. Jungfer Fröhlich. Sechs Matrosen. Die Scene ist in Amsterdam, anfangs im goldnen Schwan, hernach freier Platz am Hafen.

Lord Sieber has won 80,000 guilders, of which he has reserved 70,000 to give away equally to seven couples willing to marry by lottery and move to his plantation in the West Indies. Responding to a newspaper advertisement, fourteen willing subjects arrive, seven men first, then seven women, a scene devoted to each. From their appearance and self-introductions, it is clear that they are a motley collection of fools and tired failures. As they prepare for the lottery, Jungfer Fröhlich arrives unexpectedly, not to join in, but seeking help, for she is penniless. Lord Sieber is taken by her charm, discovers she is a distant cousin, and proposes marriage. The lottery is then drawn, the seven couples file off to the ship, Lord Sieber and his fiancée remain to start a new life together.

C (17) 41/4459

D After list of personae is a detailed description of major characters' costumes with some indicators of the characters' age, bearing, and personality type (65-8). Unusually large cast. Closing song. Highly improbable and artificially constructed action. Some humour through caricature.

A **Herr Habicht, oder der Hauswirth unter Siegel.** Nachspiel nach dem Französischen von Theodor Hell [Karl Gottfried Theodor Winkler.] Leipzig: Hinrichs, 1809. [i], [1]-48. 16 Scenen.

B Herr Habicht, Tabakshändler und Hausbesitzer. Falk, ein junger Musiker. Victorine, seine Schwester. Hannchen, ein Landmädchen. Diapazon, Lautenist und Klavierspieler, etwas taub. Kanne, Weinhändler. Ein Gerichtskommissar. Gerichtsdiener. Die Scene spielt in Habichts Hause, im fünften Stock.

Falk and Victorine owe Habicht three months' rent with no prospects of paying either him or their other creditors Diapazon and Kanne. They decide to sell their books and musical instruments, but their most valued possession, a portrait of Victorine, Falk refuses to let go. As is his custom, Habicht comes to collect while Falk is out, intending also to court Victorine; ridiculous, he throws himself at her feet, offering to cancel their debt in exchange for the portrait. He hears Falk returning and, fearing a beating, locks himself in the bookcase with the portrait, leaving his purse behind. Court officers arrive to repossess the furniture, followed closely by Falk who notices the purse and missing portrait, drawing the obvious conclusion. Creditors arrive and he pays them with Habicht's money. Discovering Habicht's hiding place, the feisty Falk threatens to throw him down the stairs in the bookcase until the terrified landlord agrees to give them three months to pay their debt and thereafter to leave Victorine alone.

C   (1a) Ys 2680

D   Despite considerable comic potential, an unremarkable work.

A   **Herrschaft der Weiber, Die.** Ein Nachspiel in einem Aufzug, von Siegmund Immanuel Mathesius. Frankfurt u. Leipzig, 1768. [1]-36. 13 Auftritte.

B   Geronte. Melusine, dessen Frau. Lorgen, dessen Tochter. Anton, ein Gerichtssecretair. Damis. Heinrich, dessen Bedienter.
Damis seeks Lorgen's hand but has offended her father by insisting that all men are ruled by their wives. We see convincing evidence in the person of Melusine who not only controls her husband but also all decisions of the local courts, and in arbitrary, hard-hearted fashion. Damis enlists Heinrich's help to convince Geronte, whereupon the servant appears as a cavalier to argue the case at length. Finally, he offers to give Geronte a horse, but Geronte is incapable of choosing the beast without his wife's approval. Thus Heinrich rests his case, crowning Geronte with a huge pair of winged spectacles. In conclusion, Damis surrenders further negotiations to Lorgen, resigned to the fact that he too must submit to the authority of her sex.

C   (ÖNB) 627601 ATh

D   While Heinrich's role has comic potential, it labours under ponderous dialogue. A blunt, unsophisticated work showing little imagination.

A   **Herr Witzling.** Ein deutsches Nachspiel in einem Aufzuge. [L.A.V. Gottsched.] Joh. Chr. Gottsched, Hrsg., *Der deutschen Schaubühne, nach den*

Regeln und Mustern der Alten. 6. Theil, Leipzig: Breitkopf, 1745. [509]-551. 9 Auftritte.

B   Herr Reinhart, ein reicher Kaufmann in Leipzig. Jungfer Lottchen, seine Unmündige. Der junge Reinhart, sein Sohn, ein junger Advocat. Herr Witzling, ein junger Mensch, der nur unlängst Studierens wegen nach Leipzig gekommen und bey dem Herrn Reinhart im Hause wohnet. Herr Rhomboides, ein junger Gelehrter. Herr Jambus, ein junger Dichter. Paul, ein Diener. Der Schauplatz ist auf Jungfer Lottchens Zimmer. Die Handlung fängt, gleich nach der Mittagsmahlzeit an, und endiget sich gegen 5 Uhr.

Lottchen's fortune is controlled by the well-meaning Herr Reinhart who, to her horror, means to pair her with Witzling, the son of a business friend. This plot line is abandoned for most of the play and resumed only at the conclusion, as Witzling escapes in panic after a confusion of letters has exposed his insincerity and stupidity. The central action consists of a humorous discussion involving Lottchen, young Reinhold, Witzling, Rhomboides, and Jambus on philosophy, poetics, mathematics, and particularly the German language. The last three characters show appalling ignorance and resolve to found a 'deutsche Sprachschnitzergesellschaft,' an appropriate order for their linguistic and literary talents.

C   (25) E4246,a-6

D   Little action or plot; essentially an amusing dramatic discussion and satire on contemporary issues, with reference to Newtonian mathematics, Wolffian philosophy, Gottsched's linguistic reforms, and the *Schaubühne* itself. Weak correction of social vice (Witzling).

In the *Vorrede* to the volume Gottsched comments on the Nachspiel, claiming to have received it from an unknown person. Since its tone and content fit his intentions for the collection, he decided to include it, but took the liberty to make some editorial changes to soften the satire and avoid all possibility of personal reference (xviiif). See analysis p 264.

A   **Heyrath aus Liebe.** Ein Nachspiel mit Arien und Gesängen [in 2 Aufzügen]. [Schack Hermann Ewald.] Gotha: Ettinger, 1781. [1]-80, 10 + 4 Auftritte.

B   Baron von Wildenberg. Caroline von Wildenberg, dessen Nichte. Wilhelm, Graf von Lingen. Konrad, sein Jäger. Junker von Krach. Junker von Rosenblatt. Hannchen, Carolinens Dienstmädchen. Lehnchen, ein Bauermädchen auf dem Guthe des Fräuleins. Die Scene ist, im ersten Akt, ein freyer auf den Seiten mit Gebüsch umgebener Platz vor dem Landhause des Fräuleins und ihres Onkels, und im zweyten Akt ein Spatziergang im Holze.

The wealthy young Wilhelm and Caroline are devoted to each other but he hides his identity, afraid that she, as others before, seeks his wealth. Both Junker and the bellicose Krach, and also the milksop Rosenblatt, seek her hand, Krach with the Baron's support. By pretending in turns to be an outcast, criminal, and gadabout, the Count tests Caroline's love before revealing his true identity and absolute devotion. The two are betrothed with the Baron's blessing.

C   (GMC)

D   Only simplistic dramatic action and dialogue, yet filled with delightful arias, duets, ensemble pieces. Wilhelm's test of loyalty and Caroline's steadfastness a humorous excess. Gentle social commentary underlying: importance of genuine feeling over social and financial status in marriage; freedom of young woman to choose partner over authority of guardian. See analysis p 254.

A   **Heyrath der Thorheit, Die.** Als ein Nachspiel zu den verliebten Thorheiten [Jean-François Regnard's 'divertissement' to his *Les Folies amoureuses*, 1704]. *Des Herrn Regnard sämtliche theatralische Werke aus dem Französischen übersetzt*, 2. Theil. Berlin: Nicolai, 1757. [145]-162. 5 Auftritte.

B   Clitander, Erasts Freund. Erast. Agathe. Albert. Lisette. Crispin. Momus. Die Thorheit. Das Carnaval. Ein Haufe Masquen.

Clitander and Erast look forward to Erast's wedding with Agathe, but fear the interference of old Albert. They are interrupted by a joyful parade of masques, led by Thorheit and Carnaval who are themselves in love and betrothed. There follows much playful talk on love and marriage, interspersed with songs and dances. Albert enters, seeking Agathe, and accepts Thorheit's advice: leave love to the young and lose yourself now in wine.

C   (ÖNB) 845000/122 ATh

D   Bright and merry theatrical fluff. Mélange of dialogue, song, dance, and costumes. The characters of the Nachspiel are taken from *Les Folies amoureuses*, with the exception of Clitander, Thorheit, Carnaval, and the masques, as is the general theme of love and marriage.

A   **hinkende Bothe, Der, oder die aufgehobene Belagerung von Neiß.** Ein Nachspiel in drey Auftritten. [Johann Heinrich Gottlob Justi.] Im November 1758. [1-6.] 3 Auftritte. Rhymed alexandrines.

B Der General Harsch. Der Französische Oberlieutenant Mr. de Cribaval. Des
   General Harsch Secretaire. Des General Harsch Adjutant.

   Just when Harsch is on the verge of taking and plundering Neiß (for his
   Empress Maria Theresia), word arrives that the enemy king (Frederick II of
   Prussia) is underway with sixty thousand men. Harsch opts for quick with-
   drawal to save his skin.

C (1a) Yr 3031

D Bound and published following *Die Rechnung ohne Wirth, oder das eroberte
   Sachsen*. Ein Lustspiel in drey Auftritten, place of publication and publisher
   unknown, 1758. Title-page to volume includes both works. *Die Rechnung*
   plays 'im grossen Garten vor Dreßden' and deals directly with the siege of
   Neiß and Harsch's withdrawal. Feldmarschall Daun prepares to profit from
   Harsch's taking of Neiß and to liberate Saxony for his empress [Maria
   Theresia], but abruptly changes plans when he hears of Harsch's difficulties.

   A second copy in (1a) is paginated [1]-10 (*Rechnung*), [11]-16 (*Bothe*), but
   otherwise identical to the one above (Sig Yr 3032). In a third printing, also
   1758 and in (1a), the texts of the two plays are the same as the above (except
   for minor differences), but *Bothe* is printed first as a 'Trauerspiel in drey
   Auftritten,' followed by *Die Rechnung*, an order more in keeping with the
   sequence of events portrayed in the two works, although it is difficult to
   understand the genre designation 'Trauerspiel' (Sig Yr 3037).

   A manuscript of *Rechnung* and *Bothe*, the same as the published versions
   (with minor differences), carrying the date 'Im November 1758,' is located in
   the ÖNB Handschriftensammlung, Cod 13935.

   Bothe is a fragmentary work, perhaps a brief version of a longer one. The
   'hinkend' reference in the title is not evident from the text, unless understood metaphorically. The geographic reference is likely to the city of Neiße
   (now the Polish Nysa) in Upper Silesia and the period perhaps the Silesian
   Wars of 1740-2 and 1744-5, although more likely the Seven Years' War 1756-
   63 because of French involvement. All three wars involved Prussian King
   Frederick II's attempts to gain possession of Silesia from Austria and Empress Maria Theresia. Authorship is uncertain, but the work may well have
   stemmed from Justi. Perhaps this would also explain its dramatic weakness,
   for creative writing was hardly Justi's vocation (see Chapter 9 above, p 271).

A **Hirten der Alpen, Die.** Ein Nachspiel. Nach der Erzählung von Marmontel.
   [David Christoph Seybold.] Leipzig: Weygand, 1777. [1]-64. 8 Auftritte.

B Sophie, Die Hirtin, eigentlich Gräfin von Orestan. Jakob, ein Hirte,
   eigentlich der Marquis von Fonrose, aus Turin. Paul, der alte Hirte, bey

dem Sophie sich aufhält. Marie, seine Frau. Frizchen. Der alte Marquis von Fonrose. Die Marquise. Ein Bürger aus dem benachbarten Städtchen. Die Scene stellt einen Wald vor.

Four months ago Jakob had seen the shepherdess Sophie, was enchanted, and followed her to this idyllic place where she has lived for four years with Marie and Paul. Both suspect noble heritage of the other, and Sophie first tells her story. She is an Austrian noblewoman who left her home against family wishes to follow her husband, Count Orestan. But the count suffered a military dishonour and before her eyes took his own life on this spot. She buried him there and has stayed to mourn him ever since. Her grief is so great that Jakob cannot hope to make her his own. Maria and Paul, Sophie's surrogate parents, arrive and tell of a lad who has been saved from drowning by a valiant anonymous shepherd. Jakob's parents, the Marquis and Marquise of Fonrose, arrive, overjoyed to have found their missing son. They hear of Sophie and are taken by her charms. Sophie then learns Jakob's true identity, and also that he is in fact the shepherd who saved the child, Frizchen. She reveals now that Frizchen is her own son, a dear reminder of her marriage with Orestan. She offers her hand to Jakob in affection and gratitude, and all rejoice at the union.

C (ÖNB) 392.620/91 A

D Marmontel's tale, *La Bergère des Alpes*, was translated into German and had appeared in three editions by 1769 (*Moralische Erzählungen* [Carlsruhe: Macklot]) under the title *Die Hirtinn der Alpen*. Marmontel also treated the same material in dramatic form, *La Bergère des Alpes* en trois actes, et en vers, mêlée de chant, with music included in the published version (Paris: Merlin, 1766).

Dedication to Hofrath von Wöllworth in Anspach (3). In a foreword directed to a dear personal friend addressed simply as 'Baron,' the author compares his play with its source and discusses some of its features (5-18). One reason for casting his ideas in this form, he explains, is 'weil ich etwa kurz zuvor in einem Journale oder in einer Zeitung Klagen über Mangel an Nachspielen gelesen hatte' (7). The work itself contains artificial characters, stilted language, and a thoroughly incongruous plot amid bucolic surroundings in the *Schäferspiel* tradition.

A **Hochzeittag.** Ein Nachspiel in zwey Akten. Von -t-. Halle: Curts Wittwe, 1789. [1]-52. 13 + 13 Auftritte.

B Eduard Reder, ein junger Arzt. Ludwig Förner, Sekretair. Elias Mehzeg, Landprediger. Bernhard Mehzeg, dessen Vater, ein Gewürzkrämer.

Schlucker, ein alter Advokat. Superintendent Mirow. Pastor Rothstof. Seine
Frau. Frau Willmer, eine reiche Wittwe, und Mutter von Wilhelmine
Willmer, Braut des Landgeistlichen. Albertine Lichter, ihre Freundin, und
Reders Wirthin. [Albertinens Mädchen. Friedrich, Reders Bedienter.
Hochzeitsgäste.]

Act I: Reder is growing more despondent as his secret love, Wilhelmine,
is to marry pastor Mehzeg tomorrow. The feeling is mutual, but Wilhelmine
must follow her mother's wishes. Frau Willmer sees no better match, thoroughly taken in by the pious and calculating cleric, oblivious to his pecu-
niary motives. Förner, a loyal friend, himself in love with Albertine,
promises to set things right with Schlucker's help. Act II: Wedding day and
Mehzeg prepares his new wig, suspicious that Frau Willmer will withhold
the dowry. Schlucker enters for a private word of advice, and beyond the
audience's hearing they appear to agree. Thereafter the pastor disappears as
the wedding guests arrive. He finally enters dramatically, holding a written
set of conditions for the dowry payment, and states that he will not proceed
until the mother has signed. Frau Willmer is suddenly enlightened as to his
motives, confronts and reproaches him, allowing Reder to step forth as able
and popular replacement.

C (ÖNB) 845000/131 ATh

D Conventional but entertaining. Unusually large cast. Comment on the values of country clergy and enlightenment of those who see through such
false piety. See analysis p 242.

A **Hypochondrist, Der.** Nachspiel. Johann Christian Brandes. Berlin: Birnstiel,
1767.

C Kayser, VI, 103

A **Instinkt, Der, oder Wer ist Vater zum Kinde?** Ein Nachspiel von J.F. Jünger
[Charles sieur de la Rivière du Fresny, *Le faux instinct*, 1707]. Aufgeführt im
k.k. National-Hoftheater. Wien: beym Logenmeister, 1785. [1]-34. 15
Auftritte.

B Frau von Seefeld, eine Hauptmannswittwe, in Trauer. Der alte Brenner, ein
Kaufmann. Madame Brenner. Wilhelm Brenner, sein Neffe. Sophie,
Schwester der Madame Brenner. Rösgen, ein kleines Mädchen. Peter, ein
Bauer. Dore, seine Frau. Frau Rinteln, Haushälterin der Frau von Seefeld.
Die Handlung ist auf einem Dorfe.

After four years of absence, the middle-aged Frau v. Seefeld and old
Brenner, now with a new young wife, return separately to claim their respective children from Peter and Dore, to whom they each entrusted a child
after birth in exchange for regular payments. But there is just one child now,
the delightful little Rösgen. Peter claims that both of their children contracted chicken-pox in infancy, that one died, and that the confusion left
them unable to identify which child survived. In sub-intrigues, Wilhelm
hopes that the child is not Brenner's, as he wishes himself sole heir, and
Frau v. Seefeld also prefers to abandon the child who might interfere with
her plans to attract a new suitor. Each offers Peter a reward for his assistance. Rösgen is then asked to identify her own parents, it being assumed
that instinct will suffice, but she chooses the young Madame Brenner and
Wilhelm, rejecting the old claimants out of hand. Finally, the sly farmer
produces documents proving that the child is in fact his own, both other infants having died years ago. He cashes in the rewards and all subsistence
monies accumulated to date as well.

C (H) 23/1028

D A complicated and interesting humorous intrigue, suitable for a longer
work. A final page added after the text [35] reports that Jünger wrote the
Nachspiel for the Vienna Hoftheater where it would soon be performed,
and that it had already been seen in the Theater in der Leopoldstadt.

A **Isaac und Rebecca, Oder die Kluge Vorsichtigkeit, Welche dey dem
Heyrathen zu beobachten,** Durch eine kurtze Theatralische Aufführung In
leichter und ungezwungener Poëtischer Schreib-Arth vorgestellet, Mit
Beyfügung eines Lustigen Nach-Spiels, Worinn der Harlequin fünff, in
einer Person sich nicht wohl zusammen schickende Bedienungen/ Nehmlich Eines Herren-Dieners, Nacht-Wächters, Bier-Rüffers, Thor-Hüters, und
Kuh-Hirtens zusammen verwaltet. Zur nüztlichen Ergötzung aufgesetzet
Von Jodoco Thüringern. Frankfurt/Oder: Schrey, 1722. *Isaac u. Rebecca*:
[i-xiii], [1]-41. 5 Handlungen. Alexandrines with arias in tetrameters. *Nachspiel*: 42-82. 20 Auftritte.

B Carsten Leberwurst, Richter in dem Flecken Rumpelsdorff. [Merten But-
termilch, sein Knecht.] Stephen Rundhut, dessen Beysitzer. Ursel Kuh-
schwantz, des Richters Base. Semper-Lustig, oder der Harlequin. Curt Fle-
derwisch, ein Rumpelsdorffischer Inwohner. Keiff-Anne, dessen Frau. Tön-
nies Lämmerfuß, Schaaffmeister zu Rumpelsdorff.
Matzpump, who had previously filled the jobs described in the Nachspiel's title, has died and Leberwurst with Rundhut must name his succes-

sor. They choose the apparently clever and adroit Harlequin on condition
that he marry Ursel, a true bumpkin. He agrees, but his first day on the job
is a disaster, leaving the town up in arms. Clever enough to anticipate his
demise, Harlequin takes leave to a merry tune, and to cherished freedom,
instead.

C   (32) 0,9:368

D   *Isaac und Rebecca* is preceded by a foreword [iii-xiii] signed 'Jodocus
Thüringer' in which the author defends the aesthetics of both works to follow. His tone suggests that he expected criticism as part of an ongoing debate. This is followed by a short plot summary of *Isaac und Rebecca* [xiiif], a
play based on Genesis, Chapter 24, in which Abraham sends one of his servants to Mesopotamia to find a wife for his son. As the story goes, Rebecca
was chosen because of her warm generosity in welcoming the servant to her
land and providing refreshment for him and his camels. She and Isaac are
thus joined in marriage in the end.

The Nachspiel is also preceded by a brief plot summary (42). The work
depends for its comic effect on verbal misunderstandings, heavy misuse of
foreign terms (Latin, French), Ursel's dialect, slapstick antics, beatings,
ridiculous characters, and satire on the pompous town officials. See analysis
p 154.

A   **Jacobiner, Die.** Ein Nachspiel in einem Aufzuge [nach dem Französischen.
Wien,] 1794. [1-5], 6-61. 16 Auftritte.

B   Secretair Neuwing. Chevalier de Morau, Marquis de Vie, Jacobiner. George,
Michel, Veist, Himpel, Conrad, Sansculotes. Wirth. Anne [Georgs Frau]. Ihr
Vater. Pfarrer. Schloßbedienter. Peter, ein Bauer-Pursch. 2 Bauern. Wache.

Neuwing is full of bitterness because his scholarly contribution to society
has not been sufficiently acknowledged and rewarded. He has become a
revolutionary, bent on upsetting the social order and overturning the lord
of the region to whom they all report. He is visited by the two Jacobins who
see in him an ally for their cause; beneath their flattery, they secretly plan to
use him and other naive German intellectuals as pawns in their revolutionary plan. The spirit of freedom and equality has also caught fire among
the Sansculotes who hold a meeting to set their strategy. But they are ignorant (and increasingly intoxicated) peasants, enamoured with ideas whose
significance for themselves and society they really fail to grasp. Their crude
understanding and motives become clear when they accept Peter as an new
member, stripping him of his few possessions and threatening execution if
he withdraws. Anne's worry about George and her father's common-sense

warnings go unheeded. In the end the pastor brings the Sansculotes down to earth with a stern warning, praise of the enlightened benevolence of their lord, and news that the two Jacobins have been arrested.

C (Mh28) G 423

D A conservative German reaction to events of the French Revolution. Pencil entry facing title-page: 'In Mannheim nicht aufgeführt.' See analysis p 241.

A **Jedem sein Lohn.** Fragment eines Nachspiels. [Heinrich Leopold Wagner.] *Theater-Journal für Deutschland,* 10, hrsg. v. Heinrich A.O. Reichard. Gotha: Ettinger, 1779. Nachdr.: *Das deutsche Theater des 18. Jahrhunderts,* hrsg. v. Reinhart Meyer. München: Kraus, 1981. 14-42. No internal divisions.

B Pfarrer Laudikius. Frau Laudikius, seine Mutter. Christine, Schwester des Pfarrers. Inspektor Spitzkopf. Stabhalter Gudjan. Doktor Belzer. Riem, ein Schneider. Der Schauplatz ist im Pfarrhaus, eine Stunde von der Stadt; die Handlung geht um drei Uhr an.

   The conscientious Pfarrer labours to repay the debts of his dead father and to comfort his sickly mother in her last years. His sister is a burden not a help, living in a world of pious fantasy. Spitzkopf, a cynic, whose own dishonesty is shown by his evasion of a debt due to Riem, assures the pastor that Belzer, who holds the pastor's note, will show no charity. Appalled, Gudjan offers a gift which the proud Laudikius refuses. Here the action breaks off, but the author, signed [Heinrich Leopold] Wagner, offers a synopsis of the unwritten conclusion (41-2): Belzer appears with the due note but burns it dramatically, freeing the pastor of debt, at the same time announcing that Spitzkopf has been found guilty of embezzlement, relieved of his post, and ordered to leave the land. To each, thus, his due!

C (25) TZ493/10/1779

D Not a comic piece; serious social themes underlie the action: the effects of money and debt; bourgeois avarice and cynicism; dishonesty among civic officials. See analysis p 253.

Johann Scherenschleifer, see bestrafte Hochmuth, Der

A **Juliane Dürrbach** in einem Aufzuge. Nach Sprickmanns Erzählung des Intelligenzblatt. *Nachspiele zum Behuf teutscher Theater,* hrsg. v. G.E.[C.] Claudius. Frankfurt u. Leipzig: Brönner, 1783. [1]-38, 18 Scenen.

B   Franz Dürrbach, ein Krämer in einem kleinen Städtchen. Marie, seine Frau.
Juliane, ihre Tochter. Wilhelm Grünwald, ein junger Advokat, Julianens
Liebhaber. Meister Elis, ein Metzger. Jakob, Grünwalds Bedienter. [Röse,
Dienstmädchen bei Dürrbachs]. Die Handlung geht in einer kleinen Stadt
vor – Darnach wird sich auch das Costume bestimmen müssen.

Juliane is betrothed to Grünwald who has gone to collect his inheritance
before marriage. Juliane fears the worst as Grünwald delays reunion upon
his return, but remains steadfast and gushingly sentimental in her loyalty.
Jakob reports that Grünwald must withdraw his wedding promise, where-
upon Juliane's father sets to avenge his misplaced confidence in Grünwald
and absorb ridicule from the coarse Elis who had sought Juliane for his own
son. Grünwald explains that his benefactor confessed upon his death to
have gained his fortune through deceit; the virtuous Grünwald hence
surrendered his claim, only to learn now that Juliane's very father was his
benefactor's victim. Herr Dürrbach of course in turn surrenders his claim
and blesses the happy couple.

C   (P) 477

D   Strong emotions and sentiment throughout. Bourgeois values and importance of money central. Virtue rewarded. Several stage directions indicating
author's conception of acting and staging needs. See analysis p 251.

A   **jungen Rekruten, Die.** Eine komische Operette in drey Aufzügen, als ein
Nachspiel gemacht für die in dem befreyten Stift zu den Wengen in Ulm
studierende Jugend, und von derselben aufgeführt am Ende des Schul-
jahres 1781. Text und Musik ist von Joseph Lederer, regulierten Chorherrn
in gedachtem Stifte, und Kaiserlichen gekrönten Dichter. Ulm: Wagner,
1781. [i-iv], [1]-35. 6 + 9 + 5 Auftritte. Songs in short rhymed iambic verse.

B   Lieutenant von Stegmann, Werbofficier. Herr Suppe, Vater eines Rekruten.
Herr Göldin, Schullehrer. Ein Feldprediger. Vier junge Rekruten [Adam,
Nemrod, Abraham, Samuel]. Ein Korporal. Ein Profos. Ein Trom-
melschläger. Frau Rindfleischinn, Frau Saurkrautinn, Mütter zweener
Rekruten. 2 Knaben.

I: The boys decide to miss school and become soldiers; they meet
Stegmann who enlists them and provides uniforms. II: After some hard
drilling, the soldier's life seems less attractive than school. All but Samuel
desert. III: The loyal Samuel is rewarded, the deserters threatened with
hanging before mercy is granted and they return to home and school.

C   (122) 17581-588

D A lively and humorous work. Double title-page, pp [i] and [1]. The first
gives two titles, 'Der Chargenverkauf, Ein militärisches Drama, gedruckt zu
Salzburg 1780,' and then 'Die jungen Rekruten' with information as on the
second title-page (cited in A above), save place and publisher, and with the
addition of 'den 3ten 4ten und 6ten des Herbstmonats 1781' as precise performance dates. It would appear that this Nachspiel was intended to follow
the *Chargenverkauf.* P [ii]: personae of both plays. Pp[iii-iv]: brief content
summary of *Rekruten* as well as 'Anmerkungen' concerned with seating in
the theatre, prices for entrance, and printed copies of the Nachspiel, time
and length of performance. These preliminary pages were likely used as
playbills.

A **Kaiser Joseph auf der Reise im Amthause.** Ein Nachspiel in zwey Aufzügen. Coburg: Ahl, 1799. [i-ii], [1]-80. 16 + 10 Auftritte.

B Kaiser Joseph, als Officier. Amtmann Krumm. Gerichtsschreiber Ehrlich.
Commissarius Voll. Pater Plump, der Dorfgeistliche. Jurist Stell. Frau
Krumm, des Amtmanns Frau. Louise, Theres, des Amtmanns Töchter. Frau
Commissarin Voll. Velten, Peter, Michel, Nickel, Herbert, Bauern. Eine
arme Frau. Ein Besenbinder. Ein armes Kind. Berbel, die Hausmagd.

   After hours of waiting, the farmers who have gathered at the Amtmann's
residence to have their produce registered grow impatient and bitter. As
they wait, they tell tales of his corruption and callous behaviour towards
them, their families, and the poor of the region, and wish their good Emperor were closer at hand to alleviate their plight. Meanwhile, the Amtmann and Commissarius Voll, Pater Plump, their wives, and Louise play
cards and drink themselves to intoxication. Ehrlich and Theres plead with
them to interrupt their game to give the poor farmers their due, but the un-
feeling party show no sympathy. Disguised as an officer, Kaiser Joseph appears, hears the farmers' plight, and takes matters into his own hands. The
Amtmann is stunned when his Emperor reveals himself, relieves the corrupt official of his post, and spreads generous donations among the waiting
farmers. The honest Ehrlich is charged with administrative responsibility
for the region and the caring Theres happily agrees to be his wife.

C (70) C III 11/14

D A dramatic testimonial to the benificence of Kaiser Joseph and the benefits
awaiting his loyal followers. Criticism of corrupt civic officials and church-
men. See analysis pp 246 and 253.

A **kindische Vater, Der.** Ein kleines Nachspiel in einem Aufzuge. [Franz
   Xaver Jann.] *Etwas wider die Mode. – Trauer- und Lustspiele ohne ärgerliche Ca-
   ressen, und Heurathen, für die studierende Jugend herausgegeben von Franz Xaver
   Jann* ... 3. Theil. Augsburg: Rieger, 1788. 496-524. 8 Auftritte.

B Der kindische Vater. Klugdünkel, dessen Bruder. Hiesel, Thomerle, Tonele,
   Söhne des kindischen Vaters. Schulmeister. Jergl, Hausknecht. Amtsknecht.
     The boys, aged seventeen, sixteen, and fourteen, are spoiled completely
   by their foolish father, himself of child's mentality. With his blessing they
   terrorize all around with tricks and pranks. Jergl and Klugdünkel convince
   him that they need schooling and he reluctantly agrees to the briefest of
   private lessons from the schoolmaster. The first lesson ends in chaos, the
   schoolmaster resorting to his cane in desperation. But through Klugdünkel's
   influence, the mayor sends a writ commanding the boys to attend regular
   school and catechism. They show first signs of begrudging obedience.

C (ÖNB) 845000/275 ATh

D *Vorbericht* printed below title (496): 'Ja einen Vater spielen wir: / Und dieser
   ist ein ganz gelinder, / Er hat drey ungezogne Kinder, / Und mit dem
   Vater sind es vier. / Es soll uns aber Niemand sagen, / Daß die Geschicht
   nicht glaublich sey; / Denn wir verpfänden unsre Treu: / Sie hat sich wirk-
   lich zugetragen.'
     A work with spirit and much comic potential in language (misunder-
   standings, colloquial flavour) and action (raucous confusion, beatings), no
   doubt of great amusement to contemporary audiences and readers. See
   analysis p 201.

A **Kirschen, Die, oder die Wißbegierde,** ein Nachspiel in einem Aufzuge.
   [Johann Baptist Hirschfeld.] [Frankfurt u. Leipzig, 1783.] [89]-110. 15
   Auftritte.

B Herr von Reinhardt. Fräulein Leonore. Ein Bauerjunge. Karl, ein Bedienter.
   Zwey Bauern. Ein Verwalter.
     Reinhardt instructs Karl to take a box of cherries to Leonore, but the cu-
   rious servant opens them, cannot resist, and eats them all. Leonore visits
   unexpectedly, and Karl is exposed, then given a letter for the Verwalter. Instead of delivering it himself – he fears it contains a directive for his punishment – he assigns the task to a peasant lad who arrives to ask for Reinhardt's help. The boy does as instructed, the Verwalter follows the directive,
   and the lad is beaten. When Reinhardt discovers the injustice, Karl confesses all and is spared for telling the truth in the end. The boy returns
   home with a purse for his poor family and to the incredulous Verwalter

Reinhardt explains the value of truth, enlightened correction, and generosity.

C (ÖNB) 845000/168 ATh

D Entertaining attributes of traditional comedy (disobedient servant, peasant class, physical beatings) mixed with functional enlightened instruction.

A **Klatschen, Die.** Ein Nachspiel in einem Aufzuge. Breßlau u. Leipzig: Daniel Pietsch, 1757. [155]-175. 15 Auftritte.

B Frau Leichtglaubinn, eine Wittwe. Papchen, ihre Tochter. Frau Klappermäulinn, ein altes Weib. Cathrinchen, Papchens Bedientinn. Herr Treulieb, Papchens versprochener Liebster. Windwend, Papchens Liebhaber. Hanns Simplex, Treuliebs Bedienter. [Der Jude]. Der Schauplatz ist das Haus der Frau Leichtglaubinn.

The devious Windwend attempts to gain Papchen by blackening Treulieb's reputation with the aid of the gossip Klappermäulinn and Simplex. He is foiled by the intervention of the Jew [despite his absence from the list of Personae].

C (CRL)

D Printed in same volume after *Die Menechmes, Oder die Zwillings-Brüder*, Ein Schauspiel ..., which is a translation of Jean-François Regnard's *Les Ménechmes ou les Jumeaux*, comédie en cinq actes et en vers (1705). There is no connection to *Die Klatschen*.

A **Klätscher, Der.** Ein Nachspiel. [François-Marie Arouet de] Voltaire. [*L'Indiscret*. Paris, 1725.] *Sammlung einiger Schriften zum Zeitvertreibe des Geschmacks*, 1. Bd, 1. St. Leipzig: Weidmann, 1746. [1]-41. 21 Auftritte.

B Euphemie. Damis [ihr Sohn]. Hortensia [eine junge Witwe, Trasimons Muhme]. Pasquin [Bekannter von Damis und Clitander]. Clitander [Marquis, Liebhaber der Hortensia]. Trasimon. Nerine [Hortensias Bediente].

Euphemie warns the haughty Damis of the dangers of boasting and gossip in court circles. He recounts his recent romantic triumph over Hortensia, but confides in a soliloquy that he plans only to marry her for her wealth, then deceive her daily with Julchen and others. Bristling with vanity, he betrays to Clitander and Trasimon Hortensia's intimate communications, a love note and a self-portrait, and tells them of his plan to deceive her. Incensed, Clitander and Trasimon, with Pasquin's assistance, cause a quarrel between the lovers, and Hortensia decides to test Damis's sincerity at the masquerade ball. Thinking she is Julchen, he unwittingly reveals his duplicity, Hortensia casts him aside and offers her hand to Clitander.

C   (26) Rara 953

D   An unremarkable comedy of French manners.

Kleider machen Leute, see **Verwechselung**

A   **kleinste Lüge ist gefährlich, Die.** Ein Nachspiel in zwey Acten. Nach Herrn von Kotzebue. Grätz, 1800. [*Neue Sammlung deutscher Schauspiele*, Bd. 60, Graz, 1800.] [1]-51. 5 + 5 Auftritte.

B   Graf Seefeld. Emilie, dessen Gemahlinn. Hauptmann Braun. Laura, dessen Gemahlinn. Doctor Waschhaus, Hausarzt beyder Familien. Lottchen, Emiliens Mädchen. Lisette, Laurens Mädchen. Franz, ein alter Bedienter des Grafen Seefeld. Friedrich, Bedienter des Hauptmanns. Die Handlung ist abwechselnd in Seefeld und Brauns Hause, zuletzt in einem Walde.

Emilie had been in love with Braun years ago, but a marriage was impossible as he lacked means. Since then, each has found a loving and devoted partner, although their old feeling for each other remains. Coincidence brings them together alone, but they are seen by Waschhaus who mischievously reports to Seefeld and Laura. Their explanations to their spouses, while not lies, are misleading and defensive, so that both spouses initially consider themselves deceived. The count demands a duel to defend his honour. Through some clever manipulation of written communications, Laura averts a tragedy by proving the innocence of both.

C   (H) 63/2442

D   Resolution of the crisis entirely unbelievable. The servant Friedrich a charming and entertaining complement to the action. *Vorerinnerung*, p [3]: 'Dies kleine Stück entstand aus einer Erzählung des Herrn von Kotzebue im zweyten Band seiner Kinder meiner Laune, unter der Ueberschrift: die kleinste Lüge ist gefährlich. [*Die jüngsten Kinder meiner Laune*, 3. verb. Aufl., Bd. 2, Berlin u. Leipzig, 1806, pp 137-63.] Es schien mir der Inhalt dieser Erzählung zu einer dramatischen Bearbeitung vorteilhaft... [signed] Der Verfasser X.Y.Z.' Author goes on to point out that he has revised Kotzebue's tragic ending to a happy one. Indeed, in Kotzebue's story, the cumulative effect of nine lies causes the count to murder the captain, who on his deathbed swears the countess's innocence, urging the count now to flee the authorities. This he does, never to see his wife again.

kluge Vorsichtigkeit, Die, see **Isaac**

A **kranke Frau, Die.** Ein Nachspiel in einem Aufzuge. Christian Fürchtegott
Gellert. Gellert, *Lustspiele*. Leipzig: Wendler, 1747. Faks-Dr mit einem
Nachwort v. Horst Steinmetz, Stuttgart: Metzler, 1966. [397]-446
[erroneously paginated as 426]. 24 Auftritte.

B Frau Stephan. Herr Stephan. Jungfer Philippine, Stephans Muhme. Jungfer
Henriette, der Frau Stephan Stiefschwester. Herr Wahrmund, ein Chiro-
mantist. Herr Richard.
   A moaning hypochondriac, Frau Stephan commands the constant attention of her doting husband and others around her. Only Philippine doubts
her illness and chastises her bluntly. Wahrmund eagerly reads her palm
and pronounces on her health and welfare, but loses credibility as family
friend Richard supplies an even better remedy, a new dress to appeal to the
patient's vanity. With this she is quickly cured.

C (25) E5175/73-75

D An inspired work.

A **Krispin der geplagte Lehenbediente.** Nachspiel von einem Aufzuge.
Deutsche Schaubühne, Bd. 124, [place of publication and date unknown, but
likely after 1769; Meyer's *Bibliographie* dates the series *Deutsche Schaubühne*
from 1770 through the turn of the century]. [1]-19. 9 Auftritte.

B Baron Scharffhau. Baron Hanenkamp. Krispin, der geplagte Lehenbediente.
Ein Kellner. Das Theater stellet einen Wirtshaussaal vor, worinnen auf beyden Seiten zwey Nebenzimmer sind.
   Attracted by the prospect of a double salary, Krispin accepts two positions at the same time, as servant to each Baron. But when his duties com-
mence, he is lost as both require him simultaneously. Nevertheless, he is
spared a beating for his duplicity by the benevolent masters. In his final
words 'Ad Auditorium' he vows never to serve two masters again.

C (ÖNB) 392620 A

D Effectiveness depends on Krispin's ability to act frantic scenes of dual service. Potential for comedy through improvisation. See analysis p 179.

A **Landprediger, Der.** Ein Nachspiel von Friedrich [Samuel Lucas von]
Eckardt. *Sammlung neuer Original-Stücke für das Deutsche Theater*, Zweyter
Band. Berlin u. Leipzig: Decker, 1778. [1]-23. 6 Auftritte.

B   Erich, ein Pfarrer. Frau Erich. Fritz, elf Jahr alt; Karoline, neun Jahr alt;
Georg, sechs Jahr alt, ihre Kinder. Der Amtsrath. Ein fürstlicher Läufer. Der
Schauplatz ist in der Dorfpfarre. Abends.

The good pastor and his family exist in abject poverty, the mother sick, a
fourth child recently deceased, only a crust to share. They are further
threatened by the harsh Amtsrath who is about to foreclose on their debts
and imprison Erich. At the point of despair, a messenger arrives from their
distant monarch who has learned of their plight and sends a generous gift.
They are now freed of debt and poverty and the Amtsrath will face prose-
cution.

C   (ÖNB) 392620/152 A

D   Melodrama in the extreme with an artificial reversal to save the day. Concern for the plight of the poor and a compliment to the benificent monarch,
but no serious attention to the social problem or its solution. See analysis p
253.

A   **Liebe im Sommer, Die, oder das Schifferstechen.** Nachspiel. Amsterdam:
Jülicher, 1790.

C   Heinsius, IV, 309

A   **Liebe und Vaterland.** Ein Nachspiel in einem Aufzuge von dem Freyherrn
von Bilderbeck. Den 24ten März 1788 auf der Dürkheimer Gesellschafts-
bühne aufgeführt. Dürkheim an der Haard: Pfähler, 1789. [1]-72. Zueig-
nung, Vorrede + 15 Auftritte. [Title in later edition, **Erste Liebe.** Ein Nachspiel in einem Aufzug. *Schauspiele von C [= correctly L(udwig)] F[ranz] von
Bilderbeck*, 2. Bd. Leipzig: Voß, 1801. [133]-211. 15 Auftritte.]

B   Madame Welser, Kaufmanns Wittwe. Sophie, ihre Tochter. Ferdinand
Steinberg, ein englischer Offizier. Carl Werner. Fischmann, Wirth. Lene,
dessen Frau. Christian, Steinbergs Bedienter. Johann, Hausknecht. Die
Handlung ist in einem Gasthofe eines kleinen Land-Städchens.

Steinberg returns excitedly to his homeland, a rich man after twenty
years' service under England in East India. He had left a sweetheart and
sister behind, with whom he has since had no contact. Madame Welser and
Sophie arrive at the same inn. As they have no means, mother urges
daughter to abandon her love for Carl. Sophie is desolate and resists, challenging her mother's understanding of true love. Her mother then speaks
from experience, when two decades ago she was forced to give up her
beloved Steinberg similarly. Sophie acquiesces and they inform the arriving

Carl. Devastated, he hears of Steinberg and gains an interview, volunteering to go to East India to make his fortune. In an extended emotional conversation, they discover that Steinberg is Carl's uncle, and that his sweetheart is in fact the present Madame Welser. The two are reunited in a climactic final scene.

C   L u V: (ÖNB) 845000/180 ATh; E L: (17) 41 3912

D   A work encumbered with pathos and melodramatic sentiment; little action. Scene 13 (54-66, Steinberg and Carl) a prime example. Author inserts instructions for actors before critical Scene 13 (54). Strong patriotic statements (57) and bizarre, distorted impression of foreign lands and cultures (58f). Text dedicated to Ifland [sic] (3). In the *Vorrede* to each edition, the author briefly discusses the Nachspiel as genre. Two other plays in the 1801 edition of Bilderbeck's dramas are designated in the table of contents as Nachspiele, *Das Manuscript* and *Kleider machen Leute*, but on their title-pages as 'Lustspiel' and 'Posse' respectively. Hence they have not been included in this bibliography. See analysis pp 257 and 262.

A   **Liebhabertheater vor dem Parlament, Das.** Ein Nachspiel mit Gesang, aufgeführt auf dem Liebhabertheater zu Reval am Stiftungsfeste desselben. [August v. Kotzebue.] [Frankfurt u. Leipzig, 1790.] [105]-139. 8 Auftritte.

B   Präsident von Güldenkalb. Weibermund / Jaja / Olim / Klatschsieb / Selten / Herz: Parlaments-Räthe. Der Sekretär. Der Fiscal. Ein Advokat. Der Wachmeister. Der Ofenheizer. Die Göttin der Mildthätigkeit. Thalia. Nymphen und Genien. Der Schauplatz ist der Gerichtssaal. In der Mitte eine lange Tafel für die Parlamentsglieder, an der Seite ein Pult für den Sekretär.

The successful local theatre group is under attack and today will be judged. In a long-winded and largely irrelevant diatribe, the Fiscal argues for expulsion claiming in traditional fashion that theatre distracts the local folk from productivity and is generally immoral. The attorney counters, dismissing his arguments and enumerating the benefits of theatre for the community historically and for his own time. However, the parliamentarians have all fallen asleep at the outset. When awakened they pass judgment nevertheless: the theatre is condemned and banned. Herz and Selten alone dissent and are overruled. When the verdict is pronounced, the heavens open to reveal the goddess of clemency, Thalia, and her entourage. With song and ceremony they denounce and overturn the verdict, singing the virtues of art. But the parliamentarians are unmoved and file off to dinner, which has been their chief preoccupation all along.

C   (ÖNB) 845000/180 ATh

D   A satire on local civic justice and philistinism. Allegorical characters and
    depth more commonly found in *Vorspiel*. See analysis p 267.

List gegen List, see Nachspiel zur berühmten Komödie

A   **Lotto, Das, oder der redliche Schulze.** Ein Nachspiel in einem Aufzug. Für
    das Landvolk. [Johann L. Huber.] Stuttgart: mit Mäntlerischen Schriften,
    1779. [1]-56. Prolog + 15 Auftritte. Prologue in loose rhymed iambic pen-
    tameter.

B   Biedermann, der Schulze. Margaretha, dessen Frau. Ehrlich, der Bürger-
    meister. Jacob, der Dorf-Schüz. Der Schulmeister. Vier Richter. Zwey Bau-
    ren. Eine im Kopf verrückte Bäurin. Zwey andere Bauren-Weiber. Zwo
    Scheinheilige. Ein Secretarius von dem Amtshauptmann. Die Scene ist auf
    dem Rathaus, das zugleich des Schulzen Wohnhaus ist, in der Gerichts-
    Stube.
        Prologue to audience (3-6): Speaker describes journey from near
    Straßburg and visit to a church along the way where upon the altar he saw
    Gabriel's goodness overcome the devil and his dice, a lesson for all. Text:
    The village has been overcome by lottery fever, citizens waste their savings
    and incomes, taxes are unpaid. Only Biedermann and the trusty Jacob rec-
    ognize the peril, foresee their collective downfall, and resolve to fight to the
    end. But even their own wives are involved, not to mention the cynical
    schoolmaster to whom Jacob turns for help. Support through the courts fails
    as the judges rule unanimously to keep the lottery. Biedermann appeals to a
    higher power, the Amtshauptmann, and awaits his reply. Meanwhile, he
    and Jacob take matters into their own hands, calling forth all lottery players
    for beatings and jail. An insurrection mounts as the prison and town hall
    are besieged, but the higher authority's reply arrives just in time: all lotter-
    ies are hereafter banned, Biedermann and Jacob rewarded.

C   (ÖNB) 845000/187 ATh

D   Strong social comment and thematics, with Biedermann and Jacob intensely
    self-righteous. Interesting question of judicial authority, for democratic de-
    cision of townfolk is clearly rejected. Severe criticism of cynical and hypo-
    critical schoolmaster for his lack of moral leadership. Tiresomely extended
    moralistic lesson and tone, saved only by dramatic excitement of citizens'
    uprising. Unusually large cast. See analysis pp 244 and 251.

A **lustige Elendt, Das.** Ein Nachspiel. 7 folio Manuskriptseiten. 15 Scenae.

B Herr v. Habenichts. Frau v. Habenichts. Leander, ein Burgers Sohn.
Anselmo, ein Kaufmann. Hanswurst, diener des Leanders. Colombina
[called Lisette], Mädl der Fr. v. Habenichts. Corporal und Wache. Isabella,
H. v. Habenichts Tochter.

The drunkard Frau v. Habenichts is joined by Leander who seeks her
support to marry Isabella. Initially thinking he is attracted to her, and delighted by Leander's gift of a fresh bottle, Frau v. H. nevertheless agrees to
convince her husband. Meanwhile Hanswurst courts Colombina/Lisette.
Frau and Herr v. H. engage in a drunken exchange of insults before
Anselmo arrives with the guards to claim a debt, failing that to have
Habenichts arrested. Leander comes to the rescue, paying the debt and receiving Isabella's hand from her grateful father.

C (ÖNB) Handschriftensammlung, Cod. 13.160, fol.

D Lively, earthy, entertaining. Full dialogue for some scenes, others only
summarized and left for the players to enact. Numerous stage directions re
set changes and improvisation. Arias and duets throughout. See analysis p
109.

Lustspiel auf der Treppe, Das, see Drei Stockwerk hoch

A **Magnetismus, Der.** Nachspiel in einem Aufzug. Von Wilhelm August
Iffland. Mannheim: Schwan u. Götz, 1787. [1]-52. Vorrede + 13 Auftritte.
[Also extant as manuscript, 28 unpaginated leaves, pp. 18^V, 19^r, 28^V blank,
title and author as above.]

B Hofrath Rosenstein, Lieutenant Linden. Konsistorial-Registrator Rendius.
Kantor Sandbach. Karoline, dessen Tochter. Grundmann, ein reducierter
Soldat, Lindens Aufwärter. Franz, Rosensteins Bedienter.

The schoolmaster (Kantor), highly vulnerable to the latest fads and
fashions in the world of learning, has promised Karoline to Rendius despite
her love for Linden. To delay the match she has feigned illness for weeks,
and is guarded by her anxious though loving father. With the help of
Rosenstein, Franz, and Grundmann (disguised as a professor), Linden attempts to steal his beloved from her guardian by staging a magnetic cure,
but the schoolmaster, first taken in, is not deceived. The desired end is
achieved nevertheless as Linden ensures Rendius's withdrawal from the
competition by threat of force. With eyes open, Sandbach gives his daughter
to the man she loves, rushing them straight off to the altar.

C (ÖNB) 626666 ATh [Manuscript: (38) ST Iffl 3555]

D A loose plot with opportunities for comic effects through pantomime, eavesdropping, the curious ceremony of magnetism, and the half-deaf Grundmann as professor. Satire on the practices of magnetism and the gullibility of its adherents, as well as on pompous scholars. Motto on title-page: 'Schließet eure Augen und sehet!' Dedication preceding *Vorrede* (2): 'Der Wahrheit gewidmet.' *Vorrede*, signed W.A. Iffland, Mannheim, 20 May 1787 (3-8): author indicates his intention to satirize extreme forms of contemporary belief in magnetism.

   Cologne manuscript is by a scribe, not the author. It is virtually identical with the published version above. There is also an emended copy of the above edition in Mannheim (Mh28-G189) which contains many written deletions as well as a few entries in at least three different hands but far fewer than the devastating deletions in the Vienna copy of *Die Martinsgänse* (see below). Facing the title-page is the pencil notation: 'Premiere am 21.11.1787.' These emendations to the text may well have been put into effect for the many productions of the work in Mannheim from 1787 on. The deletions for the most part are minor except for pp 32-3 which are struck out almost completely. They contain a discussion about magnetism involving Rosenstein and the Kantor. According to Friedrich Walter (222ff), detailed staging information for *Der Magnetismus* and many other plays performed in Mannheim was available in the so-called *Hauptbücher*, contemporary hand-written documents of the Nationaltheater there (*Der Magnetismus* in *Hauptbuch* I, 27). Unfortunately all of these *Hauptbücher* were lost in the Second World War. See analysis p 197.

A **Martinsgänse, Die.** Nachspiel von Gustav Hagemann. Eisenach: Wittekindt [1798]. [1]-80. 18 Auftritte.

B Kühnow, Prediger eines Marktfleckens. Marthe, seine Frau. Friderici, ein Schauspieldirektor. Hans, ein Bauer. Peter, Wilhelm, Aufwärter in einem Gasthofe. Görge, Ehrlich, Bauern. Anne, Margarethe, Ihre Weiber.

   For the St Martin's Day celebration Kühnow and his wife, despite extremely modest means, had acquired two geese and invited some poor folk to a feast. But the geese have been stolen. With generosity and faith in mankind nevertheless intact, Kühnow plans to offer the few scraps they still have in the house. Friderici, a dear friend from student days, visits unexpectedly and their reminiscing recalls to him that as a young man he was determined to change social attitudes and fight injustice. But he has lost hope in that venture and now strives for impact through the stage as principal of a theatre troupe. Kühnow, surprised at this occupation, neverthe-

less treats his old friend with great warmth and generosity. Hearing that
Friderici needs money, he gives him his last possession of value, a silver
watch, having previously given away his last penny to a needy farmer. But
Friderici's need is a ruse. He has arranged for a table laden with roast geese
and other treats to be delivered along with a gold watch, further gifts, and a
letter of deep appreciation and regard. Kühnow and the delighted guests sit
down to a feast after all, their faith in kindness and generosity bolstered.

C (ÖNB) 626301 ATh

D Highly interesting and provocative comments on contemporary clergy, social classes, the theatre scene, censorship, and moral values. Often biting social criticism. Copy examined is *Soufflierbuch* of Viennese production, containing the censor's handwritten deletions, additions, and notes to performance of [22] June 1800, reflecting sensitivity of contents. See analysis p 276.

A **Maskerade, Die, oder die dreyfache Heyrath.** Ein Nachspiel. [Friedrich
Wilhelm Gotter, nach Philippe-Néricault Destouches, *Le mystère ou les fêtes
de l'inconnu*, 1714.] Gotha: Ettinger, 1773. [1]-76. 20 Auftritte.

B Herr von Orme. Caroline, Rösgen, seine Töchter. Ferdinand, sein Sohn.
Wilhelmine. Julie [Ferdinands Geliebte]. Von Dahl [Carolines Geliebter,
Vetter von Wilhelmine]. Meelhorn. Marthe, Carolinens Mädchen. Heinrich,
Ferdinands Bedienter. Johann, Dahls Bedienter. Die Gräfin Lammfromm.
Michel, ein Gärtner. Masken.

   Orme has just completed the required period of mourning for his recently deceased wife and now rejoices, looking forward to the life of gaiety
which she had always forbidden. He wants a new female companion and is
holding a masquerade ball to begin celebrations. His elder daughter Caroline is promised to old Meelhorn against her will; she and Dahl are in love.
With the prospect of significant financial gain, Orme further promises his
fun-loving son Ferdinand to the fading countess, and she arrives to claim
her prize. Among the masques at the ball, however, are Julie and Dahl.
Amid much confusion made possible by masked immunity, the true lovers
vow to stay together and resist Orme's commands. All is unravelled as the
two young couples reveal that they have both married secretly, and the
good-natured father is ready now to accept the choices of his children – especially since he plays a trump on the trick by announcing that he too has
married secretly, Wilhelmine his bride. In a final flurry the countess moves
to take Ferdinand by force, but Heinrich has changed disguises with him so
that all now anticipate her pending humiliation with glee.

C (ÖNB) 845000/229 ATh

D Lively and well-constructed action. Heinrich a particularly witty, inventive, and clever servant figure.

A **Matrone von Ephesus, Die, oder Der von den Weibern leicht vergessene Tod der Männer.** Ein Nachspiel in einem Aufzuge. [Christian Felix Weiße.] 1764. [1]-16. 9 Auftritte. Rhymed alexandrines; initial aria in rhymed iambic pentameter.

B [Eunomia. Haliska. Hector.] [Ephesus.]
Eunomia mourns her dead husband, vowing to remain in his tomb and fast until death. Haliska encourages her mistress to take up a new life. The soldier Hector arrives, having heard the lament from his post where he is guarding the corpse of a hanged criminal. He joins Haliska, offering food and wine, encourages Eunomia, and finally pledges his love to her. She refuses stoically, but when it is revealed that Hector's charge has been stolen, he himself must die, and Eunomia turns to mourning for him. In a final monologue, Haliska warns against women revelling in the deaths of their husbands.

C (H) 20/888

D The work begins with a single aria. Serious theme and elevated atmosphere with touches of the macabre and black humour. No connection was found between the events of this Nachspiel and legends surrounding the classical Greek figure Eunomia (Pauly, *Real-Enzyclopädie*, 6, 1). The story of 'Die Matrone von Ephesus' has received many dramatic treatments, both in the eighteenth century and since, including an uncompleted 'Lustspiel in einem Aufzuge' with the same title by Lessing (1767). While this version has different personae from Weiße's, both are drawn from the story in Petronius. See Lessing's fragment and commentary (Lessing/Petersen, Bd. 10, 272-96).

A **Melonen, Die, oder die Zänkerinn.** Ein Nachspiel in einem Aufzuge. [An adaptation of Simon Nicolas Henri Linguet's *Intermède des melons et de la femme têtue*, which is his translation of *Entremes del melonar y la respondona*, and appeared in his *Théâtre espagnol* IV, Paris, 1770.] *Beytrag zum spanischen Theater.* Hamburg u. Riga: Hartknoch, 1771. [77]-86. 4 Auftritte.

B Michel. Lise. Ein Nachbar. Barbe.
Michel and Lise argue about how to make their fortune, by going into service or producing melons; and then about her responsibilities as wife. A concluding duet describes their roles as tyrannical husband and servile spouse.

C (H) 30/1306

D A nasty farce, the main action consisting of Michel's repeated beating of
Lise. See analysis p 182.

A **Minna oder Das unschuldige Mädchen.** Ein Nachspiel in einem Aufzug.
Von dem Uebersetzer der glücklichen Zusammenkunft. [Düsseldorf:
Schreiner,] 1799. [i-ii], [1]-34. 16 Auftritte.

B Herr von Olipan, Stadtrichter, Oheim des jungen Eduard. [Eduard]. Frau
von Haricour, eine Wittib von etlichen dreißig Jahren. Minna, ihre Tochter,
ein unschuldiges Mädchen von 16 Jahren. Frau von Pernelle, eine Wittib
von mittlerem Alter. Ludwig, der alte Gärtner der Frau von Haricour. Der
Schauplatz ist der Garten, hinter der Frau von Haricour ihrem Hause.
[Introductory orchestral accompaniment indicated.]
     Olipan and Eduard surprise each other at night in the Haricour garden,
each seeking a tryst with his beloved. Frau von Haricour comes to meet
Olipan, but is disturbed by the gossip of Frau von Pernelle, who simply
must have her pleasure in reporting an escapee from the convent and a
young man disinherited for 'Christian' reasons. Finally Frau von Haricour
gets rid of her and meets Olipan. He tries to convince her to marry him, but
she is modest and cautious, her doubts reinforced when Pernelle later
claims that Olipan has already proposed to her. In between, Eduard manages a furtive meeting with the innocent Minna who knows nothing of men
or love, but soon reveals a long-standing attraction to him. Yet her mother
has determined that she will enter the convent to be free from the evils of
the opposite sex. The busybody Frau Pernelle returns and is delighted to
discover grounds for further gossip in her friend's family, but is defused
when Olipan, who has assured his intended that he loves only her, takes
matters into his own hands, announcing that he and Frau Haricour will be
married. His willing fiancée follows suit by blessing Minna's engagement to
Eduard. In the end it is Frau Pernelle who is disgraced, for it was her own
daughter who had fled the convent, pursued by the beau she had herself
seen reduced to penury.

C (385) C868

D The tangle of furtive encounters could prove challenging and entertaining
on stage. A gentle praise of love and virtue.

A **Mis Jenny.** Ein tragisches Nachspiel, nebst drey kleinern Gedichten. [Joh. F.
Behr.] Mitau und Hasenpoth: Hinz, 1771. [4]-39. 20 Auftritte.

B   Mylord Gordon. Richard, Gordons Sohn. Amalia, Gordons Tochter. Bliefild.
    Jenny. Heinrich Greville. Bedienter. Der Schauplatz ist ein Zimmer in
    Milord Gordons Hause.

    Richard and Amalia have met the desolate Jenny in a park, heard her
    sorry tale and taken her in. Four years ago she was betrothed, but seduced
    before the wedding and deserted, thereafter bearing a child who died at the
    age of three. Her father disowned her and she is desolate. Richard and
    Amalia are sure of her innate virtue and goodness, convincing their father
    of the same. He has recently returned from a business trip and arranged a
    marriage between Richard and an associate's daughter, which will at the
    same time solve a financial crisis. But to his father's consternation Richard
    refuses the marriage, having fallen in love with Jenny and now seeking her
    hand. Mylord Grenville refuses permission as Jenny is penniless, of doubt-
    ful heritage, and already in disgrace. Bliefild, Gordon's old school chum and
    a trusted business associate, enters with news of his sadness and regret at
    the loss of his daughter, who, they discover, is none other than Jenny. All
    rejoice in the imminent union now of Jenny and Richard. Offstage, how-
    ever, Jenny's former lover and deserter, young Anton Greville, has re-
    turned. Richard runs to the rescue, but his own dagger is used by the re-
    jected Greville to kill both Jenny and him.

C   (1a) Yr 4334/2

D   Highly sentimental and contrived. A tragedy of virtue and vice and a rein-
    forcement of the class structure. See analysis pp 239 and 256.

A   **Mißtrauen und Neckerei.** Nachspiel in einem Akt v. Heinrich Gottlieb
    Schmieder. Hamburg: Vollmer, 1804.

C   Heinsius, IV, 319

A   **Mündel, Das.** Ein Nachspiel aus dem französischen. [Barthlélemy-
    Christophe] Fagan [de Lugny]. [*La Pupille*. Paris, 1734.] *Sammlung einiger
    Schriften zum Zeitvertreibe des Geschmacks*, 1. Bd, 3. St. Leipzig: Weidmann,
    1746. [187]-233. 21 Auftritte.

B   Arist. Charlotte, sein Mündel. Orgon, Arists Freund. Der Marquis [Valer],
    Orgons Neffe. Lisette, Charlottens Kammermädchen. Der Schauplatz ist in
    Arists Stube.

    The over-confident young Valer assumes Charlotte's love and seeks Or-
    gon's help in gaining Arist's blessing. But Charlotte thinks him a fool and
    secretly loves Arist, despite his advancing years. Unknown to her, he shares

the attraction, but both are too timid to confess. Yet Charlotte does reject Valer bluntly, and then attempts a ploy to win Arist. Pretending to write to Valer, she dictates to Arist a letter whose content spells out her love, but he is still too feeble to claim her heart. Only in the final scene does Arist summon his courage and snatch Charlotte from Valer's eager grasp.

C (26) Rara 953

D A tedious and precious exercise arousing limited interest.

A **Nachspiel zur berühmten Komödie, Erklärte Fehde oder List gegen List, Das.** Dem Schatten des Boileau gewidmet. [Cornelius Hermann v. Ayrenhoff.] Ayrenhoff, *Sämmtliche Werke*, 3. Bd. Wien u. Leipzig: Gräffer, 1789. [331]-366. 14 Auftritte.

B Pantalon, unter dem Nahmen Baron Stanville. Rosaura, dessen Nichte, unter dem Nahmen Lucille. Brigella, unter dem Nahmen Olive, Bedienter des Pantalon. Columbina, Kammermädchen, unter dem Nahmen Lisette. Signor Momolo, ein Gondelier von Venedig. Marquis von Dorsan. Frontin, des Marquis Bedienter. Einige Bediente, Schiffknechte, ein Scharfrichter, und ein Kind von 3 oder 4 Jahren. Die Scene ist zu Marseille in Frankreich.

The Marquis is furious at having been duped by the Baron in courting Rosaura. Loose-tongued Columbina tells him the truth about the Baron and his entourage: he is in fact Pantalon, a bankrupt merchant from Italy, Brigella his right-hand man. His niece Rosaura is betrothed to the gondolier Momolo from whom she had a child some years ago. He is to arrive soon for the wedding. Upon hearing this, the Marquis is doubly incensed, feeling national disgrace as a Frenchman having been duped by a group of itinerant Italian clowns. He gladly accepts Frontin's confident offer to set things right, as he claims Harlequin would do for his master were they part of the Italian scheme. Momolo arrives with the child and Frontin cleverly manages to manipulate him, Pantalon, and Brigella through deception and disguise to gain sweet revenge. Pantalon and Brigella are put in sacks and beaten, the Marquis withdraws his claim to Rosaura, and she is reunited with Momolo and their child, and Columbina and Frontin are paired together as well.

C (ÖNB) 622563 BTh

D On title-page, below title: 'Aux dépens du bon sens gardez de plaisanter! *Boileau dans l'art poétique*.' Personae list indicates author's conscious location of Nachspiel in *commedia dell'arte* tradition with consequences for performance style. Text preceded by 'Anmerkung des Herausgebers' in which editor clarifies the intention of the Nachspiel author. *Erklärte Fehde* is a translation of [Antoine-Jean-Bourlin] Dumaniant's *Guerre ouverte* [1786] in which the action surrounding Lucille's first fiancé, the ship captain, is left unresolved. This Nachspiel completes that sub-plot. The editor goes on to anticipate and deny vehemently claims that the Nachspiel is a satire on Dumaniant's play and style, a protestation made so strongly that it is surely done tongue-in-cheek (333f).

A clever and fast-paced work making free use of devices such as disguise, sexual innuendo, exaggeration, beatings, *commedia dell'arte* costumes, and a play within a play. Satire on French pride and customs. In final scene, comment on the state of German theatre. See analysis p 203.

Nachspiel zu Verbesserungen und Zusätze des Lustspiels Die Geistlichen auf dem Lande, see Verbesserungen

A **Naturaliensammler, Der.** Nachspiel. Christian Felix Weiße. *Beytrag zum deutschen Theater*, Bd. 1. Leipzig, 1759. 2. Aufl., Leipzig, 1765. 3. Aufl., Leipzig, 1771.

C Goedeke, IV^1, 138

neue Schätzung, Die, see Christen

A **neueste Verheyrathung, Die.** Berlin, Hamburg, Leipzig: publisher unknown, 1759. [41]-56. 12 Auftritte.

B Pantalon, des Arlequins Vater. Arlequin, der Sohn des Pantalons. Peter, ein Schuster. Liesgen, eine Liebhaberin des Arlequins. Schulmeister mit seinen Jungen. [Schauplätze:] Schuster-Liesgen / Schule.

After one failure, Pantalon tries to secure for his son a position as shoemaker's apprentice, but Arlequin sees too much work and discipline in that, so runs off. Thereafter he decides to auction himself as a husband, securing an offer from Liesgen. He then seeks employ as assistant schoolmaster, doing miserably on the simple qualifying test, but getting the post anyway by virtue of Liesgen's charms. The play ends with general mayhem in the schoolhouse.

C (H) 4/137

D Bound and published after *Der Bauer-Arzt*, ein Lustspiel in ungebundener Rede, mit einem Nachspiel, die Neueste Verheyrathung. *Bauer-Arzt* [1]-40; *N.V.* [41]-56.

 Stage directions require frequent improvisation and rowdy behaviour. Thematic connection to preceding *Lustspiel*. Indirect comment on social practice of match-making on financial grounds. See analysis p 174.

A **Neujahrstag, Der.** Ein Nachspiel für Kinder in einem Aufzuge. Vom Verfasser der Elisa [Friedrich Karl Adolf v. Trützschler]. Leipzig: Böhme, 1779. [i-xv], [i-ii], [1]-72. 20 Auftritte.

B Rosimunde, Hofmeisterin. Lottgen, Julie, Ferdinand, Lisette, Kinder des Grafen Treuwerth. Niklas Stab, ein alter Bettler. Tobias, dessen Sohn. Der Schauplatz ist im Hause des Grafen.

 Ferdinand has received a gold coin from his parents and begins this first day of a new year by writing a lengthy and effusive expression of gratitude. Tobias visits, telling of a sickly father, poverty, and woe, touching the generous Ferdinand who gives him the coin. Afraid to tell his parents, Ferdinand pretends to have lost the gift, learns that the spiteful Julie has informed their parents, and is desolate. All suspect he is lying, but even the trusty Rosimunde cannot bring him to tell the truth. Niklas Stab enters, returning the coin in the belief that young Tobias had stolen it in desperation. For his honesty, the old man is rewarded with a weekly stipend from the count and the assurance that his son will be cared for. Ferdinand's self-effacing generosity triumphs and the spiteful Julie is punished. Despite his presence among the personae, the count fails to appear.

C (7) Poet dram III, 3298f

D Illustration on title-page shows two figures, one bowing to the other, with subscript 'Hat nichts zu sagen, was will er?' [spoken by Ferdinand to Tobias, Scene 7]. Pp [iv-xi]: Dedication to Peter von Sievers, captain in Russian Imperial Army, in which the author expresses warmth and appreciation for their lifelong friendship. Pp [xii-xv]: Note describes genesis of the work, written for the pleasure and performance of a group of friends.

 The work itself is an exaggerated display of virtue, honesty, and sensitivity, to which the modern reader is likely to react as the black sheep Julie: 'Ich mag sein Geschwäz nicht länger anhören' (66). Interspersed lessons in enlightened child-rearing, based on the belief that Nature needs the strong hands of discipline and morality as a guide. See analysis p 240.

Noch war es nicht zu spät, see Weihnachtabend

A **Nur ein Stündchen war er fort.** Nachspiel aus dem Französischen des Loraux [Michel Fillette, called Loraux, *Une heure d'absence,* comédie en 1 acte, en prose. Paris: Masson, an X (1801)] von Theodor Hell [Karl Gottfried Theodor Winkler]. Leipzig: Weigel, 1805. [1]-70. 23 Scenen.

B Oberst von Sturmthal, Onkel des Lieutenant von Sturmthal, Husar. Majorin von Seelingen, dessen Tante. Ida von Arnstein. Lottchen, deren Kammerjungfer. Johann, des Lieutenants Reitknecht. [Ein Bedienter.] Die Scene spielt in einem Saale mit einer Mittelthüre, und einer Thüre auf jeder Seite; über der, die zu dem Zimmer des Obersten führt, ist oben ein sogenanntes Ochsenauge, (rundes kleines Scheibenfenster) zum Oeffnen, vor dem eiserne Gitter sind, an der Thüre selbst ist ein Riegel. Auf der Scene stehen zwey Tische, einer mit einem Schreibzeug.

   Lieutenant Sturmthal, a cocky young gadfly, has opened in error an invitation addressed to his uncle to attend a ball, and thinking it was for himself, went in his place. He returns to tell of the festivities and of a pending duel resulting from an insult. Upset at his nephew's impudence, the stalwart Oberst is nevertheless preoccupied foremost by his own concerns, the imminent arrival of Ida von Arnstein, many years his younger, whom his sister has chosen to be his bride. Young Sturmthal finds this out by a deft exchange of letters and realizes that Ida is the woman with whom he fell in love six months ago. He resolves to steal her from his uncle. Sturmthal senior meanwhile locks his nephew up and leaves on business for an hour. Just now his sister arrives with Ida who finds herself alone with young Sturmthal. Posing as his uncle, he treats her rudely. She thus resolves to refuse the planned marriage. But before departing, young Sturmthal speaks to her again, this time as himself, and their love of the past is rekindled. The scene is interrupted by Sturmthal senior who is appalled at his nephew's trickery and exposes his questionable character and past. Still, he sees that the young couple rightly belong together, and that his own age sets him apart; magnanimously in the end he steps aside and wishes them well.

C (Mh28) G 630

D A cleverly constructed, entertaining, if superficial little comedy.

A **Officier, Der.** Ein Nachspiel in einem Aufzuge. [Johann Baptist Bergobzoom.] Uebersetzte auserlesene neue Lustspiele nebst einem deutschen Nachspiele. Frankfurt u. Leipzig: Metternich, 1769. 5. Stück, [1]-32. 16 Auftritte.

B Lisidor, ein versuchter Officier. Mangold, ein reicher Mann. Barbara, seine alte Hausfrau. Lisette, seine Tochter. Lucinde, ihre arme Anverwandte.

Frontin, Lisidors Bedienter. Pernille, Mangolds Haushälterin. Der Schauplatz ist in Mangolds Vorzimmer.

After honourable service in the Seven Years' War, Lisidor and Frontin return home, having gained fortune and rank along the way, looking forward to reunions with their sweethearts Lucinde and Pernille. They find the Mangold family absorbed in snobbish affectation, rank, and money. Unaware of the recent wealth and status of the returning soldiers, the family treats them with disdain. Only poor Lucinde has remained genuine and true. When Lisidor asks for her hand, Mangold and Barbara agree only too happily, then to be rocked as they learn of Lisidor's wealth and rank. But Mangold's pleas on behalf of his own daughter are by then too late.

C (16) G5513

D Stiff characters and dialogue, dull plot. Thematic importance of honour in war and love. Frontin a strong and intelligent servant figure. Little comic potential.

A **ohnmächtige und zur Ruhe gesetzte Wolke, Die.** Nachspiel in einem Akt, als Parodie auf das Nachspiel: Die Wolken. Heinrich Wilhelm Seyfried. Frankfurt, 1783. [Ostensibly a reaction to *Die Wolken* below.]

C Goedeke, V, 396

A **Perücke, Die.** Ein komisches Nachspiel in einem Aufzug. Leopold Huber. Wien: Goldhann, 1791.

C (ÖNB) card catalogue. Library possesses only 'zweyter Theil.'

A **Perücken, Der, zweyter Theil.** Ein komisches Nachspiel in einem Aufzug. Leopold Huber. Wien: mit Goldhannschen Schriften, 1791. [107]-135. 18 Auftritte.

B Hofrath. Hofräthin. Herr von Hoburg. Johann, Diener des Hofraths. Lisette, Kammermädchen der Hofräthin. [Wien]

The Hofräthin is deceiving her gullible husband with Hoburg, manipulating servants and spouse to her ends. An anonymous letter informs the incredulous Hofrath of this, but he is convinced by his wife to don her clothes, trick her suitor, and punish him. At the same time she has Hoburg informed and ready to pounce on the unsuspecting husband in drag and deal him a beating. The Hofrath is beaten, fooled, convinced of his wife's innocence, and invites Hoburg to come and live with them, making his cuckoldry self-imposed and complete.

C (P) 272

D A depiction of feminine duplicity and masculine foolishness; licentiousness and pretension of upper middle class. Many comic devices, including humorous language mixed with shades of Viennese dialect, French affectations (often incorrect), and crudity; cuckold motif, physical beating; comic disguise, mistaken identity, eavesdropping; instructive song directed at audience by comic servant to close. Many stage directions, particularly for Johann whose role requires improvisational talent.

A **Phlegmatikus, Der.** Ein Nachspiel. Breslau: Meyer, 1799.

C Heinsius, IV, 331

A **Portrait, Das.** Ein Nachspiel des Hrn [Pierre François Godard de] Beauchamps. [*Le Portrait*, comédie en 1 acte. Paris: Dupuis, 1728.] Place of publication and publisher unknown, [1778]. 21-55. 16 Auftritte.

B Bernardin, Julchens Vater. Julchen, Bernardins Tochter. Valeri, Julchens Liebhaber. Lisette, Julchens Kammermädchen. Johann, Valers Lakay. Der Schauplatz ist zu Paris.
   With shrewish petulance Julchen has resolved never to take a husband, so that when her father announces that he has brought home an unknown suitor she rebels. From her father she has Valer's portrait, and unbeknown to her he has hers. Before Valer visits, Julchen and Lisette change clothes so that Julchen receives Valer as a servant, treats him discourteously, and does all to convince him not to pursue the marriage. Of course Valer sees through her disguise before leaving. But his character and performance have impressed Julchen so much that she has fallen in love and now regrets her actions. All is saved when he calls once more, they discover their love and join in a wish to be married.

C (33) Ob V 5, 1020 (7. Bd)

D A transparent action saved in some measure by Lisette's and Johann's impudent and lively contributions.

A **Prahler, Der.** Ein Nachspiel in Versen. Augsburg: Merz, 1761. [1]-24. 10 Auftritte. Rhymed alexandrines; rhymed iambic trimeter and tetrameter in several arias.

B Leonard, vermeinter Vater der Julia, dessen geglaubte Tochter. Wurmholtz, Liebaug, beyde in Julia verliebt. Eisenstahl, ein Prahler ohne Hertz. Vier stumme Soldaten.

Eisenstahl recounts his military triumphs, meets Julia by chance, and announces that he will carry her off to be his bride. She enlists the help of the eager Wurmholtz and Liebaug to drive him away that night. Meanwhile Leonard reveals to her that he is only her guardian, having promised her deceased father to raise and protect her from infancy. Now he wishes to marry her and secures her willing agreement. Eisenstahl, Wurmholtz, and Liebaug then meet and clash briefly, before Eisenstahl surrenders, slightly injured. They drive him off forever and join the happy couple to celebrate their wedding.

C (DI1) HV 378/79

D An amusing if simple-minded piece, baroque in tone. Eisenstahl a *miles gloriosus* type. Some mimic improvisation and coarse language. A musical piece, containing three arias, a duet, and closing chorus.

A **redliche Betrüger, Der.** Nachspiel. Wien: Doll, 1797.

C Heinsius, IV, 257

redliche Schulze, Der, see Lotto

A **Rekreation, Die.** Ein Nachspiel von einem Aufzuge. Aufgeführet auf dem kaiserl. königl. privil. deutschen Theater. 1766. [Wien:] Kraus. [1]-29. 4 Auftritte. Dramatic excerpts in rhymed alexandrines.

B Luise. Emilie. Cecilie. Eleonora. [Wien.]

The sisters' father has instructed them to practise some theatrical pieces so that they can perform for others. The action consists of their rehearsal of dramatic excerpts in French, German, and Italian. An aria (in Italian) and ballet close the piece.

C (ÖNB) 845000/273 ATh

D Personae include casting list. Trilingual work reflects taste and culture of Viennese audience. Ballet connected to Nachspiel at conclusion.

A **Rendez-vous, Das.** Nachspiel aus dem Französischen. Karl Reinhard Röpe. Hamburg, 1789.

C Goedeke, V, 252

A **Rosalia.** Ein Nachspiel mit Arien von Schink. Gotha: Ettinger, 1777. [1]-39.
No internal divisions. Arias in rhymed trochaic and iambic tetrameter.

B [Erast. Rosalia. Seline. Lucinde.] Die Scene ist ein Thal, – im Hintergrunde
eine kleine Hütte; vorn einzlne Bäume, an der einen Seite eine Rosenhecke.
– Ein schöner Morgen – heitre Sonne.
   Lucinde has toyed with Erast's love and devotion, causing him to curse
her and all of her sex. But Rosalia's tender song and secret love win Erast
anew and they are quickly betrothed. It is too late now for Lucinde, who
rejected her sister Seline's warnings and now sits alone.

C (H) 97/3030

D A simple piece, in the manner of both *Schäfer-* and *Singspiel.* Idyllic scenes
and motifs, natural imagery, sentimentality. Yet some satire on the bucolic
genres comes from the sharp-tongued Lucinde.

A **Schatzgräber, Der, oder der geprellte Geizhals.** Nachspiel nach dem
Französischen. Breslau: Meyer, 1799.

C Heinsius, IV, 342

Schifferstechen, Das, see **Liebe im Sommer**

A **Schimpf und Ernst mit gleicher Münz bezalt.** Nachgspill. [Dachau, 1760-
70]. No internal divisions.

B Hanß, Sylvinus, beide baurn mit stekhen versechen, ieder einen strikh in
den sakh. Rubelle, Casperle, zwey baurnbiebl. Liberius, ein verwögnes
Birschl.
   Hanß and Sylvinus are out hunting, and when Sylvinus pursues a fox on
his own, Hanß decides to test his boys' knowledge of the Lord's Prayer and
catechism. Appalled by their ignorance, he begins a remedial lesson but is
interrupted by the sudden entrance of the scoundrel Liberius who intends
to rob him. The boys flee, Hanß is stripped of his every belonging (trousers
included), and awaits execution from the cruel thief. But Sylvinus returns
just in time to turn the tables. Now Liberius is the victim and is hanged
from a tree in revenge. No thought of Christian charity remains from the
earlier religious instruction.

C CWR 832.08 K47

D This Nachspiel is written for the most part in Bavarian dialect and survives
   as a reprint in Oscar Brenner's collection *Altbairische Possenspiele für die
   Dachauer Bühne bearbeitet von Franz von Paula Kiennast (†1783)* (München:
   Kaiser, 1893), pp 16-21. Brenner lists his source as another reprint a few
   years earlier, A. Hartmann's *Volksschauspiele* (Leipzig, 1880), pp 439ff (p ix)
   and dates the Nachspiel between 1760 and 1770. He indicates that it was
   performed after *Die Getrukht aber nit Undertrukhte Unschuld / oder / Die heilige
   Itta / vorgestöllt / In dem churfrtl. Markht Dachau / Von / Einigen auß der Burgerschafft* (p 16), although he does not give us the text of this work. In his introduction and notes to the slim volume (40 + xvi pp), Brenner provides information on Kiennast (1728/1729-1783) who as organist and theatre director
   in Dachau from 1759 was responsible for public productions and probably
   had a hand in writing and editing the works in the volume. Brenner also
   suggests that the Nachspiel *Schimpf und Ernst* was intended to lighten the
   tone of the evening after the tragic contents of *Itta* (p xiii). Humour results
   largely from the verbal and physical interplay between Hanß and the boys,
   their general stupidity, and Hanß's disrobing before the thief. In contrast,
   the Nachspiel's conclusion is anything but jolly.
   It is interesting to note that the play was performed 'Von / Einigen / auß
   / der Burgerschafft,' in other words not by professional actors but by local
   citizens. This no doubt ensured that the dialect was true, giving the work
   immediate appeal to the audience.

A **Schleppen, Die.** Ein Deutsches Original-Nachspiel in einem Acte. Grätz,
   1797. [1]-10. No internal divisions.

B Akmee, eine junge Frau. Laura, Philinde, Cousinen der Frau Räthinn. Frau
   Räthinn Sprecher. Herr Sprecher, deren Sohn. Ein Bedienter. Eine weibliche
   Bedientinn. Die Scene ist zu Berlin in der Vorstadt. Ein gut gebautes und
   anständig meubliertes Haus, und dessen Visiten-Zimmer.
   Frau Sprecher and her son await their lady guests on this rainy day. He
   fears that they will soil the floor with the trains of their dresses and indeed
   they do. He protests politely, attempting to convince the fashion-conscious
   ladies to do away with the useless things forever, which in the end they reluctantly promise to do.

C (ÖNB) 698427 ATh

D An odd little jibe at fashion-conscious Berlin. More of the same can be seen
   in the reviews of *Die beiden Billets* (see p 190). The contemporary *Journal des*

Luxus und der Moden (1786-9) shows just how important the world of fashion was for the age.

A **sehende Blinde, Der.** Ein Nachspiel in Versen nach dem frantzösischen des Herrn le Grand. Dresden, 1752. [ii], [1]-45. 29 Auftritte. Rhymed alexandrines.

B Leonore, eine junge Wittwe. Leonore, ihre Tante. Damon, ein See-Officier. Leander, sein junger Vetter. Doctor Safft, ein junger affectirter Medicus. Lisette, Leonorens Mägdgen. Caspar, Damons Diener. Ein Notarius. Der Schauplatz ist in Damons Hause.

During Damon's lengthy absence, his fiancée Leonore has fallen in love with Leander and now dreads his return, especially since he is said to have been blinded in action. She plans to deceive him, paying Caspar to assist her. Her aunt will further the deceit by impersonating her in front of Damon in order to trick him into marriage herself. But Caspar is loyal to his master and Damon knows of Leonore's infidelity already; he is merely feigning blindness to foil their deceit. This he does upon arrival, tricking the aunt and the stupid Safft into a mutual marriage contract, then leaving Leonore and Leander to ponder their fate with each other. His good sense has overcome their foolishness; it is those with sight who are blind to truth.

C (12) P.o.germ.1522

D Light, well-paced, and at times witty. Caspar a clever comic servant. See analysis p 237.

A **sich selbst Betrügende, Der, oder Der Verwirrte Mißtrauer.** Ein Nachspiel aus dem Französischen des Herrn J[ean] B[aptiste] Rousseau [*La Dupe de soi-même ou le méfiant confondu*, 1751] in deutsche Verse übersetzt von D Georg Heinrich Behr. Frankfurt u. Leipzig, 1754. Reinhart Meyer, Hrsg., *Das deutsche Drama des 18. Jahrhunderts in Einzeldrucken. 1 Das Repertoire bis 1755.* Bd. 6, *Das Lustspiel* 3. München: Kraus, 1981. [379]-406; original pag. of 1754 printing [1]-28. 9 Auftritte. Rhymed alexandrines.

B Isabell, Eine junge Witwe. Alcipp, Damis, Liebhaber der Isabelle. Erast, Ein Hofmann, Vetter und Oheim des Damis. Morill, Bedienter des Alcipps. Der Schauplatz ist zu Paris.

Although Isabell assures Alcipp of her loyality and Damis and Erast gallantly support their union, Alcipp is suspicious of such generosity and integrity. He thus conducts an outlandish test by withdrawing his claim to Isabelle in favour of Damis. Isabelle in turn is so insulted that she does in fact redirect her favours and loyalty, leaving the sceptic Alcipp with a hard lesson learned.

C (25*) Ats 325/60 VI

D A work with little wit or imagination.

A **Sohn, Der.** Ein Nachspiel für Kinder in einem Aufzuge. Christian Friedrich Sander. *Prosaische Dichtungen*. Flensburg u. Leipzig: Korten, 1783. 1-48. 12 Auftritte.

B Herr von Nidau, Direktor einer Militairschule. Herr Golding, Lehrer und Aufseher bey Tische. Franz von Mülen, Theodor von Ihlefeld, Gottlieb von Mönzen, Leopold von Halbersau, Schüler. Ein Bedienter. Zeit, der neunte Februar, 1780. Scene, die Arbeitsstube des Herrn von Nidau.

Nidau and Golding run their school with a mixture of fatherly tenderness and strict disciplinary code. They are both fond of Franz, but his mysterious behaviour concerns them. He refuses to eat as regulations prescribe, restricting himself to bread and water. At table he is reluctant to enjoy the company of the other boys, answering in monosyllables. But in academics and conduct, Franz is exemplary. We learn that he comes from a poor but noble family and was taken in as a gesture of kindness by Nidau. His behaviour also troubles the other boys. Theodor and Gottlieb ask the director to relieve them of his company, while Leopold requests the special task of befriending this strange classmate. Nidau, with best intentions, delivers Franz an ultimatum: to explain his behaviour or leave the school. Reluctantly, and only if Nidau agrees to be his surrogate father, Franz agrees, explaining that he cannot bring himself to enjoy his meals while his family is starving. His father has served the king [of Prussia] loyally for years as a major, but receives no pension or income. Nidau resolves his plight through a personal contact in the ministry, arranging for an immediate pension, and hence well-being for the boy's family. Overjoyed, Franz becomes fully integrated into school life.

C (COP) 52-151

D Highly sentimental and moralistic, yet interesting. Franz's mature language and attitude somewhat artificial and unconvincing. Odd repeated emphasis on the importance of the precise date of the action (9 Feb. 1780) throughout the work, as if referring to an actual event.

A **Trentleva, Das.** Ein Nachspiel. [Ernst Heydevogel.] *Theater der Deutschen,* 14. Theil. Königsberg u. Leipzig: Kanter, 1774. [507]-541. 14 Auftritte.

B Leander. Wilhelmine, seine Geliebte. Heinrich, sein Kammerdiener. Magnocaballo, ein Aventurier. Ruhländer, ein Kaufmann. Gumprecht, ein Jude.

Leander is an addicted gambler, even deigning to play with the swindler
Magnocaballo. As a result he is deeply in debt. Wilhelmine arrives with a
marriage contract which will bring him not just her but a hefty dowry; tomorrow they shall marry. Ruhländer arrives to collect a debt and allows Leander just one more day's grace, but at the cost of his contract which he
hands over in trust. Unexpectedly Ruhländer meets Wilhelmine and inno-
cently recounts the episode to her. She is shattered, breaks the engagement,
and leaves Leander to suffer the consequences of his folly. With heavy heart
he accepts an offer from Ruhländer to go to Peru where he can make a new
start and cast off his dreaded vice.

C (24) d.D 12363

D A drama of social folly and correction in the Gottschedian manner with little imagination or merit. See analysis p 243.

A **Tugend auf der Schaubühne, Die, oder Harlekins Heirath.** Ein Nachspiel
in einem Aufzuge von J.[ustus] Möser. Berlin u. Stettin: Nicolai, 1798. [1]-38.
17 Auftritte.

B Herr Berthold, Principal der Bühne. Kolombine, seine Tochter. Harlekin,
Scapin, Isabelle, Valer, Schauspieler. Peter, Lichtputzer. Der Schauplatz ist
auf dem Schauplatze.

Harlekin asks Berthold for Kolombine's hand and gains his blessing. But
he has doubts about her virtue and, with Berthold's approval, plans to put
her to a test. The other actors wager confidently on her good reputation.
Aided by Peter and Scapin, Harlekin disguises himself as a captain and
tempts Kolombine with flattery and gifts, but she resists indignantly. When
he reveals the guise she rejects him for his lack of confidence in her. Nevertheless, she softens at the end and agrees to give him another chance.

C (ÖNB) 627698 BTh

D Footnote on p [3]: 'Man sehe über dies scherzhafte Stück die Nachricht,
welche ich in Mösers Leben S. 81f. davon gegeben habe. Da es in seiner Art
merkwürdig ist, habe ich es auch besonders abdrucken lassen. N.[icolai].' In
his account of Möser's life, Nicolai devotes two pages to this Nachspiel,
telling us that it was written in 1763 when Möser was on a trip to England;
he sent it to Nicolai, thus beginning their correspondence. On Nicolai's re-
quest, Döbbelin promised to perform it but never did. The work was lost for
many years before being rediscovered. Nicolai himself says that 'es gleich
als theatralisches Stück wenig Verdienst hat,' but adds that it was important

'den alten Geckorden wieder zu erneuern … Es würde dies eine wichtige Verbesserung vieler jetzigen, theils sehr hochweisen, theils sehr hochsteifen, theils sehr hochnaserümpfenden, theils sehr hochspielenden Gesellschaften sein. Ich bitte nachzulesen, was Möser darüber sagt, wie es zugegangen, daß unsere Vorfahren so gesund, so hungrig, so aufgelegt zur Freude gewesen; doch auch seine feine Cautel, daß die Geckheit zünftig, nicht aber unzünftig sein müsse, dabei wohl zu beherzigen' (Nicolai, *Leben*, 64f). The Möser quotation is from the latter's essay 'Den alten Geckorden sollte man wieder erneuern' (*Phantasien II*), in which the author recalls the 'Geckorden' founded by Herzog Adolf von Kleve in which persons of all classes joined equally to take on fictitious dramatic roles, thus breaking down social barriers at least temporarily. He surveys similar impulses in other periods and literary forms back to medieval times (*Sämtliche Werke*, II, 207-14). Beyond the presence of traditional comic figures, the work includes many comic devices such as pantomime, disguise, exaggeration in language, and sexual allusions. See analysis p 207.

A **Unerwartete im Heyrathen, Das, oder die Frau mit zwenen Männern zugleich,** ein Nachspiel, von J.H. Steffens, Rector der Zellischen Schule. Zelle: Gsellius, 1765. [1]-28. 12 Auftritte.

B Philanide, eine schon etwas bejahrte Kaufmanns Frau. Dorimon, ihr zweiter Mann. Angelike, Philanidens Stieftochter von ihrem ersten Manne. Dorante, Dorimons Stief-Sohn. Megador, ihr erster Mann, den man für todt gehalten. Argutius, ein angesehener Advocat, und Angelikens Curator. Viereck, ein Kaufmann, Dorantes Vormund. Die Scene ist in Philanidens Hause, in einer berühmten Residenz-Stadt eines benachbahrten Königreiches.

Dorante has just won a fortune in the lottery which removes for him any impediment to his marrying Angelike. But she refuses, feeling her lack of means disqualifies her for the match. Viereck works to block the marriage, hoping to gain his charge, along with the fortune, for one of his nieces. Argutius clears a path by announcing that Angelike is now also of independent means – a trust has been established for her by unnamed friends. Megador then reappears after nine years, to the delight of all. He recounts his adventures and changed fortune since leaving in bankruptcy. Both Philanide and Dorimon accept him warmly, agreeing to a tripartite marriage, which Argutius is to arrange!

C (ÖNB) 628647 ATh

D Highly improbable action, but entertaining and with a remarkable conclusion in the *ménage à trois*. Underlying emphasis on the importance of money for happiness. See analysis p 251.

unschuldige Mädchen, Das, see **Minna**

A **Vater in Cadix, Der.** Nachspiel aus dem Französischen. Karl Reinhard Röpe. Hamburg, 1788.

C Goedeke, V, 252

A **verachtete Eitelkeit der Welt, Die.** In einem Musicalischen Nach-Spiele Auf dem Merseburgischen Schul-THEATRO vorgestellet. Anno M DCC II. Merseburg: Gottschick, [1702]. [1-16]. No internal divisions. Iambic and trochaic tetrameters with several arias in shorter verses.

B Dulcimene, Eine Dame. Fortunatus, Ein Cavailler. Hercules, Ein Officirer. Spinosa, Ein Doctor. Euclio, Ein Kauffmann. Ignatius, Ein Abt.
   Dulcimene has sworn to protect her virtue and purity by avoiding marriage. Four men, each representing an occupation in society, seek a bride and woo the reluctant lady. She rejects each in turn, along with the life-style he represents, finally accepting the abbot's invitation to enter a convent, forever rejecting temptations of the mortal world.

C (32) 0,9:364

D Ostensibly a purely musical/operatic work containing distinct arias as well as inter-rhymed dialogue exchanges. Light and humorous interchanges between Dulcimene and her suitors, but a sober commitment in the end.

A **Verbesserungen und Zusätze des Lustspiels die Geistlichen auf dem Lande in zweien Handlungen samt dessen Nachspiel.** Frankfurt u. Leipzig: publisher unknown, 1744. [Nachspiel:] [107]-126, 2 Auftritte + Postscripts.

B [Commissarii. von Kohlstengel. Haferstroh].
   An undramatic interrogation of Kohlstengel and Haferstroh by the Commissarii on the subject of their mistreatment of the clergyman in the preceding *Verbesserungen*. Judgment and punishment meted out in first Postscript, including fines, release from office (Haferstroh), and confession of guilt (Kohlstengel). Second Postscript gives [fictitious] account of unexpected death of author of preceding works, brief biography, and tribute.

C (7) 1942 388

D The *Verbesserungen* were written in direct response to Johann Christian
   Krüger's Lustspiel *Die Geistlichen auf dem Lande* (1743). They consist of a
   counterplay which extols the virtues of the clergy in contrast to Krüger's
   strident satire of that profession. Those judged and punished in the Nachspiel are the *Verbesserung*'s principal culprits, defamers of the clergy. Other
   than thematic contrast, the *Verbesserungen* have no connection with Krüger's
   comedy. The Nachspiel has little dramatic character or merit. See commentary in Johann Christian Krüger, *Werke*, p XXII, note 25.

A **Verlobung bei Kaiserslautern.** Nachspiel in einem Aufzuge. Weissenfels u.
   Leipzig: Severin, 1795. [1]-78. 15 Auftritte.

B François de Bercheau, ehemals Banquieur in Lion, jezt Nationalgarden-Of-
   ficier und Kommandeur eines kleinen Korps. Toinon, Wittwe, Charlotte,
   seine Töchter. Walter von Kronau, ein gefangener preussischer Officier und
   Liebhaber der Charlotte. Von Linkheim, ein preussischer Husarenofficier.
   La Soliere, ein französicher Bürger. Ein Kommissarius des Nation-
   alkonvents. Zween Nationalgarden. Ein französicher Unterofficier. Eine Or-
   donnanz. Ein Soldat. Französische Soldaten. Preussische Husaren. Volk.
   Der Schauplatz ist in einem französischen Grenzstädtchen ohnweit Kaiserslautern.

   The action occurs soon after the French Revolution during the First
   Coalition War (the date of publication) when a climate of violence, intrigue,
   and fear prevailed. The loyal Frenchman Bercheau despises what has hap-
   pened to his homeland and family. His wife has been executed by the revolutionaries, his daughters forced to flee before finding their father again.
   Still, an intense sense of honour keeps him at his post. In his official function he orders a justified whipping for two guards, who then vow revenge.
   Charlotte's cold rejection of the Kommissarius's advances also leads him to
   plot against the family. In addition, Toinon learns that her husband has
   fallen in battle. The climax approaches as the vindictive guards and
   Kommissarius combine to jail the innocent Toinon and strip her father of
   office. Just as all seems lost, Prussian Hussars break through to liberate their
   colleagues and with them the Bercheau family. Walter is reunited with
   Charlotte, Von Linkheim offers his love to Toinon, and all prepare to begin
   a new and happier life on German soil.

C (ÖNB) 129408 A

D Despite much exaggerated pathos and the contrived conclusion, an exciting
   work which captures the fear, intrigue, and horror in the aftermath of the

French Revolution. By contrast, the work is a patriotic praise of Germany and its people. Unusually large cast with a number of stage directions intended to guide the actors' performance technique. See analysis p 240.

A **vermeynten Nebenbuhler, Die.** Ein Nachspiel in Versen. *Neue Erweiterungen der Erkenntnis und des Vergnügens*, Bd. 4. Frankfurt u. Leipzig: Lankisch, 1754. 47-63. 11 Auftritte. Rhymed alexandrines.

B Marine, eine alte Jungfer. Erast, derselben jüngerer Bruder, in Rosetten verliebt. Rosette, eine Waise, die sich bey diesem aufhält. Clarice, verkleideter Bedienter des Erasts unter dem Namen Damis. Sergest, Freund des Erasts. Der Schauplatz ist in Erasts Hause.

Encouraged by his malicious sister, Erast doubts Rosette's devotion to him, suspecting her of loving Sergest, then Damis (Clarice). Sergest suffers from the guilt of jealously stabbing his lover years ago before learning of her innocence. Marine eagerly seeks a partner, cornering and ostensibly convincing Damis (Clarice) to marry her. In the end Clarice reveals herself as Serget's lover who has survived and returned to be reunited with him. Rosette and Erast are likewise joined, his suspicions now dispelled. Only the malevolent Marine is left abandoned.

C (21) Kb 80a

D Rapid turnabouts, little dramatic development, producing a fragmented work.

A **Versuch, Der, oder Eitelkeit und Herzensgüte.** In einem Aufzuge von [Johann Heinrich] Decker. *Neueste deutsche Schaubühne für 1806*, Bd. 4. Frankfurt u. Leipzig, 1806. [1]-54. 28 Scenen.

B Heinrich Brandt, Kaufmann. Sophie, dessen Gattin. Jenny, Titus, deren Kinder. Ludwig Brandt, Bruder des Kaufmanns Brandt, Oekonom. Hanns Brandt, dessen Sohn. Die Handlung geht im Hause des Kaufmanns Brandt vor.

Heinrich Brandt is on the verge of financial ruin caused by the extravagance of his wife and children who bow to every whim of social convention, from attire and parties to reading and sport. He tries to enforce budget restraint but is too weak to change their ways and is intimidated by Sophie's threat to divorce him. His brother arrives with son Hanns from the country and Ludwig steps in, admonishing Heinrich for his weakness. Heinrich agrees to put things into his brother's hands, transferring in name all financial authority, whereupon drastic restrictions on family spending result, to the horror of Sophie and the children. Despite Sophie's repeated threats of divorce, Ludwig convinces his brother to stand firm, and indeed the family soon acquiesces, promises to reform, and to move to a country estate, away from the city's temptation and falseness. Hanns will, however, stay to hone his skills in the urban world.

C   (59) I Fr 11a7

D   Table of contents: 'Deckers Nachspiele: Der Versuch. Die Brandschatzung.' Although at times ponderous and self-righteous in tone, an interesting comment on the falseness of urban convention as opposed to rural values and integrity. Hanns's *Plattdeutsch* an amusing linguistic contrast to the others, parallel to his solid personal values. He also expresses his values in a closing address to the audience, inviting them to leave the city. See analysis p 252.

A   **Verwechselung, Die, oder Kleider machen Leute.** Nachspiel. Theodor Hell [Karl Gottfried Theodor Winkler]. *Neue Lustspiele von Theodor Hell*, Bd. 2. Leipzig: Hinrichs, 1808. [233]-303. 22 Scenen.

B   Herr Rund. Diane Rund, seine Schwester. Adelheid, beider Nichte. Stern. Narzissus Klarwasser. Lotte, Adelheids Kammermädchen. Franz, Sterns Bedienter. Ein Bedienter. Die Scene ist in Runds Hause.
      The aging and wealthy, but vain and fashion-conscious Diane Rund refuses to allow her niece to marry until she herself has found a husband. Her brother has arranged a suitor for Adelheid: Narzissus Klarwasser, son of an old friend from the provinces. Adelheid loves the young Stern, but her aunt is determined to marry him herself. Lotte plays the major role in manipulating the two pairs into acceptable position by utilizing Diane's bizarre attraction to youth and fashion and Narzissus's gullible naivety and avarice. Two marriages are contracted in the end, Diane with Narzissus, Adelheid with Stern.

C   (Mh28) S47, Bd. II

D   Predictable and without particular merit save the clever figure of Lotte.

verwirrte Mißtrauer, Der, see sich selbst Betrügende, Der

A   **Vetterschaft, Die.** Nachspiel. Friedrich Wilhelm Gotter. Leipzig: Dyk, 1784.

C   Heinsius, IV, 366

A **Virtuoso und Irena.** Ein tragisches Nachspiel.

C Plümicke, 279

von den Weibern leicht vergessene Tod der Männer, Der, see Matrone

A **Was ist's?** Ein Nachspiel in einem Aufzuge. [J.H.F. Müller.] Für das kais.
kön. National- Hoftheater. Wien: Jahn, 1786. [1]-58. 15 Auftritte.

B Herr von Raden. Amalie, dessen Tochter. Lieutenant Streitberg. Herr von
Wendheim. Herr Winkel. Nannette, Amaliens Mädchen. Zwey
Hausknechte.
   The fiery Streitberg is passionately in love with Amalie and wants to
marry, but in keeping with a long-standing agreement her father plans to
match her with Wendheim, the son of an old friend. Wendheim is introduced, a thorough milquetoast, fool, and narrow legal pedant. Raden instructs his daughter in her wifely obligations and leaves the two alone to
discover blissful harmony. Much his better in intellect and wit, Amalie reduces her suitor to childlike impotence, and Streitberg's anger at the
prospect of losing her brings him to propose a duel. By now Wendheim
wants only to escape, and on Winkel's advice pretends to be a nincompoop.
When Raden witnesses his performance, he abandons all thoughts of the
match. Relieved, Wendheim departs for a less challenging marriage at home
and father gives daughter to Streitberg.

C (ÖNB) 698427/213A ATh

D A work with tremendous comic potential on stage. Rapidly paced action
and dialogue. Many classic devices of improvised comedy (eavesdropping,
disguise, physical threats). Spirited and realistic language with potentially
hilarious exchanges. Many stage directions requiring mimed comic improvisation (Wendheim's performance as imbecile, 10. Auftritt, particularly).
Satire on bombastic scholars of law and on reactionary ideas of the role of
women (4. Auftritt). See analysis p 191.

A **Weihnachtabend, Der, oder Noch war es nicht zu spät.** Nachspiel in zwei
Akten. [Printed at end of text:] Wittenberg, gedruckt bei Adam Christian
Charisius. *Kleinere Theaterstücke für gesellschaftliche Bühnen von A.K. Walder,*
2. Bändchen. Freyberg: Craz u. Gerlach, 1803. [1]-40. 5 + 7 Auftritte.

B Rittmeister von Sindel, verabschiedet. Fritz von Sindel, Referendarius, sein
Neffe. Räthin Ludolph, Wittwe. Hannchen, ihre Tochter. Ein Briefträger.

Joseph Richter, gewesener Wachtmeister, als Invalid in des Rittmeisters
Diensten. Im ersten Akte, stellt das Theater das Zimmer des Rittmeisters,
im zweiten das Zimmer der Räthin vor.

Fritz asks von Sindel's blessing to marry the commoner Hannchen,
daughter of von Sindel's beloved deceased friend, but she is reluctant, having given her heart to the painter Braun. The Rittmeister endeavours to dissuade his nephew from marrying below his class, although he secretly ad-
mires Hannchen and is inclined to support the marriage. Von Sindel inter-
views the girl's mother, who is anxious to see the match, and so instructs
Hannchen to forget her true love. In an interview with von Sindel, the in-
tensity of Hannchen's dilemma prevents her from uttering a word, which
von Sindel misinterprets as a desire to marry Fritz. But as all gather to announce the engagement, Braun appears as a postman with the startling
news that he is in fact von Sindel's illegitimate son. With joy von Sindel
blesses his marriage with Hannchen, her mother approves, and Fritz bows
out graciously.

C (ÖNB) 3923 A

D An interesting work with much indirect social commentary on the privilege
and rights of the nobility, their eroded social position and integrity. At
times stage directions place heavy demands on actors; Hannchen's interview with von Sindel (II, 3), in which she is silent but must convey a range
of reactions, is especially noteworthy. The painter/artist Braun is an unusual Nachspiel figure, perhaps representing the value of that profession
over the upper class. See analysis pp 246 and 263.

Wer ist Vater zum Kinde? see **Instinkt**

Wiederfinden der Tochter, see **Brandschatzung**

A **Wildheit und Großmuth. Der erste Dank.** Zwey Nachspiele von J.K.
Wezel. Leipzig: Dyk, 1784. Aus dem dritten Theile der Lustspiele von J.K.
Wezel. *Wildheit u. Großmuth*: [3]-7, 240-62 [irregular pagination]. 2 Akte.
Dank: [263]-298. 1 Akt.

B *Wildheit*: Mentzikow, ein russischer Offizier. Romigny, ein kranker Offizier,
ehemals in russischen Diensten. Franz, sein Sohn. Ein Gastwirth. Im
Gasthofe einer kleinen Stadt.

For years Mentzikow has been searching for Romigny who was responsible for ruining his reputation. At the inn he hears of a crippled sol-

dier who has been displaced to the attic to make room for him, and he is en-
raged at the innkeeper's callousness. After befriending the invalid's son, he
discovers that the soldier is his arch-enemy Romigny. He confronts him
with pistols, and Romigny, who despises Mentzikow equally, struggles to
join the duel but is too lame. When he sees this, Mentzikow admirably fires
his weapon out the window. On discovering that his own hatred is unjusti-
fied and based on a misunderstanding, Romigny agrees to write a public re-
traction, and the fiery Mentzikow leaves satisfied, departing with honour
and the generous offer of a financial gift.

Dank: Herr Arend, ein Kaufmann. Madam Arend, seine Frau. Wilhelm,
der älteste Sohn. Otto, der jüngste. Zwey Gerichtspersonen. Ein Bedienter.
In Madam Arend's Stube.

Madam Arend is sewing a waistcoat for her husband's birthday as the
two boys quarrel in a typical domestic scene. They wonder about their father who has recently seemed dejected because of a family suddenly
bankrupted. Father returns with the sad news that they themselves are that
family. They prepare to leave their home as officials arrive to seal the doors
and possess their belongings. Despite the boys' naive offer to contribute everything they own, the family leaves sadly but honourably to begin a life of
penury elsewhere.

C (ÖNB) 629304 BTh

D *Wildheit*: fiery language and serious masculine tone unusual for Nachspiel
genre. *Dank*: melodramatic pathos mixed with the incongruous antics of the
boys. See analysis p 252.

Wißbegierde, Die, see Kirschen

A **Witwe, Die.** Nachspiel in einem Aufzug. Johann Baptist Bergobzoom.
Wien, 1772.

C Goedeke, V, 311

wohlthätige Kommissionär, Der, see Cangé

A **Wolken, Die.** Ein Nachspiel mit Musik u. Tanz. Vorgestellt von der Böh-
mischen Gesellschaft in Frankfurt am Main, den 12ten April 1782. Frankfurt: Eichenberg, 1782. [1]-16. 4 Auftritte. Arias, duets, chorus in irregular,
short, rhymed iambic and trochaic verses.

B Apoll. Theon, ein Schäfer. Venus. Theone, eine Schäferin. Grazien und
   Liebesgötter. Die Scene ist auf Cythere.

   Venus and Apollo use their powers, magic potions, and clouded visions
   to separate the two lovers Theon and Theone, intending to test their fidelity
   and the strength of mortal love. The deities offer themselves as new partners and deceive the shepherds with false visions of infidelity. Theon and
   Theone despair, but stand faithful to each other nevertheless. Venus and
   Apollo finally praise their steadfastness and reunite the mortal couple in a
   celebration of their love.

C (ÖNB) 3.796 A

D 'Vorerinnerung' (iiif) calls the work a replacement for the usual ballet and
   describes its enthusiastic reception, yet also the storm of criticism it
   aroused. It was published so that readers could judge its merits themselves.
   Pantomimic actions indicated for the non-speaking personae (Grazien,
   Liebesgötter) throughout as well as in a closing ballet. Elements of the bucolic *Schäferspiel*.

   Another work entitled *'Wolken. Ein Nachspiel Sokratischer
   Denkwürdigkeiten. Cum Notis Variorum in Usum Delphini. '[Johann
   Georg Hamann.]* Altona, 1761, [1]-72, 3 Aufzüge [(1) Sig Yy5256[a]] is, despite
   its title and internal division, not a dramatic work in any sense, but rather a
   satirical philosophical treatise written in reaction to a publication in the
   Hamburgische Nachrichten aus dem Reiche der Gelehrsamkeit, 57. Stück (1760).
   Hence, it has not been included as a separate item in this bibliography. The
   publication in question was a review by Christian August Crusius, Professor of Theology in Meißen (in the *Hamburgischen Nachrichten* [1760, 452-
   5]) of the *Sokratische Denkwürdigkeiten für die lange Weile des Publikums
   zusammengetragen von einem Liebhaber der langen Weile* (Amsterdam, 1759),
   published anonymously by Hamann. The place of publication was
   fictitious, the work in fact having appeared in Königsberg (see Hamann,
   1968, p 4). Crusius's review is a bitter indictment of the work and its
   anonymous author. Of its '4 Bogen in klein Oktav,' Crusius writes: 'Gewis
   stark genug, und zu stark, für eine Schrift, die lauter Aberwitz und Unsinn
   in sich hält' (452). Hamann's Nachspiel is his response and extends the debate.

   Any work entitled *Wolken* in this age naturally conjured up Aristo-
   phanes' original and carried connotations related to broad aesthetic debate.
   Witness a further treatment of the subject, Lenz's *Die Wolken* and the ensuing dispute in the mid-seventies involving the author, Goethe, and Wieland
   (Lenz, *Vertheidigung des Herrn W. ...*, 1776).

Zänkerinn, Die, see Melonen

zwei Billets, Die, see beiden Billets, Die

zwei Portraits, Die, see beyden Portraits, Die

SECONDARY WORKS CITED

The following bibliography is arranged in alphabetical order by author, editor, or title (in the case of anonymous works). All works listed here are secondary sources in the sense that they are relevant to the Nachspiele but are not themselves Nachspiel texts, regardless of the time period in which they were written. These have been used to support the central argument of the book. The primary works, the Nachspiel texts, are listed alphabetically in the Annotated Bibliography of the German Nachspiel.

(ADB) *Allgemeine Deutsche Biographie.* Hrsg. durch die Historische Commission bei der Königlichen Akademie der Wissenschaften. 56 Bde. Leipzig: Duncker u. Humblot, 1875-1912.

Aikin-Sneath, Betsy. *Comedy in Germany in the First Half of the Eighteenth Century.* Oxford: Clarendon, 1936.

Alth, Minna von, u. Gertrude Obzyna. *Burgtheater 1776-1976. Aufführungen und Besetzungen von zweihundert Jahren.* Hrsg. v. österreichischen Bundestheaterverband. 2 Bde. Wien: Ueberreuter, no date.

Asper, Helmut G. *Hanswurst. Studien zum Lustigmacher auf der Berufsschauspielerbühne in Deutschland im 17. und 18. Jahrhundert.* Emsdetten: Lechte, 1980.

– *Spieltexte der Wanderbühne. Ein Verzeichnis der Dramenmanuskripte des 17. u. 18. Jahrhunderts in Wiener Bibliotheken.* Wien: Verband der wiss. Gesell. Österreich, 1975.

Barnett, Dene. The Art of Gesture: *The Practices and Principles of 18th Century Acting.* Heidelberg: Winter, 1987.

Bauer, Anton. *Opern und Operetten in Wien. Verzeichnis ihrer Erstaufführungen in der Zeit von 1629 bis zur Gegenwart.* Graz, Köln: Böhlau, 1955.

– *Das Theater in der Josefstadt zu Wien [1788-1956]*. Wien: Manutius, 1957.

– Unpublished card catalogue of performances of eighteenth-century plays. Austrian National Library. Theatersammlung. Wien, [1935].

Bergobzoom, Johann Baptist. *Theaterspiegel aller Trauer- Schau- Lust- Sing- und Nachspielen, Balletten und Nebenvorstellungen welche auf dem königlichen Brünner städtischen Theater vom 2.11.1786 bis … 5. Hornung 1788. aufgeführt worden sind*. Brünn: Traßler, 1788.

Best, Otto F. *Handbuch literarischer Fachbegriffe. Definitionen und Beispiele*. Überarb. u. stark erweiterte Ausgabe. Frankfurt/M: Fischer, 1982.

Bilderbeck, Ludwig Franz Freiherr von. Foreword to *Schauspiele*. 2 vols. Leipzig: Voß, 1801.

Bing, Anton. *Rückblicke auf die Geschichte des Frankfurter Stadttheaters von dessen Selbstständigkeit (1792) bis zur Gegenwart*. 2 Bde. Frankfurt/M: Verlag der Wochen-Rundschau für dramatische Kunst, Literatur u. Musik, 1892-6.

Binger, Norman. *A Bibliography of German Plays on Microcards*. Hamden, Connecticut: The Shoe String Press, 1970.

Birbaumer, Ulf. *Das Werk des Joseph Felix von Kurz-Bernardon und seine szenische Realisierung. Versuch einer Genealogie und Dramaturgie der Bernardoniade*. 2 Bde. Wien: Notring, 1971.

Blümml, Emil Karl, u. Gustav Gugitz. *Alt-Wiener Thespiskarren. Die Frühzeit der Wiener Vorstadtbühnen*. Wien: Schroll, 1925.

Brachvogel, Albert Emil. *Geschichte des Königlichen Theaters zu Berlin*. 2 Bde. Berlin: Janke, 1877-8.

Brenner, Clarence D. *A Bibliographical List of Plays in the French Language 1700-1789* (1947). Repr. Michael A. Keller, Neal Zaslau ed. New York: AMS, 1979.

Brenner, Oscar, Hrsg. *Altbairische Possenspiele für die Dachauer Bühne bearbeitet von Franz von Paula Kiennast (†1783)*. München: Kaiser, 1893.

Brockhaus Enzyklopädie. Wiesbaden: Brockhaus, 1971.

Burkhardt, Carl August Hugo, Hrsg. *Das Repertoire des Weimarischen Theaters unter Goethes Leitung 1791-1817*. Hamburg u. Leipzig: Voß, 1891.

Catholy, Eckehard. *Das deutsche Lustspiel. Vom Mittelalter bis zum Ende der Barockzeit*. Stuttgart: Kohlhammer, 1969.

– *Das deutsche Lustspiel. Von der Aufklärung bis zur Romantik*. Stuttgart: Kohlhammer, 1982.

Critische Nachricht von der Schuchischen Schauspielergesellschaft. Danzig: publisher unknown, 1758.

Deutscher Biographischer Index. 4 Bde. Hrsg. v. Willi Gorzny. München: Saur, 1986.

Devrient, Eduard. *Geschichte der deutschen Schauspielkunst* (1867). 2 Bde. Neue Ausgabe. Berlin: Elsner, 1905.

Devrient, Hans. *Johann Friedrich Schönemann und seine Schauspielergesellschaft* (1895). Repr. Nendeln: Kraus, 1978.

Driesen, Otto. *Der Ursprung des Harlekin. Ein kulturgeschichtliches Problem.* Berlin: Duncker, 1904.

Eichhorn, Herbert. *Konrad Ernst Ackermann. Ein deutscher Theaterprinzipal. Ein Beitrag zur Theatergeschichte im deutschen Sprachraum.* Emsdetten: Lechte, 1965.

Engel, Johann Jakob. *Ideen zu einer Mimik.* Bd. 7, 8 of *Schriften* (1801-6). 12 Bde. Repr. Frankfurt: Athenäum, 1971.

Flasdieck, Hermann M. 'Harlekin. Germanischer Mythos in Romanischer Wandlung.' *Anglia,* 61 (1937), 225-340.

Frankfurter Gelehrte Anzeigen. Hrsg. v. Johann Heinrich Merck, Johann Georg Schlosser, Karl Friedrich Bahrdt. Frankfurt/M.: Eichenberg, 1722-90.

Fratzke, Dieter. 'Die maßstabgerechte Nachbildung des Theaters am Gänsemarkt von 1765, des späteren Hamburger Nationaltheaters. Ein literaturmusealer Beitrag zur Vorgeschichte des Themas "Lessing und Hamburg".' *Lessing Yearbook,* XX (1988), 1-14.

Friedrichs Theaterlexikon. Hrsg. v. Henning Rischbieter. Velber bei Hannover: Friedrich, 1969.

Fromm, Hans. *Bibliographie deutscher Übersetzungen aus dem Französischen 1700-1948.* 6 Bde. (1950-3). Repr. Nendeln: Kraus, 1981.

(FZ) Frankfurt *Theaterzettelsammlung.* Playbill collection of the Stadt- u. Universitätsbibliothek, Frankfurt/M.

(GAD) *German and Austrian Drama in the Houghton Library, Harvard University: Guide to the Microfilm Collection* compiled by James E. Walsh. Woodbridge, Connecticut: Research Publications, 1985.

Gebhardt, Walther. *Spezialbestände in deutschen Bibliotheken. BRD einschließlich Berlin (West).* Berlin, New York: de Gruyter, 1977.

Gellert, Christian Fürchtegott. *Lustspiele.* Hrsg. v. Horst Steinmetz. Faks.-Dr. n. d. Ausg. v. 1747. Stuttgart: Metzler, 1966.

Genée, Rudolf. *Lehr- und Wanderjahre des deutschen Schauspiels. Vom Beginn der Reformation bis zur Mitte des 18. Jahrhunderts.* Berlin: Hofmann, 1882.

Gesamtverzeichnis des deutschsprachigen Schrifttums 1700-1910. Bearb. unter der Leitung v. Peter Geils u. Willi Gorzny. 160 Bde. + 1 Bd. Nachträge. München: Saur, 1979-87.

Glaser, Horst Albert, Hrsg. *Deutsche Literatur. Eine Sozialgeschichte.* 7 Bde.ff. Reinbeck bei Hamburg: Rowohlt, 1980ff.

Goedeke, Karl. *Grundriß zur Geschichte der deutschen Dichtung. Aus den Quellen.* 2. u. 3. Aufl., 22 Bde. Dresden: Ehlermann; Berlin: Akademie-Verlag, 1884-1966.

Goethe, Johann Wolfgang von. 'Regeln für Schauspieler.' *Werke*. Weimar Ausgabe, I, 40. Weimar: Böhlau, 1901.
- *Tagebücher 1775-1787*. Weimar Ausgabe, III, 1. Weimar: Böhlau, 1887.
- *Wilhelm Meisters theatralische Sendung*. *Werke*. Weimar Ausgabe, I, 51. Weimar: Böhlau, 1911.
[Goethe, Katharina Elisabeth.] *Briefe der Frau Rath Goethe*. [8. Aufl. Frankfurt:] Insel, [1968].
Gottsched, Johann Christoph. *Ausführliche Redekunst*. *Ausgewählte Werke*, Bd. 7. Hrsg. v. P.M. Mitchell. Berlin, New York: de Gruyter, 1975.
- *Versuch einer Critischen Dichtkunst vor die Deutschen* (1730). [5]1751. Repr. Darmstadt: Wiss. Buchgesell., 1962.
- Hrsg. *Die deutsche Schaubühne nach den Regeln und Exempeln der Alten*. 6 Bde. (1742-5), also referred to as *DS*. Repr. Stuttgart: Metzler, 1972.
- Hrsg. *Nöthiger Vorrath zur Geschichte der deutschen dramatischen Dichtkunst oder Verzeichniß aller Deutschen Trauer- Lust- und Singspiele, die im Druck erschienen, von 1450 bis zur Hälfte des jetzigen Jahrhunderts* [1757-65], also referred to as *NV*. Repr. Hildesheim: Olms, 1970.
Gottsched, Luise Adelgunde Victorie. *Der Witzling*. Hrsg. v. Wolfgang Hecht. Berlin: de Gruyter, 1962.
Grandaur, Franz. *Chronik des Königlichen Hof- und Nationaltheaters in München*. München: Ackermann, 1878.
Grimm, Jacob u. Wilhelm. *Deutsches Wörterbuch*. 16 Bde. Leipzig: Hirzel, 1854-1954.
Grimminger, Rolf. *Deutsche Aufklärung bis zur Französischen Revolution 1680-1789*. *Hansers Sozialgeschichte der deutschen Literatur*, Bd. 3. München: Hanser, 1980.
Gryphius, Andreas. *Gesamtausgabe der deutschsprachigen Werke*. Bd. 8, *Lustspiele II*. Hrsg. v. Hugh Powell. Tübingen: Niemeyer, 1972.
- *Verliebtes Gespenst, Gesangspiel*. *Die geliebte Dornrose, Scherzspiel*. Hrsg. v. Eberhard Mannack. Berlin: de Gruyter, 1962.
Hadamowsky, Franz. *Bücherkunde deutschsprachiger Theaterliteratur*. 2 Teile. Wien: Böhlau, 1982.
- *Ein Jahrhundert Literatur- und Theaterzensur in Österreich (1751-1848)*. *Die österreichische Literatur. Ihr Profil an der Wende vom 18. zum 19. Jahrhundert (1750-1830)*. Hrsg. v. Herbert Zeman. Teil 1, 289-305. Graz: Akademische Druck- u. Verlagsanstalt, 1979.
- *Das Theater in der Wiener Leopoldstadt 1781-1860*. Wien: Höfels Witwe, 1934.
- *Die Wiener Hoftheater (Staatstheater) 1776-1966. Ein Verzeichnis der aufgeführten Stücke mit Bestandsnachweis und täglichem Spielplan*. Teil 1. Wien: Prachner, 1966. Teil 2. Wien: Hollinek, 1975.

Haider-Pregler, Hilde. *Des sittlichen Bürgers Abendschule. Bildungsanspruch u. Bildungsauftrag des Berufstheaters im 18. Jahrhundert.* Wien: Jugend u. Volk, 1980.

Hamann, Johann Georg. *Sokratische Denkwürdigkeiten. Aesthetica in nuce.* Hrsg. v. Sven-Aage Jørgensen. Stuttgart: Reclam, 1968.

Hamburgische Nachrichten aus dem Reiche der Gelehrsamkeit. [Hamburg:] Schröder, 1758-71.

Hansen, Günther. *Formen der Commedia dell'Arte in Deutschland.* Emsdetten: Lechte, 1984.

Heine, Carl. *Das Schauspiel der deutschen Wanderbühne vor Gottsched.* Halle/S.: Niemeyer, 1889.

Heinsius, Wilhelm. *Allgemeines Bücherlexikon oder Vollständiges alphabetisches Verzeichnis aller von 1700-1894 erschienenen Bücher.* 19 Bde. Leipzig: Heinsius, 1812-94.

Herloßsohn, Karl, u. Hermann Marggraff, Hrsg. *Allgemeines Theaterlexikon oder Encyklopädie alles Wissenswerthen für Bühnenkünstler, Dilettanten und Theaterfreunde.* Neue Ausg., Bd. 1-7. Altenburg: Expedition, 1846.

Hinck, Walter. *Die deutsche Komödie des 17. und 18. Jahrhunderts und die italienische Komödie, commedia dell'arte und théâtre italien.* Stuttgart: Metzler, 1965.

Hodermann, Richard. *Geschichte des Gothaischen Hoftheaters 1775-1779* (1894). Repr. Nendeln: Kraus, 1978.

Holl, Karl. *Geschichte des deutschen Lustspiels.* Leipzig: Weber, 1923.

Holzmann, Michael, u. Hanns Bohatta. *Deutsches Anonymen-Lexikon.* 7 vols. (1902-28). Repr. Hildesheim: Olms, 1961.

– *Deutsches Pseudonymen-Lexikon* (1906). Repr. Hildesheim: Olms, 1961, 1970.

Houben, Heinrich Hubert. *Der ewige Zensor. Längs- u. Querschnitte durch die Geschichte der Buch- u. Theaterzensur.* 1926. Repr. Kronberg/Ts.: Athenäum, 1978.

Iffland, August Wilhelm. *Almanach fürs Theater.* Berlin: Salfeld, 1808.

– *Theorie der Schauspielkunst für ausübende Künstler und Kunstfreunde.* Hrsg. v. Christian Gottfried Flit[t]ner. 2 Bde. in einem. Berlin: Neue Societas, 1815.

Jacob, Martin. *Kölner Theater im 18. Jahrhundert bis zum Ende der reichsstädtischen Zeit (1700-1794).* Emsdetten: Lechte, 1938.

Jöcher, Christian Gottlieb. *Allgemeines Gelehrten-Lexicon.* 4 Thle. nebst Fortsetzungen u. Ergänzungen. Leipzig: Weidmann, 1750-1897.

Jördens, Karl-Heinrich. *Lexikon deutscher Dichter und Prosaisten.* 6 Bde. Leipzig: Weidmann, 1806-11.

Journal aller Journale. Oder Geist der vaterländischen Zeitschriften. Hrsg. v. J.L. Heß. 10 Bde. Hamburg: Chaidron, 1786-7.

Journal des Luxus und der Moden. Hrsg. v. F.J. Bertuch u. G.M. Kraus. Jg. 1-42 (1786-1827). Gotha: Ettinger; Weimar: Landes-Industrie Comptoir. Partial repr., hrsg. v. Werner Schmidt. Edition Leipzig, 1967.

Jung, Johann Heinrich. *Lehrbuch der Staats- Polizey-Wissenschaft.* Leipzig: Weidmann, 1788.

Justi, Johann Heinrich Gottlob von. *Die Grundfeste zu der Macht und Glückseligkeit der Staaten; oder ausführliche Vorstellung der gesamten Policey-Wissenschaft.* 2 Bde. Königsberg u. Leipzig: Hartung (Bd. 1), Woltersdorf (Bd. 2), 1760-1.

— *Grundsätze der Polizey-wissenschaft.* Göttingen: Vandenhöck, 1756.

Kayser, Christian Gottlob. *Vollständiges Bücher-Lexikon, enthaltend alle von 1750 bis 1910 in Deutschland und den angrenzenden Ländern gedruckten Bücher.* 36 Bde., 6 Reg.-Bde. Leipzig: [wechselnde Verlage], 1834-1911.

Kindermann, Heinz. *Conrad Ekhofs Schauspieler-Akademie,* also referred to as *CE.* Wien: Rohrer, 1956.

— *Theatergeschichte Europas.* 10 Bde. Salzburg: Müller, 1957-74.

— *Theatergeschichte der Goethezeit.* Wien: Bauer, 1948.

Kleines literarisches Lexikon. Begr. v. Wolfgang Kayser. 4. neu bearb. Aufl. hrsg. v. Horst Rüdiger u. Erwin Koppen. Bd. 3, *Sachbegriffe.* Bern: Francke, 1966.

Kleist, Christian Ewald von. *Sämtliche Werke,* 1. Theil. Reuttlingen: Fleischhauer, 1774.

Klinger, Friedrich Maximilian. *Das leidende Weib. Mit Anhang: Die frohe Frau und Klingers Entgegnung.* Hrsg. v. Ludwig Jacobowski. Halle: Hendel, [1889].

— *Historisch-kritische Gesamtausgabe,* Bd. 1. Hrsg. v. Edward P. Harris. Tübingen: Niemeyer, 1987.

Koffka, Wilhelm. *Iffland und Dalberg.* Leipzig: Weber, 1865.

Kosch, Wilhelm. *Deutsches Literatur-Lexikon. Biographisches und bibliographisches Handbuch.* 2. Aufl. Bern: Francke, 1949-58.

— *Deutsches Theater-Lexikon. Biographisches und bibliographisches Handbuch.* Bd 1-2. Klagenfurt: Kleinmayr. Bd. 3. Fortgeführt v. H. Bennwitz. Bern, München: Francke, 1965ff.

Krause, Markus. *Das Trivialdrama der Goethezeit, 1780-1805. Produktion und Rezeption.* Bonn: Bouvier, 1982.

Krüger, Johann Christian. *Werke. Kritische Gesamtausgabe.* Hrsg. v. David G. John. Tübingen: Niemeyer, 1986.

Krywalski, Dieter, Hrsg. *Handlexikon der Literaturwissenschaft.* 2. Aufl. München: Ehrenwirth, 1976.

Küpper, Heinz. *[Pons-] Wörterbuch der deutschen Umgangssprache.* Stuttgart: Klett, 1987.

[Lawätz, Heinrich Wilhelm.] *Die Diamanten. Schauspiel in einem Aufzuge. (Wahre Geschichte).* 'Vorerinnerung' von L[awätz]. *Deutsche Schaubühne,* 6. Jg., Bd. 4. Nach der Ordnung 64. Bd. Augsburg: publisher unknown, 1794.

Lebrün, Carl. 'Geschichte des Hamburger Theaters, von seiner Entstehung an bis zum Jahre 1817.' *Jahrbuch für Theater und Theaterfreunde.* Bd. 1, 56-362. Hamburg: Perthes, Besser u. Mauke, 1841.

Legband, Paul. *Münchener Bühne und Litteratur im 18. Jahrhundert.* München: Historischer Verein v. Oberbayern, 1901-4.

Lehr, Walter. 'Die szenischen Bemerkungen in den Dramen des Alt-Wiener Volkstheaters bis 1752.' Diss. Wien, 1965.

Lenz, Jakob Michael Reinhold. *Vertheidigung des Herrn W. gegen die Wolken von dem Verfasser der Wolken* [1776]. *Werke und Briefe in drei Bänden,* hrsg. v. Sigrid Damm, Bd. 2, 713-36. München: Hanser, 1987.

Lessing, Gotthold Ephraim. *Werke.* Vollständige Ausgabe in 25 Teilen. Hrsg. v. Julius Petersen, Waldemar v. Ohlhausen, Waldemar Oehlke et al. Berlin: Bong, [1925].

– *Werke.* 8 Bde. Hrsg. v. Herbert G. Göpfert. München: Hanser, 1970-9.

Liss, Konrad. 'Das Theater des alten Schuch. Geschichte und B[e]trachtung einer deutschen Wandertruppe des 18. Jahrhunderts.' Diss. Berlin, 1925.

Litteratur- und Theater-Zeitung. Hrsg. v. Christian August Bertram. Jg. 1-7 (1778-84). Repr. hrsg. v. Reinhart Meyer. München: Kraus, 1981.

Litzmann, Berthold. *Friedrich Ludwig Schröder.* 2 Teile. Hamburg u. Leipzig: Voß, 1890/94.

Lochter, Ulrich. *Justus Möser und das Theater. Ein Beitrag zur Theorie und Praxis im deutschen Theater des 18. Jahrhunderts.* Osnabrück: Wenner, 1967.

Lowack, Alfred. *Die Mundarten im hochdeutschen Drama bis gegen Ende des achtzehnten Jahrhunderts.* Leipzig: Hesse, 1905.

Macchi, Vladimiro, Hrsg. *Wörterbuch der Italienischen und Deutschen Sprache,* 1. Teil (Ital.-Dt.). Wiesbaden: Brandstett; Firenze/Roma: Sansori, 1970.

Magazin der Sächsischen Geschichte. Hrsg. v. Johann Christian Hasche. Th. 1-8 = St. 1-96. Dresden: Gerlach, 1784-91.

Mannack, Eberhard. *Andreas Gryphius.* 2. Aufl. Stuttgart: Metzler, 1986.

– 'Andreas Gryphius' Lustspiele – ihre Herkunft, ihre Motive und ihre Entwicklung.' *Euphorion,* 58 (1964), 1-40.

Martens, Wolfgang. 'Obrigkeitliche Sicht. Das Bühnenwesen in den Lehrbüchern der Policey und Cameralistik des 18. Jahrhunderts. *Internationales Archiv für Sozialgeschichte der deutschen Literatur,* 6 (1981), 19-51.

Martersteig, Max, Hrsg. *Die Protokolle des Mannheimer Nationaltheaters unter Dalberg aus den Jahren 1781 bis 1789.* Mannheim: Bensheimer, 1890.

Maurer-Schmoock, Sybille. *Deutsches Theater im 18. Jahrhundert.* Tübingen: Niemeyer, 1982.

Mayer, Wolfgang. 'Historisches Leben und Treiben am Wiener Spittelberg.' *Renovation*, 1 (1985), 14f.

Mentzel, Elisabeth. *Geschichte der Schauspielkunst in Frankfurt a. M. von ihren Anfängen bis zur Eröffnung des städtischen Komödienhauses.* Frankfurt/M: Völcker, 1882.

Metzler Literatur Lexikon. Hrsg. v. Günther u. Irmgard Schweikle. Stuttgart: Metzler, 1984.

Meusel, Johann Georg. *Lexikon der vom Jahr 1750 bis 1800 verstorbenen teutschen Schriftsteller.* 15 Bde. Leipzig: Fleischer, 1802-16.

Meyer, Elise Marie. 'Der Einakter in der deutschen Dichtung des 18. Jahrhunderts.' Diss. Leipzig, 1920.

Meyer, Reinhart. *Bibliographia dramatica et dramaticorum: kommentierte Bibliographie der im ehemaligen deutschen Reichsgebiete gedruckten und gespielten Dramen des 18. Jahrhunderts nebst deren Bearbeitungen und Übersetzungen und ihrer Rezeption bis in die Gegenwart,* Abt. 1, Bd. 1-3. Tübingen: Niemeyer, 1986.

– 'Von der Wanderbühne zum Hof- u. Nationaltheater.' See Grimminger, pp 186-216.

Mohr, Albert Richard. *Frankfurter Theater von der Wandertruppe zum Komödienhaus.* Frankfurt/M.: Kramer, 1967.

Möser, Justus. 'Harlekin, oder Verteidigung des Groteske-Komischen.' *Sämtliche Werke,* Bd. 2. Bearb. v. Oda May. Oldenburg (Oldb.), Hamburg: Stalling, 1981.

– 'Den alten Geckorden sollte man wieder erneuern.' *Sämtliche Werke,* Bd. 5. Bearb. v. Ludwig Schirmeyer. Oldenburg (Oldb.), Berlin: Stalling, 1945.

Müller, Johann Heinrich Friedrich, Hrsg. *Genaue Nachrichten von beyden kaiserlich-königlichen Schaubühnen und andern öffentlichen Ergötzlichkeiten in Wien.* Wien: Ghelen, 1772.

– Hrsg. *Geschichte und Tagbuch der Wiener Schaubühne.* Wien: Trattner, 1776.

Mylius, Christlob. 'Abhandlung, daß die Wahrscheinlichkeit der Vorstellung bey den Schauspielen eben so nöthig ist, als die innere Wahrscheinlichkeit derselben.' *Beyträge zur Critischen Historie der deutschen Sprache, Poesie und Beredsamkeit.* Hrsg. v. Johann Christoph Gottsched. Bd. 8, 30. Stück, VII, 297-322. Leipzig: Breitkopf, 1743.

(MZ) Munich *Theaterzettel.* Playbill collection of the Theatermuseum, Munich.

Neue Erweiterungen der Erkenntnis und des Vergnügens, Bd. 4. Frankfurt u. Leipzig: Lankisch, 1754.

Nicolai, Friedrich. *Leben Justus Möser's.* Mit Beilagen. *Justus Mösers sämmtliche Werke,* 10. Theil. Hrsg. v. B.R. Abeken. Berlin: Nicolai, 1843.

Niessen, Carl. *Kleine Schriften zur Theaterwissenschaft und Theatergeschichte.* Hrsg. v. Günter Seehaus. Emsdetten: Lechte, 1971.

Pauly-Wissowa. *Realenzyklopädie der classischen Altertumswissenschaft*. Neue Bearbeitung, 12. Halbband. Stuttgart: Druckenmüller, 1909.

Pazarkaya, Yüksel. *Die Dramaturgie des Einakters. Der Einakter als eine besondere Erscheinungsform im deutschen Drama des 18. Jahrhunderts*. Göppingen: Kümmerle, 1973.

Pichler, Anton. *Chronik des Großherzoglichen Hof- und Nationaltheaters in Mannheim*. Mannheim: Bensheimer, 1879.

Pies, Eike. *Prinzipale. Zur Genealogie des deutschsprachigen Berufsttheaters vom 17. bis 19. Jahrhundert*. Ratingen: Henn, 1973.

Pirker, Max, Hrsg. *Teutsche Arien, Welche auf dem Kayserlich-privilegirten Wienerischen Theatro in unterschiedlich producirten Comoedien, deren Titul hier jedesmahl beygerucket, gesungen worden*. 2 Bde. Wien, Prag, Leipzig: Strache, 1927, 1929.

Plümicke, Carl Martin. *Entwurf einer Theatergeschichte von Berlin* (1781). Repr. Leipzig: Zentralantiquariat, 1975.

Prick, Elisabeth. 'Heinrich Gottfried Koch und seine Schauspielergesellschaft bis zum Bruche mit Gottsched.' Diss. Frankfurt/M., 1925.

Raab, Ferdinand. *Johann Joseph Felix von Kurz genannt Bernardon*. Frankfurt/M: Rütten u. Loening, [1898].

Reallexikon der deutschen Literaturgeschichte (1925-31). Begr. v. Paul Merker u. Wolfgang Stammler. 2. Aufl. Bd. 1ff. Berlin: de Gruyter, 1958ff.

Reden-Esbeck, Friedrich Johann von. *Caroline Neuber und ihre Zeitgenossen* (1881). Repr. mit einem Nachwort und einer Ergänzungsbibliographie von Wolfram Günther. Leipzig: Zentralantiquariat der DDR, 1985.

Rieger, Max. *Klinger in der Sturm- und Drangperiode dargestellt. Mit vielen Briefen*. 2 vols. Darmstadt: Bergstraesser, 1880.

Riha, Karl. *Commedia dell'Arte. Mit den Figuren Maurice Sands*. Frankfurt: Insel, 1980.

Rischbieter, Henning, Hrsg. *Theater-Lexikon*. Zürich: Orell Füssli, 1983.

Rommel, Otto. *Die Alt-Wiener Volkskomödie. Ihre Geschichte vom barocken Welt-Theater bis zum Tode Nestroys*. Wien: Schroll, 1952.

– Hrsg. *Die Maschinenkomödie*. Deutsche Literatur in Entwicklungsreihen, Reihe 13, 1. Leipzig: Reclam, 1935.

Roob, Helmut. *Sondersammlungen in Bibliotheken der DDR. Ein Verzeichnis*. 2. überbearb. u. erw. Aufl. Berlin (Ost): Methodisches Zentrum für wissenschaftliche Bibliotheken beim Minister für Hoch- u. Fachschulwesen, 1982.

Der Sammler, ein Unterhaltungsblatt. Hrsg. v. Franz Castelli et al. Jg. 1-21. Wien: Schaumburg (Strauß), 1809-29.

Sammlung Oskar Fambach (SOF). Archival materials in the Seminarbibliothek of the Deutsches Seminar, Bonn University.

Sasse, Hannah. *Friedericke Caroline Neuber. Versuch einer Neuwertung.* Freiburg i. B.: Wild, 1937.

Schäffer, Carl, u. C. Hartmann. *Die königlichen Theater in Berlin. Statistischer Rückblick auf die Tätigkeit und die Personal-Verhältnisse während des Zeitraums 1786-1885.* Berlin: Comtoir, 1886.

Schenda, Rudolf. *Volk ohne Buch. Studien zur Sozialgeschichte der populären Lesestoffe 1770-1910.* Frankfurt: Klostermann, 1970.

Schindler, Otto. 'Theatergeschichte von Baden bei Wien im 18. Jahrhundert. Mit besonderer Berücksichtigung der "Badner Truppe" und ihres Repertoires.' Diss. Wien, 1971.

Schlegel, Johann Elias. 'Abhandlung, daß die Nachahmung der Sache, der man nachahmet, zuweilen unähnlich werden müsse' and 'Abhandlung von der Nachahmung.' *Aesthetische und dramaturgische Schriften,* hrsg. v. Johann v. Antoniewicz, pp 96-160. Heilbronn: Henninger, 1887.

– *Werke.* Hrsg. v. Johann Heinrich Schlegel. Bd. 2 (1773). Repr. Frankfurt: Athenäum, 1971.

Schlienger, Armin. *Das Komische in den Komödien des Andreas Gryphius. Ein Beitrag zu Ernst und Scherz im Barocktheater.* Bern: Lang, 1970.

Schlösser, Rudolf. *Vom Hamburger Nationaltheater zur Gothaer Hofbühne 1767-1779. Dreizehn Jahre aus der Entwickelung eines deutschen Theaterspielplans* (1895). Repr. Nendeln: Kraus, 1978.

Schmeller, Johann Andreas. *Bayerisches Wörterbuch.* Neudruck der 2. bey R. Oldenburg 1872-77 in 2 Bänden erschienen Auflage v. G. Karl Frommann, mit Vorwort v. O. Basler. 2 Bde. Aalen: Scientia, 1961.

Schmid, Christian Heinrich. *Chronologie des deutschen Theaters* (1775). Neu hrsg. v. Paul Legband. Berlin: Gesellschaft für Theatergeschichte, 1902.

Schmidt, Friedrich Ludwig. *Denkwürdigkeiten des Schauspielers, Schauspieldichters und Schauspieldirektors.* 2 Thle. Hrsg. v. Hermann Uhde. Hamburg: Mauke, 1875.

Schneider, Max. *Deutsches Titelbuch.* Berlin: Haude u. Spener, 1927.

Schrickel, Leonhard. *Geschichte des Weimarer Theaters von den Anfängen bis heute.* Weimar: Panses, 1928.

Schulte-Sasse, Jochen. 'Drama.' See Grimminger, pp 423-99.

Schuster, Ralf S. *Gedruckte Spielplanverzeichnisse stehender deutscher Bühnen im Ausgang des 18. Jahrhunderts bis 1896.* Frankfurt/M., Bern, New York: Lang, 1985.

Schütze, Johann Friedrich. *Hamburgische Theatergeschichte* (1794). Repr. Leipzig: Zentralantiquariat der DDR, 1975.

Scott-Prelorentzos, Alison. *The Servant in German Enlightenment Comedy.* Edmonton: University of Alberta Press, 1982.

Sichardt, Gisela. *Das Weimarer Liebhabertheater unter Goethes Leitung*. Weimar: Arion, 1957.

Sommerfeld, Kurt. *Die Bühneneinrichtungen des Mannheimer Nationaltheaters unter Dalbergs Leitung (1778-1803)*. Berlin: Schriften der Gesellschaft für Theatergeschichte 36, 1921.

Sonnenfels, Joseph von. *Briefe über die Wienerische Schaubühne* (1768). Wiener Neudrucke, 7. Wien: Konegen, 1884.

– *Grundsätze der Polizey, Handlung und Finanzwissenschaft*, Bd. 1 (1765). 3. Aufl. Wien: Kurzböck, 1770.

– *Handbuch der inneren Staatsverwaltung mit Rücksicht auf die Umstände und Begriffe der Zeit*. Wien: Camesina, 1798.

Steinmetz, Horst. *Die Komödie der Aufklärung*. 3. Aufl. Stuttgart: Metzler, 1978.

Tagebuch der Mainzer Schaubühne. Hrsg. v. Aloys Wilhelm Schreiber. St. 1-13 (1788-9). [Frankfurt/M.: Eichenberg]. Fortgesetzt u. d. Titel *Dramturgische Blätter*. Frankfurt/M.: Eßlinger.

Tagebuch der Mannheimer Schaubühne. Hrsg. v. Trierweiler. Bd. 1-2. Mannheim, 1786-8.

Teatralia Zámecké Knihovny v Českém Krumlově, ed. Jitka Šimáková and Eduarda Macháčková. 3 vols. Prag: Národní Muzeum, 1976.

Teatralia Zámecké Knihovny z Křimic, ed. Jitka Šimáková and Eduarda Macháčková. Prag: Národní Muzeum, 1970.

Teatralia Zámecké Knihovny z Radenína, ed. Pravoslava Kneidla. 3 vols. Prag: Národní Muzeum, 1962, 1963, 1969.

Trautmann, Karl. 'Italienische Schauspieler am bayerischen Hofe.' *Jahrbuch für Münchener Geschichte (JMG)*, Bd. 1 (1887), 193-312. München: Lindau. 'Französische Schauspieler am bayerischen Hofe.' *JMG* 2 (1888), 185-334. 'Deutsche Schauspieler am bayerischen Hofe.' *JMG* 3 (1889), 259-430.

Trilse, Christoph, Klaus Hammer, Rolf Kabel et al. *Theaterlexikon*. Berlin: Henschel, 1977.

Uhlich, Adam Gottfried. *Erste / Zweyte Sammlung neuer Lustspiele*. Danzig u. Leipzig: Rüdiger, 1746, 1747.

Van Cleve, John Walter. *Harlequin Besieged: The Reception of Comedy in Germany during the Early Enlightenment*. Bern: Lang, 1980.

Verzeichnis der Tragödien und Komödien von fünf und drey Ackten, welche vom Jahr 1750 an auf dem Kochischen Theater und wann solche zum erstenmale aufgeführet worden. Hamburg: Spieringk, date unknown.

(VZ) Vienna *Theaterzettel*. Playbill collection of the Stadtbibliothek, Vienna.

Walter, Friedrich, Hrsg. *Archiv u. Bibliothek des Grossh. Hof- u. Nationaltheaters in Mannheim 1779-1839*. 2 Bde. Leipzig: Hirzel, 1899.

Weilen, Alexander von. *Geschichte des Wiener Theaterwesens von den ältesten Zeiten bis zu den Anfängen der Hoftheater.* Wien: Gesellschaft für vervielfältigende Kunst, 1899.

– [Notes on an adaptation of Gryphius's *Peter Squentz* with reference to *Die Bauren.*] *Euphorion,* 2 (1895), 632.

– Review of Ferdinand Raab, *Johann Joseph Felix von Kurz ... Euphorion,* 6 (1899), 350-61.

Wentzlaff-Eggebert, Friedrich Wilhelm u. Erika. *Andreas Gryphius 1616-1664.* Darmstadt: Wiss. Buchgesell., 1983.

Williams, Simon. *German Actors of the Eighteenth and Nineteenth Centuries: Idealism, Romanticism, and Realism.* Westport, Connecticut: Greenwood, 1985.

Wilpert, Gero von, Hrsg. *Sachwörterbuch der Literatur.* 6. verb. u. erw. Aufl. Stuttgart: Kröner, 1979.

Winds, Adolf. *Geschichte der Regie.* Berlin: Dt. Verlagsanstalt, 1925.

Wollrabe, Ludwig. *Chronologie sämtlicher Hamburger Bühnen [1230-1846].* Hamburg: Berendsohn, 1847.

Zechmeister, Gustav. *Die Wiener Theater nächst der Burg und nächst dem Kärntnerthor von 1747 bis 1796.* Graz, Wien, Köln: Kommissionsverlag der Österreichischen Akademie der Wissenschaften, 1971.

INDEX OF NAMES

Names are followed by dates of birth and death, if known. Otherwise, b. signifies date of birth, d. date of death. Chief sources are the *Deutscher Biographischer Index*, *Allgemeine Deutsche Biographie*, Pies's *Prinzipale*, and Brenner's *Bibliographical List of Plays in the French Language 1700-89*.